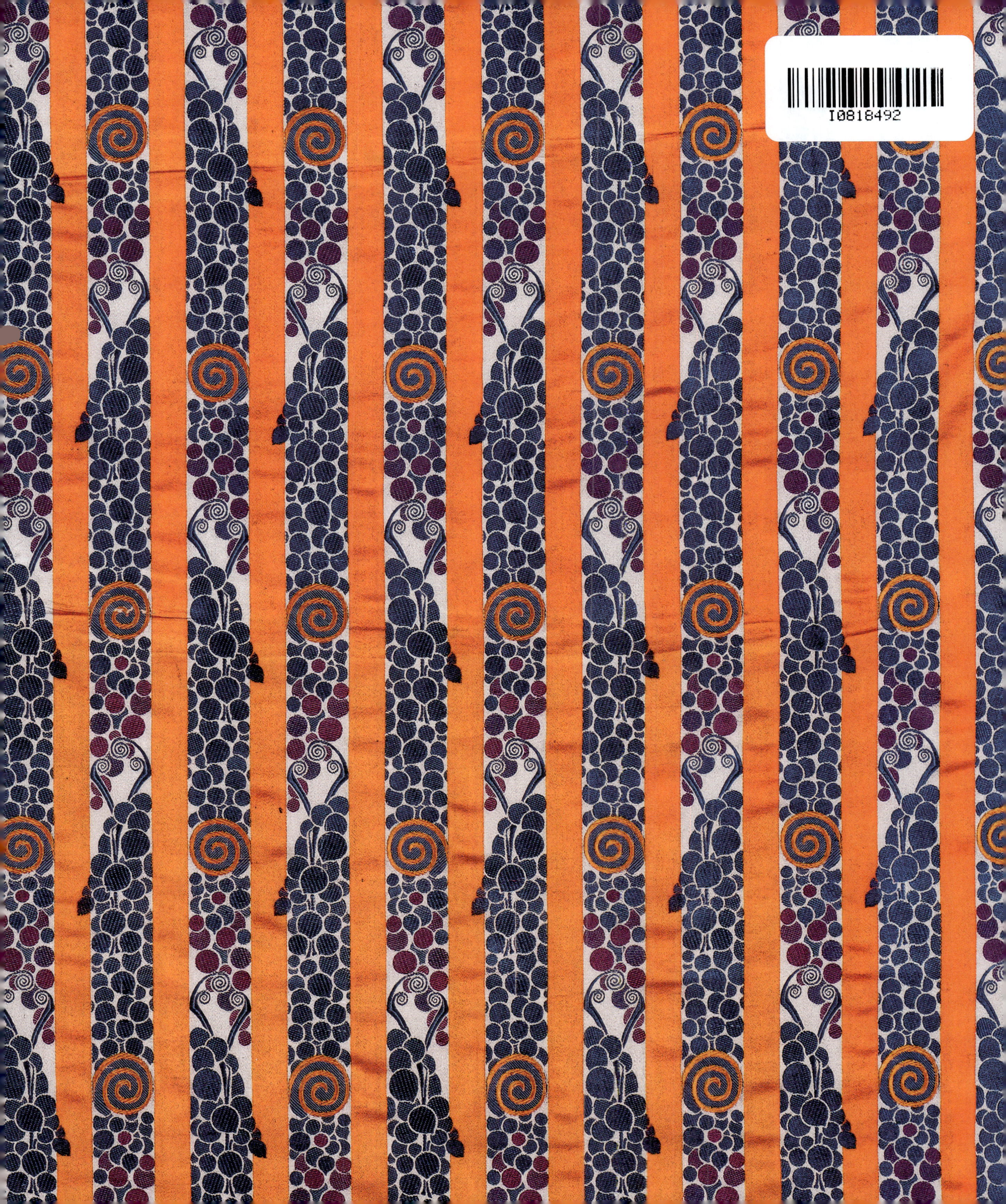

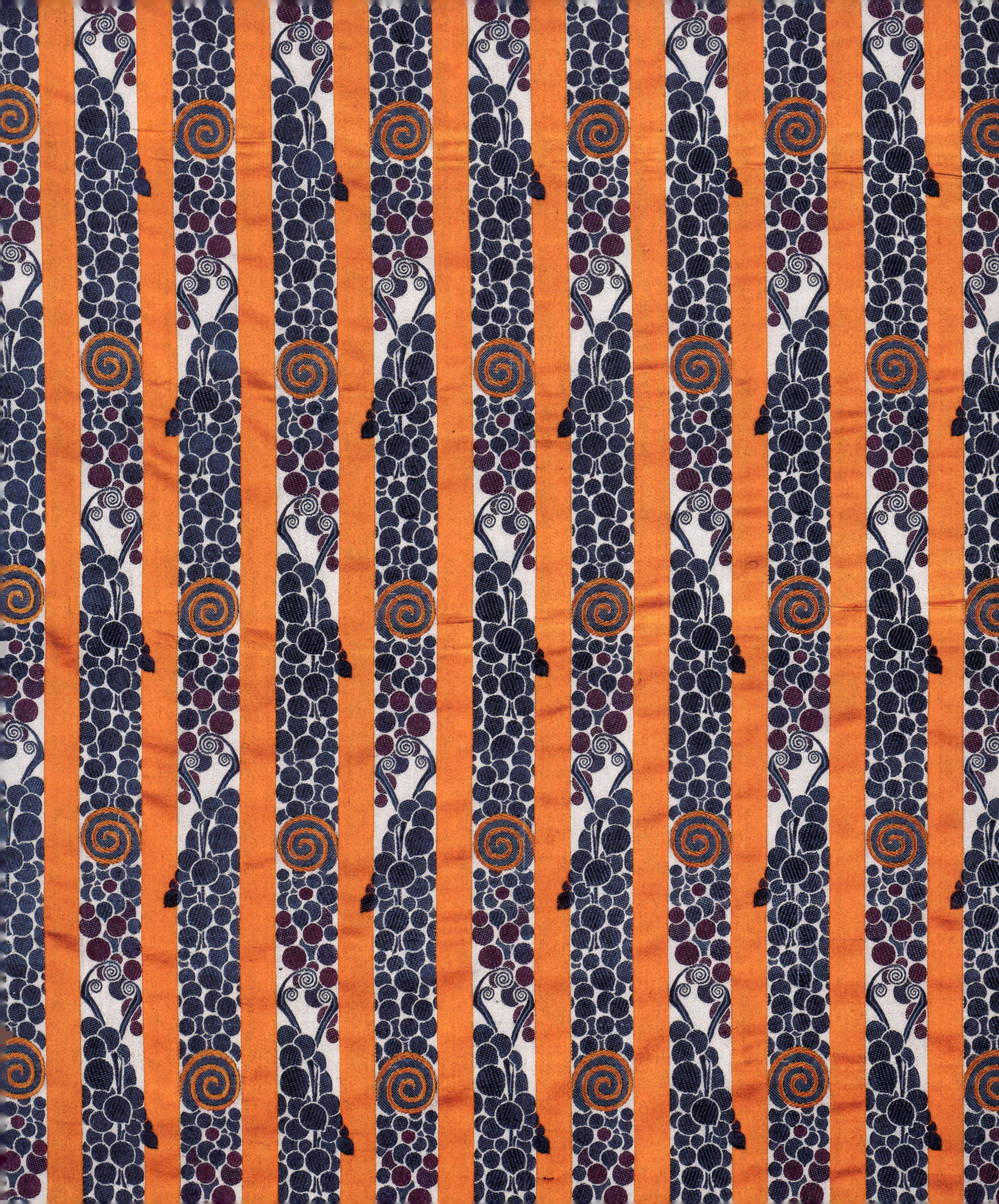

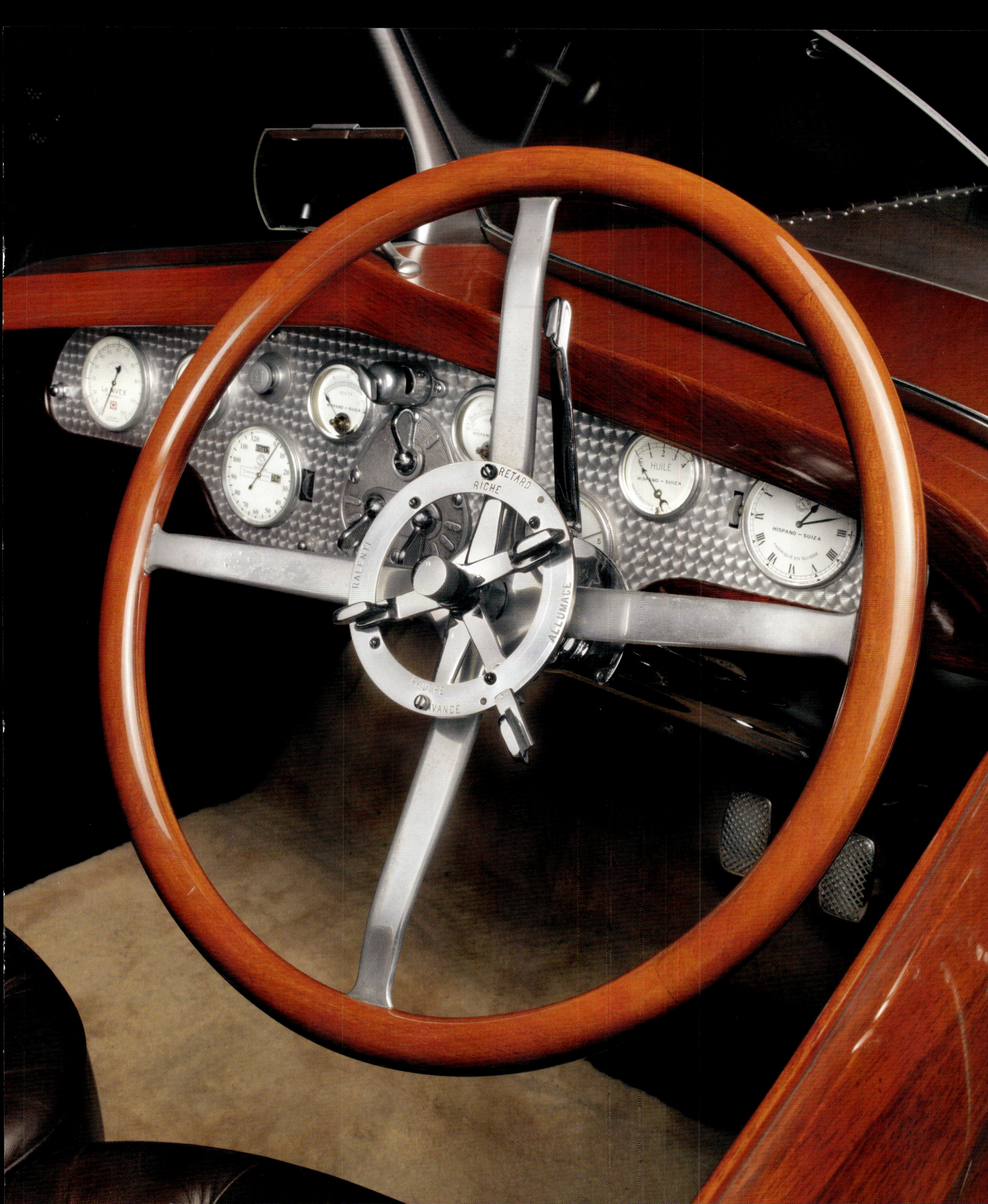
RETARD
RICHE
RALENTI
ALLUMAGE
HUILE
HISPANO – SUIZA

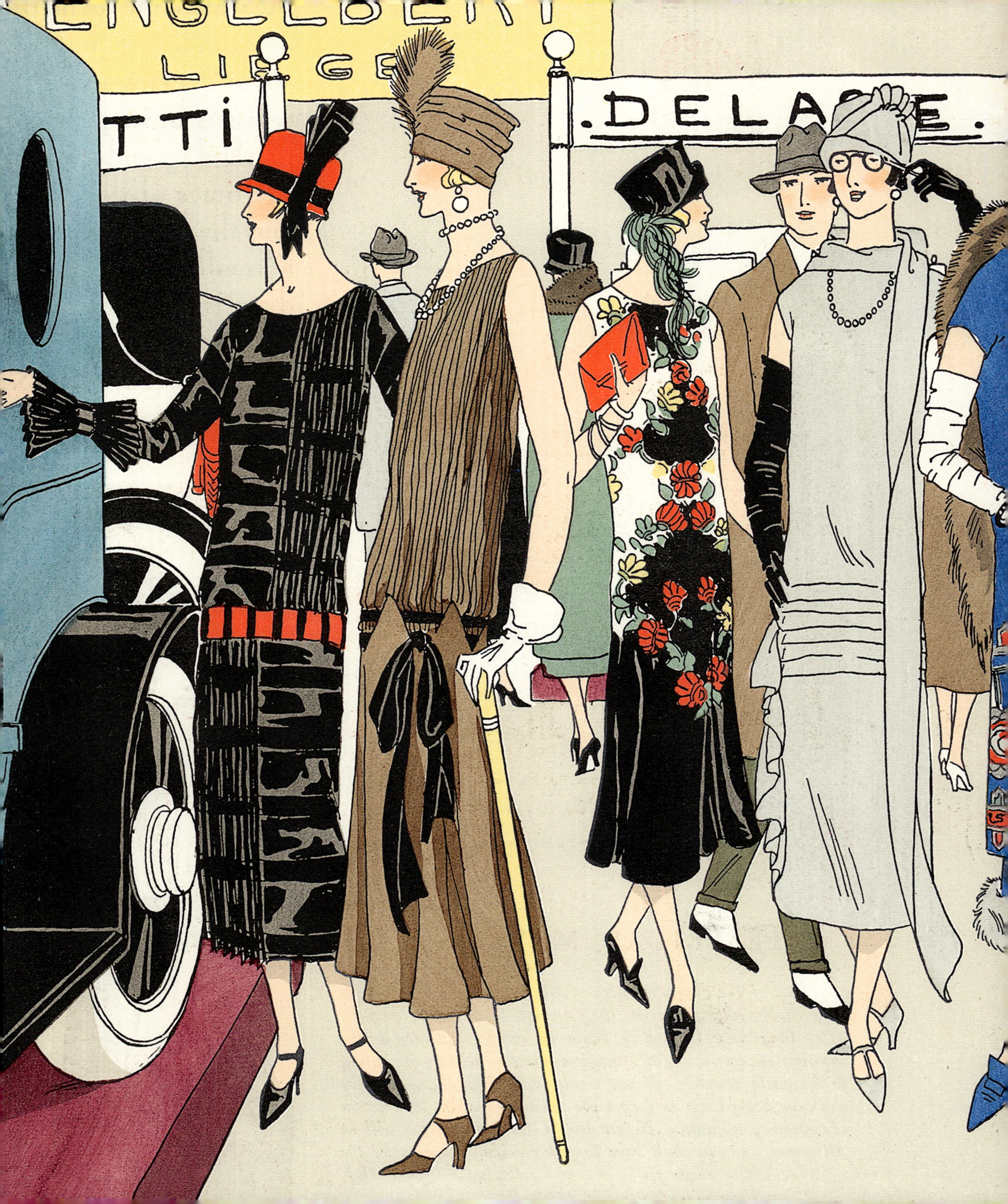

TTI
.DELA E.

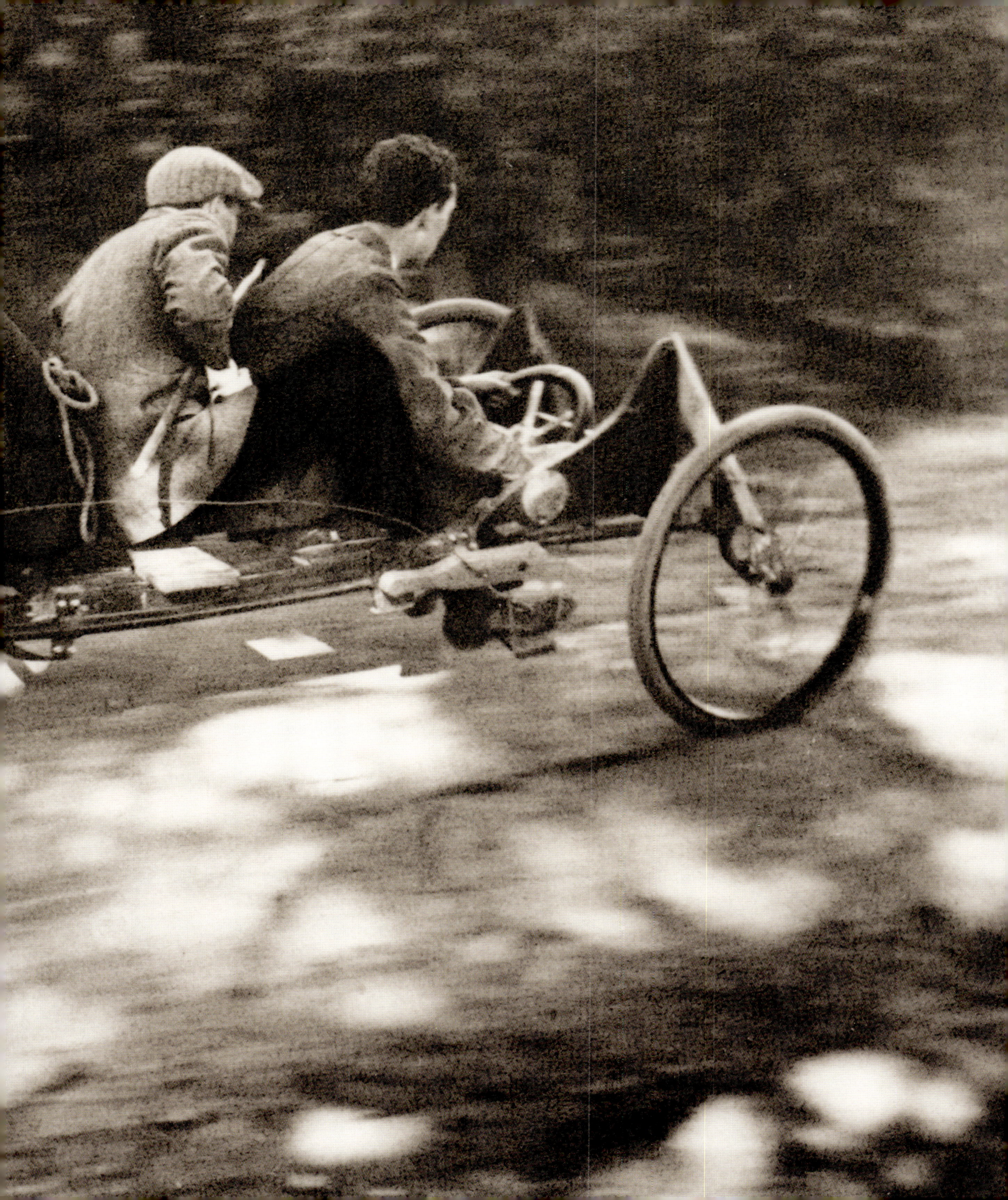

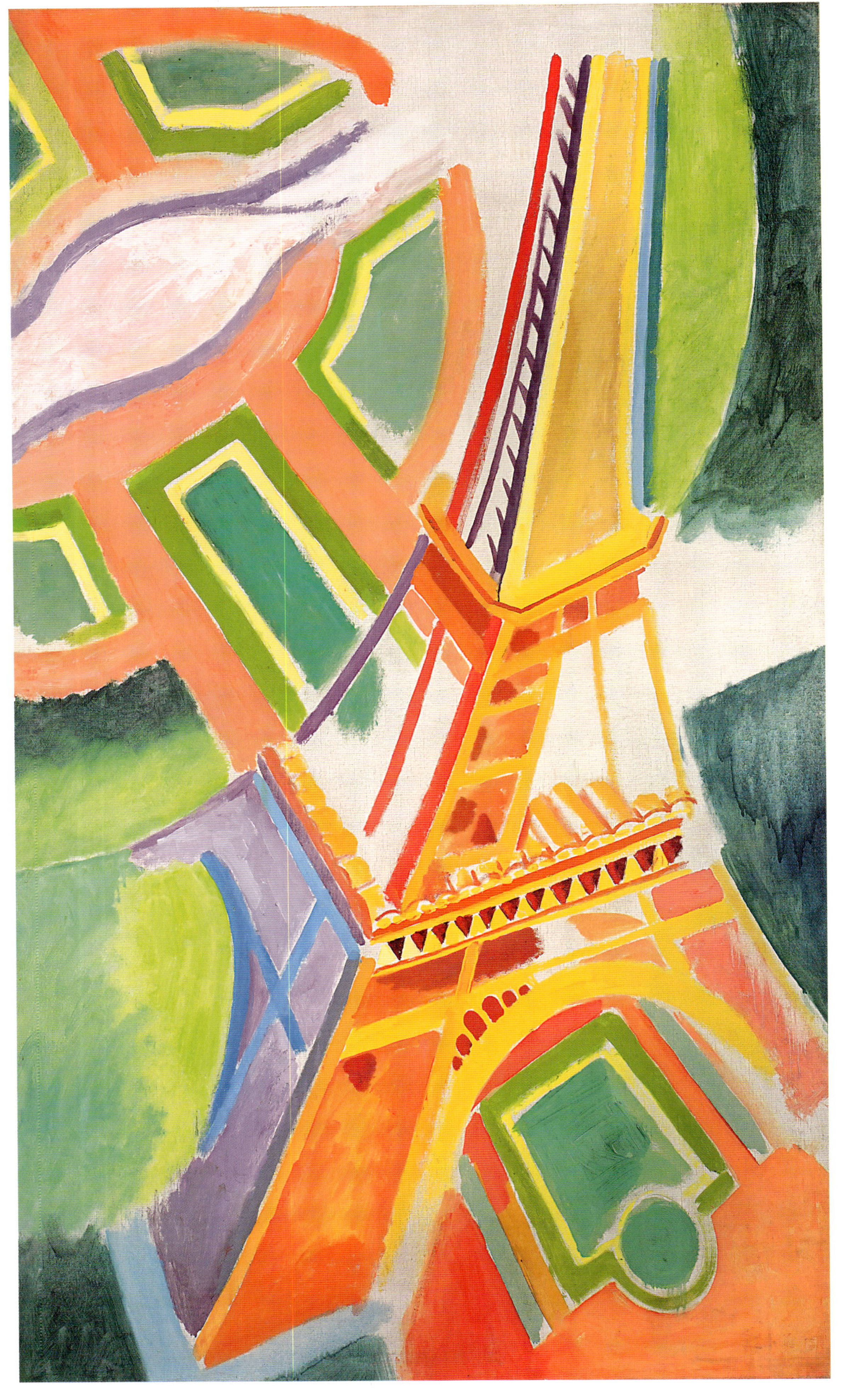

FIG. 1
Robert Delaunay, French, 1885–1941; *Eiffel Tower*, 1924; oil on canvas; 63 ⅝ × 38 ⅛ in.; Saint Louis Art Museum, Gift of Mr. and Mrs. Morton D. May 536:1956

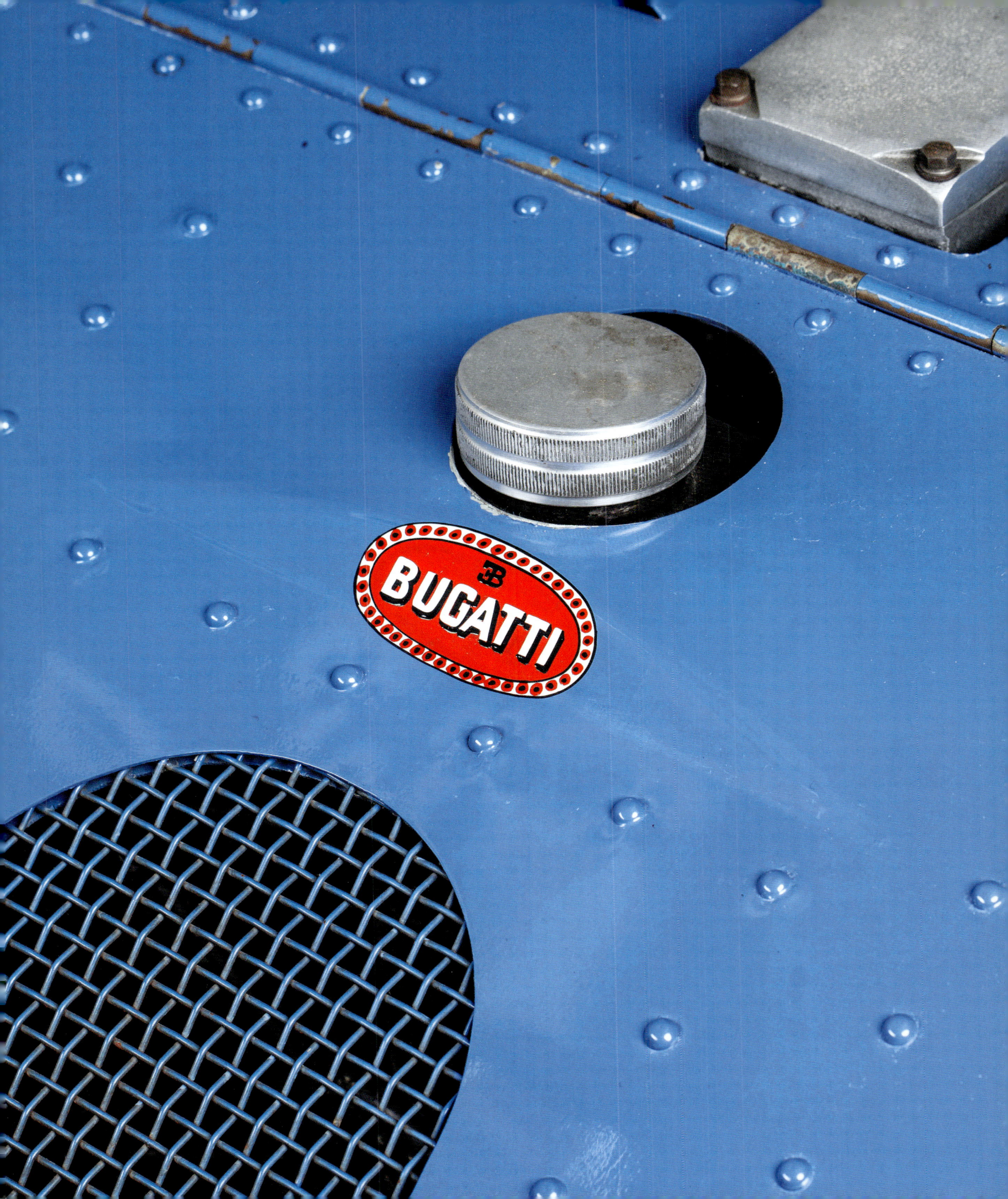
BUGATTI

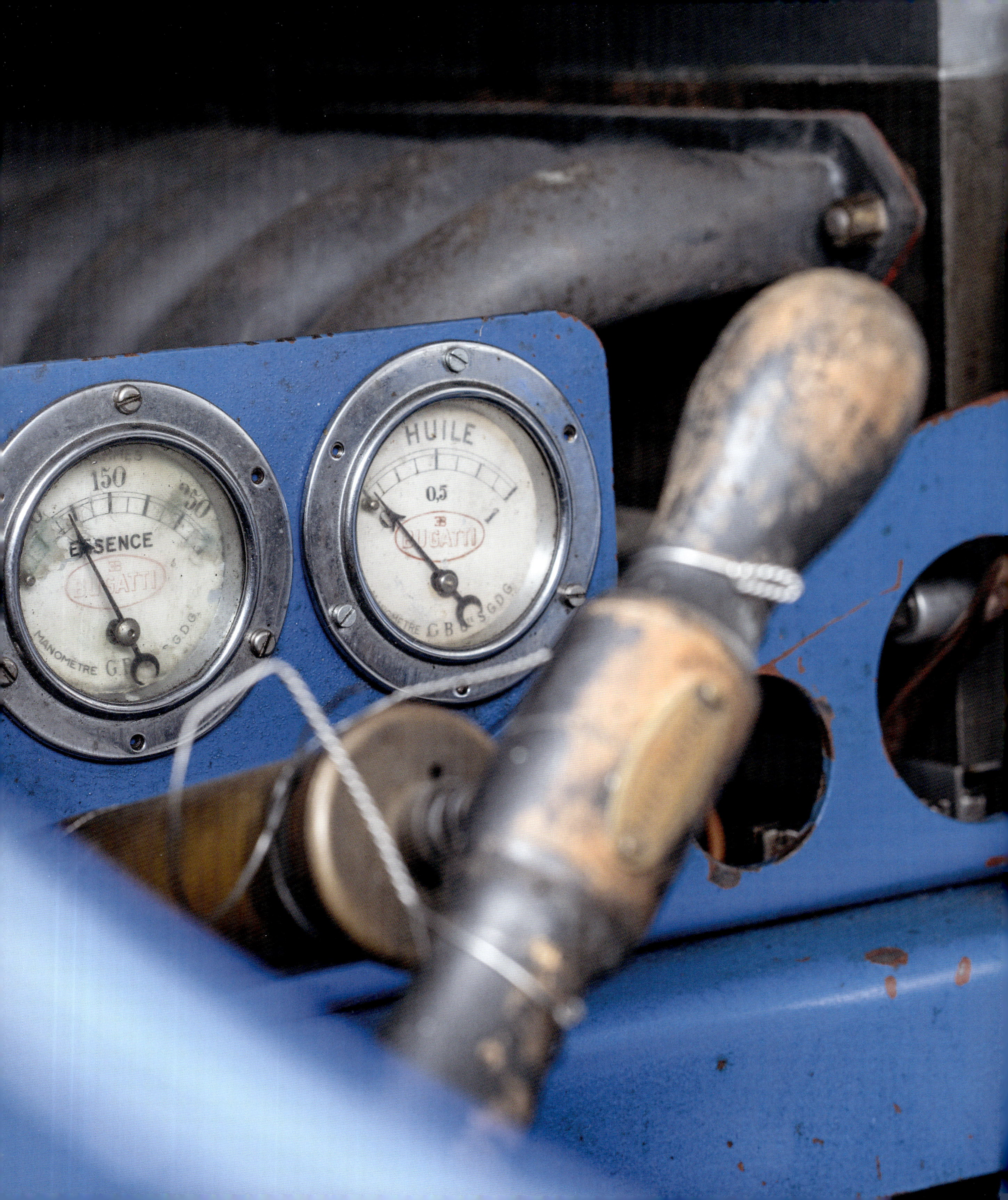
150
250
ESSENCE
BUGATTI
MANOMETRE
HUILE
0,5
1
BUGATTI

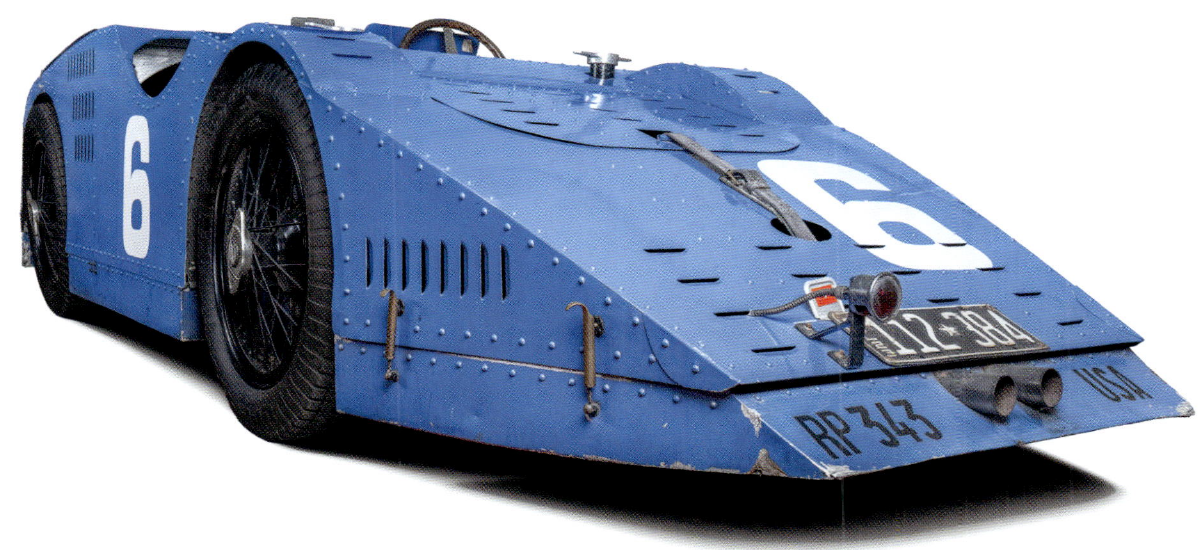

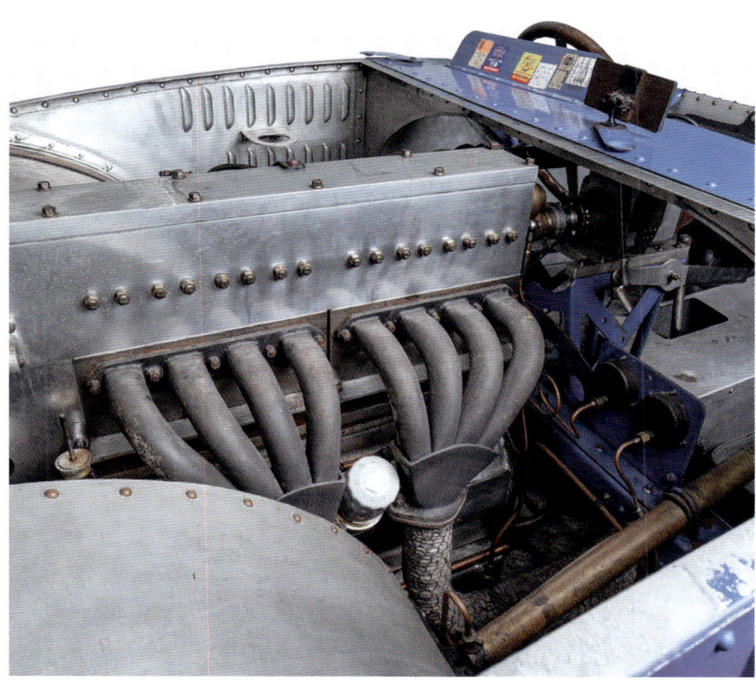

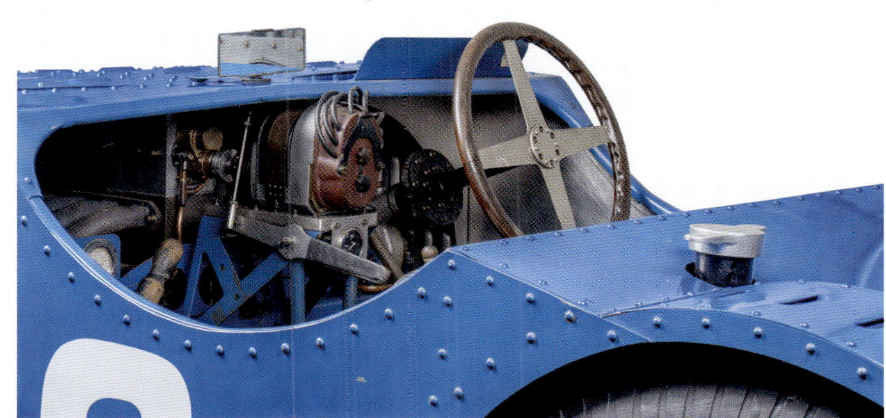

Paul Foulkes-Halbard, who had duplicated many original Tank components. The recreation was completed in 1981 in time for the Bugatti Centenary in Alsace. Some 58 years after its debut at Tours, the born-again Tank was driven around the original Tours Grand Prix course.

Writing in *Pur Sang*, the American Bugatti Club magazine, in 1981, Sutherland noted: "You can well imagine that with no firewall there is intimate communication between driver and machinery. The clutch whirrs dangerously close to one's left leg, the pipes get hot, oil splatters all over you, and there is a lot of exhaust, hot water, steam, noise and danger. The exhaust glows, gas dribbles steadily on your feet, and backfires light up the universe. All very exciting."[1]

Loaned by the Mathews Family

1 Bob Sutherland, "Building the T32 Tank Replica," *Pur Sang* 21 (1981): 2.

1925 HISPANO-SUIZA H6B LABOURDETTE SKIFF-TORPEDO

KEN GROSS

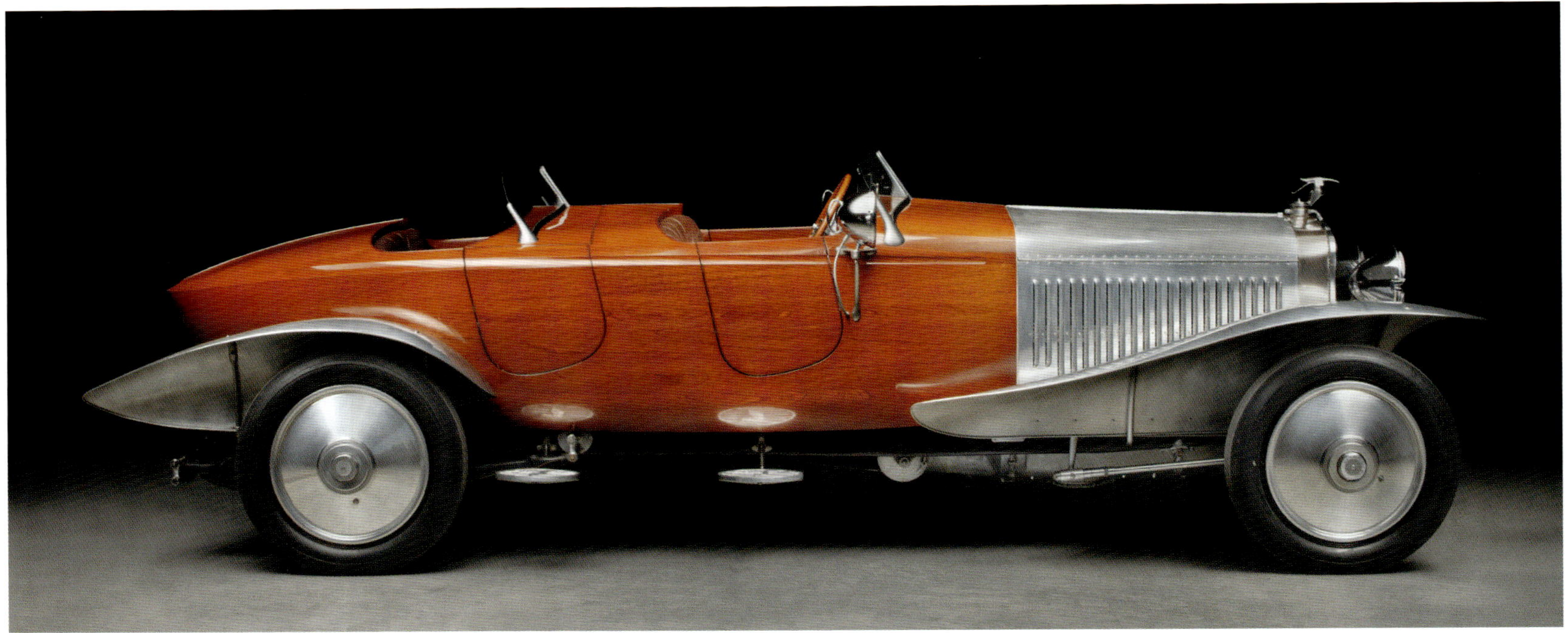

After Jean Henri-Labourdette, French, 1888–1972; Hispano-Suiza, Barcelona, Spain, founded 1904; *Skiff-Torpedo*, 1925; 65 × 219 × 70 in.; The North Collection

The Swiss engineer Marc Birkigt (1878–1953) moved to Barcelona in 1899 to build an electric autobus for a company called La Cuadra. When that project foundered, Birkigt built two gasoline-powered automobiles, but that effort also failed. In 1904, partnering with Damián Mateù and Francisco Seix, Birkigt established Hispano-Suiza, literally "Spanish-Swiss," a luxury automobile company.[1]

Early competition successes, including the Coupe des Voiturettes Boulogne with the racing driver Jean Chassagne, attracted the attention of King Alfonso XIII of Spain. He purchased a chassis and raced an eponymous sports roadster, helping to ensure the fledgling firm's success. When France proved to be a stronger market for luxury cars, Hispano-Suiza built a factory near Paris in 1911 and expanded it in 1914.

During World War I, Birkigt, working with his chief engineer, Louis Massuger, turned to the development and manufacture of advanced aircraft engines. The duo developed an overhead camshaft aluminum block V8 with steel liners—most aircraft engines used individual cylinders bolted to a common crankcase—resulting in a stronger, simpler, and lighter configuration. The Hispano V8 engine powered the famous SPAD S.VII, the fighter plane used by the legendary French ace Georges Guynemer (1894–1917), who shot down fifty-four enemy aircraft before he was killed in action. Guynemer's *Escadrille Cigogne* (Stork Squadron) emblem became the enduring symbol for Hispano-Suiza.

After the war, Hispano-Suiza resumed auto production, introducing the all-new H6 in 1919. Its massive 6.7-liter, in-line, single overhead six was essentially half of a Hispano-Suiza V-12 aircraft engine. The H6 featured full-pressure lubrication; dual ignition; a rugged seven main bearing crankshaft; and a unique, light alloy, four-wheel drum braking system that was amplified by a gearbox-driven brake booster that used the car's momentum to drive the brake servo and provide sure, four-wheeled stopping in an era when most autos made do with two-wheel brakes. It was so effective that Rolls-Royce used it for years under license. The H6C, which followed in 1924, was equipped with an eight-liter I6 engine for more power and torque.

The splendid 133-inch wheelbase H6 chassis attracted the finest coachbuilders: Million-Guiet, Jacques Saoutchik, and Jean Henri-Labourdette in France; Hooper & Co. in England; and Walter M. Murphy Company in the United States. Hispano

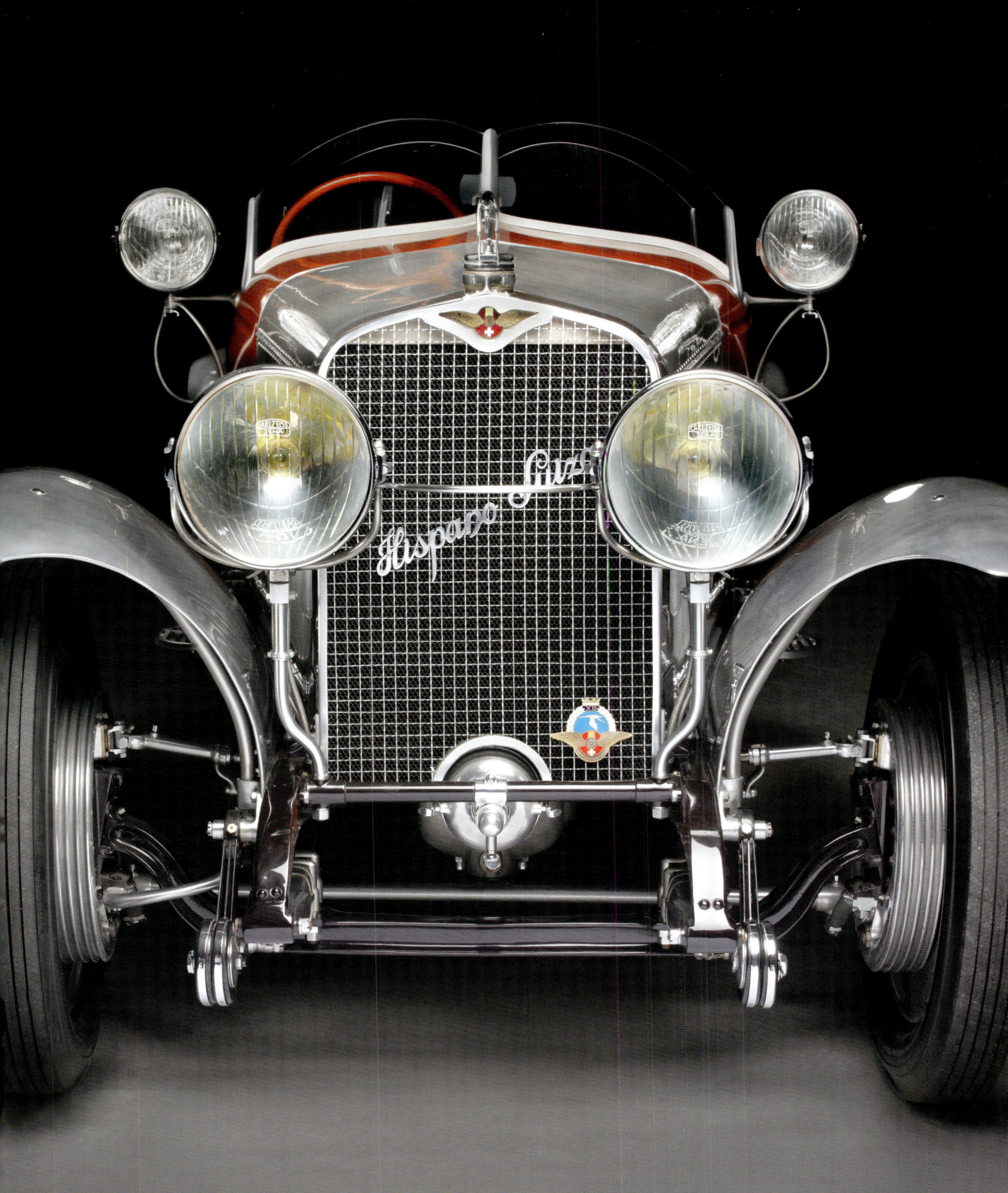
Hispano

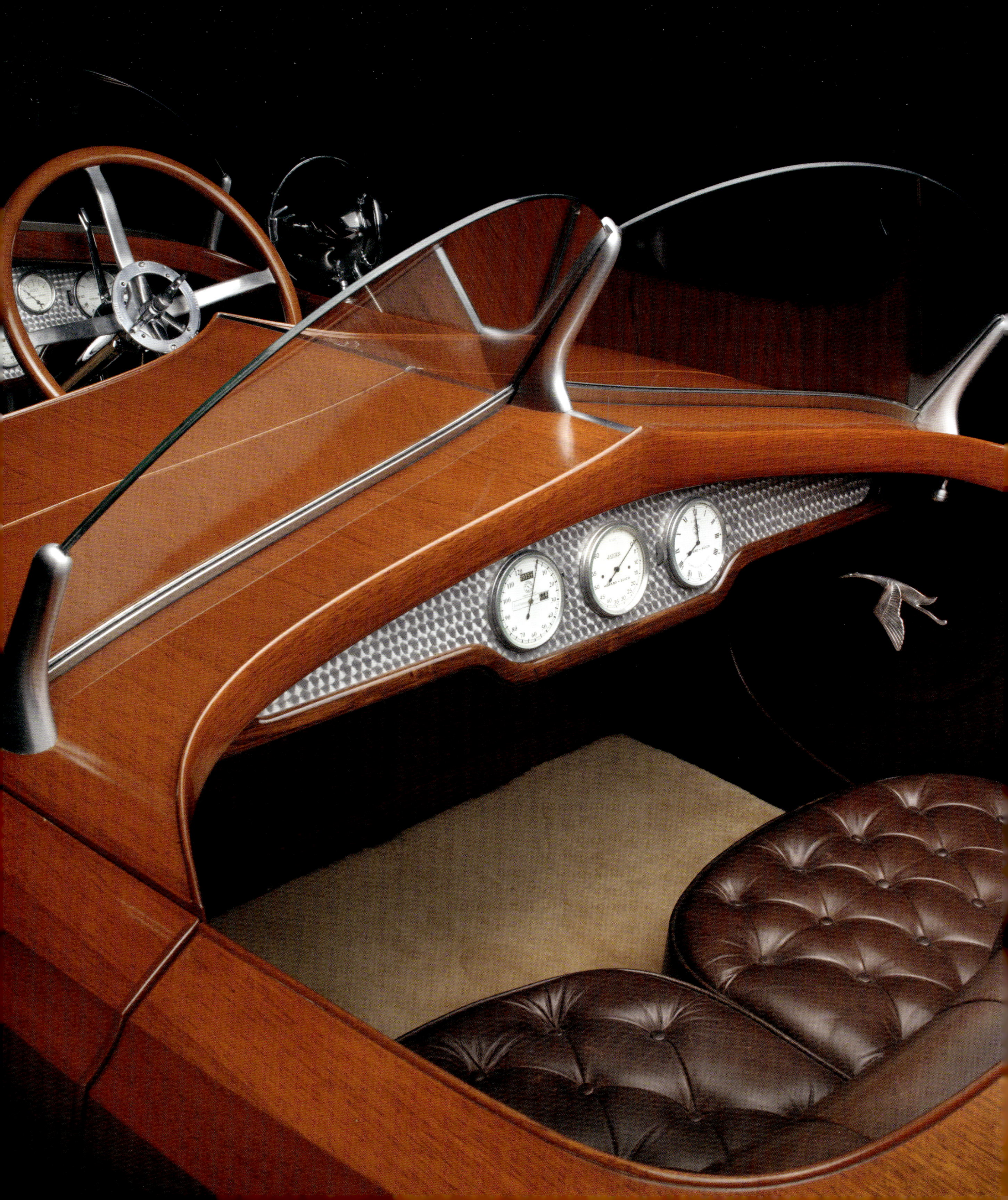

clients included Indian maharajahs and the aperitif distiller André Dubonnet (1897–1980), who had the aircraft engineer Jean Édouard Andreau (1890–1953) design a special torpedo-shaped, aerodynamic coupe with gull-wing windows built by Saoutchik. Dubonnet also owned an H6C Boulogne Targa Florio speedster with a tulipwood "skiff" body.[2]

This car, chassis no. 11256, was invoiced, according to original factory records in 1925, to a "Prince Cito," whose full name was Prince Carlo Cito Filomarino (Italian, 1891–1954, active France). When Judge John North bought this H6 in 1966, it had been stored outdoors and had suffered damage from a fire. The original body by Million-Guiet was beyond saving. A new "skiff" body after the style of Labourdette was designed and constructed in traditional fashion, made of Spanish cedar over white ash framing, by Maryland artisans Don Loweree and John Todd.

Loaned by the North Collection

1 Johnnie Green, *The Legendary Hispano-Suiza* (Londor: Dalton Watson Fine Books, 1977), 13–15.

2 Green, *Legendary Hispano-Suiza*, 140.

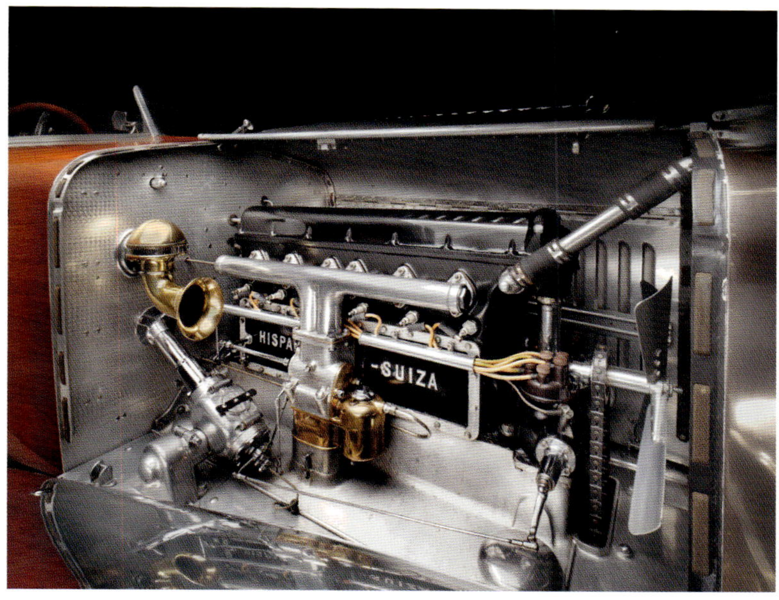

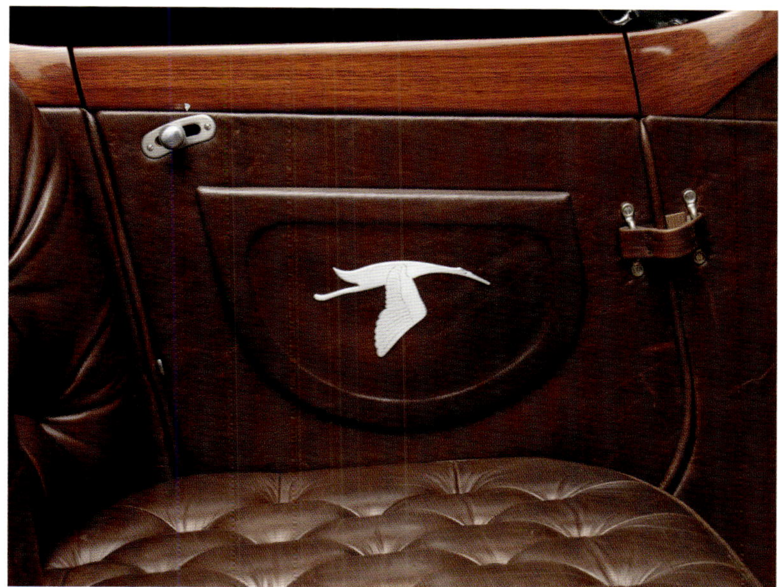

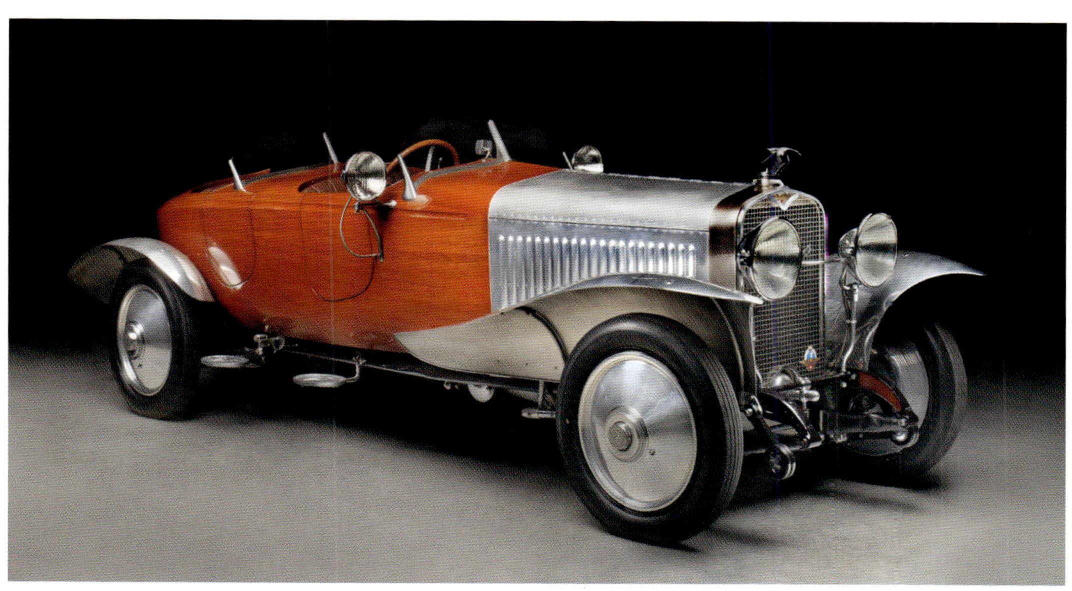

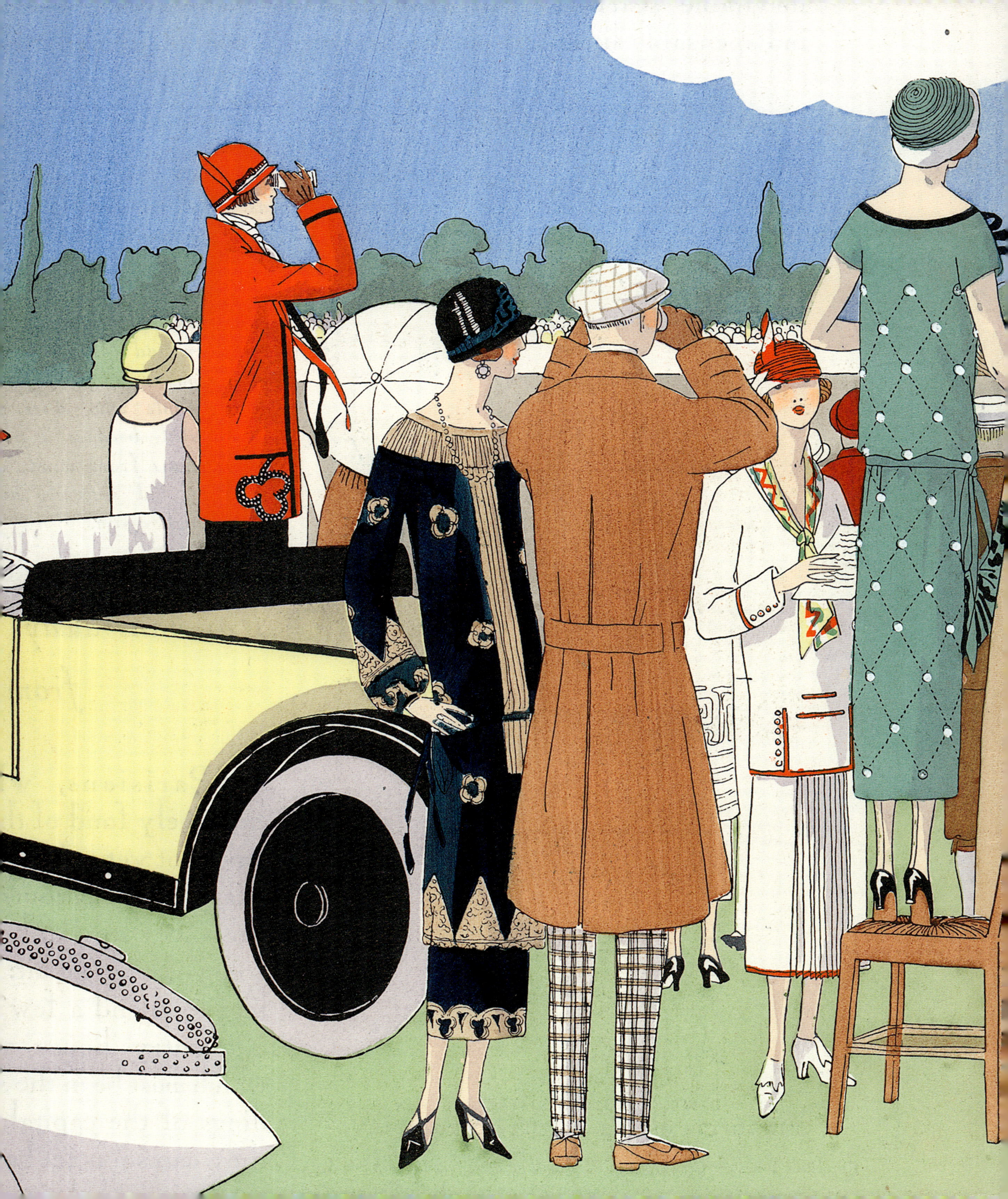

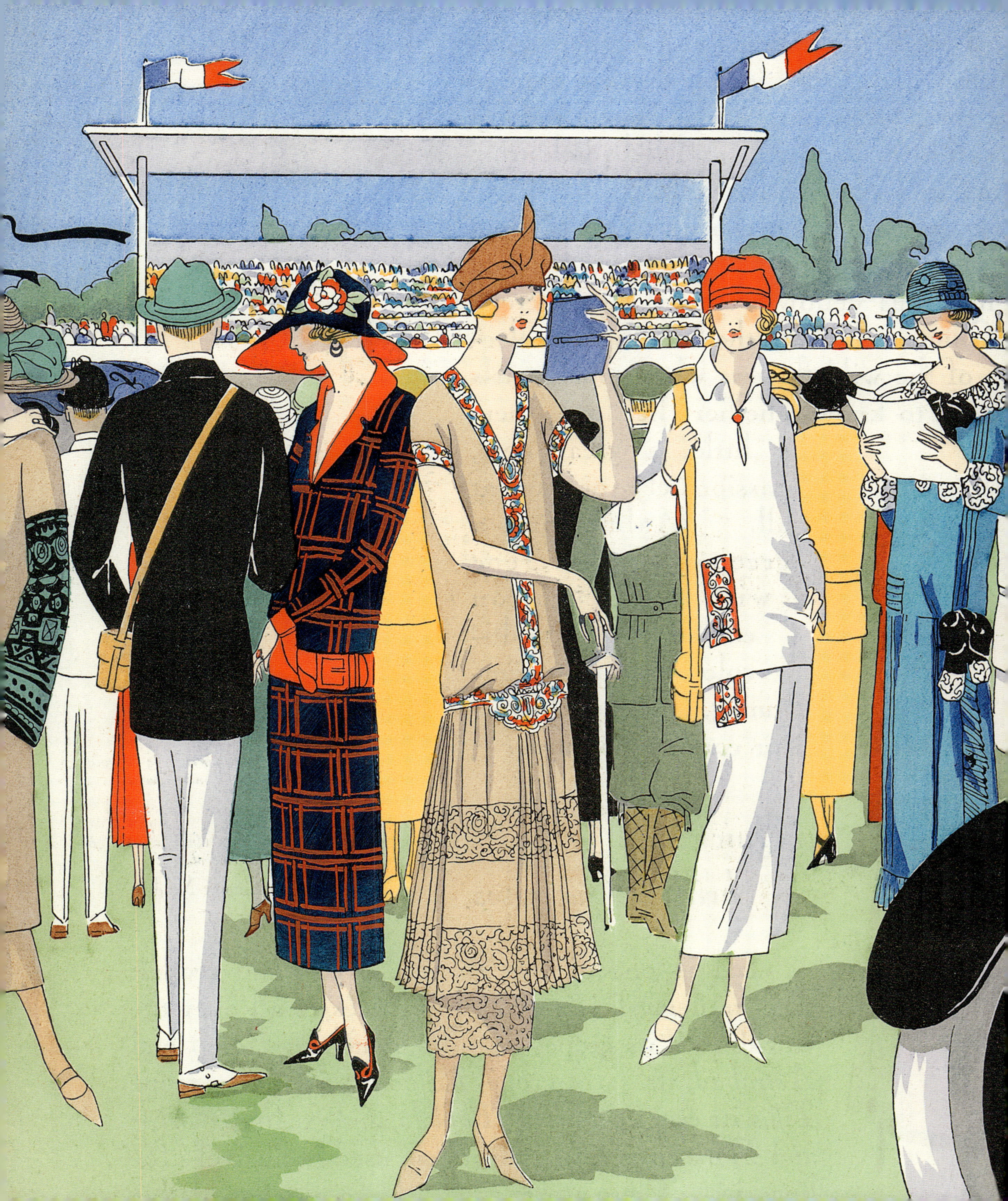

CLOSED-BODY PROBLEMS

Modernism, Gender, and the *Esthétique de l'automobile*

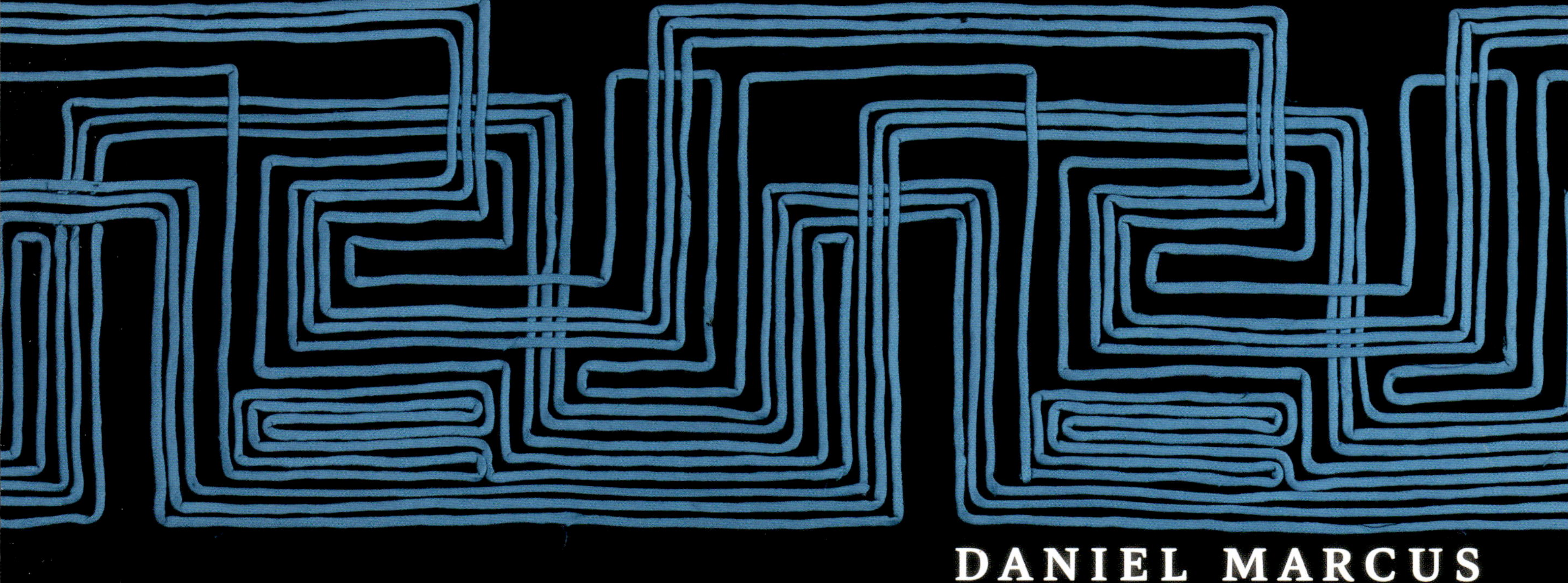

DANIEL MARCUS

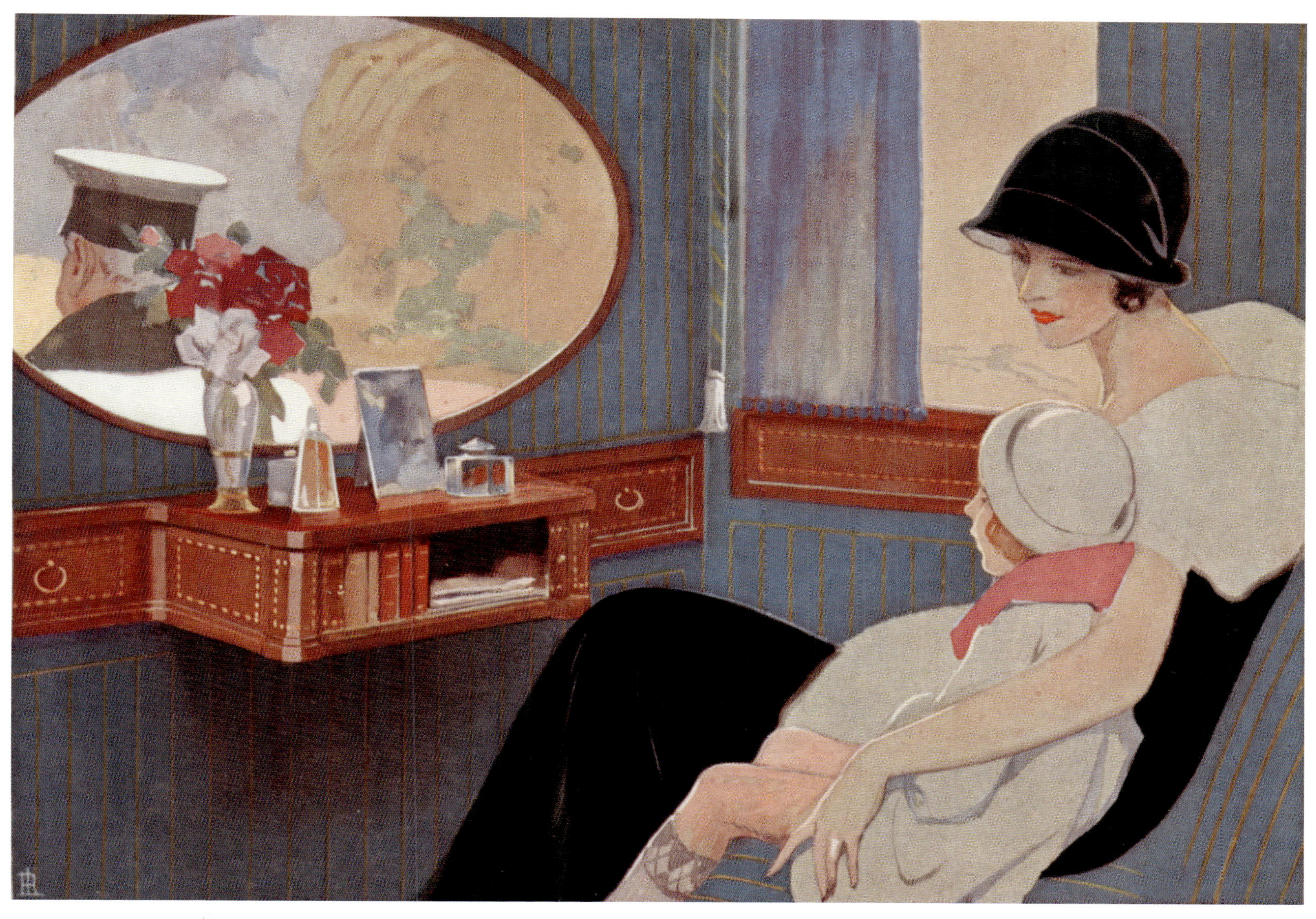

FIG. 14
Illustrated by René Lelong, French, 1871–1933; printed by Draeger, Paris, founded 1886; "Essai de carrosserie, Coupé de ville" (detail), in *Description des chassis Delaunay Belleville*, 1924; ink on paper; 9 ½ × 10 ¼ in.; Private collection

In 1997, the Los Angeles-based artist Jason Rhoades exhibited a sculptural homage to Francis Picabia, the Surrealist-affiliated modernist who, like Rhoades, professed an obsession with race cars (FIG. 15). Irreverently titled *Fucking Picabia Cars with Ejection Seat*, the sculpture resembled a pair of automobiles only in the loosest sense (FIG. 16). Constructed from metal scaffolding, plywood, plastic buckets, and various other materials, Rhoades meant the work to suggest two vehicles locked in mechanical coitus. Photocopied images of Picabia's automobile collection adorn the sculpture's wooden exterior, including one taken by Man Ray in 1924, in which the race car's forward thrust seems to bend the image around the passing machine. Atop one of the vehicular forms sits a screen playing a loop of pornographic images, linking the assemblage to the spectacle of sleaze and the automobile's long-standing role as a space of sexual encounter. Rhoades specified that Picabia's paintings were to be installed adjacent to the work, implying a causal relationship between reckless driving, vehicular sex, and the making of modern art.

From the vantage of Southern California in the 1990s, the relevance of automobilism to modernism hardly needed pointing out. At the dawn of the motor era, however, artists embraced the automobile timidly, if at all. Few could afford to own a car in the first decade of production, and those who did—such as Claude Monet, who acquired a Panhard et Levassor in 1901—left no trace of its impact in their art. The same cannot be said of the literary avant-garde, which seized upon the motorcar more or less immediately, incorporating the disorienting, frequently elliptical experience of the road journey as a narrative and poetic trope. For visual artists, however, the new technology proved more difficult to handle aesthetically. Adapted from existing coachwork design, early automobiles often repelled spectators accustomed to seeing the horse tethered to the coach; lacking a visible source of movement, these horseless carriages seemed malproportioned. While early automobilists often

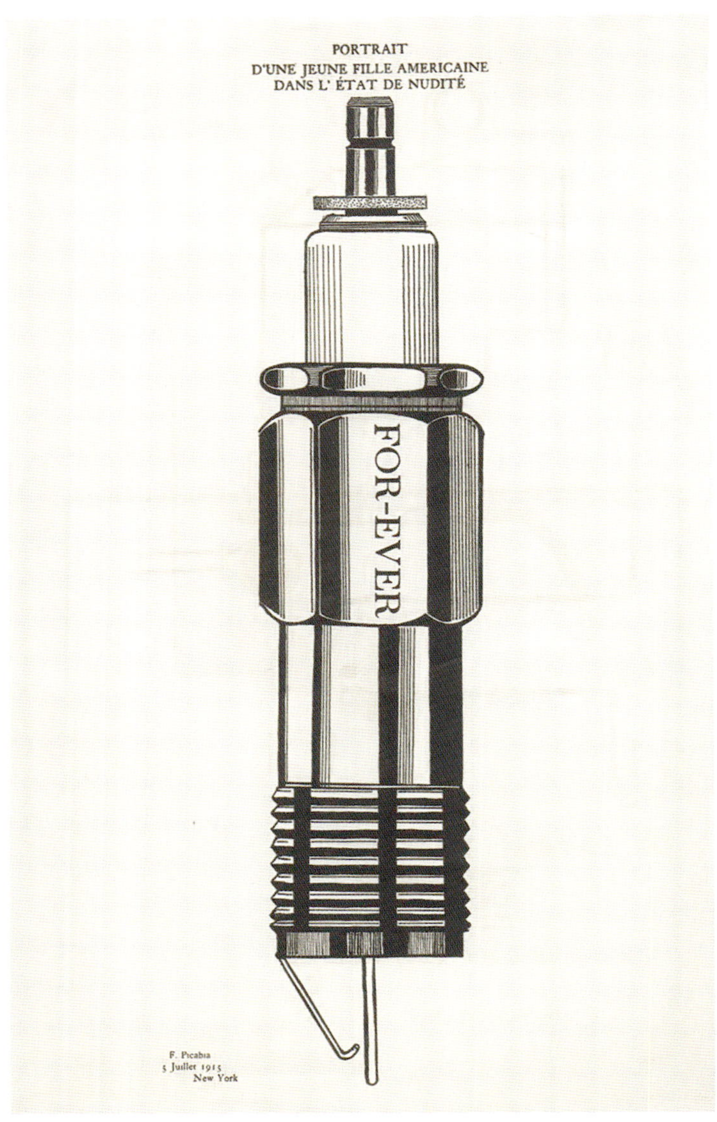

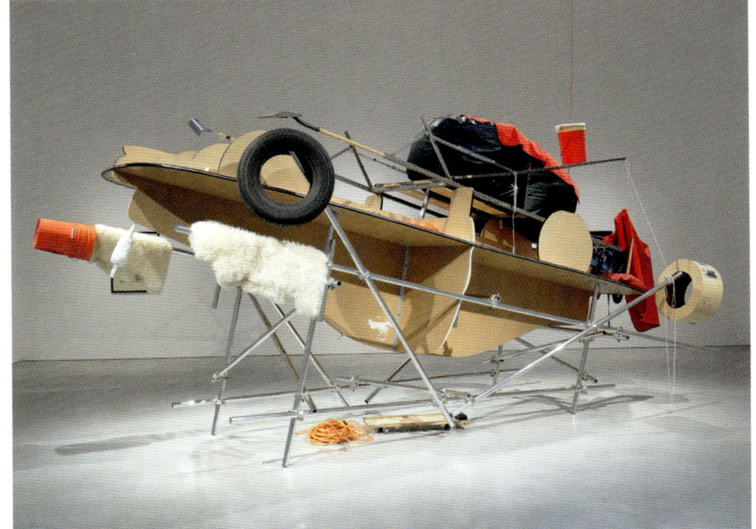

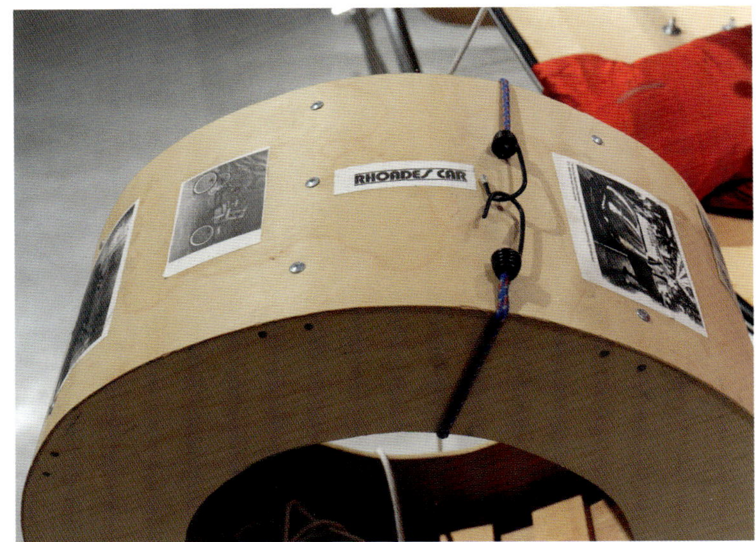

described the cinematic qualities of the motor journey, the car represented a means to this end rather than an object of aesthetic interest in its own right. The rugged conditions of prewar automobilism violated most, if not all, codes of bourgeois sensitivity: in a car, travelers risked exposure to noxious fumes, noise, jolts, and an ever-juddering vista of the fugitive landscape (FIG. 17). For riders in open cars, the threat of inclement weather necessitated the provisioning of oilskin coats, goggles, and veils; in closed cars, precipitation left the windows fogged and the cabin damp. In the nascent visual culture of the automobile, beauty rode astride the bestial machine, a metaphor equally present in print advertisements and Futurist poetry. The car barely registered as an aesthetic object, however, and questions of visual appeal figured only peripherally, if at all, to the buyer.

As aesthetics took on a larger role in automotive marketing, this balance began to shift, giving artists greater purchase upon the vehicle. Gender distinctions were key to this change, which the historian Gijs Mom describes as one "from technology to appearance and aesthetics . . . which according to some contemporary observers (and historians in their footsteps) led to a crucial increase in the role of women in co-constructing the car."[1] Affording protection from dust and wind, closed cars allowed passengers to travel in everyday clothing rather than a driving costume, an advantage deemed particularly relevant to women motorists and their families, who became their target audience. Marketed as an extension of the bourgeois apartment, these vehicles, which the French called *conduites intérieures*, provided opportunity for decorative embellishment (FIGS. 18–22). A 1911 issue of the women's magazine *Fémina*, for example, advertised a luxuriously appointed *conduite intérieure* as a "Home sur la route" (the English "home" evoking a distinctively British style of domesticity), in which "one can eat, make a cup of tea, write a letter, powder and fix one's hair; and if

FIG. 15
Francis Picabia, French, 1879–1953; *Portrait of a Young American Girl in the State of Nudity, 291* 5–6, July–August 1915

FIG. 16 A, B
Jason Rhoades, American, 1965–2006; *Installation view of Fucking Picabia Cars with Ejection Seat*, 1997/2000; mixed media; 126 × 240 1/8 × 110 ¼ in.; Private collection

the road becomes unpleasant or boring, one can even play a game of bridge . . . or sleep."[2] Likewise, an advertisement for a Belgian manufacturer of luxury car accessories, P. L. Bozon et Cie, presents the interior of a stately limousine as a boudoir, complete with a vanity, electric ceiling light, a thermometer, and a heating vent (FIG. 23). Clad in furs, the haute-bourgeois passenger sniffs a flower taken from a small vial, while a visitor and chauffeur wait at the door. Created a decade apart, both documents represent the automobile as a static chamber: in each case, the car is shown parked, as if to imply that domesticity increases as celerity declines.

These changes in the logic of car design, which Mom describes as the "domestication" of the automobile, made an impact on the avant-garde. On the eve of World War I, the Futurist movement had famously embraced automotive technology for its masculinist poetics, juxtaposing the violent power of the motorcar with the comforting calm of bourgeois domesticity. The growing popularity of the *conduite intérieure* scrambled these associations, linking automobilism with a set of values and gender codes antithetical to Futurist machismo. No single artwork better exemplifies this reversal than Henri Matisse's painting *The Windshield, On the Road to Villacoublay* (FIG. 25), which was originally exhibited as *La conduite intérieure*. In 1917, Matisse acquired his first automobile, a 1911 Renault 6 CV, from an Orleans garage where it had been stored since the first days of the war.[3] With its closed coachworks, the Renault functioned both as a family car and as an extension of Matisse's studio, allowing him to take painting equipment along on drives with his son Pierre, who played the role of chauffeur. (Matisse *père* had not yet learned to drive.) It was on one such occasion that Matisse turned his attention to the car interior, treating the Renault as a frame for the surrounding greenery. The presence of Matisse's sketchbook propped against the front seat marks the car as both a portable workspace and camera lucida—that is, a device for recording changing aspects of the landscape. As the critic Roger Fry noted in a 1924 review, however, the painting belonged equally, if not more so, to the genre of still life, trading on the "odd distortion of things seen half through glass and half directly."[4] True to the work's title, Matisse devoted special attention to the panoramic frieze of windows, especially the front windshield. Rather than depict this apparatus as a limpid aperture, however, he subtly permits each windowpane its own pictorial autonomy; on the left, for example,

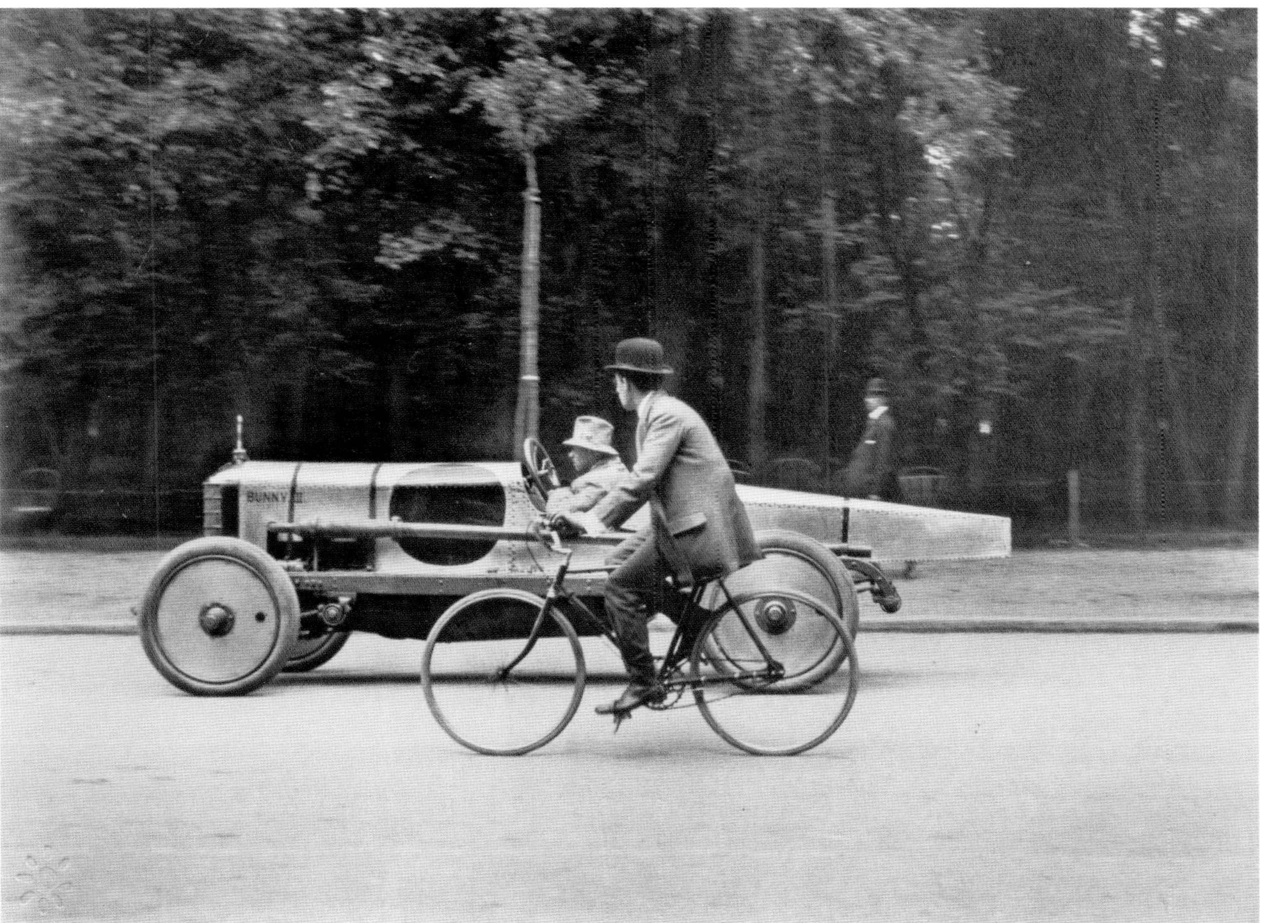

FIG. 17
Jacques-Henri Lartigue, French, 1894–1986; *The Singer Racing Car "Bunny III,"* from "The Lartigue Portfolio," 1912, printed 1977; gelatin silver print; 6 3/8 × 8 3/8 in.; Saint Louis Art Museum, Gift of Frederick P. Currier 305:1995.8

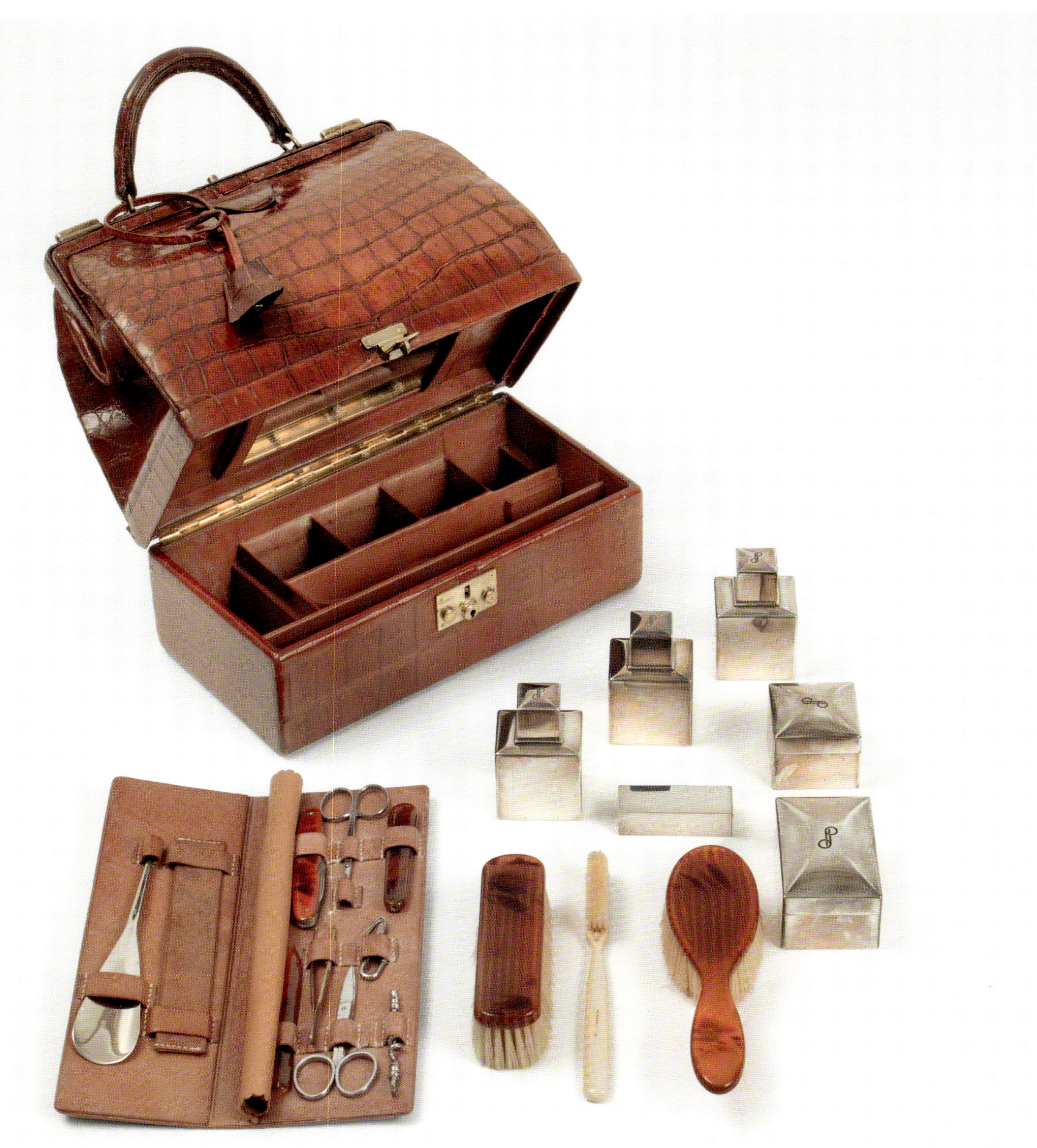

FIG. 18
Hermès, Paris, founded 1837; *Sac Mallette with Accessories,* 1929; saltwater crocodile, ivory, silver-plated metal, stainless steel, bovid horn, boar's hair, tortoiseshell, glass, mirror, morocco goatskin, silk, and gold-plated brass Conservatoire des Créations Hermès, Paris CSV-0666

Introduced by Hermès in the early 1920s, the Sac Mallette was one of the company's first designs aimed at car travelers. The sturdy base kept it upright during bumpy rides, and the dual compartments ensured maximum storage in minimum space. Begun as a horse harness and bridle maker in 1837, Hermès adapted its leatherwork expertise to the demands of modern transport, especially automobiles.

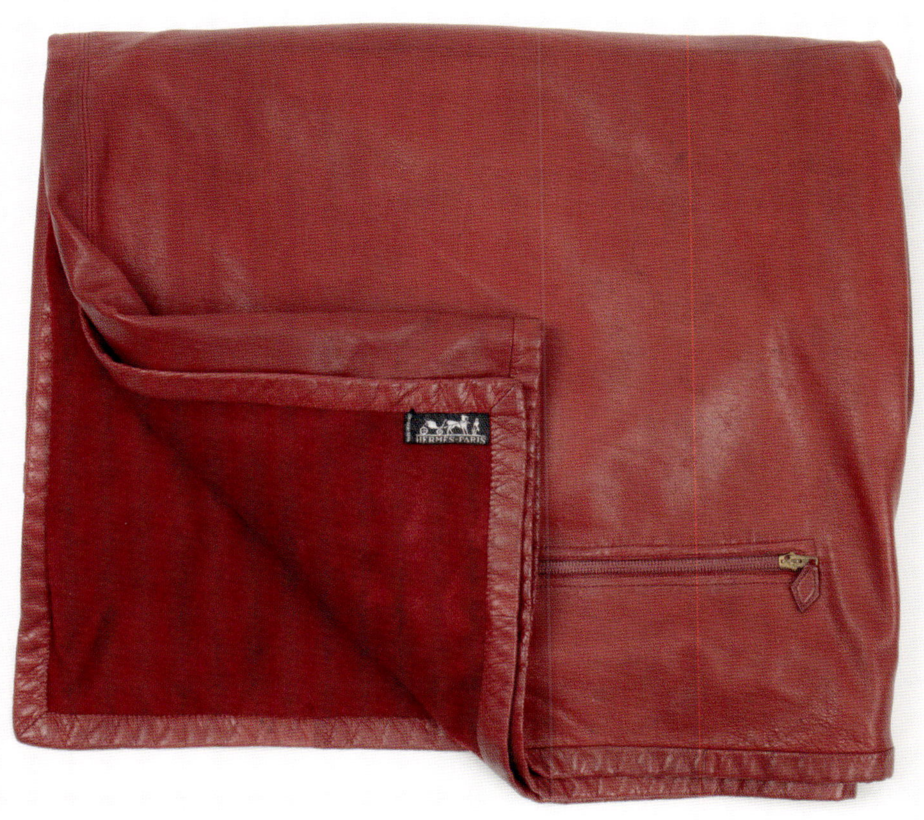

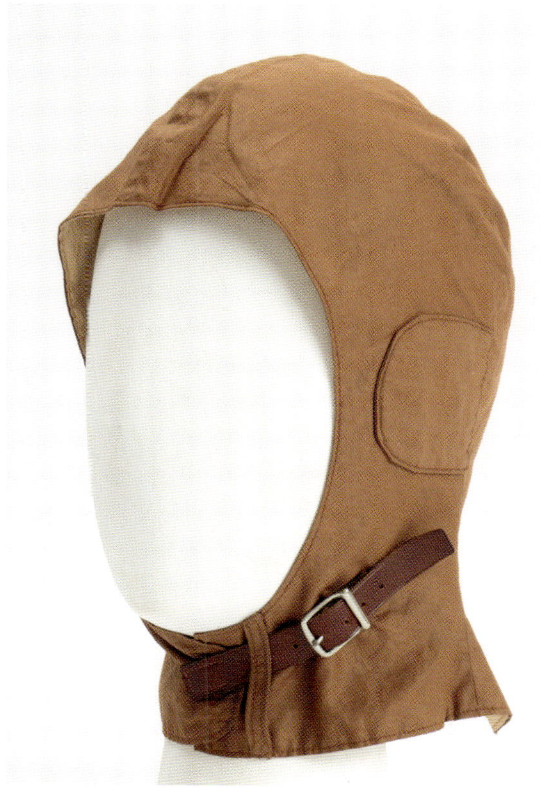

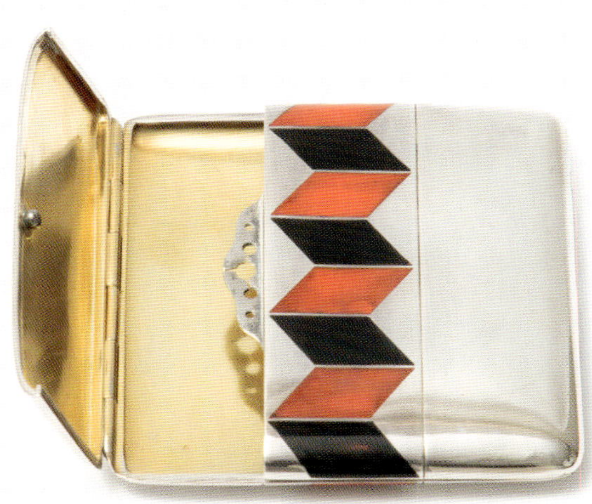

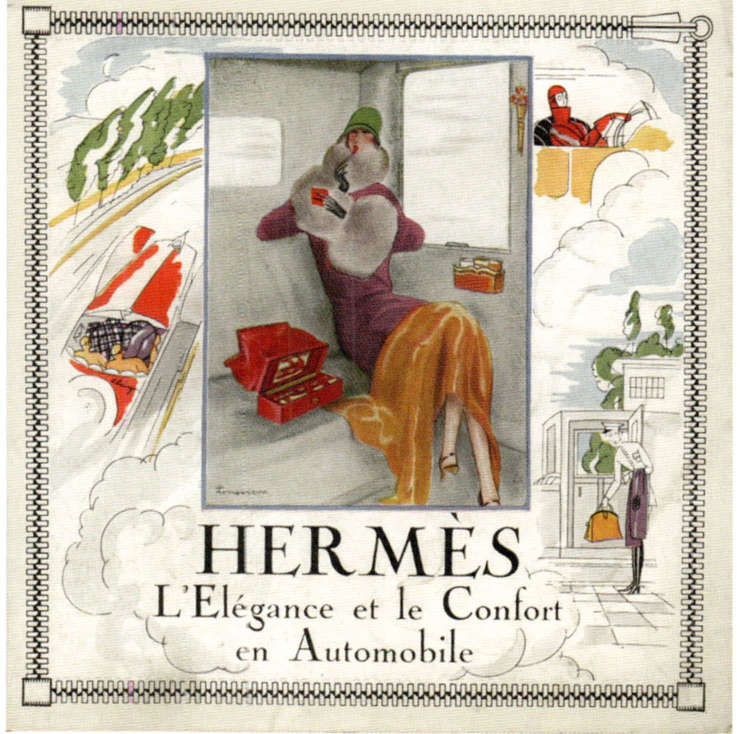

FIG. 19
Hermès, Paris, founded 1837; *Automobile Travel Blanket*, designed c.1925, made c.1950; lambskin and cashmere; Conservatoire des Créations Hermès, Paris

FIG. 21
Hermès, *Cigarette Case*, 1930s; silver, lacquer, and vermeil; Conservatoire des Créations Hermès, Paris

FIG. 20
Hermès, Paris, founded 1837, *Driving Hood*, late 1930s; cotton canvas, silk canvas lining, and box-calf; Conservatoire des Créations Hermès, Paris

FIG. 22
Illustrated by Jose Zinoview; Léon Benigni, French, 1892–1948; published by Draeger, Paris, founded 1886; Hermès catalogue cover, *L'Elégance et le Confort en Automobile* (Automobile elegance and comfort), 1925; Courtesy of the Hermès Archives

This catalogue's "zipper" border references Hermès's French patent for the sliding zipper that head Émile-Maurice Hermès first encountered on a trip during World War I to North America, where he noticed the metal-toothed fastener on canvas automobile roofs.

the upper pane seems to project outward, while the right side slants inward, subtly overlapping the pillar.[5] The resulting landscape is not only fragmented but also discounted, calling into question the car's function as a perceptual apparatus.

As depicted in *The Windshield*, the interior of Matisse's car offers little in the way of domesticity. Yet the painting fits comfortably within a suite of works from 1917 that depict the painter's family life in the Paris suburbs during wartime. Contemporaneous with his large canvas *The Music Lesson* (FIG. 24), a fragmentary group portrait of the Matisses at home, *The Windshield* attests to the automobile's function in domestic life, documenting a journey that united father and son in compressed proximity.[6] Although not portrayed directly, Pierre's role as chauffeur can be felt in absentia: sketching the interior of the parked car, Matisse made no effort to hide the car's motionlessness, a condition he had no direct power to alter. This stasis was immediately apparent to Fry, who begins his description of *The Windshield* by noting, "The chauffeur has gone off," effectively abandoning the painter—and, by association, the viewer—to his backseat vista. Had Pierre returned, however, he would have blocked the view through the front windshield. Removing his son from the scene, Matisse projects himself into the imaginary position of driver, a perspective he could at best grasp vicariously, from a parental remove.

While domesticity continued to be associated with closed cars well into the 1920s, marking the vehicle as implicitly (and often explicitly) feminine-gendered, a new set of aesthetic concerns began to coalesce around the values of comfort, privacy, and mechanical silence. Anxious to improve the performance of *conduites intérieures*, the heavy bodies of which were prone to drafts, rattling, and wear from use, coachbuilders on both sides of the Atlantic developed new systems of body construction, often drawing from advances in the aeronautic industry. In 1922, for example, the French entrepreneur Charles Weymann patented a system of fabricating closed car bodies based on the construction of airplane fuselages; garnering wide acclaim in the automotive press, these supple-jointed coachworks promised to eliminate the squeaks and creaks that had plagued early sedans, while also improving fuel efficiency. Branding his company a purveyor of silence, Weymann sought to appeal to customers' acoustic sensitivities, as suggested by a 1925 advertisement accompanied by the tagline "A Weymann body satisfies the most delicate ear" (FIG. 26).

In addition to satisfying the passenger's ear, the improvement in sound had the unintended consequence of diminishing other forms of sensory input from the exterior world, such as the driver's field of vision. Yet the coachbuilders' pursuit of hermetic enclosure played a key role in augmenting the visual appeal of the automobile, and spectators were met with increasingly unified shapes and contours in motorcars. Modernists, responding

FIG. 23
Advertisement for P. L. Bozon et Cie, 1921 (detail), in *L'Équipement automobile: Le chic français de l'automobile* 50, July 1921

FIG. 24
Henri Matisse, French, 1869–1954; *The Music Lesson*, 1917; oil on canvas; 96 ½ × 83 in.; The Barnes Foundation, Philadelphia, BF717

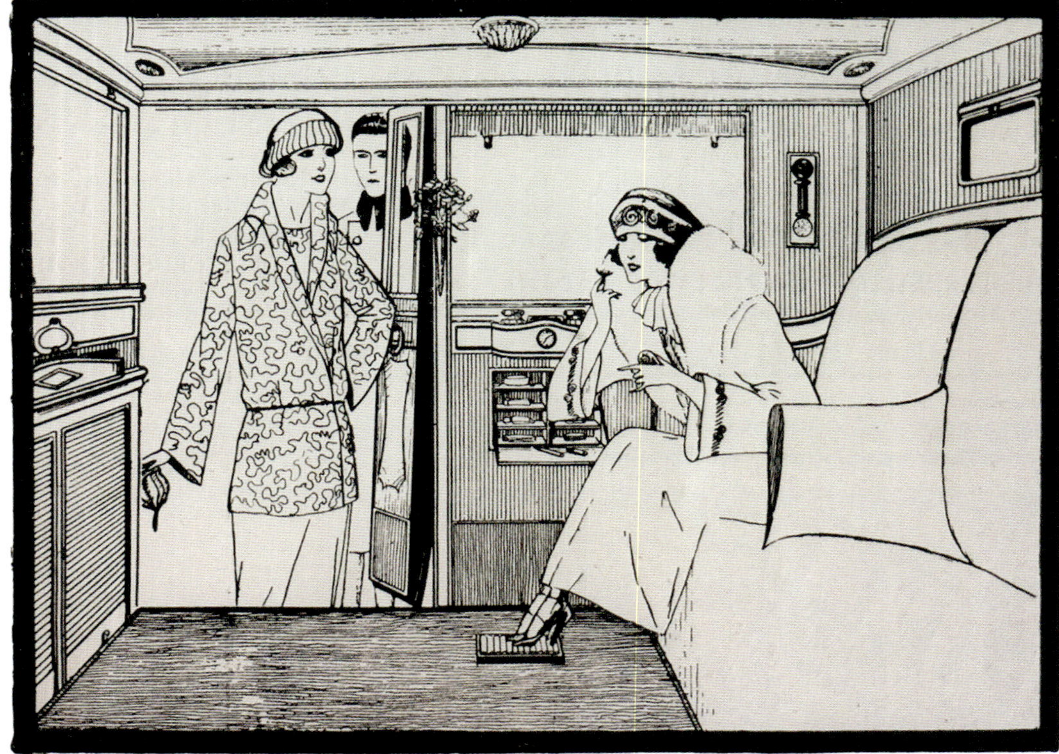

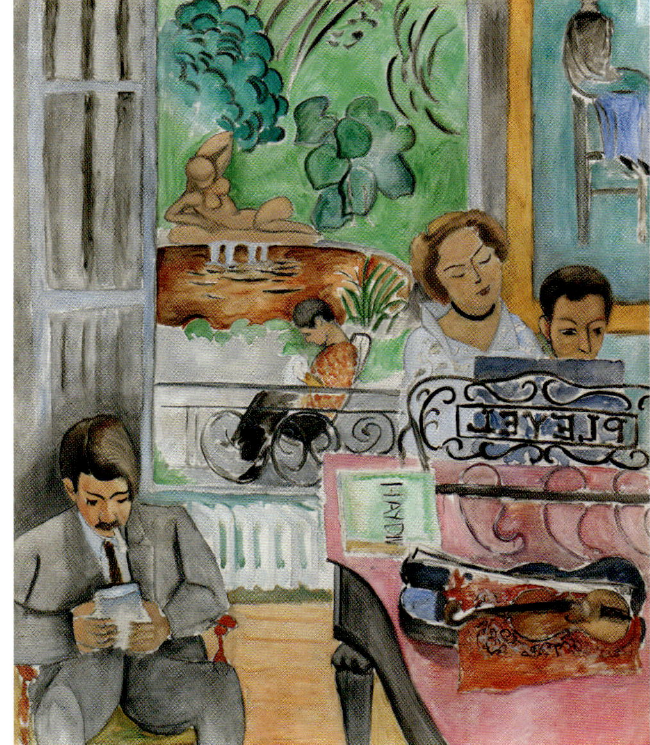

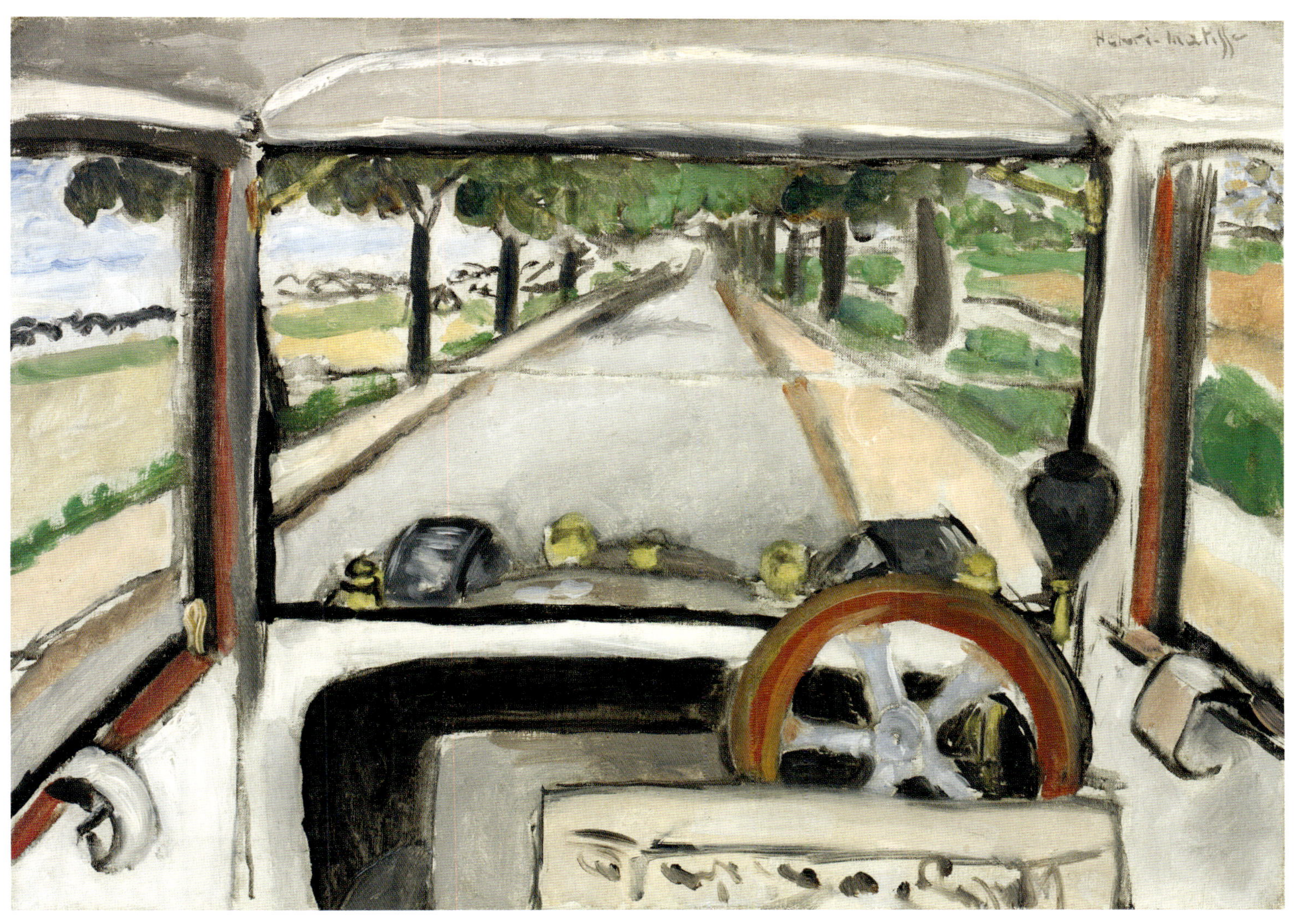

to the "look" of the latest automobiles, gathered under the banner of a new *esthétique de l'automobile* that married comfort and ease of operation with a masculine-coded formal rigor. Key to this discourse was the specter of Fordist mass production: "A new development is upon us, hastened by the arrival of the Americans," announced the journalist Olivier de Carfort in 1919, diagnosing the advent of a novel "vehicle-type, belonging to the domain of the ideal, [which] receives the name of *standard* and its construction, intended for mass production, that of *standardisation.*"[7] Although Carfort rejected the formal "monism"—in other words, the uniform styling—wrought by the Fordist assembly line, he nonetheless recognized a "beauty in this simplification, which consists of covering up buttons or rocker arms, valves, tubes, rods, gaskets, and even spark plugs within tombs of aluminum."[8] Likewise, for the critic Guillaume Janneau, the best car designs hailed from "the engineer's workshop," conforming to "a universally accepted general form, which engineers and coachbuilders have perfected under the direction of a sovereign master: necessity."[9]

FIG. 25
Henri Matisse, French, 1869–1954; *The Windshield, On the Road to Villacoublay*, 1917; oil on canvas; 15 1⁄16 × 21 3⁄4 in.; The Cleveland Museum of Art, Bequest of Lucia McCurdy McBride in memory of John Harris McBride II 1972.225

Among the most vigorous advocates of this new aesthetic were Amédée Ozenfant and Le Corbusier, co-editors of the influential modernist journal *L'Esprit nouveau.* Reviewing the 1921 Salon de l'Automobile, the journal singled out the car manufacturer Gabriel Voisin for praise, attributing his success to the firm's engagement with track racing, a field of motor sports suspended during World War I and now reanimated:

> The Salon de l'Automobile obviously still offers us these ridiculous diplodocuses (Elizalde); but the return of racing has given us *Voisin,* and we must congratulate G[abriel] Voisin and his collaborators, such as M. Noël [André Noël-Noël Telmont], for their search for the organic, for homogeneity linked to a perfection of construction that no foreign manufacturer can equal: they have created chassis that are truly admirable tools; the economy of their organism has yielded magnificent objects.[10]

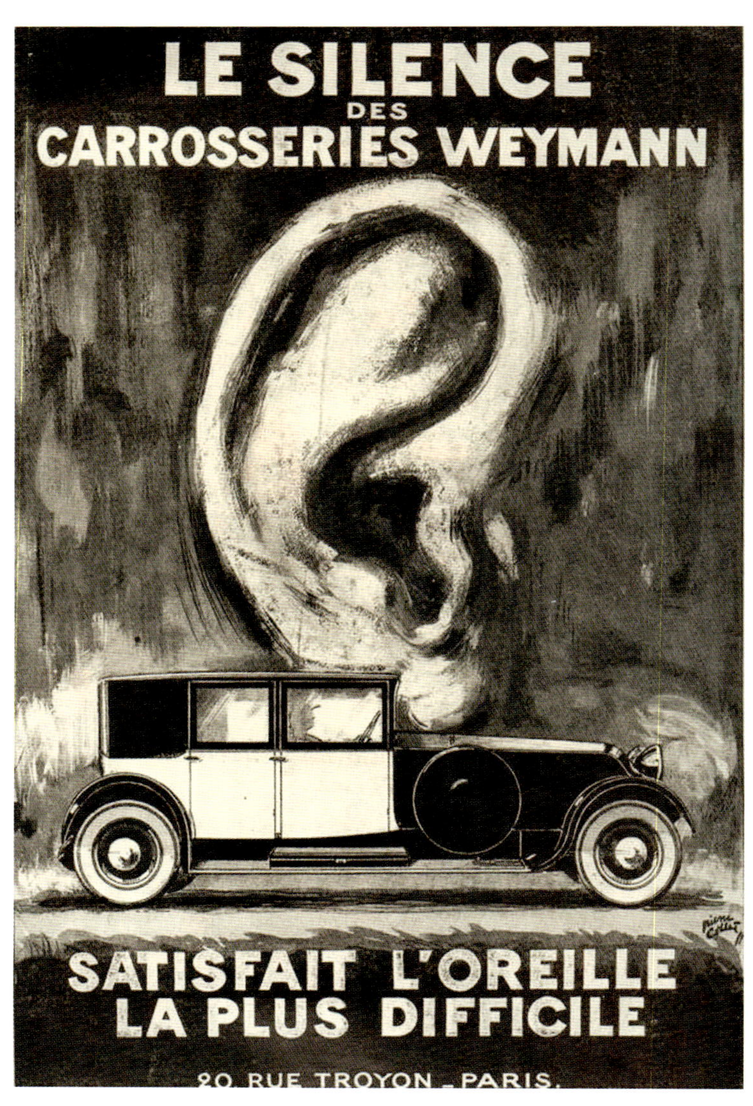

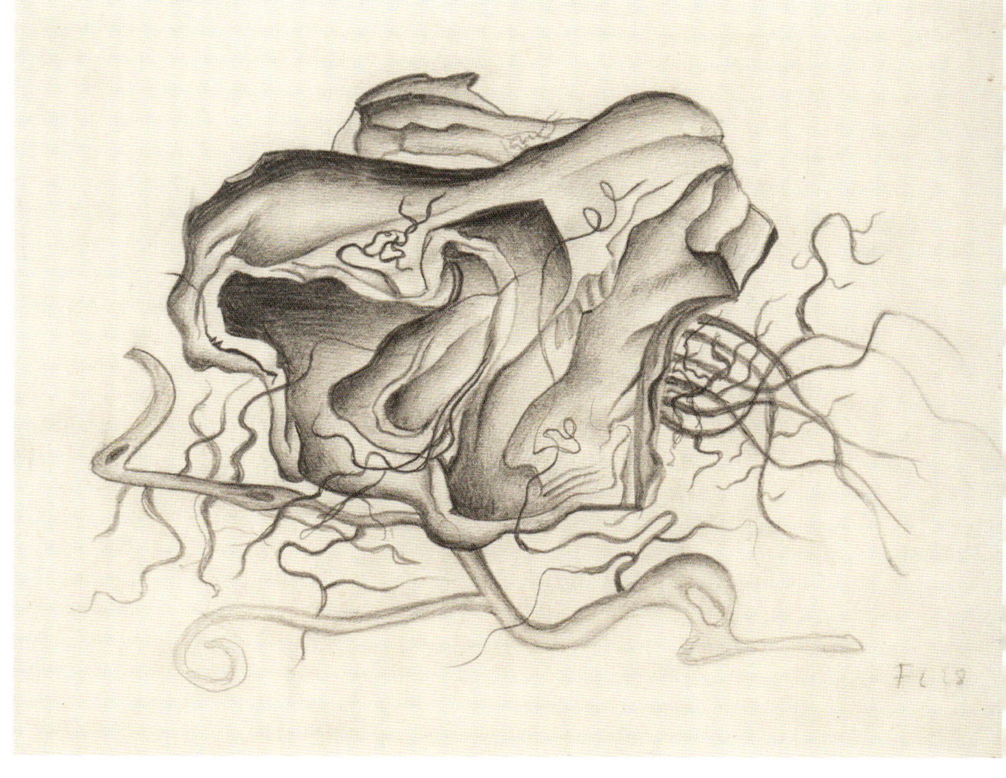

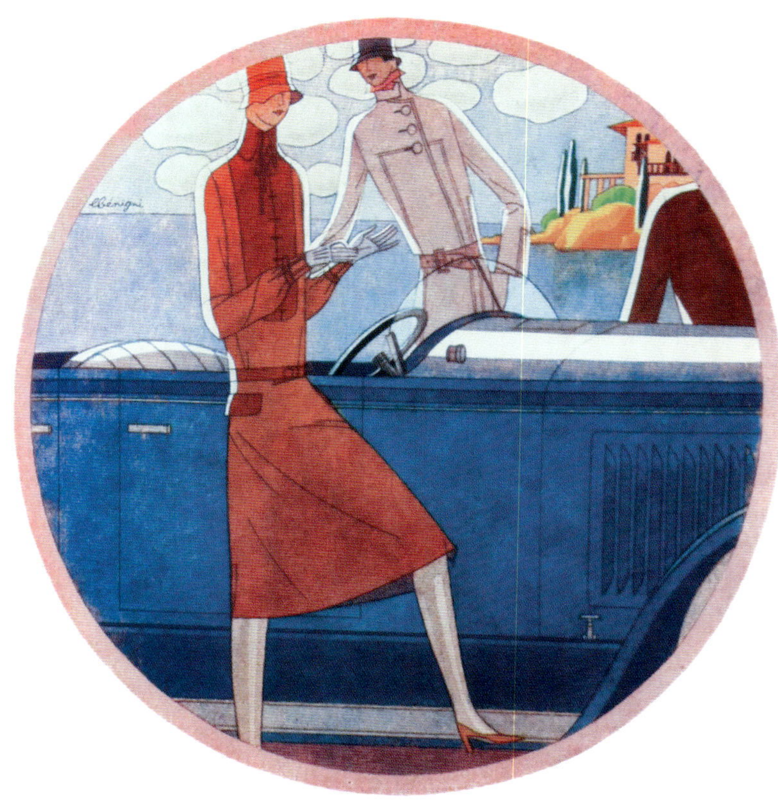

FIG. 26
"A Weymann body satisfies the most delicate ear," advertisement in *Omnia, revue pratique de locomotion*, June 1, 1925

FIG. 27
Fernand Léger, French, 1881–1955; *Root (Racine)*, 1928; graphite on paper; 10 ⅜ × 14 ¼ in.; The Menil Collection 1985-026 DJ D

FIG. 28
Léon Benigni, French, 1892–1948; Jane Régny advertisement, "Sport pour tous," *Fémina*, 1926

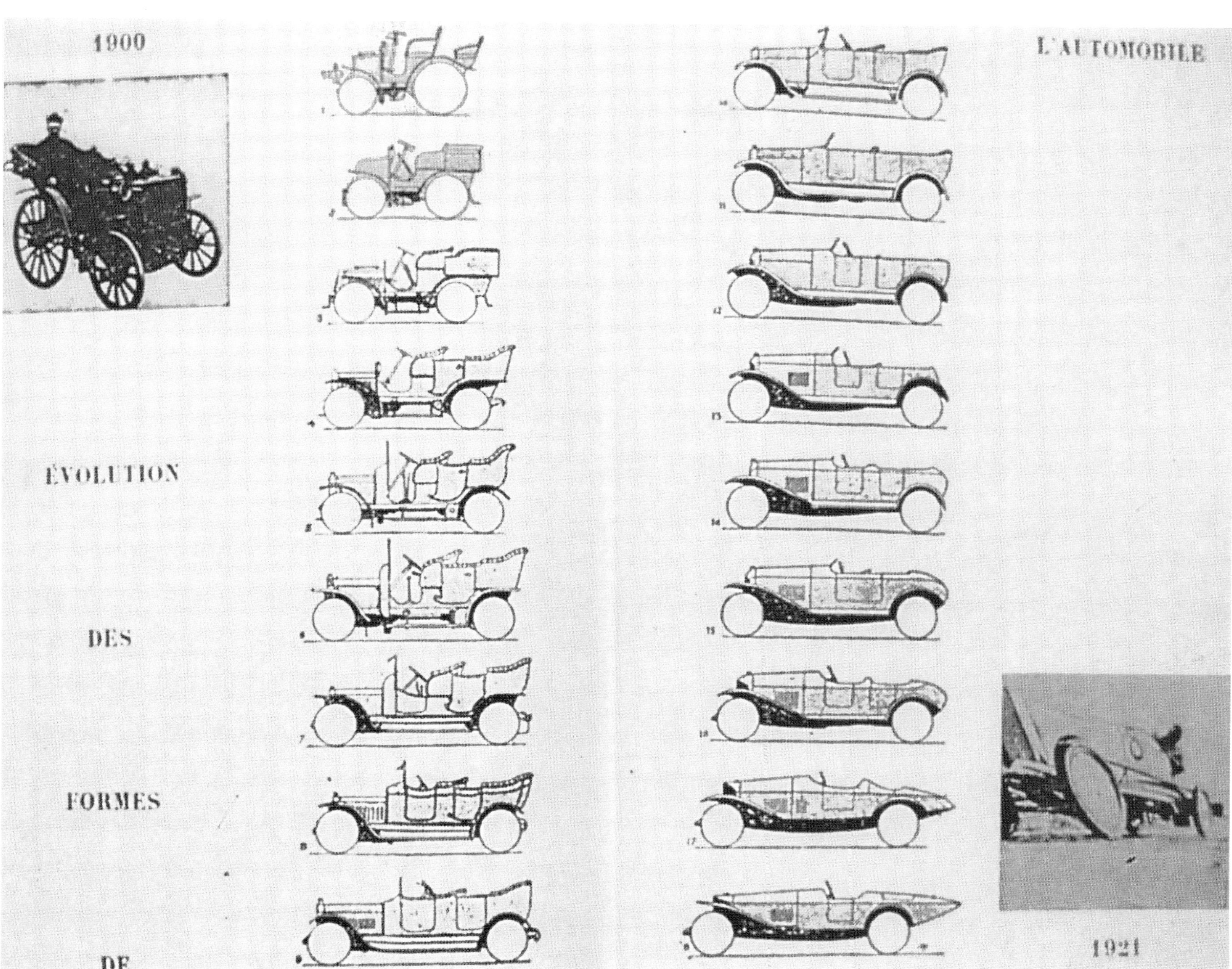

FIG. 29
"Évolution des formes de l'automobile 1900–21," *L'Esprit nouveau* 13 (1921): 1570–7

Of the two co-editors, Ozenfant held a personal stake in this argument, having previously designed a celebrated aluminum race car body for the luxury marque Hispano-Suiza in 1911. A competitive racer in his own right, Ozenfant wrote the journal's review of the Salon, lamenting that car manufacturers, "hypnotized by commercial problems," had squandered the war years by privileging the whims of the market over technical innovation. Convinced of the positive impact of racing on the field of automotive design, he and Le Corbusier repub-

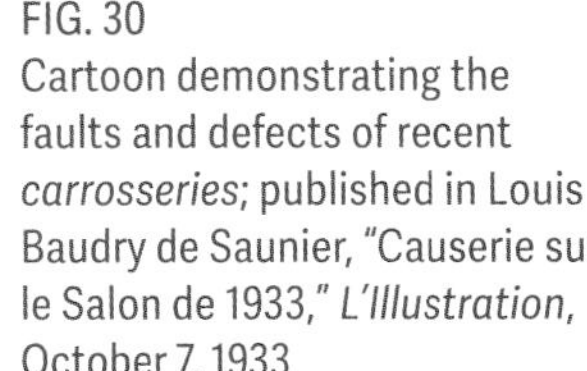

FIG. 30
Cartoon demonstrating the faults and defects of recent *carrosseries*; published in Louis Baudry de Saunier, "Causerie sur le Salon de 1933," *L'Illustration*, October 7, 1933

FIG. 31
Tamara de Lempicka, Polish (active France and United States), 1898–1980; *Self-Portrait (Tamara in the Green Bugatti)*, 1928; oil on panel, 13 ¾ × 10 ⅝ in.; Private collection

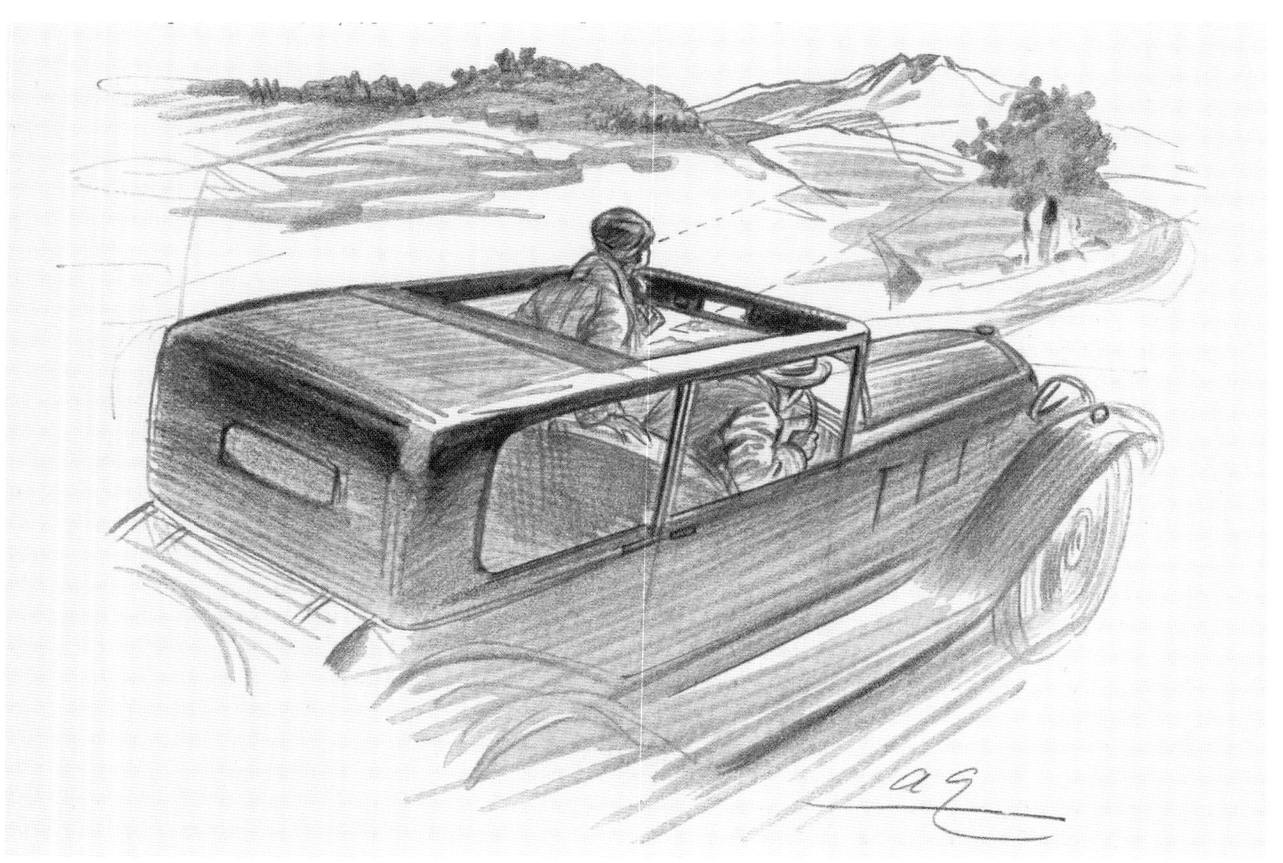

lished a comparative diagram of car body types, organized in chronological sequence from 1900 to 1921, that had first appeared in the British journal *The Autocar* (FIG. 29). In the original publication, this genealogical diagram was meant to reveal the progressive streamlining of the ideal sports car, the "Torpedo Body," which the author Gordon Crosby defended as expressive of automotive sportsmanship in its purest form.[11] For Le Corbusier and Ozenfant, the diagram illustrated a general evolutionary tendency, applicable to art and technology alike, which they called "standart," emphasizing the generative duality of reason and aesthetic genius (hence stand-*art*). In the field of automotive design, they argued, a *standart* was imposed both through the refinement of industrial production (which imposed "an imperious necessity to standardize") and in the Hobbesian struggle of the market, as a result of which "each [firm] has found itself under obligation to dominate the competition, and, on top of the standard for realized practical things, there has intervened a search for perfection and harmony outside of brute practical fact, a manifestation not only of perfection and harmony, but of beauty."[12]

Intending a rebuke to the field of decorative arts, including the art of *carrosserie*, Le Corbusier and Ozenfant rested their account of *standartisation* upon the double appeal of well-machined objects, which were both functional *and* beautiful, as contrasted with the merely extraneous appeal of ornamentation. In 1925, Le Corbusier clarified this argument, identifying the beauty of machines with the harmonious geometry of "shining disks, spheres, and cylinders of shining steel."[13] His position served as a rallying cry within the Paris avant-garde, gathering a loose coalition around the ideal of a "machine aesthetic." Notable within this group, the artist Fernand Léger cited the "evolution" of automotive body types as the sign of a new rapprochement between form and function, following the principle that "the more the car has fulfilled its functional ends, the more beautiful it has become." This was a beauty born of speed, Léger argued, and refined according to an overriding

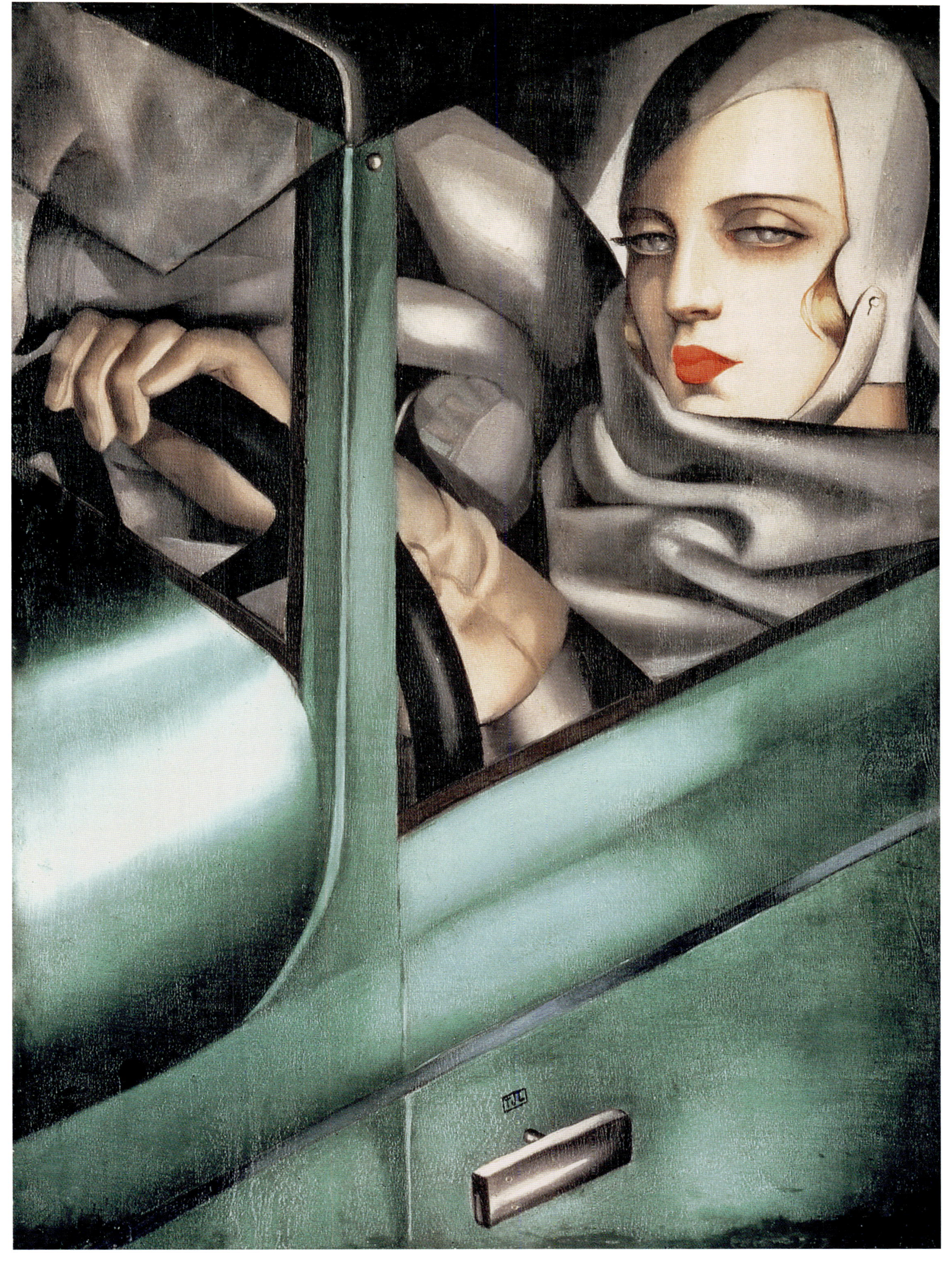

geometric ideal: "Because of the necessity for speed, the car was lowered and elongated . . . consequently, horizontal lines balanced by curves became dominant, it became a perfect whole, logically organized towards its purpose; and it was beautiful."[14] Echoing this observation, the critic André Fréchet noted that the new standards of taste in car design imposed a single horizontal line "from the hood to the rear," providing a visual unity previously lacking in the body.[15] While this linear purification of external form added neither clear mechanical function nor aerodynamic support, critics and artists alike saw it as the outward sign of an inward, teleological evolution. Indeed, many of the vehicles most admired by modernist critics flouted the laws of aerodynamics: for example, Voisin's preference for a vertical front windshield invited wind resistance to the vehicle's forward thrust—a deficit offset by the exceptional lightness of the aluminum bodyworks that were his firm's stock in trade. Nevertheless, this geometrical aesthetic proved ideally suited to the commodification of the automobile in advertising imagery, which paired the bodies of cars with those of women models, a contrast of extreme verticality and horizontality (FIG. 28). As noted by the fashion critic Maud, the latest preferences in automotive aesthetics shared a common language with haute couture: "One no longer says 'Look at the lovely ornamentation,' but rather 'What a beautiful line!'"[16]

The new "linear" aesthetic of coachwork styling reflected the influence of motor sports. It also marked the translation of a functional principle—namely, aerodynamics—into a stylistic signifier: the "look" of speed. However, while the look implied aerodynamic functionalism, no necessary relationship existed between the two. Bowing to the pressures of market competition, Mom writes, "One of the new engineer's tasks was to follow the constant pounding of the sales department to further lower the body, making it appear 'speedy' even as it stood at the curb."[17] To a growing segment of commentators, the trend toward ever lower, sleeker coachwork designs heralded the triumph of style over functionality, a betrayal of the logic of *standartisation*. Reviewing the 1928 Salon de l'Automobile, Léger addressed the glaring deficiencies of the latest car designs:

> Incontrovertible renaissance of metallic coachworks, end of coachworks in leather, shagreen, ruberoid, etc., that is to say feminine coachworks. Do not forget, after all, that "these Ladies" have also attempted the "laying on of hands." The automobile fattened up, the car inside an *étui*. It was on their account that all our major coachbuilders labored. . . . Renaissance of beautiful metal, hard, fixed, gleaming. The car becomes once more a beautiful polished mechanism, clean, striking, living (the reflection of light is the "sign of life" of metal). . . . And then it becomes more and more elongated, lowering itself to the ground, gluing itself to the road. One hunches over to get a look at it. In this race towards the horizontal, the doors become flattened, the windows diminished, nothing more remains except the eye that drives. Nothing more to see, to look at. To see what? The landscape? End of the Landscape. Ask a modern painter what a landscape is. He doesn't know. He knows a tree, a branch, a leaf. He knows the objects of the landscape, that's all.[18]

For Léger, this terminal horizon—the landscape's reduction to an alienated nub—represented a Pyrrhic victory of modern technology over nature. It was a dynamic he knew from personal experience: since 1926, Léger had divided his time between the Paris studio and a farmhouse in rural Normandy, a journey he undertook by car, chauffeured by his wife. By the late 1920s, the main road from Paris through Normandy, which ran close to Léger's hamlet at Lisores, had become heavily traveled by motorists, placing the car in a landscape dominated by vehicular traffic, exhaust, and wrecked automobiles. Informed by this alienated relationship to his *pays natal*, Léger's drawings and paintings from the countryside addressed the "end of the landscape" through a pictorial language of object fragments, aligning his work with Surrealism's aesthetics of the marvelous (a pursuit of symbolic forms beyond the grasp of reason).[19] Rather than reestablish a bond with the landscape, these works—for example, his *Root (Racine)* of 1928 (FIG. 27)—presented isolated fragments of tree trunks and root systems, marking the implied perspective of the deracinated motor tourist.

If the terms of Léger's critique held personal meaning, his appraisal of the new direction of car design resonated broadly during the Great Depression. As the 1920s lurched to a ruinous close, critics began to question the new automotive aesthetic, taking issue with its impracticality. Writing in 1930, the journalist Roland Alix worried, tongue in cheek, that the excessive streamlining of the bodyworks would end up deforming the passengers' bodies: "Hypnotized by the profile of the car, manufacturers came to see the gap between the floor and the ground as disagreeable. It's true, but what can one do about it? By lowering and flattening and elongating their cars, they may well end up deforming the human figure: what gnomes, what strange reptilian monsters in tortoiseshell glasses will we become?"[20]

Linking the "deformity" of the passenger with the obfuscation of vision, Alix's complaint touched on what was perhaps the most serious deficiency of the new automotive aesthetic, which prevailed at the expense of the motorist's sensory experience. In a 1933 article, the journalist Louis Baudry de Saunier charged that the most aggressively low-slung coachworks placed the driver such "that it becomes impossible for him to see below the top of the front fenders," illustrating this point with a series of drawings showing drivers in various states of contortion—for example, a husband hunched pitifully at the wheel while his wife, hoping for a better view of the landscape, peeks out of the open roof (FIG. 30).[21] This impoverishment of visibility was considered so severe that one reader of the industry journal *La Vie automobile* penned a satirical letter to the editor to propose the use of periscopes in automobile design, thus completing the teleology of form:

> The new coachworks will be more closed than ever. No more openings, no windows, neither in front nor at the sides, nor in the rear; the ideal of *carrosserie*: a chassis, a marvelous hermetically sealed box, a line, the definitive triumph of form.
>
> Commodiously installed, seated upon cushions of unprecedented comfort, supporting them up to the neck, the passengers will enjoy the admirable landscapes of France, so varied, so picturesque, so striking, a vision as unexpected as it is comfortable; nothing will escape their astonished gaze in these coachworks as silent as the grave.[22]

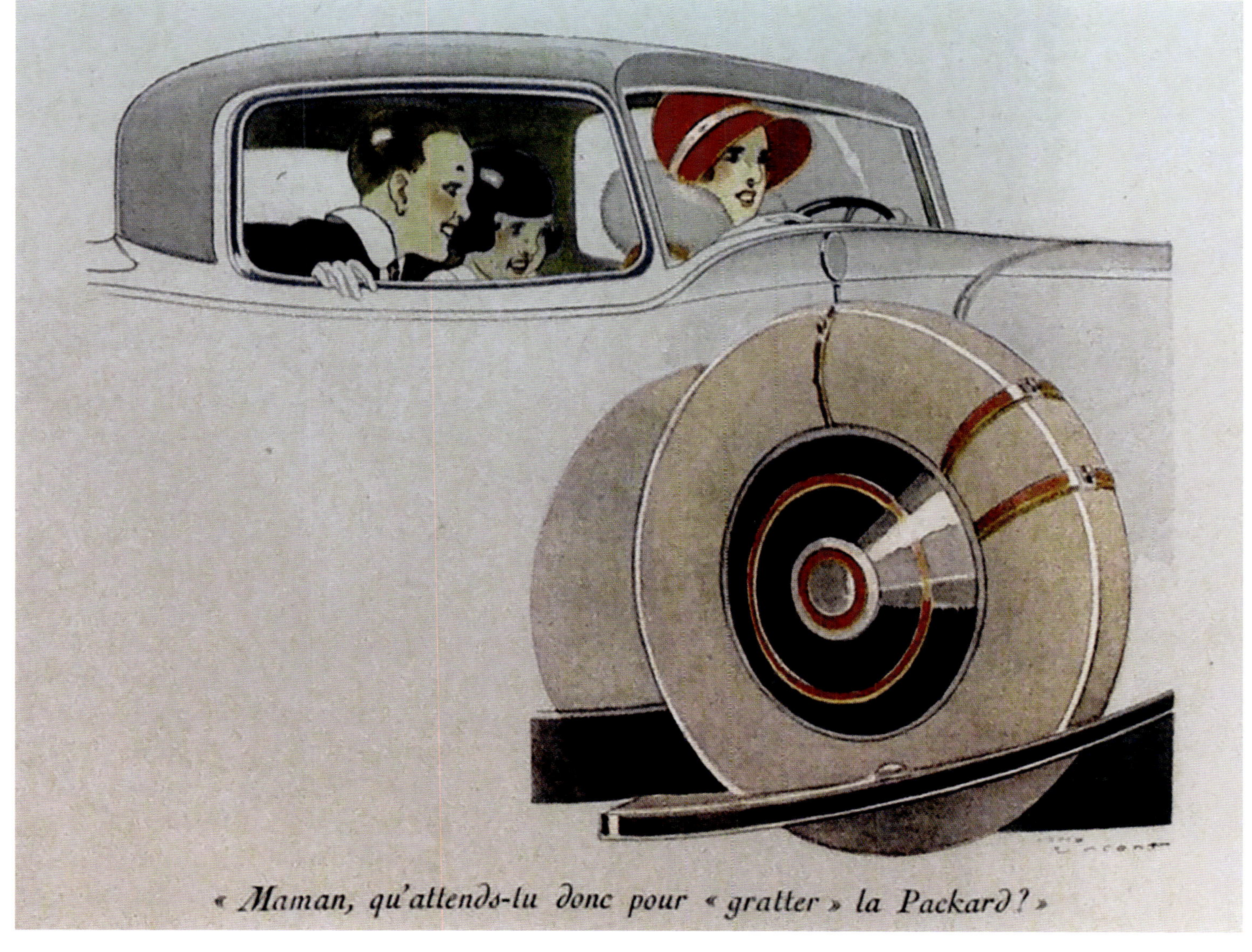

FIG. 32
René Vincent, French, 1879–1936; illustration in *L'Illustration*, October 1930

Taken in sum, these complaints delivered a critique of the proposed integration of beauty and functionality: after all, for the mock "inventor" of the automobile periscope, the "triumph of form" represented an impediment to the car's safe operation, not an enhancement. In relation to gender, this critique joined with broader currents of conservative backlash, denying the utopian—feminist—dimension of modernist aesthetics. Within the visual culture of the "New Woman," the symbolic merger of women's bodies with the automobile had offered a power trope of liberated femininity, and one that car manufacturers had initially encouraged. Looking to changing codes of fashion, the industry sought to appeal to women consumers for practicality and comfort, identifying the simplification and rationalization of the car body with the streamlining of dress silhouettes. Just as French fashion expressed an increasingly androgynous ideal of liberal femininity, so too did modernism's linear aesthetic suggest a parallel defeminization—and un-domestication—of the family car. In 1926, for example, *Fémina* instructed readers to dial back on decorative flourishes, restricting the palette to "a sober body colored green or pitch black. Banish all preciousness, all cushions not made of leather. Leave the flower bouquets to the taxis, and dashboard fetishes, to everyone else."[23] Meanwhile, at the 1925 International Exhibition of Modern Decorative and Industrial Arts, the artist Sonia Delaunay included a custom-painted Ariès Torpédo as part of her display of textile and fashion designs. A few years later, Tamara de Lempicka painted her iconic *Self-Portrait (Tamara in the Green Bugatti)* for the July 1929 cover of the German magazine *Die Dame* (FIG. 31), in which the artist's figure merges seamlessly with the machine-picture assemblage, becoming yet another sharp-edged surface in an image world of metal and industrial varnish. "I was always dressed like the car, and the car like me," remarked de Lempicka, framing the relationship between driver and vehicle as a sartorial tautology.[24]

As enthusiasm for modernism waned, however, the image of women's automobility suffered. In 1927, the editors of *Fémina* urged readers to "leave to racers the rumbling, greasy sports car, and the wild escapades on the open road. There's no goddess in a cloud of dust, and adventure, when it doesn't end in tragedy, quickly becomes ridiculous."[25] This was less an appeal for women to abandon driving than a call to order: as Virginia Scharff has noted, the expansion of car ownership among middle-class families left women "increasingly responsible for producing transportation" as part of their domestic duties, blurring the line "between women's work and play."[26] In the 1930 automotive issue of *L'Illustration*, a feature article on women motorists follows the path of a young woman from her first driving lesson to her entry into motherhood, concluding with an image of her crouched behind the wheel

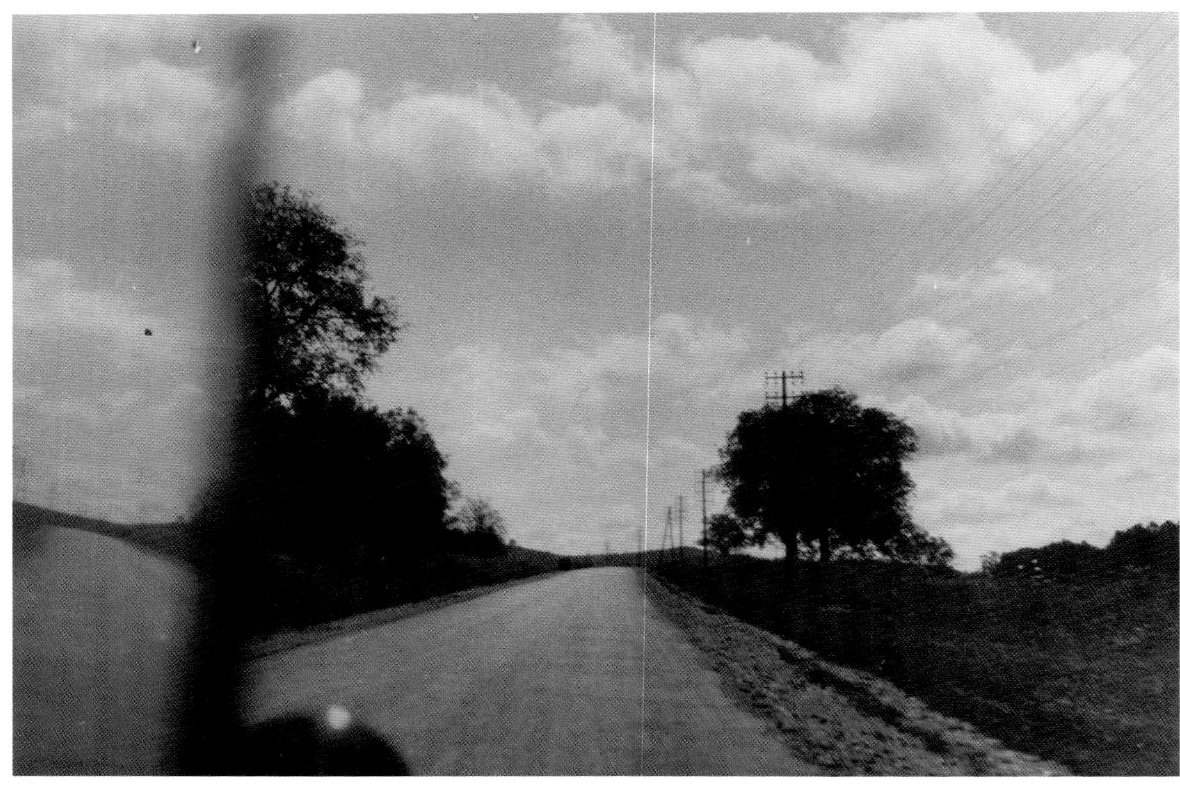

FIG. 33
Germaine Krull, French (born Poland), 1897–1985; *Untitled*, from the series "Sur la route: Huit photographies prises entre Paris et Marseille ou entre Paris et Biarritz," 1930; gelatin silver print; 5 1/2 × 8 5/16 in.; Art Institute of Chicago, The Mary and Leigh Block Endowment Fund, 2002.63.1

FIG. 34
Germaine Krull, French (born Poland), 1897–1985; *Untitled*, from the series "Sur la route: Huit photographies prises entre Paris et Marseille ou entre Paris et Biarritz," 1930; gelatin silver print; 5 ⅜ × 8 ⅜ in.; Art Institute of Chicago, The Mary and Leigh Block Endowment Fund, 2002.63.4

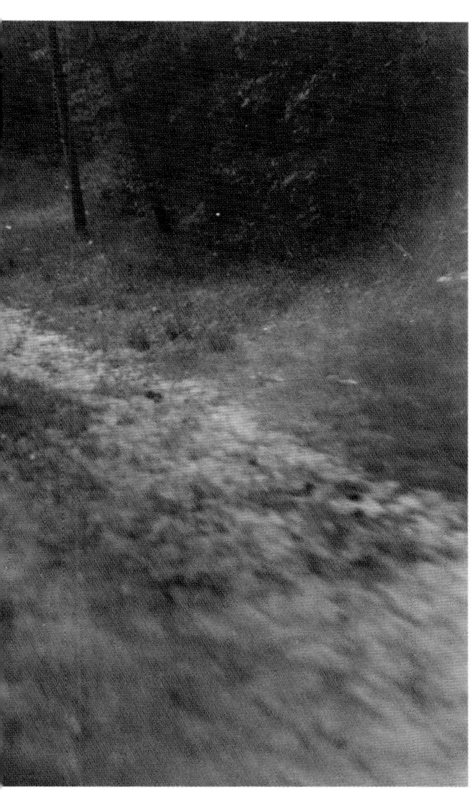

as her children cajole her to "thrash" the car in front of them: "Maman, qu'attends-tu donc pour 'gratter' la Packard?" (Mama, what are you waiting for to "thrash" the Packard?) (FIG. 32).[27] Dispensing with the ideal of hermetic enclosure ("the definitive ideal of form . . . silent as the grave"), this cartoon serves as a reminder of what the car had become and what it remains today: a tool for accelerating the rhythms of home and workplace, often at the driver's expense.

While the antimodernist backlash rejected the image of women's automotive liberation, it sought to preserve the car's role in the routines of heterosexual courtship. This discourse contrasted the supposed virility of early automobilism with the feminization of the car during the interwar years, expressing nostalgia for a time when, per journalist Robert de Beauplan, "the woman was simply a passenger, if not timid, at least passive, and visibly ignorant of the mysteries of the internal combustion engine or the caprices of the carburetor. When the car broke down, she left the driver to his perplexity with habitual resignation. Today, it is the woman who takes the wheel. She doesn't need anyone else."[28]

For de Beauplan, the car's newfound ease of operation threatened the romantic privileges of an earlier generation of male motorists, whose breakdown-prone vehicles allowed opportunity for sexual advances. As the Roaring Twenties subsided, the notion of the back seat as a scene of amorous coupling came to supplant modernism's ideal of emancipatory solitude, cementing a masculinist fantasy of women's sexual availability.

For an alternative vision of the automobile, we might look to the photography of Germaine Krull, a Prussian émigré living in Paris during the Depression. In 1929, Krull received her first car, an open-top Peugeot 201, as payment for a photographic assignment she had undertaken for its manufacturer, and the following year she set out to document a motor trip from Paris to Biarritz. Accompanied by the editor Philippe Lamour, Krull ceded to him the role of driver so that she could operate the camera with the car in motion. Flouting convention, she approached her task with death-defying recklessness, shooting from atop the retractable top while the car drove at top speed.[29] This process left the surrounding landscape largely illegible, she conceded, yet Krull's violation of photographic norms perfectly suited her purpose: "We didn't get a single clean photo, they were all unusable, but that's how we felt, and *voilà*."[30]

As indicated by her use of the plural pronoun ("that's how *we* felt"), Krull understood these blurred images as documents of an emotion that traversed driver and passenger equally. In her photographs, too, viewing positions are noticeably unclear; one photo seems to locate us at the outer limit of the car body, while another confronts the viewer with a double perspective, showing the road ahead and behind through the rearview mirror (FIGS. 33, 34). Although taken by the passenger, Krull's images simulate the phenomenological conditions of driving, and in so doing pry loose each position from the gender binary. Nearly a century later, this "wild escapade on the open road" remains a potent ideal—and a strong rejoinder to the libidinal economy of Rhoades's *Fucking Picabia Cars*, with its closed circuit of (masculine) desire and satisfaction. With Krull, we might dream of a machine that would disorient not only space and time but the matrix of gender as well.

1 Gijs Mom, *Atlantic Automobilism: Emergence and Persistence of the Car, 1895–1940* (New York: Berghahn Books, 2015), 385.

2 "Le Home sur la route," *Fémina*, August 1911, 413: "[L'auto] devient un hôtel en miniature où l'on peut manger, faire une tasse de thé, écrire un mot, se poudrer et se recoiffer, et au besoin même, si la route est laide et monotone faire un bridge . . . ou dormir."

3 Pierre Matisse, letter to Jane E. Boruff, October 23, 1976, Archives of the Cleveland Museum of Art.

4 Roger Fry, "French Pictures at the Lefevre Gallery," *The Nation and Athenaeum*, November 29, 1924, 329.

5 Sara Danius has also noted this effect, although she reads it in terms of a pictorial synthesis mediated by the automobile: "A study in perspective, the painting foregrounds the way in which the view is framed, exploring how the three windows delimit the spectator's field of vision and divide the seen into separate yet related visual spaces. These spaces, in turn, transform themselves into a pictorial suite, into three distinct images—it is as though they were only waiting to be lifted into the artist's sketchbook." Danius, *The Senses of Modernism: Technology, Perception, and Aesthetics* (Ithaca, NY: Cornell University Press, 2002), 136.

6 Pierre Matisse recalls that heavy road traffic required Matisse to work with the windows shut, evidently an uncomfortable experience. See Matisse to Boruff, 1976.

7 Olivier de Carfort, "Au Salon de l'Automobile," *L'Opinion*, October 18, 1919.

8 Carfort, "Au Salon de l'Automobile."

9 Guillaume Janneau, "Le Mouvement moderne: L'Esthétique de l'automobile," *La Renaissance de l'art français et des industries de luxe* 4, no. 11 (November 1921): 562.

10 Dr. St-Quentin [Amédée Ozenfant], "La Renaissance des courses: Le Salon de l'Automobile," *L'Esprit nouveau* 11–12 (November 1921): 1366: "Le Salon de l'Automobile montre évidemment encore de ces diplodocus ridicules (Elizalde); mais le retour des courses nous a donné la *Voisin* et il faut féliciter G. Voisin et ses collaborateurs, comme M. Noël, de leurs recherches de l'organique, de l'homogène joint à une perfection de construction qu'aucune construction étrangère n'égale: ils ont créé des châssis qui sont d'admirables outils; l'économie de leur organisme en fait des objets magnifiques."

11 Gordon Crosby, "The Harmony of Outline, Part I," *The Autocar*, July 2, 1921, 9.

12 Le Corbusier, *Toward an Architecture*, trans. John Goodman (Los Angeles: Getty Publications, 2007), 182–83; originally published as *Vers une architecture*, 2nd ed. (Paris: G. Crès, 1924).

13 Le Corbusier, *The Decorative Art of Today*, trans. James Dunnett (Cambridge, MA: MIT Press, 1997), 103; originally published as *L'Art décoratif d'aujourd'hui* (Paris: G. Crès, 1925).

14 Fernand Léger, "The Machine Aesthetic: The Manufactured Object, the Artisan, and the Artist," in *Functions of Painting*, ed. Edward F. Fry, trans. Alexandra Anderson (New York: Viking, 1973), 53; originally published as "L'Esthétique de la machine: L'objet fabriqué, l'artisan et l'artiste," *Bulletin de l'Effort Moderne*, January–February 1924. It was first delivered as a lecture at the Baraque de la Chimère, boulevard St. Germain, Paris, June 1, 1922.

15 André Fréchet, "L'Art de la Carrosserie et l'Automobile de luxe," *Art et décoration*, February 1921, 63.

16 Maud, "Mode," *La femme, le sport, la mode*, February 1926, 10: "Dans la mode actuelle, ce qui surprendra peut-être le plus la prochaine génération, c'est la géométrie qui préside à la création de presque tous les modèles. D'ailleurs, même dans le langage des couturières, la ligne a pris une importance considérable, et dans leur esprit, ce seul mot résume les lignes brisées, droites ou courbes. On ne dit plus voilà de beaux ornements, mais quelle belle ligne!"

17 Mom, *Atlantic Automobilism*, 385.

18 Fernand Léger, "Au Salon de l'Automobile: Gloire du métal," *L'Intransigeant*, October 10, 1928, 6: "Renaissance indiscutable de la Carrosserie métallique, finie la carrosserie de cuir, de galuchat, de ruberoïd. etc., c'est-à-dire la carrosserie féminine. Car n'oubliez pas que 'ces Dames' ont essayé aussi de 'mettre la main là-dessus.' L'auto étoffée, la voiture dans un étui. C'était pour elles que tous nos grands carrossiers travaillaient. . . . Renaissance du beau métal, luisant, fixe, dur. L'auto redevient une belle mécanique astiquée, nette, criante, vivante (le reflet est 'le signe de vie' du métal). . . . Et puis, elle s'allonge de plus en plus, elle s'abaisse, elle se colle à la route, On se courbe pour la voir. Dans cette course à l'horizontale, les portes s'aplatissent, les fenêtres diminuent, il ne reste plus rien que pour l'œil qui conduit. Plus rien pour voir, pour regarder. Pour voir quoi? Le paysage? Fini paysage. Demandez à un peintre moderne ce que c'est qu'un paysage? Connaît pas. Il connaît un arbre, une branche, une feuille. Il connaît les objets du paysage, c'est tout."

19 I address this relationship in my dissertation, "Traffic: On the Displacement of Art in Early Twentieth-Century Paris" (PhD diss., University of California, Berkeley, 2017).

20 Roland Alix, "L'Esthétique et la vie," *L'Européen: Hebdomadaire, économique, artistique et littéraire*, October 29, 1930, 3: "Hypnotisés par le profil de la voiture, les constructeurs se rendent compte que le hiatus du sol au plancher est désagréable. C'est vrai, mais qu'y faire? A force de baisser et d'aplatir et d'allonger leurs voitures, ils déformeront peut-être le corps humain: quels gnomes, quels étranges monstres reptiles à lunettes d'écaille, deviendrons-nous?"

21 Louis Baudry de Saunier, "Causerie sur le Salon de 1933," *L'Illustration: L'Automobile et le tourisme*, October 7, 1933, n.p.

22 J. Lagrange, "Les Carrosseries modernes vues de l'intérieur," *La Vie automobile*, December 25, 1927, 675: "Fermées, grâce à moi, les nouvelles carrosseries le seront plus que voiture ne l'a jamais été. Plus d'ouvertures, plus de glaces, ni devant, ni sur les côtés, ni derrière; l'idéal des carrosseries: un châssis, une merveilleuse boîte hermétiquement close, une ligne, triomphe définitif de la forme.

Commodément installés, étendus sur des coussins d'un confort inespéré, les soutenant jusqu'à la nuque, les passagers auront des admirables paysages de France, si variés, si pittoresques, si prenants, une vision aussi inattendue que confortable; rien n'échappera à leur regard émerveillé dans ces carrosseries aussi silencieuses que la tombe."

23 "Le Dernier mot de l'élégance," *Fémina*, March 1926, 26.

24 De Lempicka quoted in Giles Néret, *Tamara de Lempicka* (Cologne: Taschen, 2000), 7.

25 "Comment elles font du sport," *Fémina*, January 1927, 10: "Mais de grâce! ô Célimène! laissez aux coureurs la voiture de course ronflante et graisseuse, et les folles escapades sur la route 'billard.' Il n'est pas de déesse dans un nuage de poussière et l'aventure, quand elle n'est pas tragique, devient bien vite ridicule. Et votre bonnet d'aviateur, vos gants à crispins, vos bottes lacées peuvent être reléguées au magasin des accessoires inutiles."

26 Virginia Scharff, *Taking the Wheel: Women and the Coming of the Motor Age* (Albuquerque: University of New Mexico Press, 1992), 136.

27 René Vincent, "Madame conduit," in *L'Illustration: L'Automobile et le tourisme*, October 1930, n.p.

28 Robert de Beauplan, "L'automobile et la mode, 1906–1929," *L'Illustration: L'Automobile et le tourisme*, October 1929, n.p.: "La femme n'était que la passagère, sinon timorée, du moins passive, et visiblement ignorante des mystères du moteur à explosion ou des caprices du carburateur. Lorsque le panne survenait, elle laissait le conducteur à sa perplexité, avec la résignation de l'habitude. Aujourd'hui, c'est la femme qui est au volant. Elle n'a besoin de personne."

29 Germaine Krull, *La Vie mène la danse* (Paris: TEXTUEL, 2015), 132–33.

30 Krull, *La Vie*, 132–33: "Cela ne donnait pas une seule photo nette, elles étaient toutes inutilisables, mais nous le sentions comme cela, et voilà."

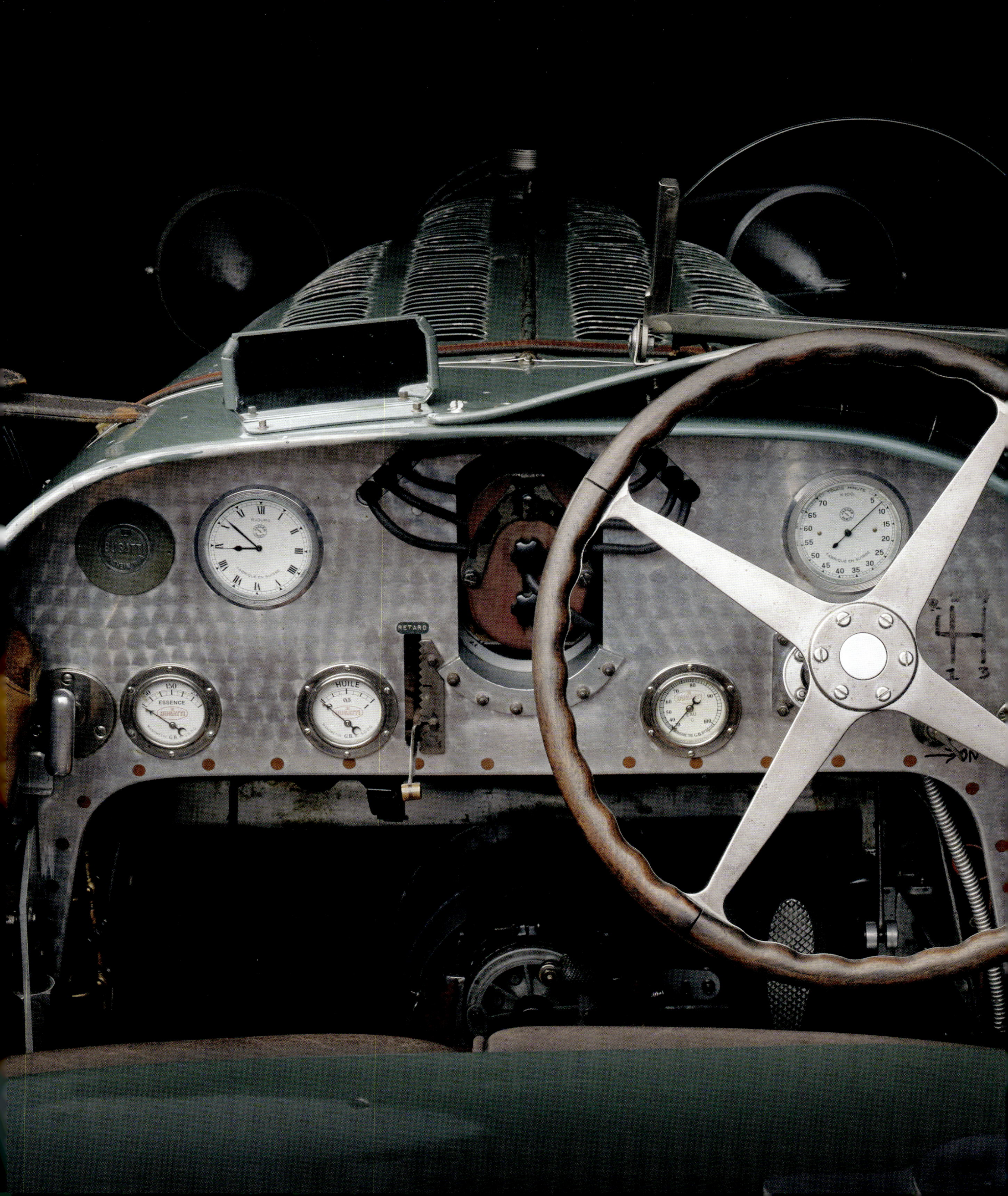
TOURS MINUTE
RETARD
ESSENCE
HUILE
ON

1927 BUGATTI TYPE 35B HELLÉ-NICE GRAND PRIX

KEN GROSS

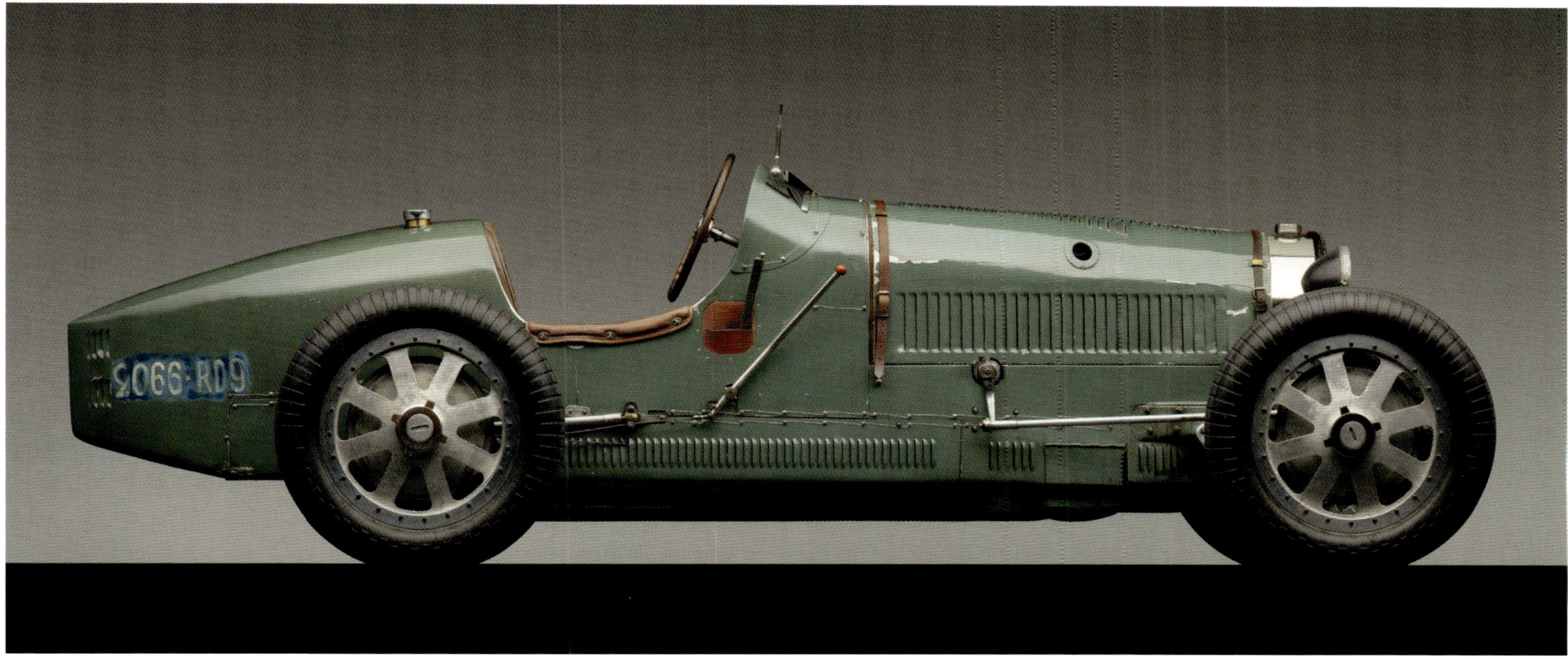

Ettore Bugatti, French (born Italy), 1881–1947; Automobiles Ettore Bugatti, Molsheim, France, active 1909–63; *Type 35B*, 1927; 42 × 145 × 52 in.; William E. Connor Collection

The Bugatti Type 35 debuted at the Grand Prix of Lyon in 1924. With its delicate horseshoe-shaped radiator; sharply chiseled, minimalist aluminum coachwork; high-revving 24-valve (two exhausts/one intake), single overhead camshaft straight eight, with a clever crankshaft setup that employed five mains running in ball bearings; a four-speed non-synchromesh gearbox; distinctive center-lock, flat-spoked alloy wheels with cast-in brake drums; and a hollow front axle that enclosed quarter-elliptic springs, the Type 35 and variants, including the supercharged Types 35C and 35B, were the most successful race cars of their era.[1]

Bugatti Type 35s won Sicily's grueling Targa Florio every year from 1925 through 1929. Actual numbers vary, but the Type 35 won the Grand Prix World Championship in 1926, as well as more than one thousand other races in its era. In addition to factory teams, dozens of privateers had great success with this model. About 635 Type 35/37/39s were built.[2]

This Type 35B, chassis no. 4863, was originally delivered to Marco Andriessi in Amsterdam, as a two-liter Type 35C. It was subsequently equipped with a 2.3-liter engine and supercharger and sold to Hellé Nice (1900–1984) in September 1929 for factory-backed speed-record work.[3] Born Mariette Hélène Delangle in 1900, near Chartres, Nice became an exotic dancer and nude model in Paris. A skiing accident in 1929 ended her dancing career. That same year, using her stage name, Hellé Nice, she won a ladies' race in Montlhéry in an Oméga-Six, which prompted Ettore Bugatti to loan her a Type 43A Gran Sport. She won the ladies' category at the Actor's Championship Grand Prix and set the fastest time for both women and men. Ettore had wanted to replace Elisabeth Junek, his retiring Czech racing champion, so he loaned Hellé Nice another car, in which she set a 197.7 kph women's speed record. After she bought this Type 35, Ettore invited her to compete in the Bugatti Grand Prix at Le Mans, where she finished in third place.[4]

Racing cars from several marques, Hellé Nice became a sensation in France. She raced Millers on dirt tracks in America, then returned to Europe in 1931, competing in hill climbs and Grands Prix. She won several races at a time when it was unusual for a woman to compete and was successful against famous male drivers like Louis Chiron, René Dreyfus, Marcel Lehoux, and Philippe "Fifi" Etancelin. Beautiful and vivacious, Nice led an exciting life, taking many lovers, adding to her fame and notoriety.

In 1936, at a race in Brazil, her Alfa Romeo hit a hay bale and crashed into the grandstand, killing six people and injuring others. Thrown out of the car, she spent three days in a coma. Returning to France, she was implicated in a scandal involving other drivers and the illegal importation of cars. Hellé Nice was convicted and fined. Actively continuing to compete, she won her last race in 1939. After the war, she was denounced by Chiron and falsely accused of being a Nazi collaborator. While she was eventually exonerated, the adverse publicity ruined all hope she had of resuming her career. Sadly, she died in obscurity in 1984. *Bugatti Queen*, a 2004 biography by Miranda Seymour, eventually helped restore her reputation.[5]

Loaned by the William E. Connor Collection

1 Chas Parker, *Bugatti Type 35 Owners Workshop Manual* (Somerset, UK: Haynes, 2018), 6–7.
2 Parker, *Bugatti Type*, 18–19.
3 Sandy Leith, *American Bugatti Register and Data Book* (Dedham, MA: American Bugatti Club, 2003), 57.
4 Parker, *Bugatti Type*, 34–35.
5 Miranda Seymour, *Bugatti Queen: In Search of a French Racing Legend* (New York: Random House, 2004), 255–58.

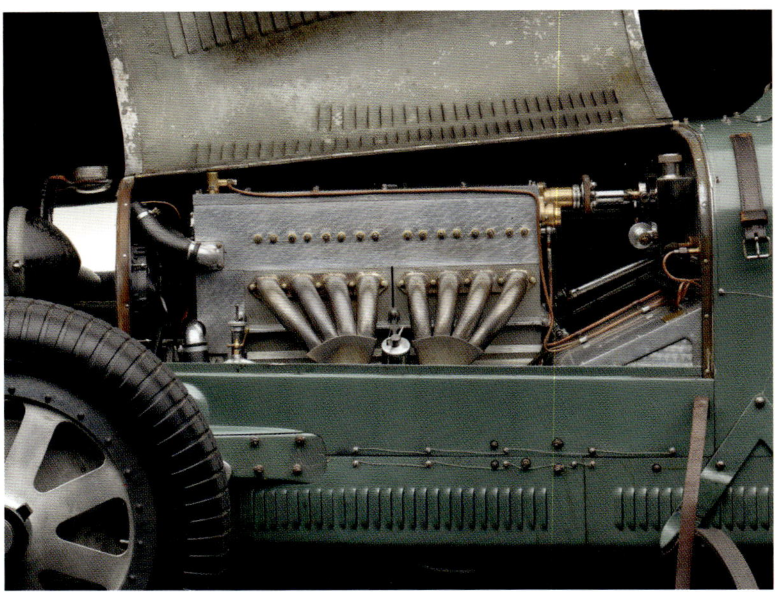

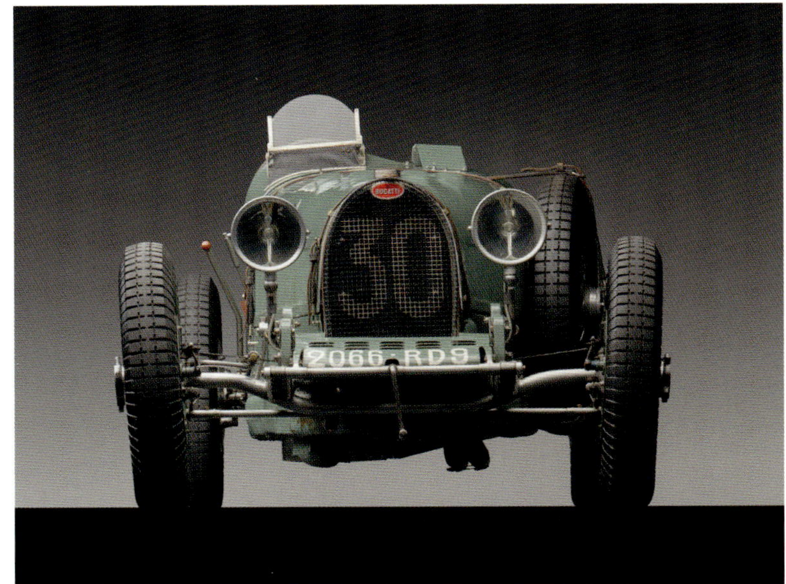

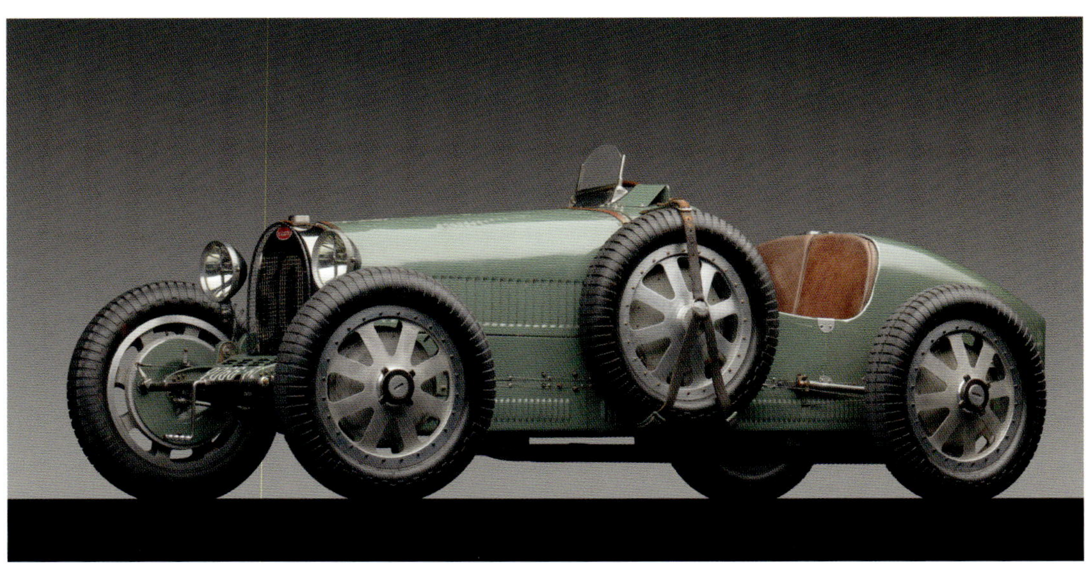

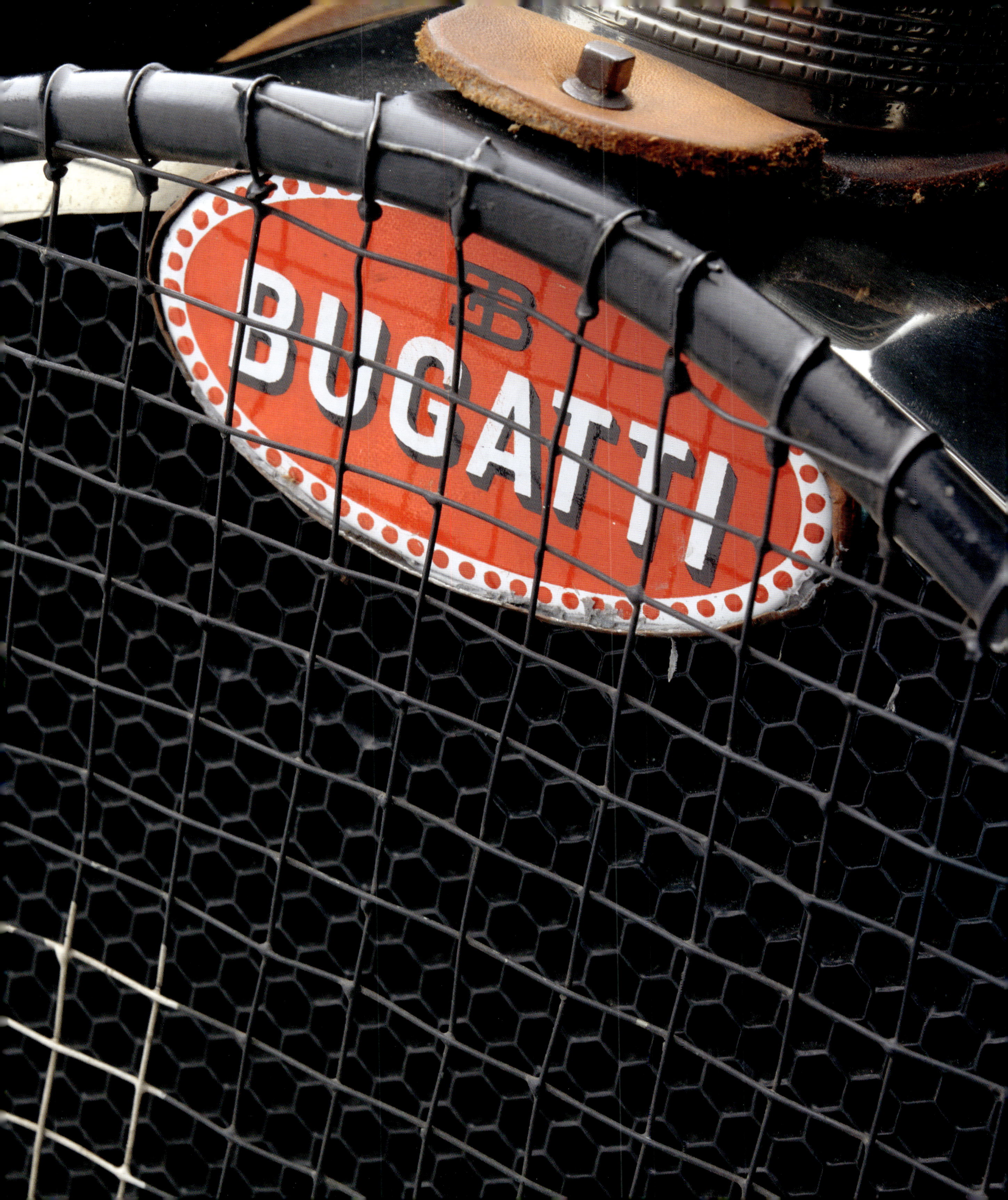
BUGATTI

1928 CITROËN B14 FAUX CABRIOLET

KEN GROSS

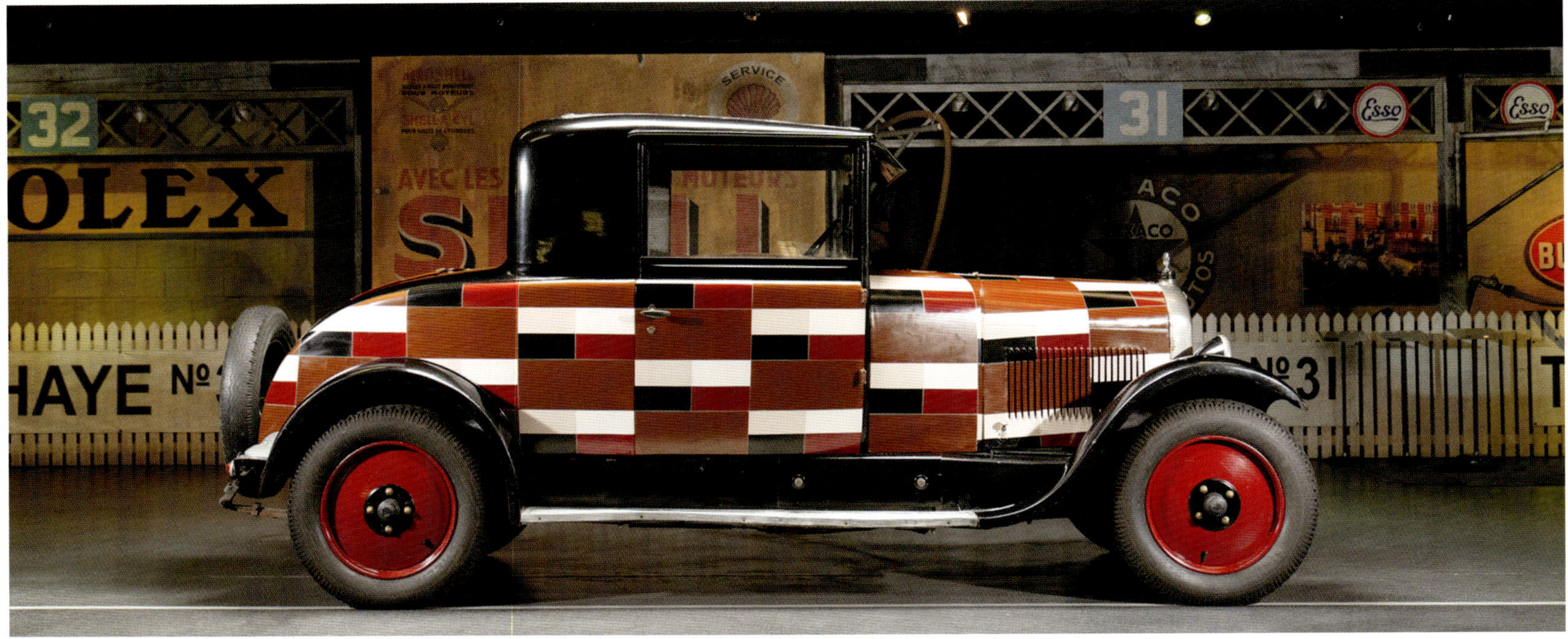

Citroën, Saint-Ouen-sur-Seine, France, founded 1919; repainted by Bernadette Ramaekers, Dutch, b. 1954; *B14 Coupe*, 1928; 71 × 164 × 56 in.; Courtesy of Edward F. Niedzweicki

The energetic and inventive André-Gustave Citroën (1878–1935) had worked for Mors, a pioneer French automaker. He subsequently became an armaments supplier to the French military, producing munitions in large quantities. When World War I ended in 1919, his company began to manufacture automobiles. Anticipating the end of that conflict, in 1916 he contracted with a former Panhard engineer, Louis Dufresne, to design a car that could be built in great numbers. Following Henry Ford, Citroën felt his best opportunity would be with a mass-produced, robust but lightweight, well-equipped, and affordable automobile. The first Citroën Type A was sold in 1919. That year, Citroën began negotiations for the company's sale to General Motors, but the acquisition did not take place.

In 1924, Citroën partnered with Edward G. Budd (1870–1946), whose company built steel car bodies for American manufacturers. Most autos at that time still used wood-framed bodies. That year, the Citroën B10 became the first all-steel-bodied European car. The Citroën company enjoyed a meteoric rise. Citroën's name appeared in lights from 1925 to 1934 on the Eiffel Tower, qualifying it for the Guinness Book of Records as the world's largest advertising sign (FIG. 70). Beginning in 1925, Citroën pioneered auto financing, established factories all over Europe, and even manufactured model cars. Citroën's versatile Kégresse all-wheel-drive vehicles generated considerable publicity in the 1930s when they crossed the heretofore impenetrable Sahara Desert and other inhospitable regions.

The Citroën B14, which superseded the B12, was introduced at the Paris Motor Show in October 1926 with a wide array of open- and closed-body styles. Period Citroën advertising emphasized the B14's comfortable, new, lightweight chassis and continued to improve on the brand's characteristically advanced and effective engineering principles, with a smoother running engine and new four-wheel brakes. Initially powered by a 1,539 cc four-cylinder powerplant, subsequently upsized to 1,628 cc, the popular B14 was offered in three progressively improved variants from 1926 through 1928.

The early history of this handsome, well-proportioned, Citroën B14 two-passenger "faux cabriolet" is unknown. The two-door coupe with a leatherette roof was sold from France to a Belgian owner in 1971. Subsequently, the car was repatriated to France. In 2010, a *carte grise* registration certificate was issued for it. Prior to its 2016 acquisition by the Mullin Collection

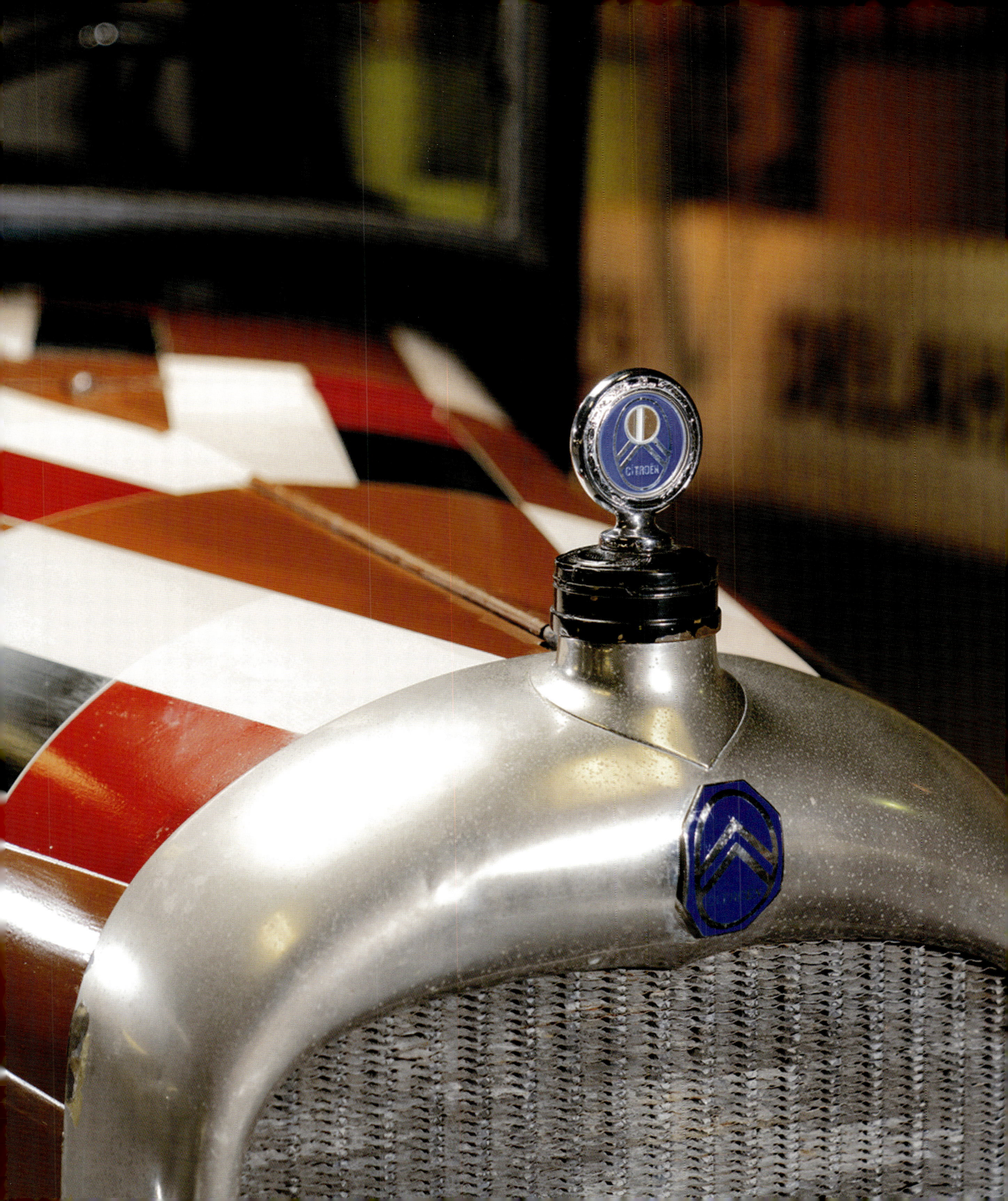
CITROEN

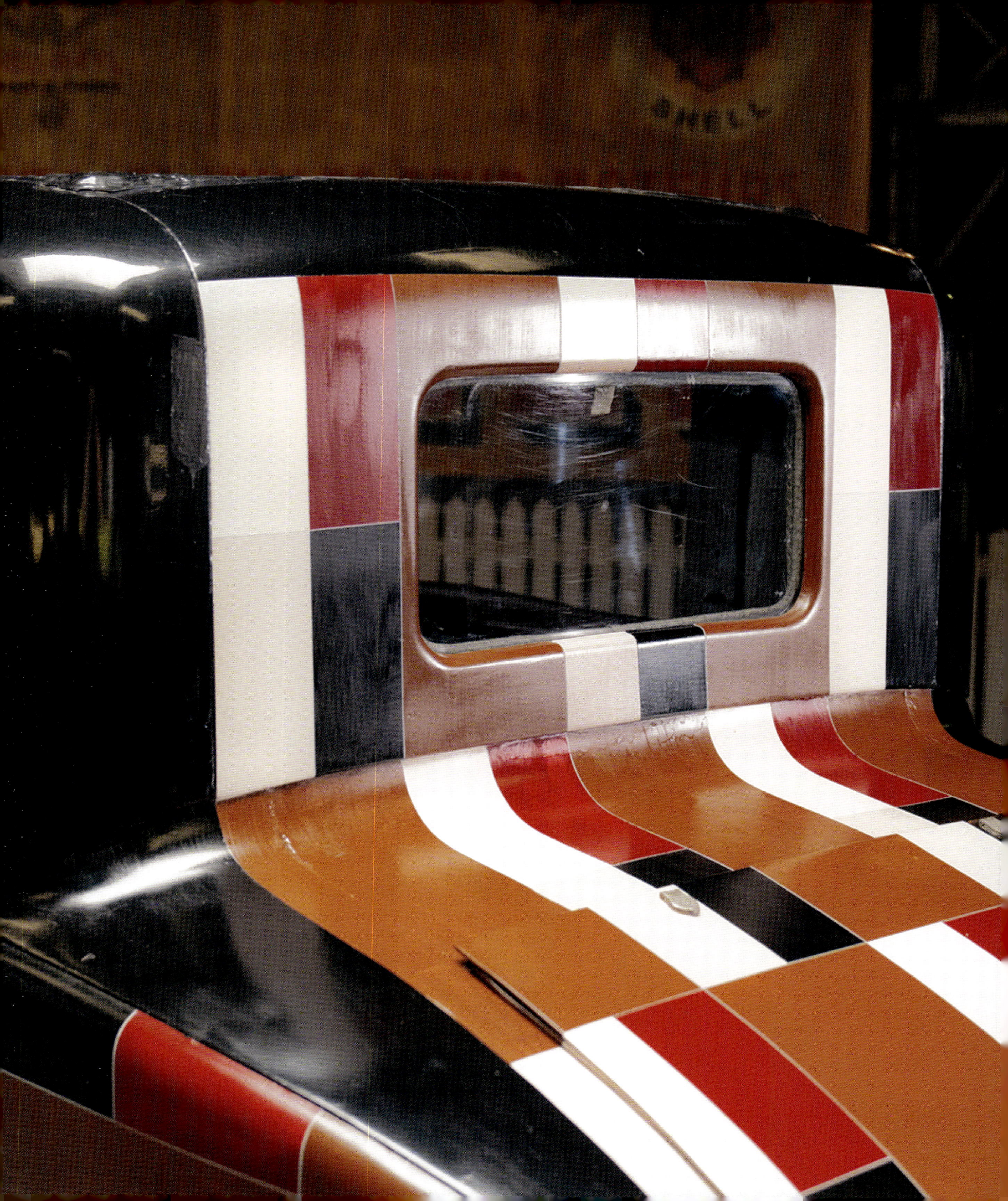
SHELL

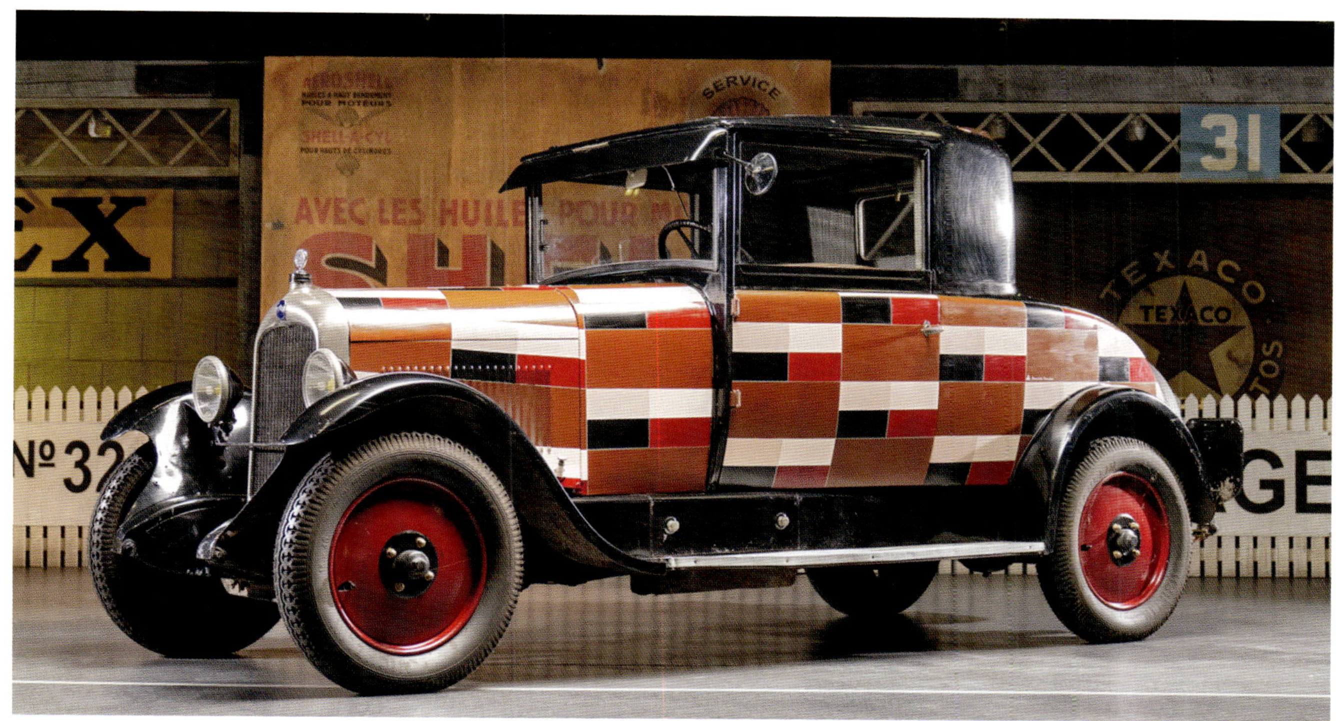

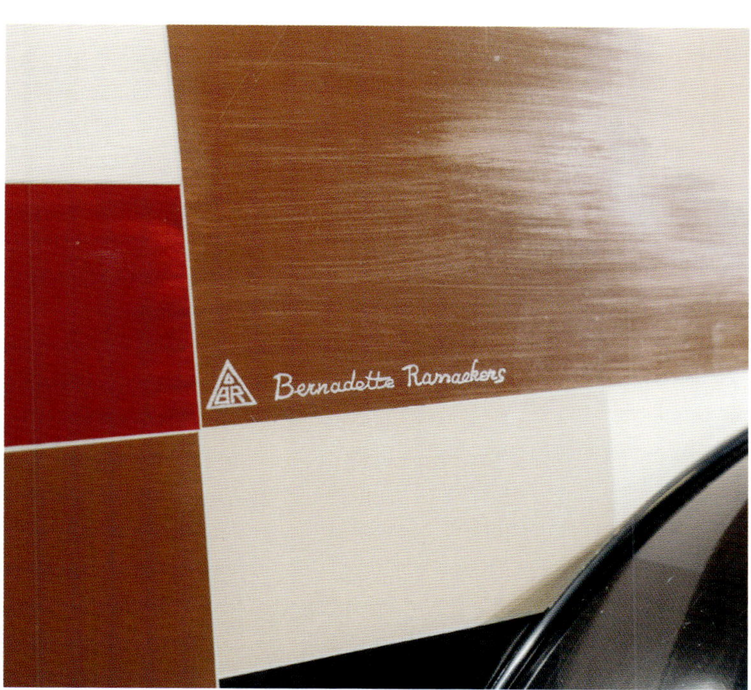

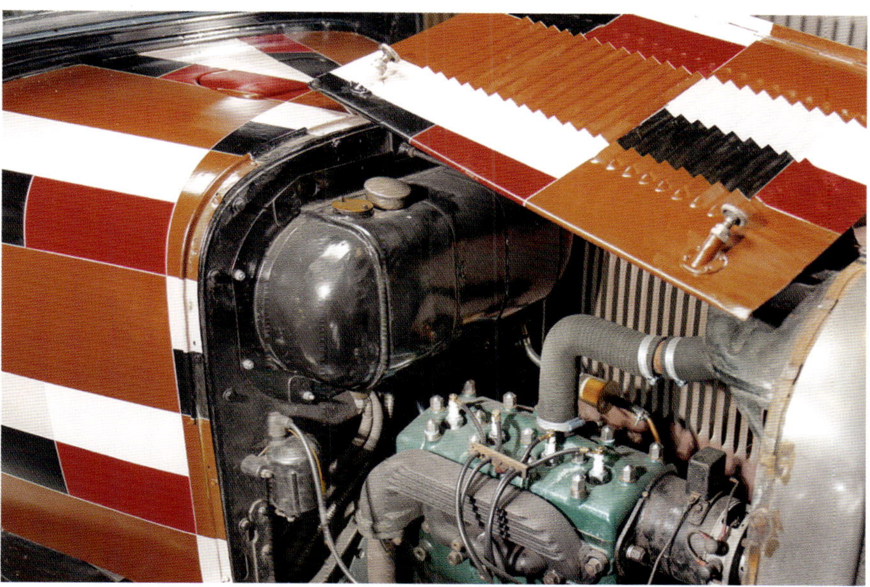

in Oxnard, California, Dutch artist Bernadette Ramaekers adorned this B14 with brightly painted accents in the style of Sonia Delaunay, who famously presented a car with a similar painted body at the 1925 International Exhibition of Modern Decorative and Industrial Arts in Paris.

Delaunay, an acclaimed French artist born to Jewish parents in the Russian Empire (now Ukraine), trained in Russia and Germany before moving to France, where she worked in many media, including textiles, fashion, furniture, wall coverings, and set design. Part of the School of Paris, she was married to Robert Delaunay, and together they founded a style of art known as Orphism.

Loaned by Edward F. Niedzwiecki

ALFA ROMEO, ROBERT MALLET-STEVENS, AND THE PLASTIC SPECTACLE OF THE MODERN SHOWROOM

GENEVIEVE CORTINOVIS

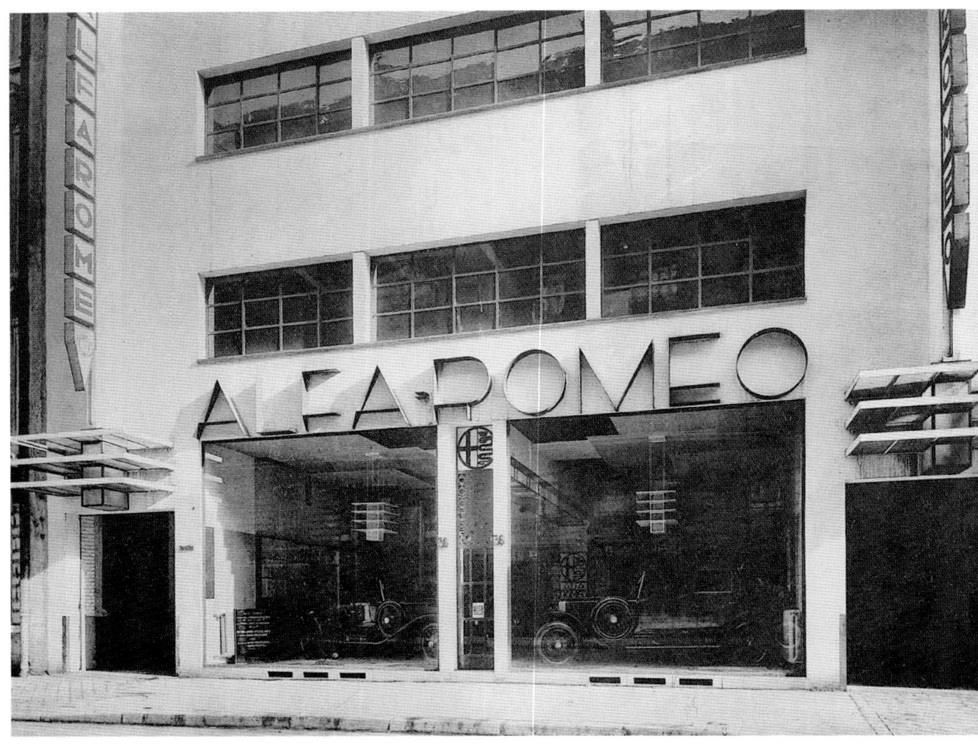

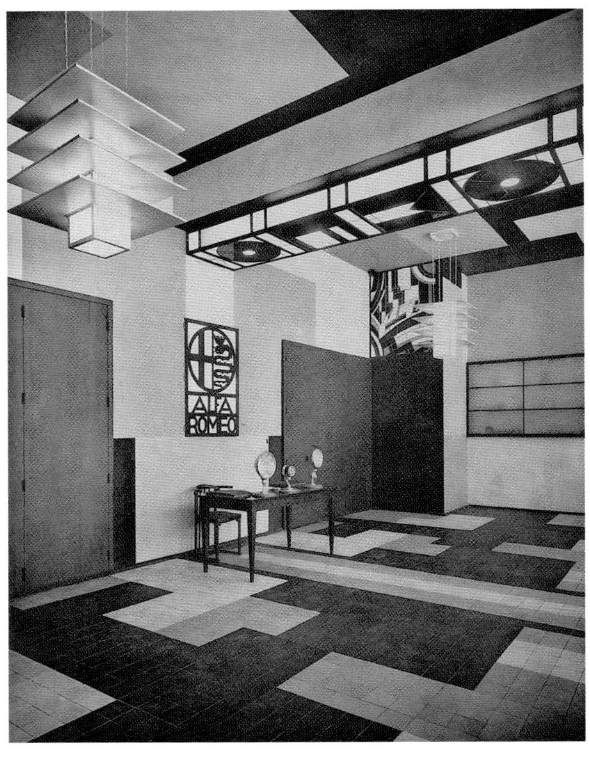

FIG. 35 A, B
Photograph by Hélio Faucheux, French; printed by John Tiranti & Company, London, England, founded 1895; exterior and interior, the Alfa Romeo showroom, Paris, c.1927; photograph in René Herbst, *Modern French Shop-fronts and Their Interiors*, 1927

On July 27, 1926, Alfa Romeo's new Paris showroom was finally complete (FIG. 35A). A multistory, white-skimmed brick and glass building, it stood out conspicuously among its nineteenth-century neighbors on rue Marbeuf, just off the Champs-Élysées.[1] The French architect Robert Mallet-Stevens had been tapped to design the Italian automobile manufacturer's headquarters, which splashily reannounced its incorporation in France in late 1923 as the Société Anonyme Française Ingénieur Nicola Romeo & Cie. Mallet-Stevens's brother-in-law Piero Manusardi, who represented the Milan-based company in France, probably made the introduction. The resulting full-throttle modernist interior was a far cry from the elaborate ancien régime–styled shops of French luxury carmakers like Delage nearby. Open barely a year, the showroom nonetheless represented a key moment in the trajectory of both Mallet-Stevens and Nicola Romeo, and the many designers and craftspeople who entered their orbits.[2]

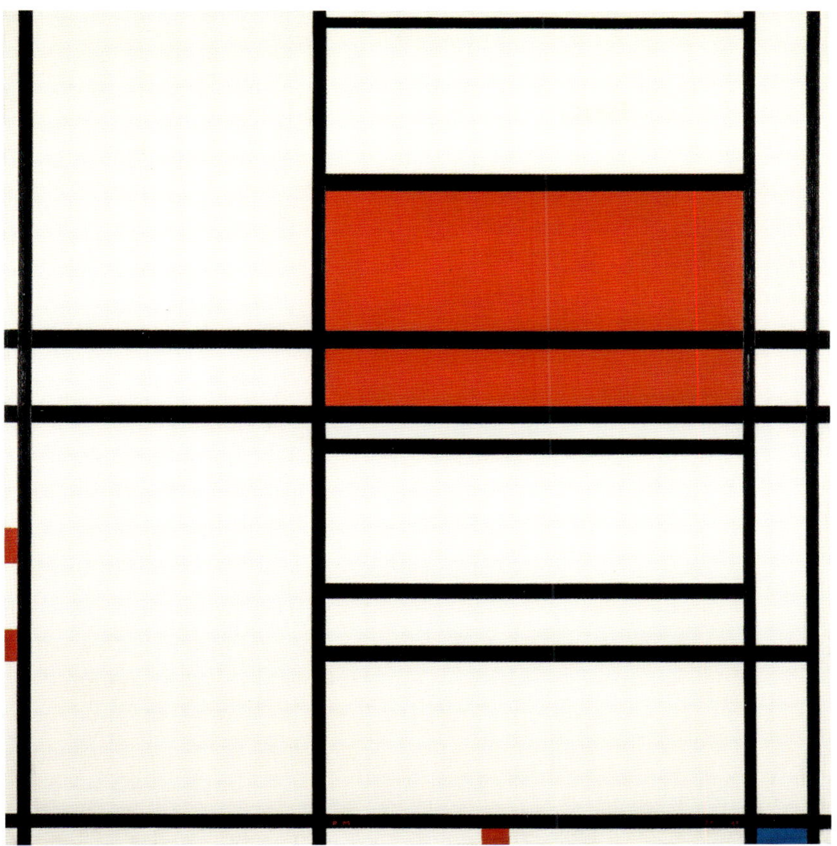

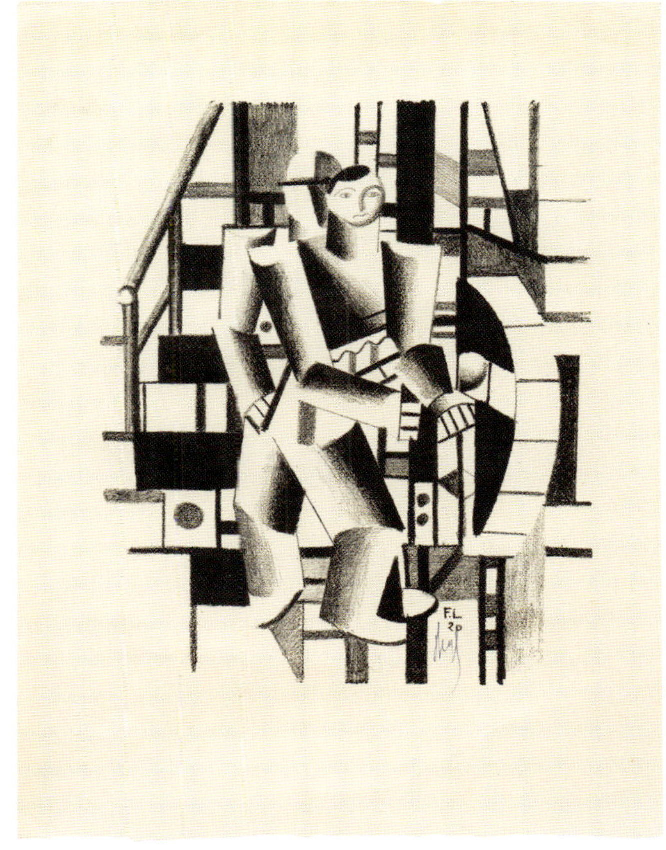

Mallet-Stevens completely transformed the existing gray marble-clad garage, which the critic Marie Dormoy described as a pinnacle of "simplicity" and "haughty sobriety,"[3] into a "cheerful, colorful, harmonious façade" that became, for Dormoy, a utilitarian "work of art."[4] The ground-floor windows were enlarged and combined into two enormous glass panels, inviting light and curious shoppers into the dazzling interior. Dormoy describes the showroom's "geometric décor—red, pink, black, white, gray" and its "invisible" lighting "filtered by the stained-glass windows of [Louis] Barillet." Down the room's central ceiling beam, Barillet created an illuminated sign—Alfa Romeo—rendered in bold, block lettering (FIG. 35B). At the room's far corners, large stained-glass panels depicted a stylized car racing through a jagged landscape of quarter circles and parallelograms. Floor tiles, arranged in abstract meanders, echoed the color-blocked walls. Two large metal hanging lanterns intersected by four stacked square planes further illuminated the interior. A single chair, its back splats running to the floor in the style of the Austrian designer Josef Hoffmann, sat at a simple table displaying headlamps. Similar lanterns surmounted the exterior entryways, linking the building's facade with its dynamic showroom, clearly visible from the street.

With its graphic floor and related lighting, Mallet-Stevens's Alfa Romeo interior closely followed his design for the pavilion of the Société des Artistes Décorateurs at the 1925 Exposition Internationale des Arts Décoratifs et Industriels Modernes. Conceived as a hall for a French embassy, Mallet-Stevens invited Louis Barillet to execute a recessed stained-glass ceiling, Henri Laurens to create a bas-relief, and Robert Delaunay and Fernand Léger to supply large paintings for the project. At the embassy pavilion and Alfa Romeo, each surface—walls, ceiling, and floor—became a canvas for collective visual expression in a "profusion still unparalleled" by the architect.[5] Of Mallet-Stevens's oeuvre, these two projects arguably bear the strongest influence of De Stijl (FIG. 36).[6] Taking its name from the Dutch journal founded in 1917 by Theo van Doesburg, the affiliation of painters, architects, and designers embraced pure geometric abstraction as the universal expression of order and unity. Throughout his career, Mallet-Stevens excelled in harmonizing divergent voices into a dynamic but cohesive ensemble, especially as the leader of the Union des Artistes Modernes (UAM).

FIG. 36
Piet Mondrian, Dutch, 1872–1944; *Composition of Red and White: Nom 1/ Composition No. 4 with Red and Blue*, 1938–42; oil on canvas; 39 ½ × 39 in.; Saint Louis Art Museum, Friends Endowment Fund 242:1972

FIG. 37
Fernand Léger, French, 1881–1955; published by Gustav Kiepenheuer, German, 1880–1949; *Composition à Deux Personnages*, 1920; lithograph; 14 7/16 × 11 7/16 in.; Saint Louis Art Museum, Gift of Julian and Hope Edison 336:2020

Although Léger had no documented involvement, his imprint on the Alfa Romeo showroom was evident in Barillet's stained-glass panels.[7] Both Mallet-Stevens and Barillet had served in the aerial photography unit during World War I, and fittingly, their first collaboration was in 1922 for the Aéro-Club pavilion. The innovative Atelier Barillet, which included Jacques Le Chevallier and Théodore-Gérard Hanssen, incorporated mirrors and impressed glass to achieve dazzling graphic effects in their increasingly abstract compositions. The subject matter of the panels—the machine in the city—was a favorite of Léger, who sought to capture the rising sensorial overload of modern life where "speed is the law."[8] In his 1919 painting *Disque dans la Rue*, Léger juxtaposed fragments of signage, scaffolding, and buzzing traffic in a patchwork of shapes and color (SEE FIG. 10). The figure took on importance for Léger following the war, as he imagined the human body in a mechanical world. One of Léger's first prints, *Composition à Deux Personnages*, depicts overlapping figures rendered in shaded volumetric forms, their bionic limbs taking on the hard edges and luminous surfaces of their mechanized surroundings (FIG. 37).

Léger further explored these human-machine interfaces in his influential film *Ballet mécanique*, which he co-directed with Dudley Murphy (FIG. 38). Set at a frantic pace, footage of a woman gently swinging is quickly interrupted by flashes of everyday objects—wine bottles, a boater hat, a cake pan—and the pointed pout of the avant-garde artist and muse Kiki de Montparnasse. As the frenzy continues, carnival rides and speeding cars are interspliced with prismatically fractured images.

Both Léger and Mallet-Stevens designed sets for Marcel L'Herbier's proto-sci-fi film *L'Inhumaine* (The inhuman woman). Léger's mechanical laboratory for the protagonist, the Swedish scientist Einar Norsen, is housed inside a Mallet-Stevens-designed villa, an asymmetrical mass of rectangular blocks that cast especially dramatic shadows under studio lights (FIG. 39). One of the film's most striking scenes follows the anguished scientist's suicidal drive in a Rolland-Pilain race car, ending in its jolting tumble down a hill.

René Herbst led his 1927 publication *Modern French Shop-fronts and Their Interiors* with an image of Alfa Romeo's rue Marbeuf showroom, one of the few photographs with cars visibly parked on the colorful terrazzo floor. "Everything is in its place," proclaimed Herbst. The circles of automobile tires are repeated in the letters of the company's signage and logo. The horizontal strips of grided windows echo the lanterns, color-blocked ceiling, and stained glass.[9] The result is a "persuasive, pervasive atmosphere"—a plastic spectacle with the automobile as its star performer.[10]

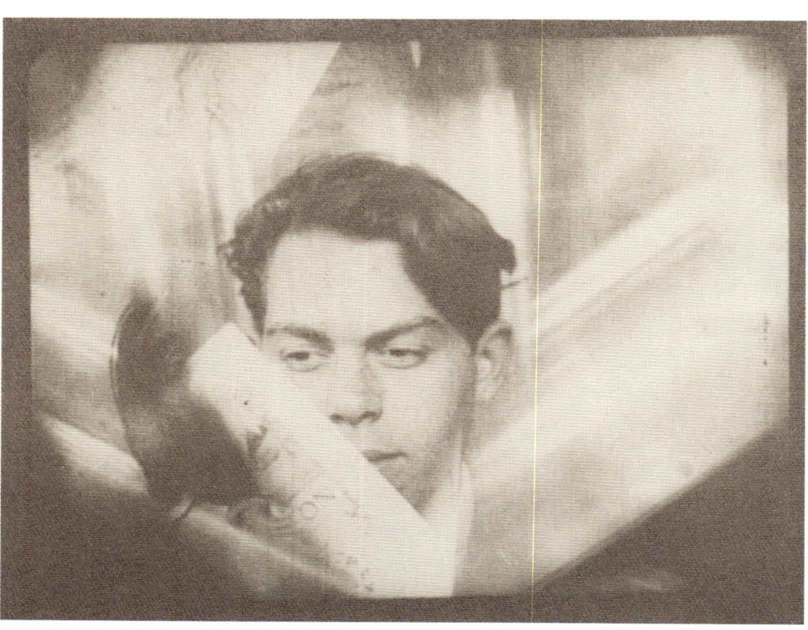

FIG. 38
Fernand Léger, French, 1881–1955; still from the film *Ballet mécanique (Dudley Murphy)*, c.1923–24; gelatin silver print; 3 ½ × 4 ⅝ in.; Saint Louis Art Museum, Funds given by donors to the 1995 Annual Appeal 5:1996

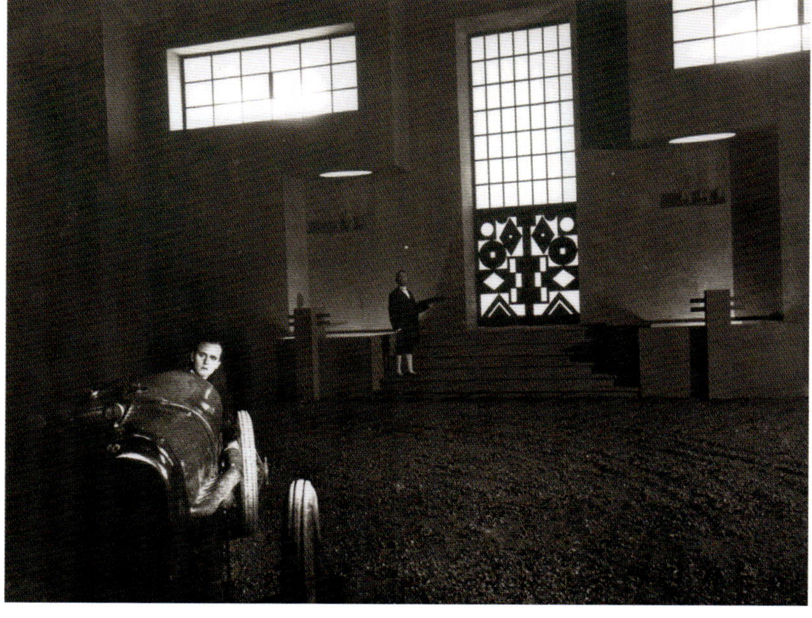

FIG. 39
Directed by Marcel L'Herbier, French, 1888–1979; sets by Robert Mallet-Stevens, French, 1886–1945; still from the film *L'Inhumaine*, 1924

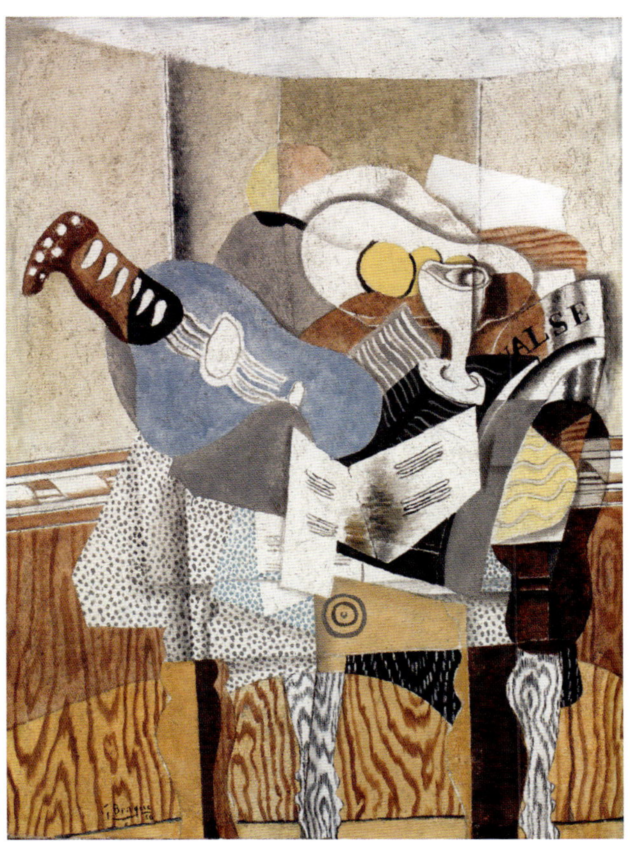

Amplifying their cars' impressive racing records in period advertisements, Alfa Romeo courted clients seeking speed, efficiency, and advanced mechanics, even if, as the automotive scholars Peter Larsen and Ben Erickson noted, their merchandise at rue Marbeuf was subpar.[11] Mallet-Stevens's avant-garde showroom expressed the company's aspirations, foretelling an experience of fragmentation, abandonment, and even oblivion. The co-founder of Cubism Georges Braque was a famous devotee of the brand (FIG. 40). In 1927, Braque reported to his dealer Paul Rosenberg on the delivery of a new Alfa Romeo, possibly ordered at rue Marbeuf.[12] The poet Blaise Cendrars described driving an Alfa Romeo purchased from Braque, its coachwork designed by the artist. Braque's friend Jean Bazaine conceded, "Like everyone else, I would refuse only, politely, to join him in his little sports car, which he drove, at seventy years of age, like a madman."[13]

FIG. 40
Georges Braque, French, 1882–1963; *The Blue Mandolin*, 1930; oil with sand on canvas; 46 × 35 in.; Saint Louis Art Museum, Museum Purchase 125:1944

NOTES

1 Peter Larsen and Ben Erickson, *Joseph Figoni: Le Grand Couturier de la Carrosserie Automobile*, vol. 1, *Alfa Romeo* (Copenhagen: Moteurs, 2021), 53.

2 Following financial troubles, Alfa Romeo leased the showroom to General Motors importer Compagnie Maryland. In an April 23, 1927, issue of *L'Information financière, économique et politique*, the new tenant advertised their "recently installed" address as 36, rue Marbeuf.

3 Marie Dormoy, "L'Architecture française moderne," *L'Amour de l'art* 3 (March 1925): 113–25. Dormy writes that this earlier structure was also designed by Mallet-Stevens but misattributes its location to the boulevard Haussmann. A January 1924 article on these same Alfa Romeo headquarters in *La Renaissance de l'art français* lists the correct location but does not cite Mallet-Stevens as the architect. According to Olivier Cinqualbre (*Robert Mallet-Stevens: L'Oeuvre complète* [Paris: Centre Pompidou, 2005], 118), Dormoy's article is the only record of Mallet-Stevens's involvement.

4 Marie Dormoy, "Garage Moderne," *L'Art vivant*, January 1927, n.p.

5 Cinqualbre, *Robert Mallet-Stevens*, 141.

6 Cinqualbre, *Robert Mallet-Stevens*, 56.

7 Jean-François Archieri and Cécile Nebout, *Atelier Louis Barillet: Maître verrier* (Paris: Éditions 15, 2005), 42–44.

8 Fernand Léger, "The Spectacle," in *Functions of Painting by Fernand Léger*, ed. Edward F. Fry, trans. Alexandra Anderson (New York: Viking, 1973), 35.

9 René Herbst, *Modern French Shop-fronts and Their Interiors* (London: John Tiranti, 1927), n.p., plate 1.

10 Léger, "Function of Spectacle," 36. "Industry and commerce, swept along in a frantic competitive race, have been the first to grab everything that could serve as an attraction. They admirably sense that a 'shop window,' a department store must be a spectacle. They had the idea of creating a pervasive, persuasive atmosphere by using only the objects at their disposal."

11 Larsen and Erickson, *Joseph Figoni*, 53.

12 Georges Braque, *La Ciotat*, letter to Paul Rosenberg, August 30, 1927, Literary and Historical Manuscripts (LHMS), The Morgan Library and Museum, MA 3500.21.

13 Jean Bazaine, *Couleurs et mots* (Paris: Cherche-Midi, 1997), 18. Braque sold one of his Alfa Romeo automobiles to the poet Blaise Cendrars. According to Miriam Cendrars, Braque had designed the coachwork and painted the body of the Alfa himself. This was also repeated in the article "La Vie des Livres" by Pierre Loewel in *L'Aurore*, July 17, 1946, and "Le Goût du Risque" by J. L. Chardans in *V: magazine illustré du MLN*, October 27, 1946, reporting on the automobile adventures of Blaise Cendrars during World War II. See Miriam Cendrars, *Blaise Cendrars* (Paris: Ballas, 1984), 327.

1930 ALFA ROMEO 6C 1750 ZAGATO SPIDER

KEN GROSS

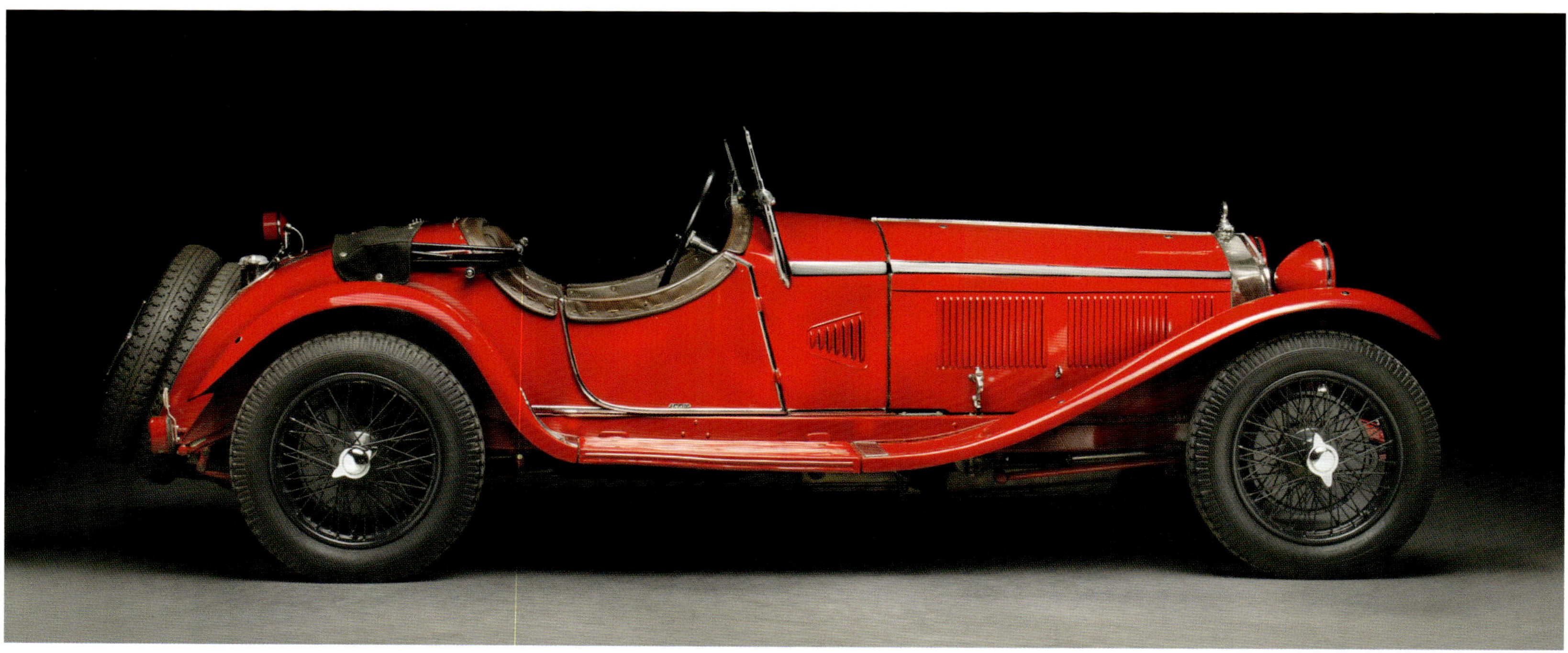

Alfa Romeo rivaled Bugatti in the 1920s and 1930s with successful and well-engineered road-going and racing cars. Ken W. Purdy (1913–1972), the great American mid-century auto writer, quipped, "a Bugattiste, even an advanced Bugattiste, will talk to an Alfa Romeo owner on terms of near equality."[1]

The marque extended its sporting heritage in 1925 when it replaced its aging RL and RM models with the new 6C 1500, the first in a long line of successful six-cylinder racing and Sports/Grand touring (GT) cars. Designed by Vittorio Jano (1891–1965), who was responsible for Alfa's successful P2 Grand Prix racers, the 6C 1500 was powered by a sophisticated alloy, twin-cam I6 engine. Alfa Romeo only sold the chassis. Initially the cars were bodied by James Young (UK) and Carrozzeria Touring Superleggera (Milan): "The whole design was ahead of its time, a small, high-revving engine in a light and agile chassis with a performance that ensured respect and with regard to the supercharged version, a performance to dominate much larger contemporaries."[2] The French artist Georges Braque (1882–1963) owned a 6C 1500 that he later sold to the modernist poet Blaise Cendrars (1887–1961).

In 1929, Alfa introduced the 6C 1750, adding more power and a more flexible chassis, with C-shaped frame rails. Produced in six series, from 1929 to 1933, the new model was a great success, winning every race in which it competed, including the Mille Miglia, co-driven by Giuseppe Campari and Giulio Ramponi. The following year, the 6C 1750 repeated its Mille Miglia triumph and also won the grueling Spa 24 Hours race. Some 2,579 examples were sold. Most 1750s were bodied with sporty styling by Zagato and Carrozzeria Touring. A few cars had bodies by James Young. Top-of-the-line Super Sport variant engines, equipped with a Roots-type supercharger and one Weber carburetor, developed 85 bhp at 4,800 rpm; Gran Sport engines upped that to 102 bhp at 5,000 rpm. Top speed was between 103 and 110 miles per hour.

Purdy noted, "This was definitely a fast car, and full of evidence of the careful design and meticulous machining that was to characterize Italian craftsmanship in mechanics until World War II."[3] The 6C 1750 was succeeded by the 6C 1900 and the 6C 2500. The latter, with increased power, either one or three Weber carburetors, and stylish, often very streamlined coachwork from a host of European firms, persisted in various iterations from 1938 to 1952.

Records indicate that this Zagato-bodied roadster (chassis no. 8513095) was initially owned in Italy from 1930 to

Ugo Zagato, Italian, 1890–1968; Alfa Romeo Automobiles S.p.A., Milan, Italy, founded 1910; *6C 1750 Spider*, 1930; 43 × 144 × 64 in.; The North Collection

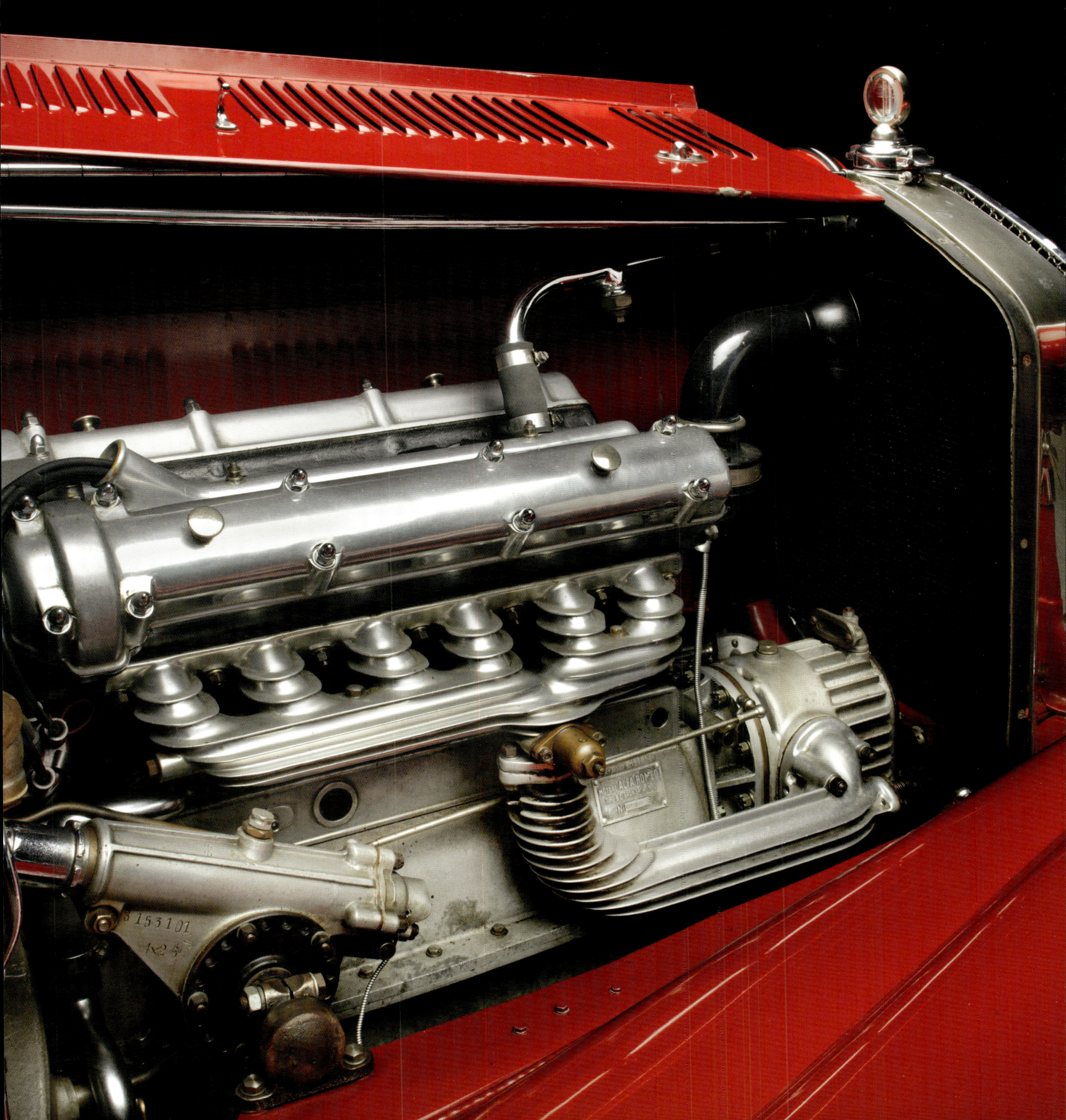
8153101

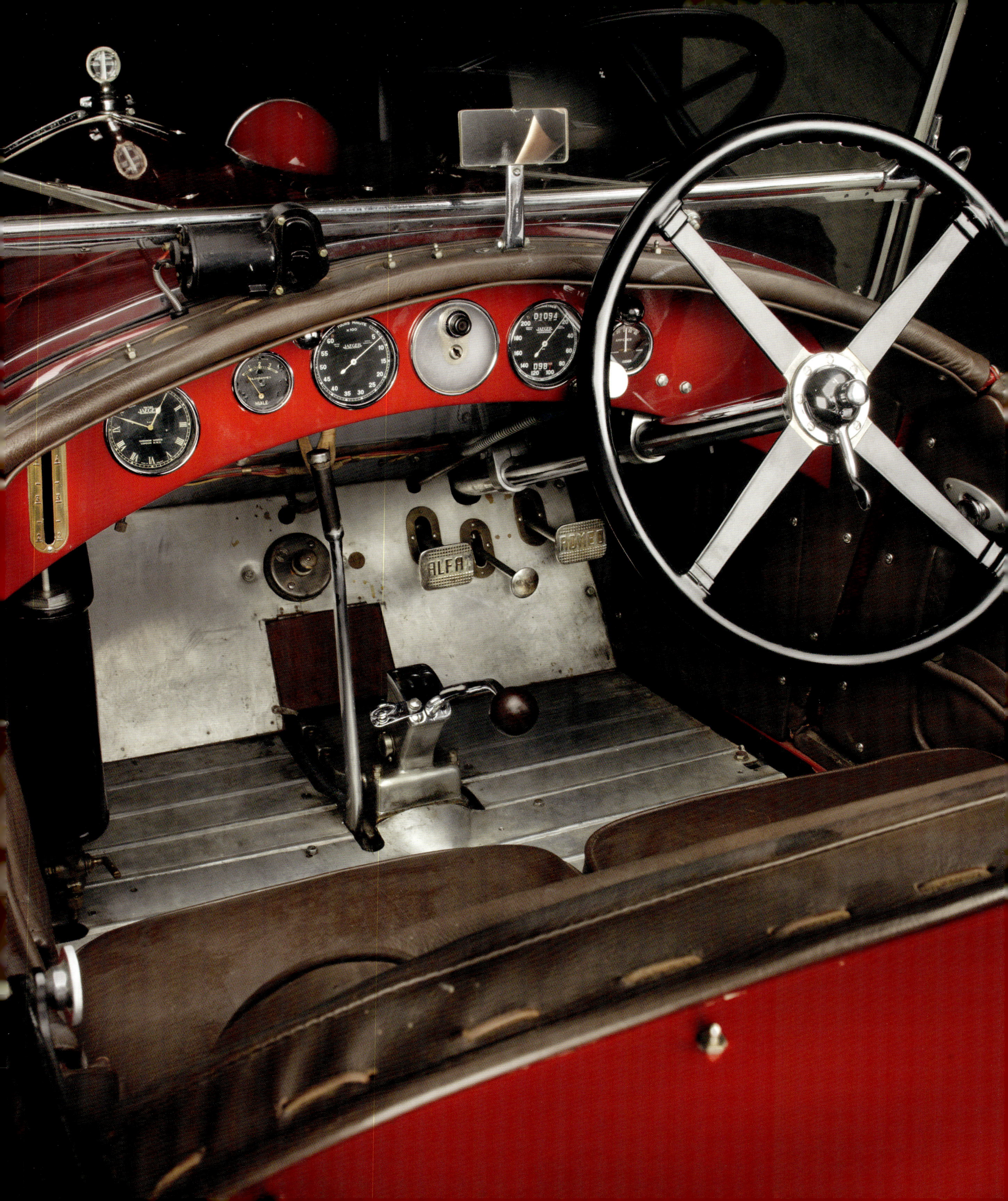
ALFA
ROMEO

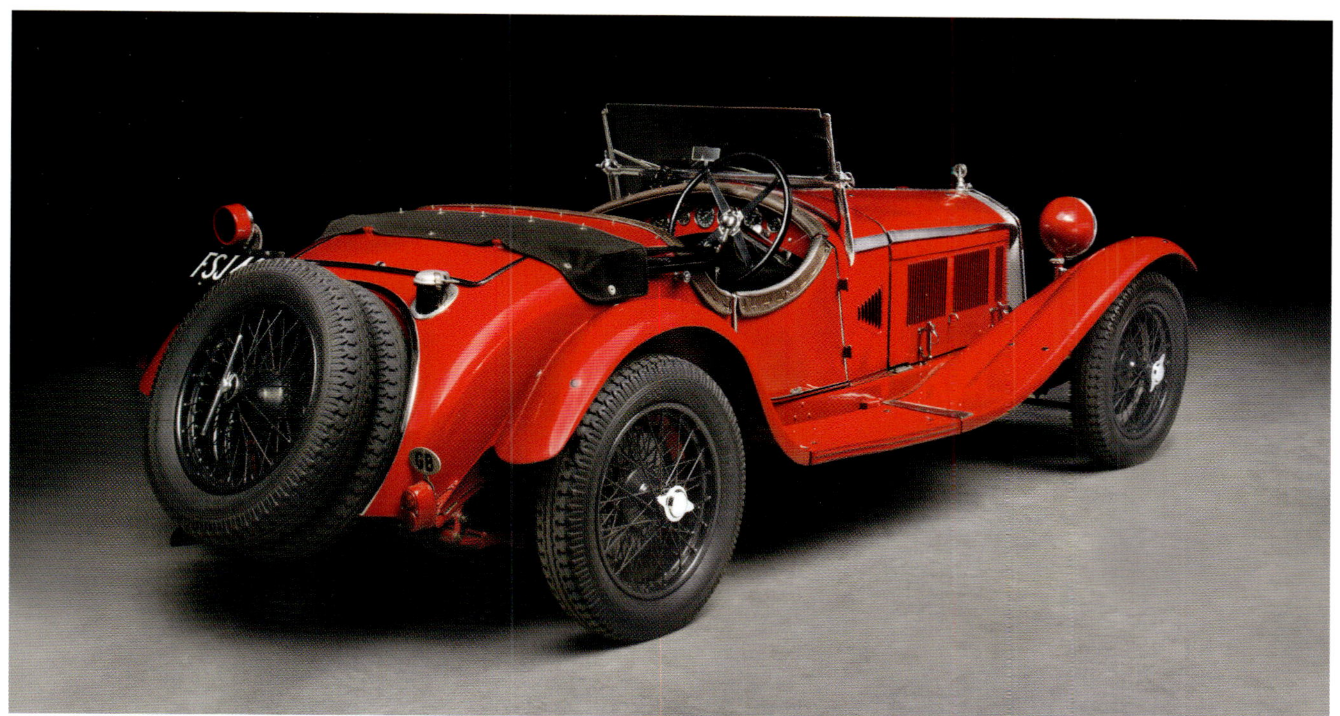

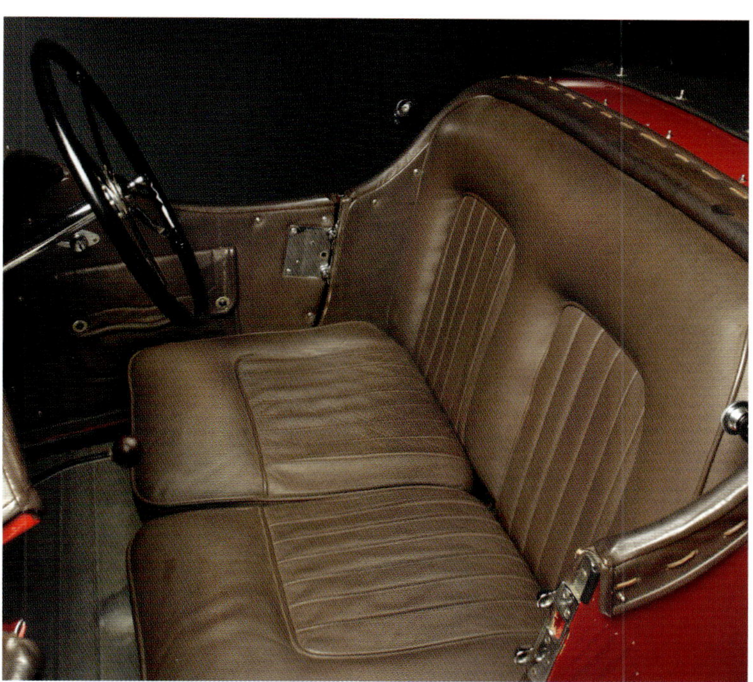

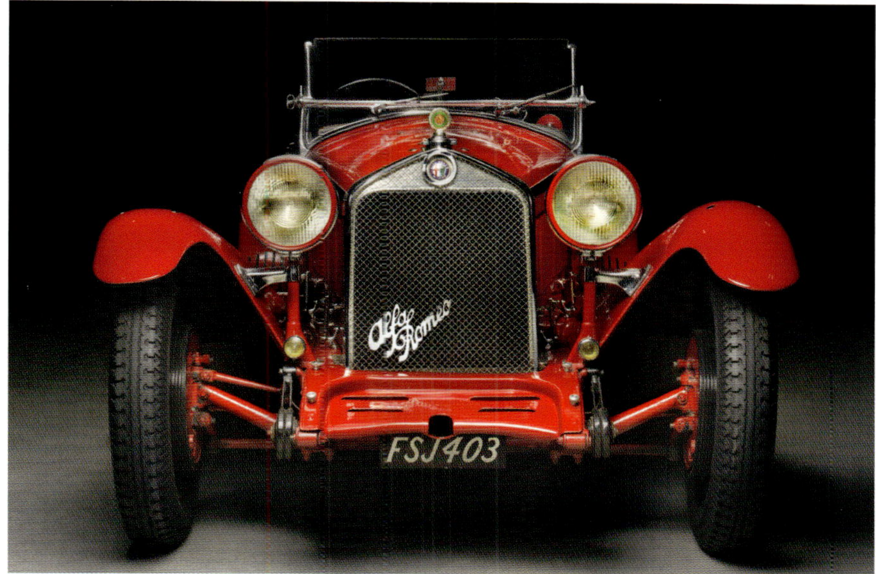

1935. It found its way to England for a while, and in the 1950s it came to the US. Subsequently owned by several collectors, it was found in California, when Judge John North acquired it twenty years ago. It was in excellent restored condition and remains so.

Loaned by the North Collection

1 Ken W. Purdy, *The Kings of the Road* (Boston: Little, Brown, 1952), 89.
2 Luigi Fusi and Roy Slater, *The 6C 1750 Alfa Romeo* (London: MacDonald, 1967), 20.
3 Purdy, *Kings of the Road*, 92.

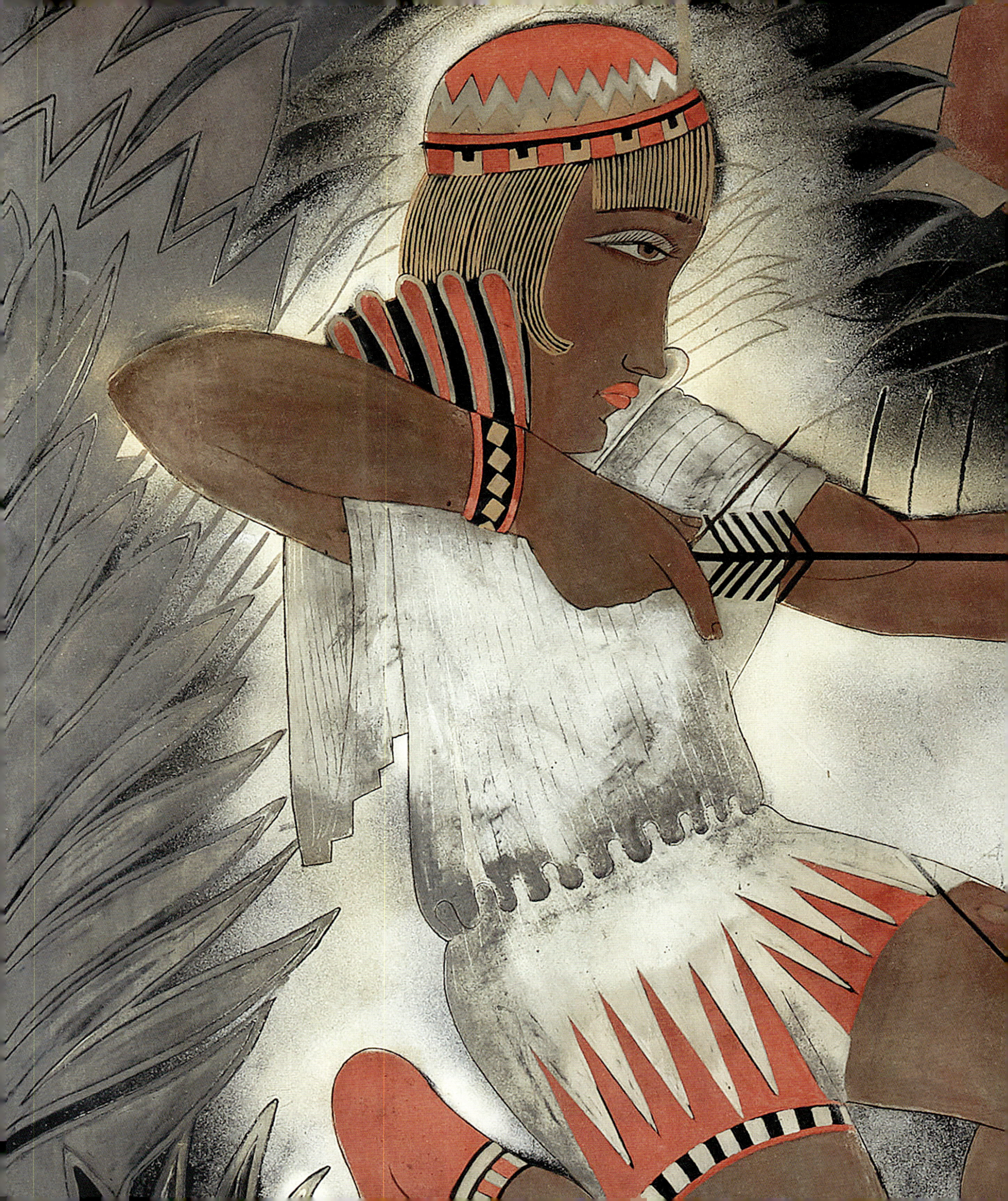

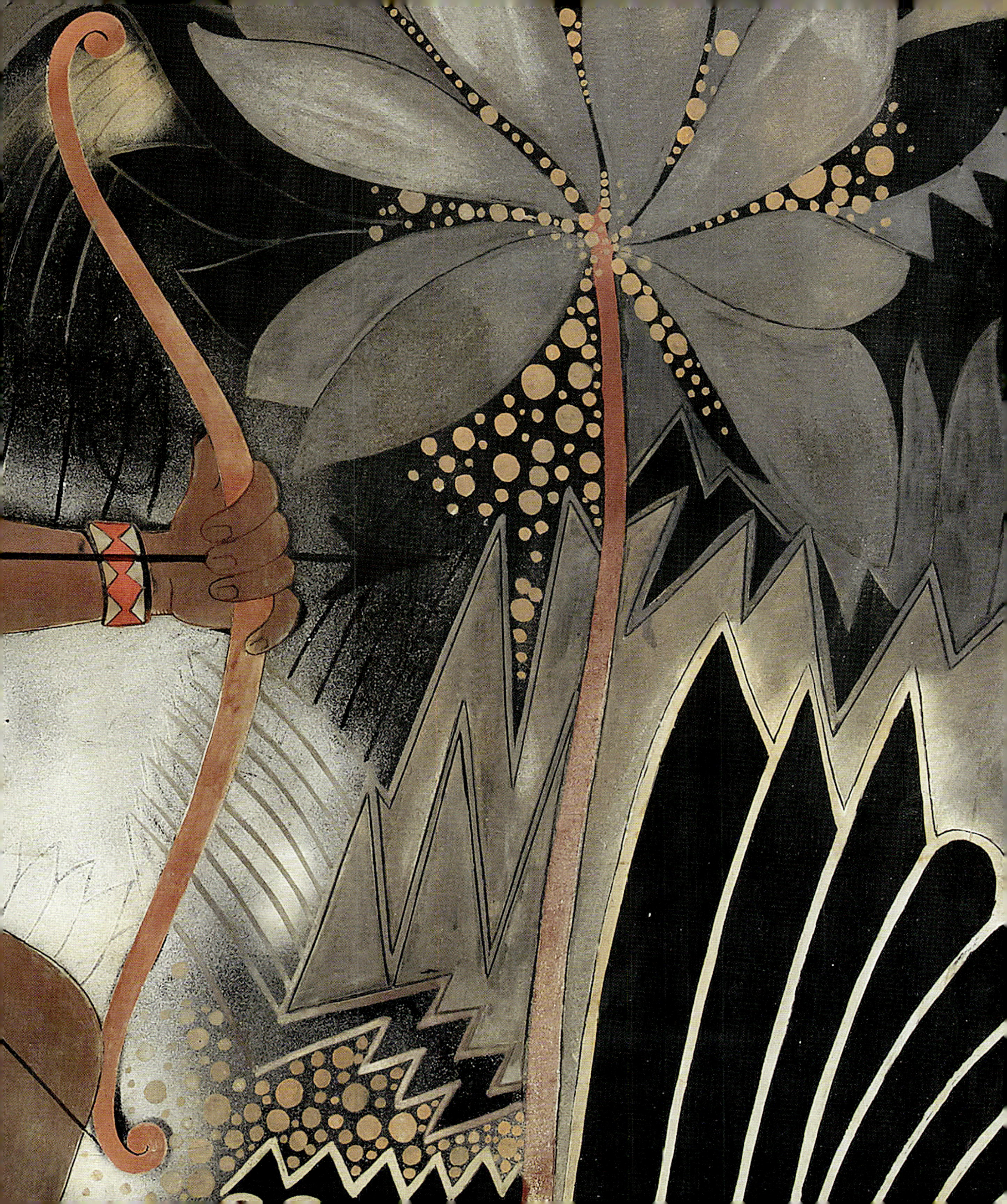

SLOW WORK IN FAST TIMES

Craft, Industry, and Technology at the 1925 International Exhibition of Modern Decorative and Industrial Arts

GENEVIEVE CORTINOVIS

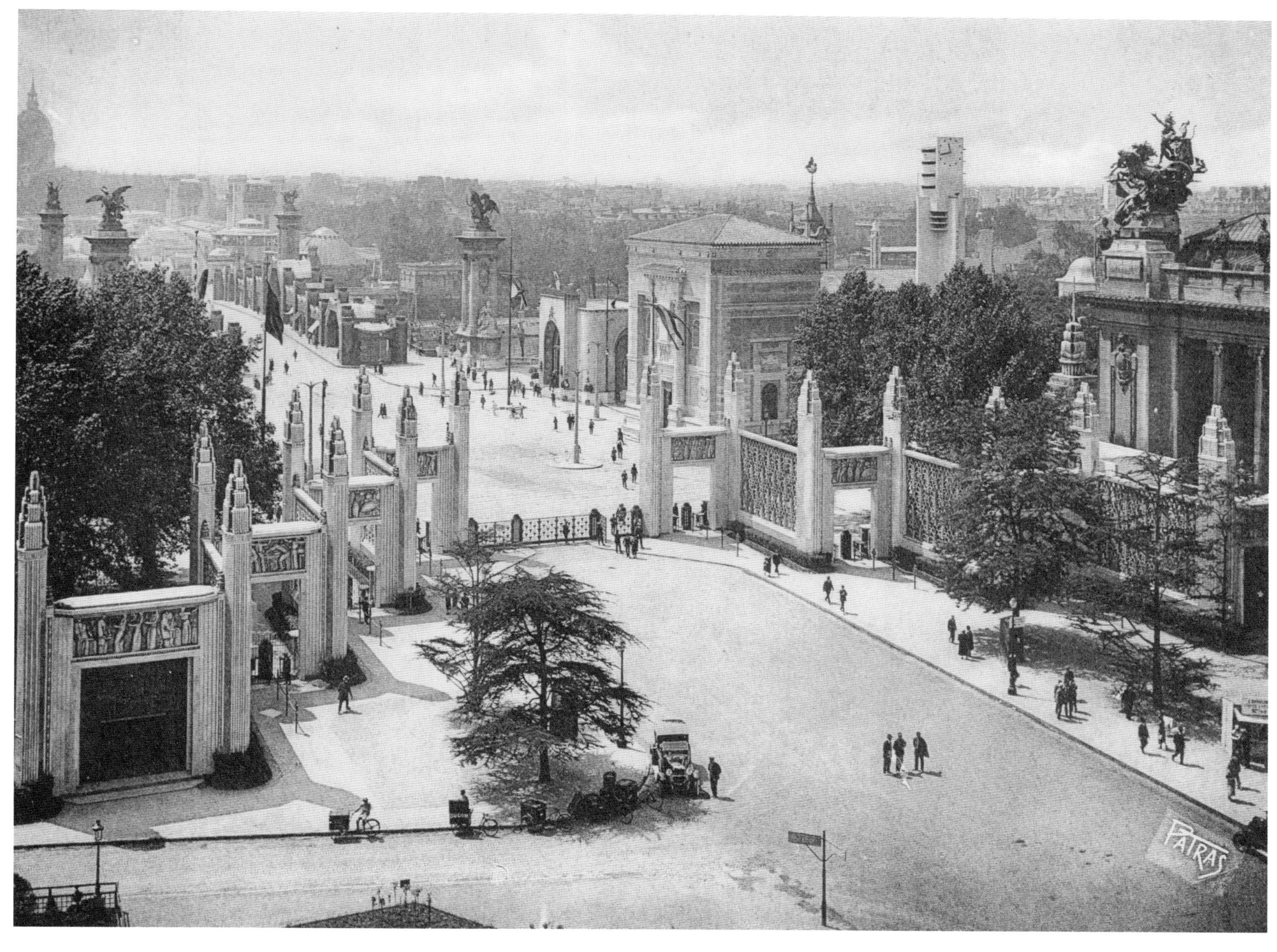

FIG. 41
Printed by Éditions d'Art L. Patras; "Main Entrance," illustration in *Exposition des arts décoratifs et industriels modernes, Paris, 1925*, 1925; book closed: 7 × 9 3/4 × 1/4 in.; Steedman Architecture Collection, St. Louis Public Library

In 1925, Paris was awash in cars: "taxi cabs . . . snub-nosed Renaults and the ubiquitous Citroëns . . . faithful old family limousines with antique hoods round as locomotive boilers. Motorized commerce—roaring dreadnaught trucks and the gleaming vans of the department stores . . . and a fifteen-thousand-dollar Hispano-Suiza impatient for the right of way."[1] The industries responsible for the astounding panoply of wheeled vehicles clogging the city's medieval streets and thundering down its wide boulevards had a surprisingly peripheral position in Paris's marquee event that year. The glittering International Exhibition of Modern Decorative and Industrial Arts (Exposition Internationale des Arts Décoratifs et Industriels Modernes) (FIG. 41) devoted a tiny fraction of the 55 acres it covered in central Paris to automobiles.

The fair was initially conceived to foster collaboration between decorative artists and manufacturers and improve and increase French exports in the face of rising competition from Germany, whose architects, designers, manufacturers, craftspeople, and retailers were successfully forging partnerships that brought modern, often machine-made, goods to middle-class consumers. Yet by the time it opened on April 28, 1925, its organizers had abandoned the focus on cross-industry collaboration. Instead, they sought to reaffirm the superiority of French luxury production and recenter Paris as an international leader in taste and fashion.[2] The organizers stipulated objects on view had to be modern, but only in the sense that they could not copy historic styles. Presenters were not required to embrace mass manufacturing or new materials or technologies. The fair's pavilions brimmed with shimmering textiles, sharkskin-covered furniture, and gem-encrusted couture reinforcing the "delusion" among outsiders that "Parisian life is

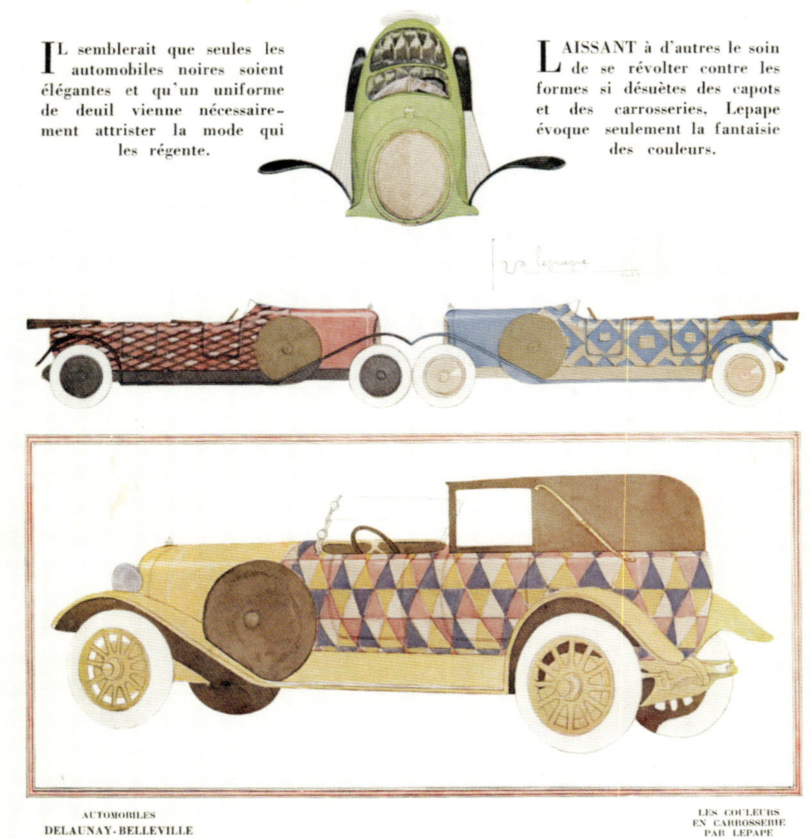

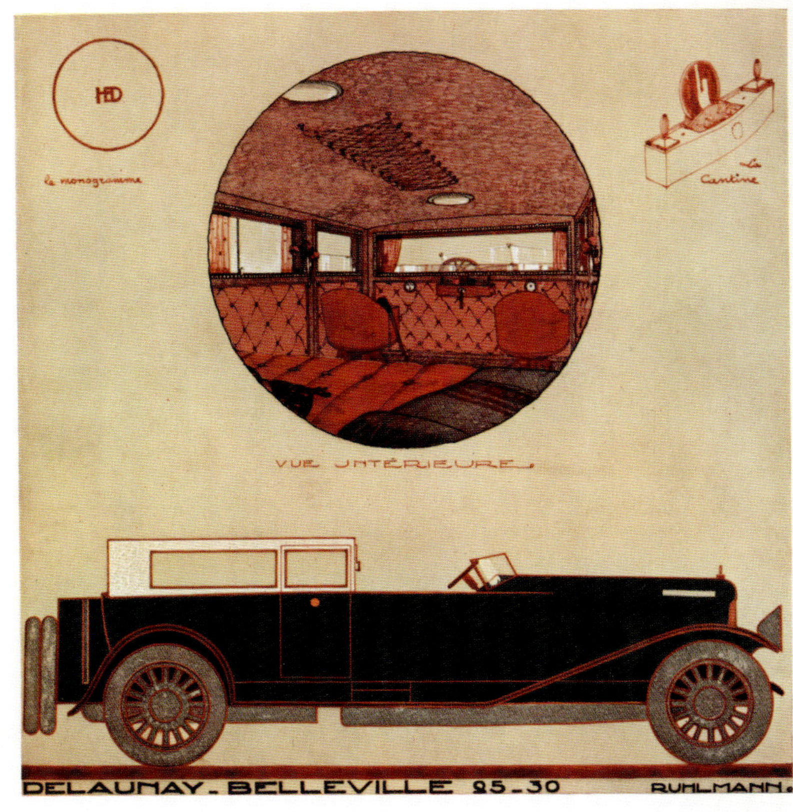

maintained against a backdrop of exotically colored and perfumed boudoirs,"[3] not exhaust-filled streets congested with cars.

Visitors were largely delighted with the artful fantasy, but many critics bemoaned the fair's seeming lack of interest in the defining developments of the era. In his review of the fair in the journal *Art et décoration,* Gaston Varenne advised attendees looking for "a truly modern style" to seek out the fair's small transport section, "disdainfully relegated to the sidelines."[4] He argued these works on view—trains, planes, and especially automobiles—were poised to "transform art" just as they had transformed life.

The marginalization of the automobile, a key French export, reflected not only the shifting objectives of the fair organizers but also larger debates around France's path to prosperity in the modern world. The complexity of the auto industry, which included designers, engineers, craftspeople, manufacturers, and advertisers making mass-produced and artisan-made cars, further complicated its position in the hierarchy of French art and culture. If the fair revealed serious hurdles in unifying modern decorative arts and industry at an institutional level, it also showed the automobile—pinnacle of luxury craft, feat of engineering, fashionable accessory, symbol of standardization, icon of liberation—to be an unruly nexus of creativity. Ultimately, the influence of the "ubiquitous Citroëns" and "fifteen-thousand-dollar Hispano-Suiza[s]" could not be defined by a single person, entity, or pavilion.

Real Bodies and False Chassis

In his essay "Introduction to the Exposition of Decorative Arts," in *Art et décoration*, the critic Guillaume Janneau opened with a drawing for a limousine from the celebrated designer Émile-Jacques Ruhlmann.[5] Leading up to the exhibition, the automobile manufacturer Delaunay-Belleville had invited Ruhlmann and several of "the most inventive decorators," including Süe et Mare and the illustrators Georges Lepape and Eduardo Benito, to submit sketches for coachwork that might "stimulate new forms" for the "automobile of the future" (FIGS. 14, 42, 43).[6] Ruhlmann's sleek black-and-white limousine boasted tufted upholstery, a patterned ceiling with a mesh pocket for storage, and a collapsible dressing table. The eye-catching illustrations followed pages of detailed diagrams of Delaunay-Belleville's chassis, and descriptions of

FIG. 42
Illustrated by Georges Lepape, French, 1887–1971; printed by Draeger, Paris, founded 1886; "Les Couleurs en Carrosserie," in *Description des Chassis Delaunay Belleville*, 1924; ink on paper; 9 ½ × 10 ¼ in.; Private collection

FIG. 43
Illustrated by Émile-Jacques Ruhlmann, French, 1879–1933; printed by Draeger, Paris, founded 1886; illustration in *Description des Chassis Delaunay Belleville*, 1924; ink on paper; 9 ½ × 10 ¼ in.; Private collection

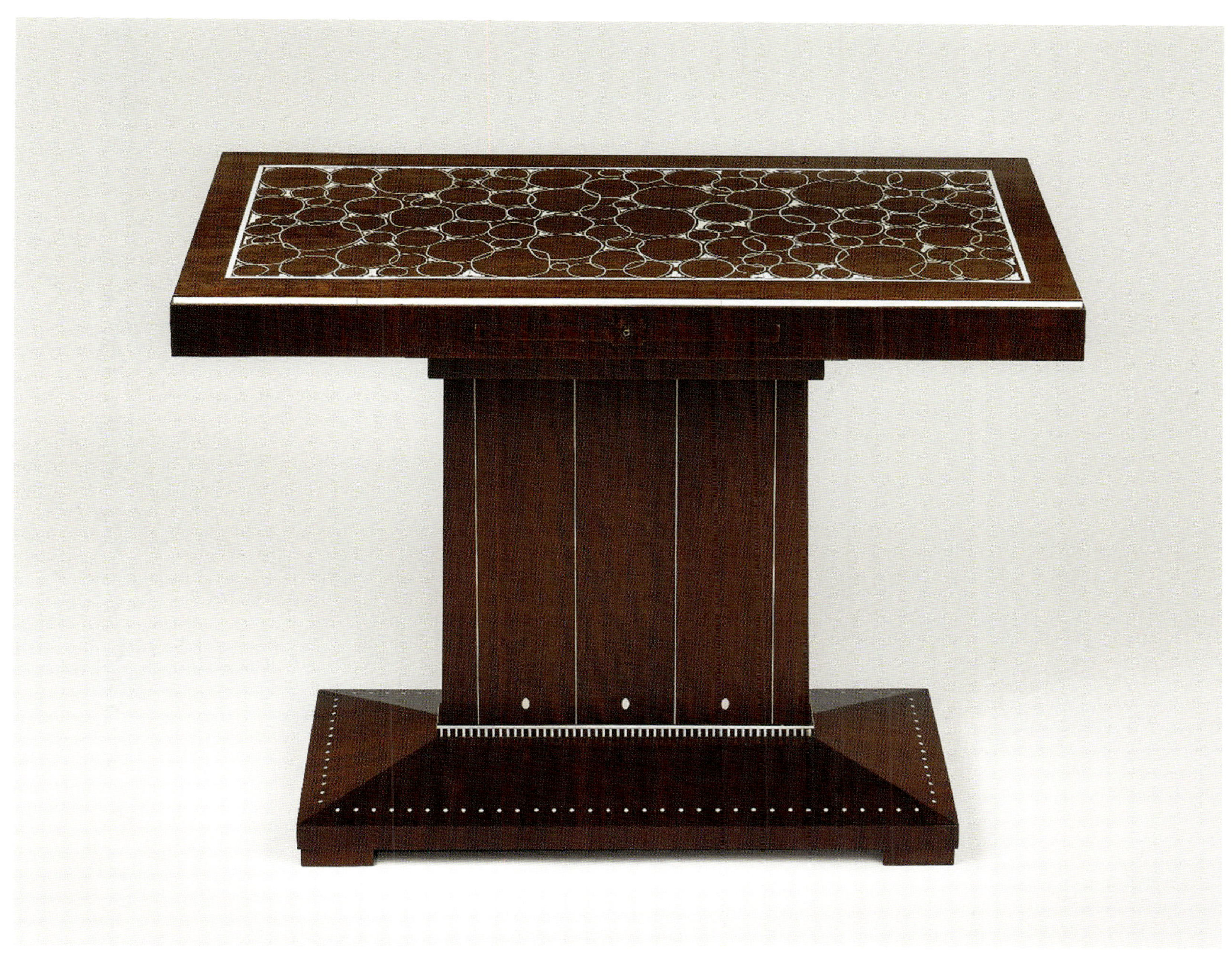

FIG. 44
Émile-Jacques Ruhlmann, French, 1879–1933; *Table*, c.1923; Kingwood veneer on mahogany and oak with ivory inlay; 22 ⅛ × 15 ⅜ × 30 ¾ in.; Brooklyn Museum, Purchased with funds given by Joseph F. McCrindle, Mrs. Richard M. Palmer, Charles C. Paterson, Raymond Worgelt, and an anonymous donor

the four- and six-cylinder engines and soft suspensions promised not only a powerful vehicle but also a comfortable and quiet ride. By harnessing the prestige of France's decorators, Delaunay-Belleville hoped the automobile industry might one day rival that of its home and fashion sectors

Ruhlmann was particularly suited to coordinating the mélange of materials and techniques required in the construction of motor cars. Best known today for his refined furniture veneered in precious woods, Ruhlmann, in his larger role as an *ensemblier*, designed and managed the execution of all aspects of an architectural interior, not only furniture but also lighting, wallpaper, and window and floor coverings. Highly sought after by Paris's elite, Ruhlmann oversaw a bustling studio in the 1920s with more than 100 employees and forged successful partnerships with manufacturers, artists, and independent designers.

Emerging in mid-nineteenth-century France, the *ensembliers* profoundly shaped the 1925 exposition, organizing its most admired pavilions. Ruhlmann supervised the interiors of the Pavillon du Collectionneur (Pavilion of a Collector), a classicizing white building with a stepped roof and porticos designed by the architect Pierre Patout. Inside, Ruhlmann's furniture—slim cabinets, softly curving chairs, and spare tables veneered in Macassar ebony and ivory (FIG. 44), both products of France's extensive colonial empire—mingled with designs by Henri Rapin and Francis Jourdain. The walls of its grand oval living room were covered in a cotton and silk textile patterned with large, burgundy stylized vases, floral garlands, and birds by Henri

FIG. 45
Designed by Henri Stephany, French, 1880–1934; made by Cornille Frères, Paris, active 1875–1926; *Tissu pour Ameublement Collectionneur* [Furnishing fabric for Ruhlmann's Pavillon du Collectionneur] (N° 214754, Patron 11141), c.1925; cotton and silk "damas satin de 5"; 77 3/8 × 50 9/16 in.; Musée des Tissus et des Arts décoratifs de Lyon

FIG. 46
Auguste Léon, French, 1857–1942; "Paris, France, The Decorative Arts Exhibition, the rotunda lounge of the Ruhlmann pavilion, decorative panel by Jean Dupas, *Les Perruches*," 1925; autochrome; 4 11/16 × 3 1/2 in.; Musée Albert-Kahn, Boulogne-Billancourt, France A47059S

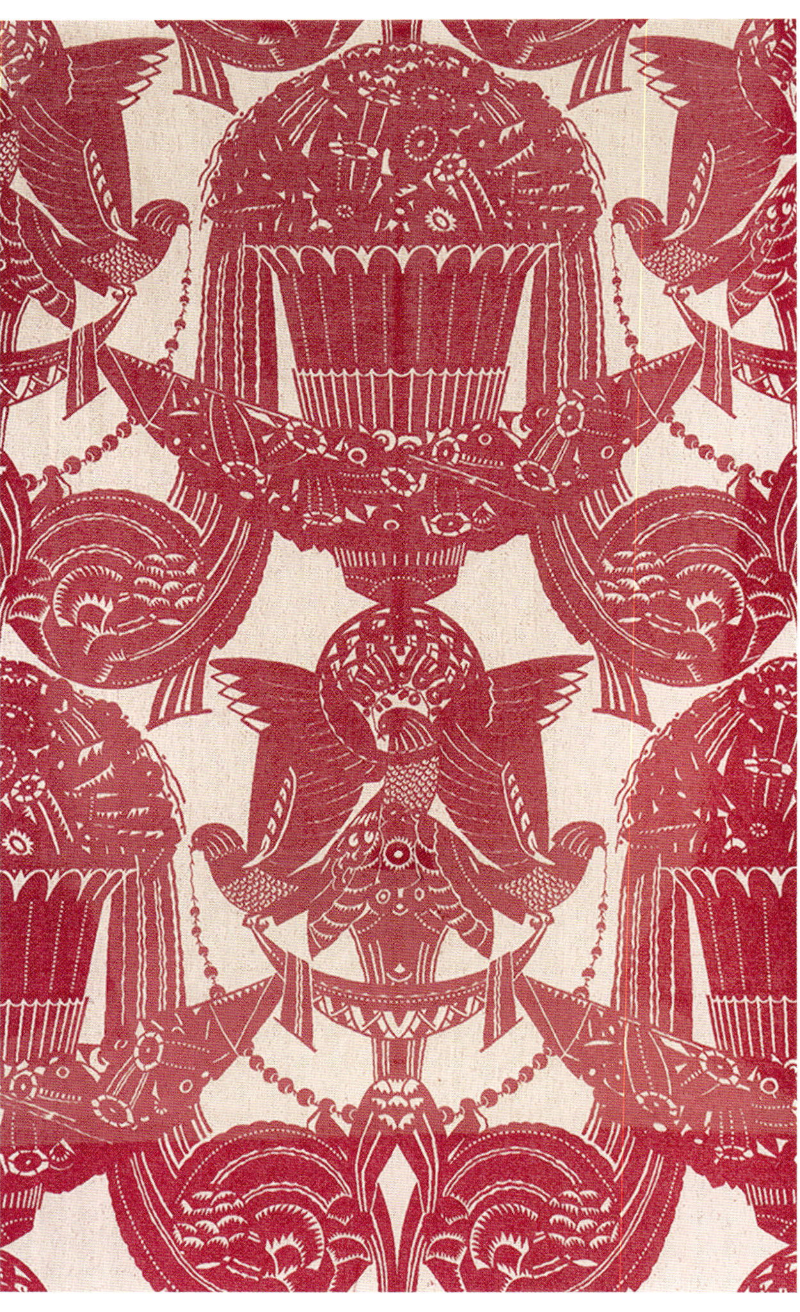

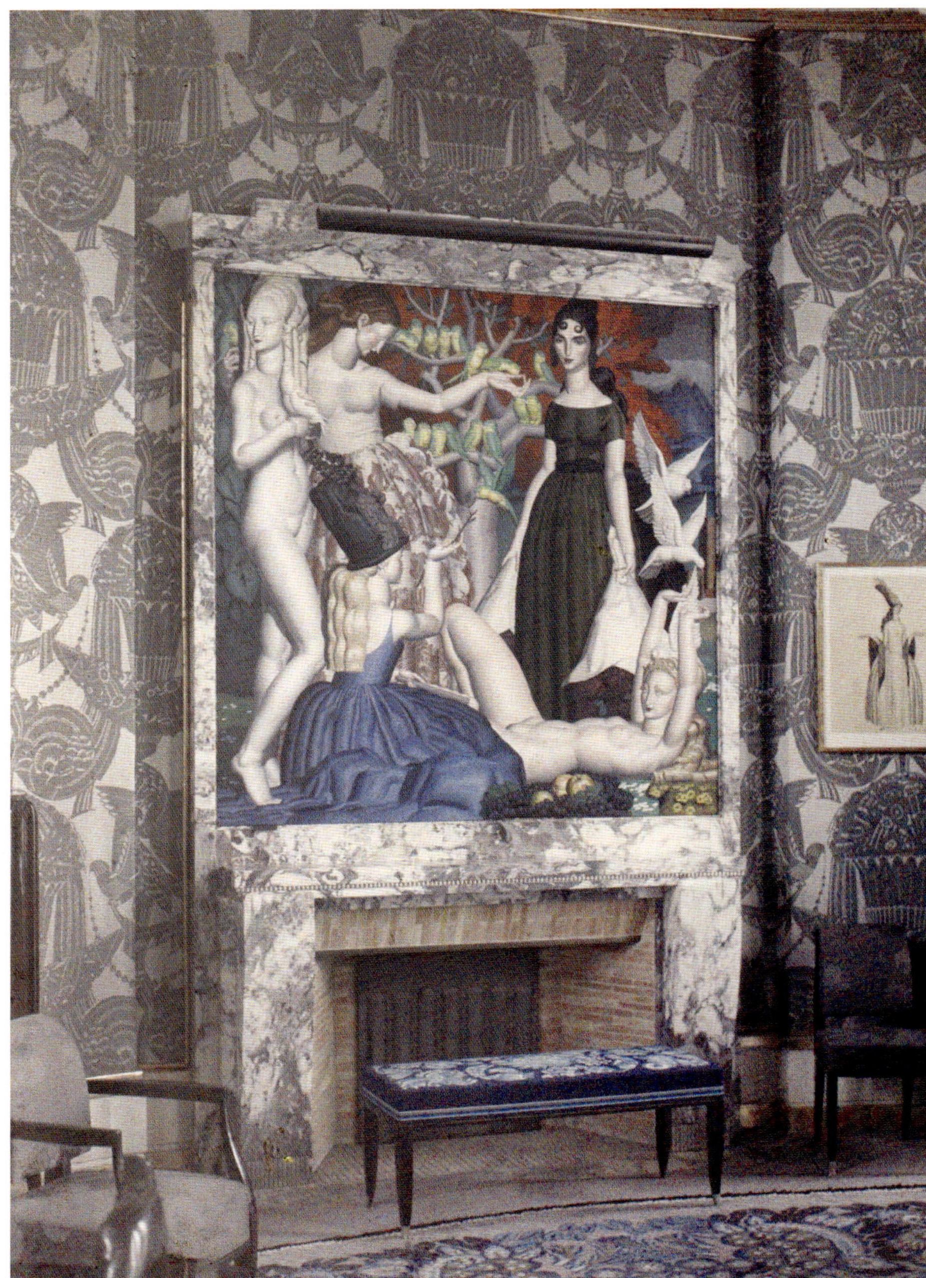

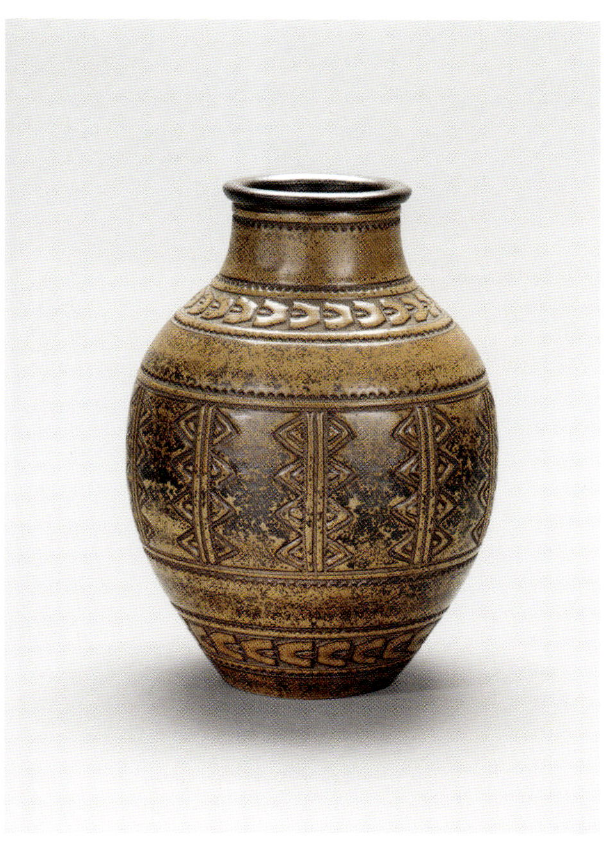

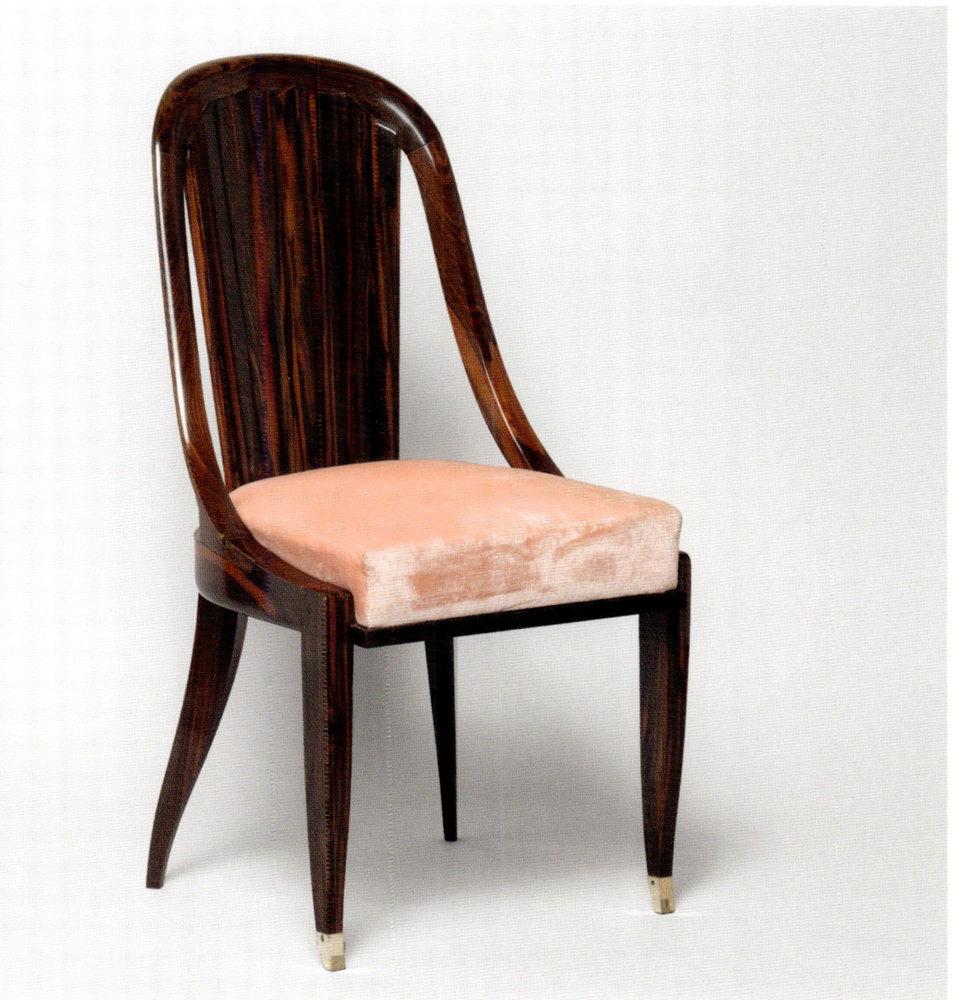

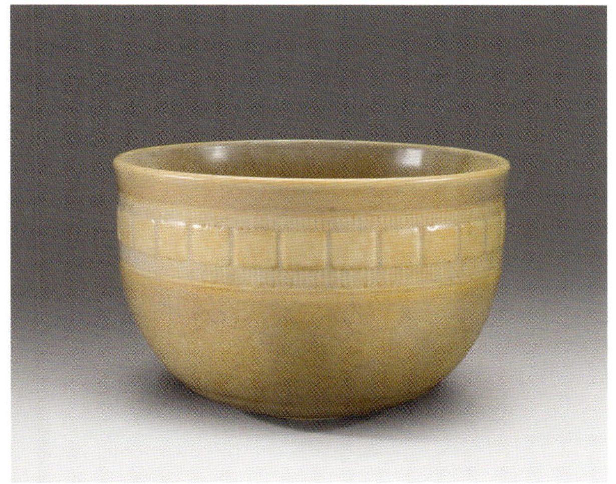

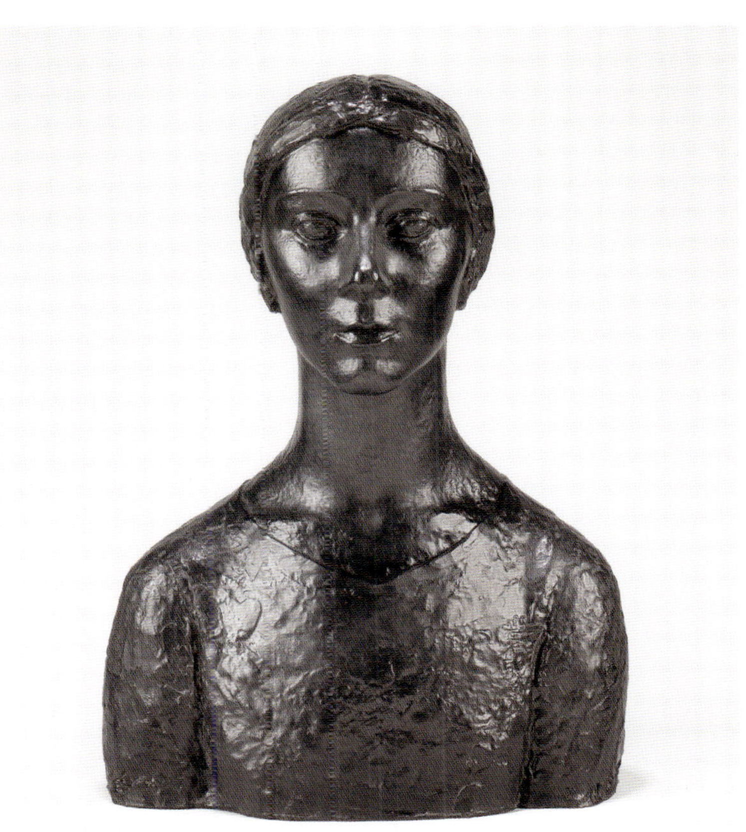

FIG. 47
Émile Lenoble, French, 1875–1940; *Jar*, c.1930; glazed stoneware; 11 ¼ × 9 in.; Saint Louis Art Museum, Bequest of Ezra H. Linley by exchange 61:1937

FIG. 49
Émile Decoeur, French, 1876–1953; *Bowl*, c.1920–25; glazed stoneware; 6 ¼ × 9 ⅝ in.; Saint Louis Art Museum, Museum Purchase 14:1927

FIG. 48
Émile-Jacques Ruhlmann, French, 1879–1933; *Side Chair*, 1926; Macassar ebony, silvered bronze, replacement silk, and cotton velvet; 37 ¼ × 17 ¾ × 20 in.; Saint Louis Art Museum, Gift of Mr. and Mrs. Stanley Hanks 110:1972

FIG. 50
Charles Despiau, French, 1874–1946; *Portrait of Line Aman-Jean*, 1925; bronze; 21 × 15 ⅜ × 10 ¾ in.; Saint Louis Art Museum, Gift of Mr. and Mrs. Joseph Pulitzer Jr. 411:1952

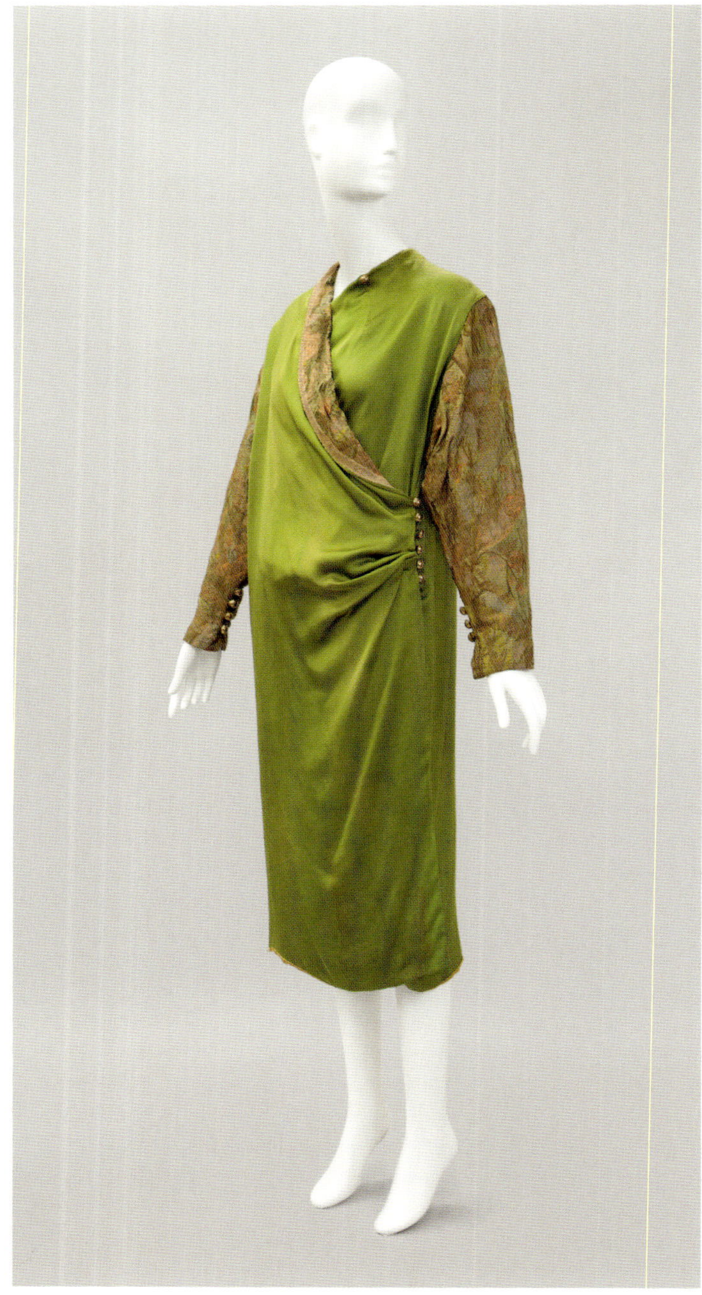

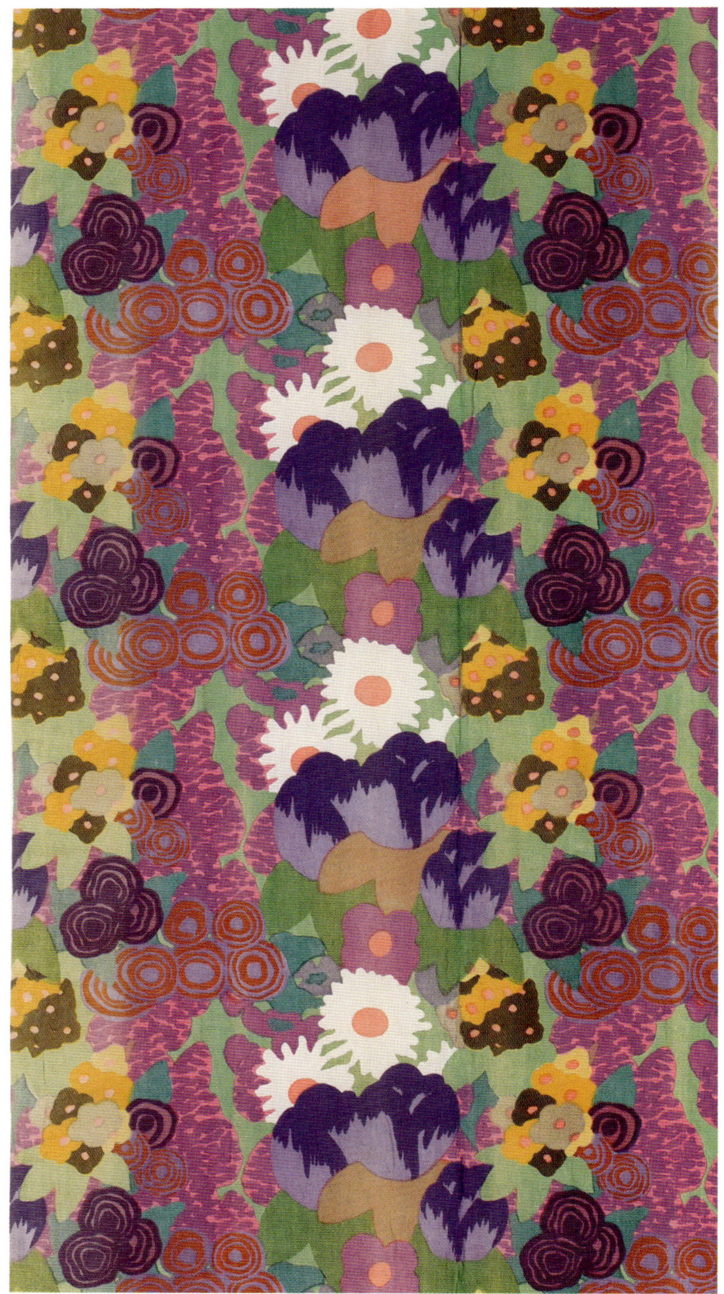

Stephany (FIGS. 45, 46). Ceramics by Émile Decoeur and Émile Lenoble, as well as other objets d'art, lined the shelves of the palatial structure's many rooms, suggesting the wealth and discernment of its imagined owner (FIGS. 47, 49). Classicizing sculptures by Alfred Auguste Janniot, Joseph Bernard, and Charles Despiau (FIG. 50) topped furniture and punctuated windows and doorways. Although taking clear cues from historic French styles and deeply engaging the country's craft industries, the Pavillon du Collectionneur offered a distinctly fresh perspective.[7] Ruhlmann and his many associates simplified architectural and furniture forms, abstracted patterns, and stripped and flattened applied ornament. For their outsized role in creating the exposition's stylistic cohesion, the *ensembliers* are credited with articulating the style that would be named after the fair: Art Deco.[8]

Ruhlmann's treatment of the automobile body as a lush architectural interior was consistent with the work presented by contemporary coachbuilders. Displayed on the Quai d'Orsay, "Moyens de Transport" featured trains, planes, automobiles, and boats. The couturier Paul Poiret's three barges—*Amours*, *Orgue*, and *Delice*—riotously outfitted inside and out by his interiors branch, the Atelier Martine, were the splashiest and most lavishly publicized components of the section (FIGS. 51–53). Reports of Poiret's "fashion parades" staged on his "transformed" riverboats reached the *St. Louis Post-Dispatch* within days of their unveiling.[9] In contrast, the automobiles on view attracted considerably less attention. The fair's *General Report* conceded they were not presented with the "desired magnitude."[10]

FIG. 51
Paul Poiret, French, 1879–1944; Poiret, Paris, active 1903–29; *Evening Coat*, 1924; silk charmeuse, silk and metallic thread brocade, and brass buttons; Courtesy of the Missouri Historical Society, St. Louis

FIG. 52
Atelier Martine, Paris, active 1911–29; *Curtain Panel*, c.1923; printed cotton with metal hardware; 105 × 46 in.; Saint Louis Art Museum, Richard Brumbaugh Trust in memory of Richard Irving Brumbaugh and Grace Lischer Brumbaugh 26:2016

Reeling from the news that the Grand Palais, the preferred venue for the Salon de L'Automobile (Paris Motor Show), had been promised to the fair organizers for most of 1925, the Chambre Syndicale des Constructers, the trade union for automobile manufacturers, forbade their members from participating in the exposition. In a press release dated March 1925, the trade union emphasized that to maintain "priority" over its European competitors, the Salon had to open the first week in October, not after the fair ended on October 25; as the venue would not be available, the Salon would be canceled. Why the fair's planners could not accommodate a larger presentation of French car manufacturers is unclear, but the rift between organizers was undeniable. The manufacturers feared losing the Grand Palais as a long-term venue, citing their "interloper" status, and complained about the lack of support from related "organizations of painters and sculptors."[11]

Today, most automobiles are unit-built; the frame, or chassis, and body are conceived and manufactured as a whole. Until the 1930s, however, these two parts were designed and executed separately (see Ken Gross's essay in this volume). In the case of most luxury cars, manufacturers produced the undercarriage, which included the engine, wheels, and steering shaft, while *carrossiers*, or coachbuilders, conceived and constructed the bodies and interiors. A "collaboration of the engineer and the artisan," as the writer André Fréchet detailed in 1921, the luxury automobile flourished thanks to advances in modern science and craft knowledge passed down over generations.[12]

Largely independent contractors with small artisan ateliers, the coachbuilders had their own trade union, and they valiantly attempted to convey the vibrancy of French automobile design at the fair under peculiar and challenging circumstances. Without engines, chassis, and hoods, the "cars" presented by leaders in the field, such as Henri Binder, Jean Henri-Labourdette, and Jacques Saoutchik, were visibly and uneasily incomplete (FIG. 99). A review in *Omnia* lamented that the work of France's great automobile "couturiers" deserved better than a "neutral" presentation in a few bays. It went on to contrast the animated gestures of the French couturiers' mannequins, arranged in evocative scenes in the neighboring Pavillon de l'Élégance, to the "suddenly broken lines" of the car bodies (FIGS. 54–56).[13]

Practically speaking, coachbuilders were closer to *ensembliers* or architects, yet *Omnia*'s characterization of them as "automobile couturiers," employing a fashion term, was more typical.[14] At

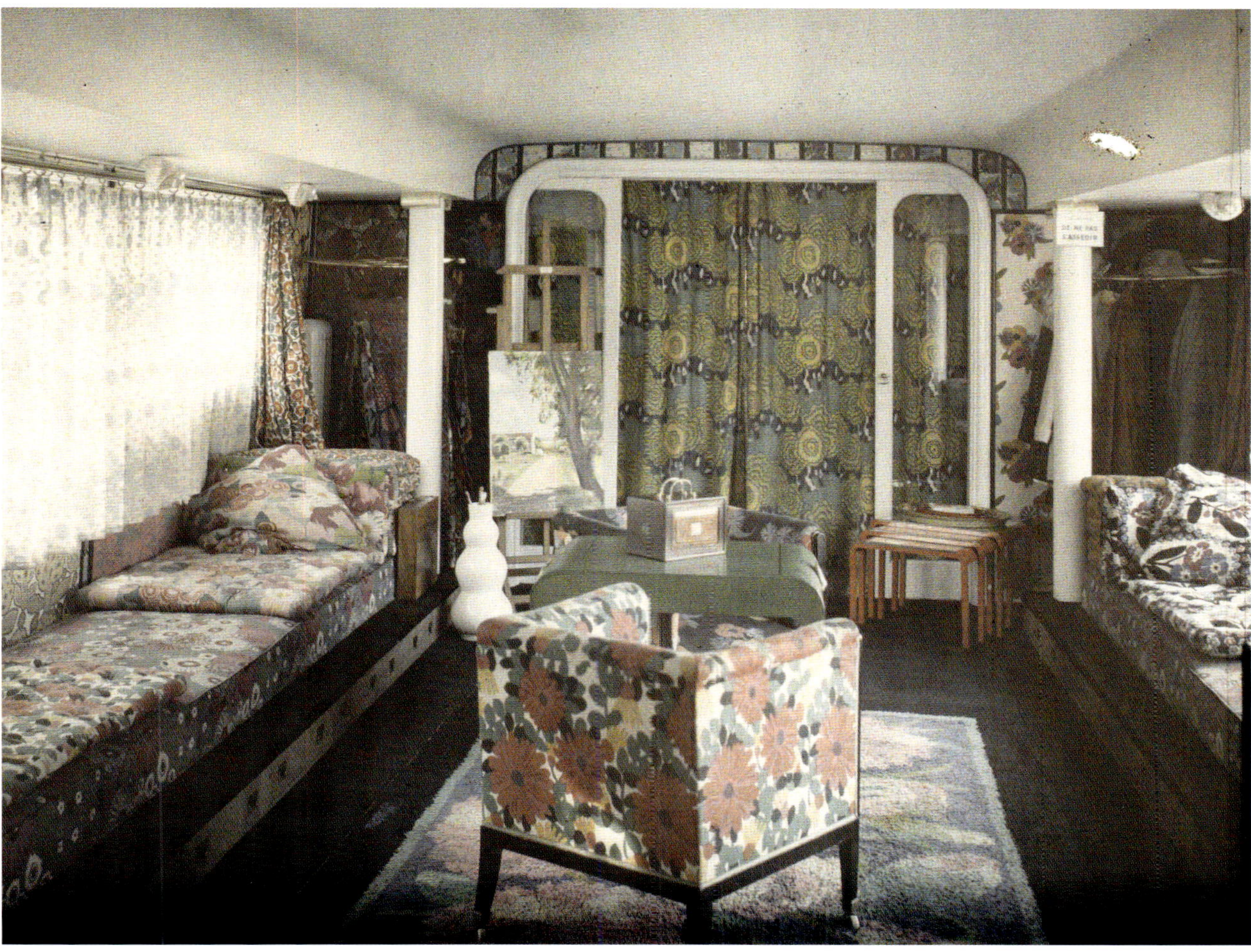

FIG. 53
Auguste Léon, French, 1857–1942; salon for the Péniche Poiret at the Exposition Internationale des Arts Décoratifs et Industriels Modernes, Paris, 1925. Musée Albert-Kahn, Boulogne-Billancourt, A47193

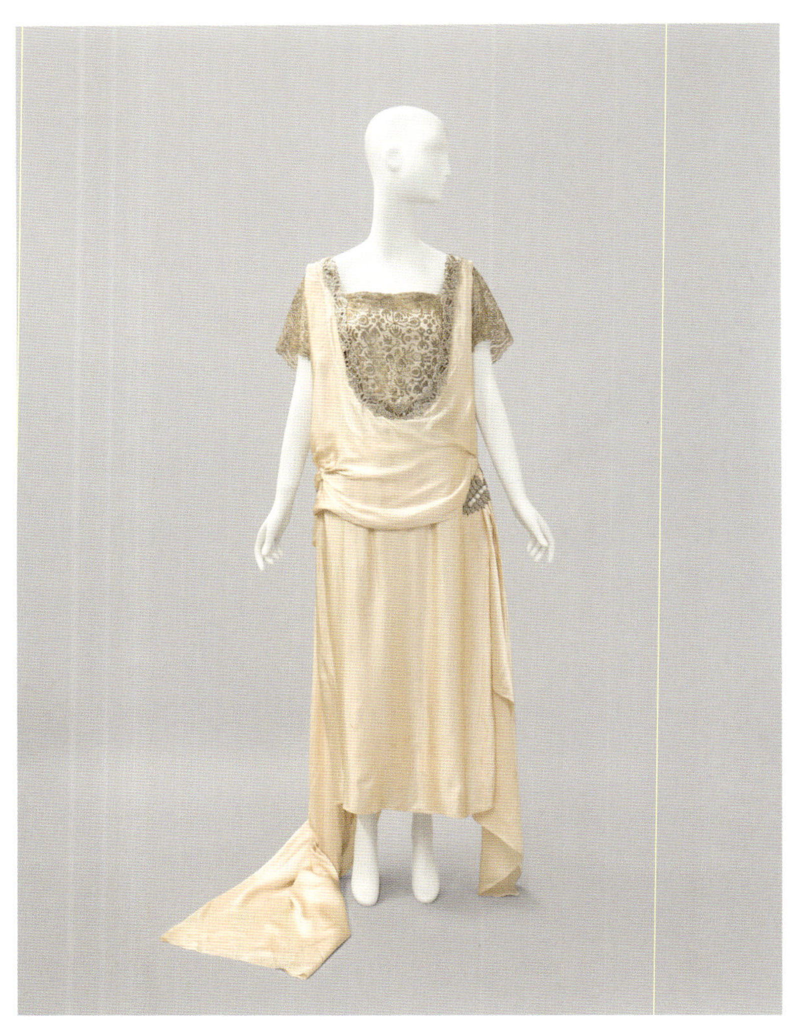

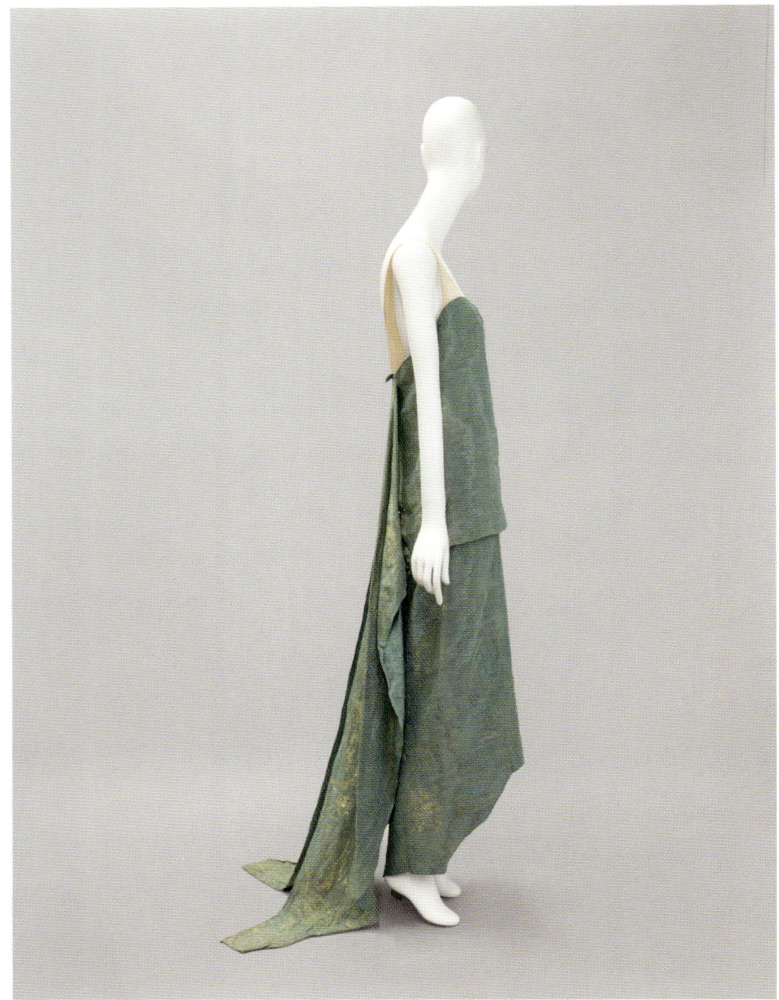

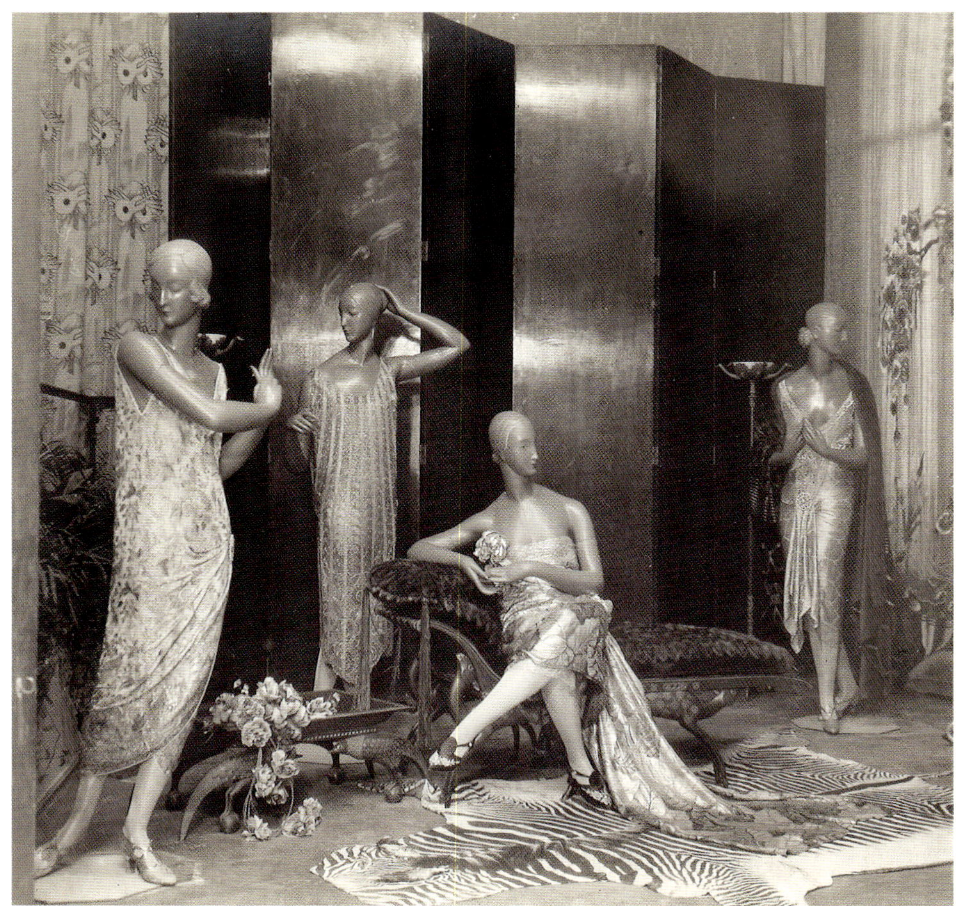

FIG. 54
House of Worth, Paris, active 1858–1956; *Evening Dress*, c.1925; silk charmeuse, silk plain weave, metallic thread lace, crystal, glass and plastic beads, and metallic thread; Courtesy of the Missouri Historical Society, St. Louis

FIG. 55
Callot Soeurs, Paris, active 1895–1937; *Evening Dress*, c.1920; moiré silk and metallic thread faille, silk charmeuse, and silk net; Courtesy of the Missouri Historical Society, St. Louis

FIG. 56
Salon of the Maison Callot Soeurs in the Pavillon de l'Élégance at the Exposition Internationale des Arts Décoratifs et Industriels Modernes, Paris, 1925; Musée des Arts décoratifs, Paris, Jean Collas Collection

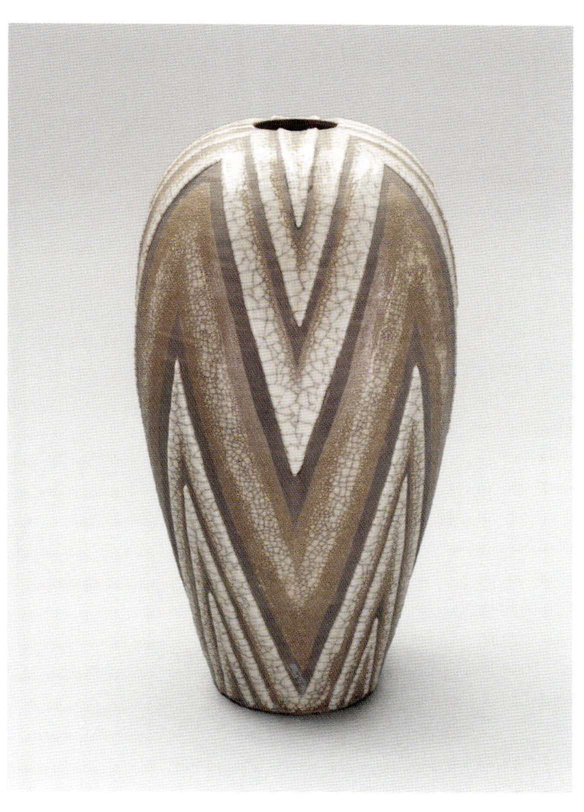

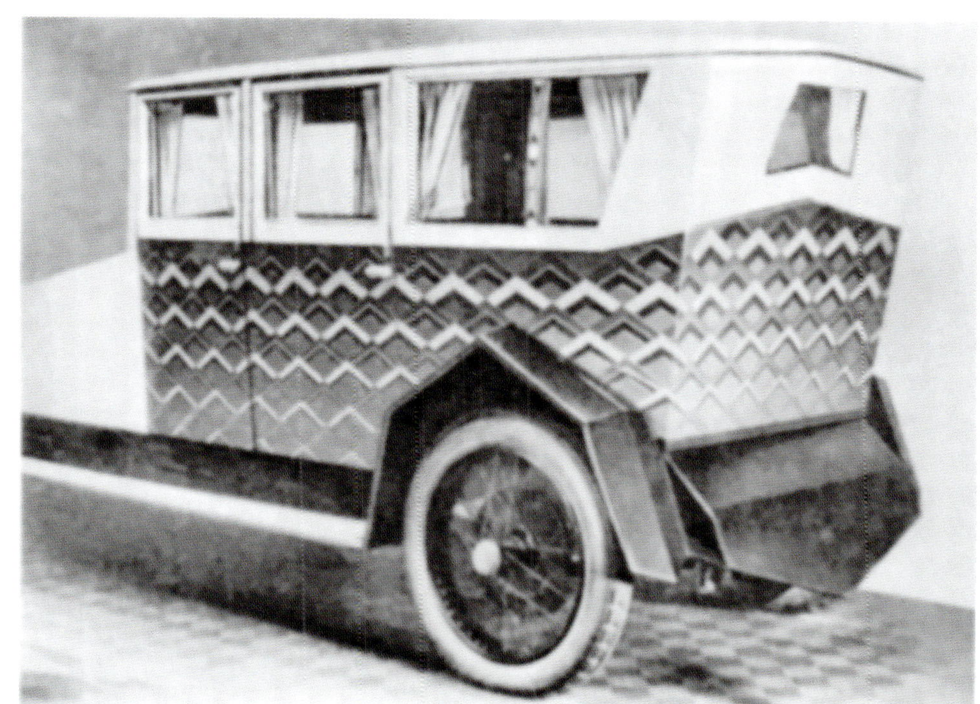

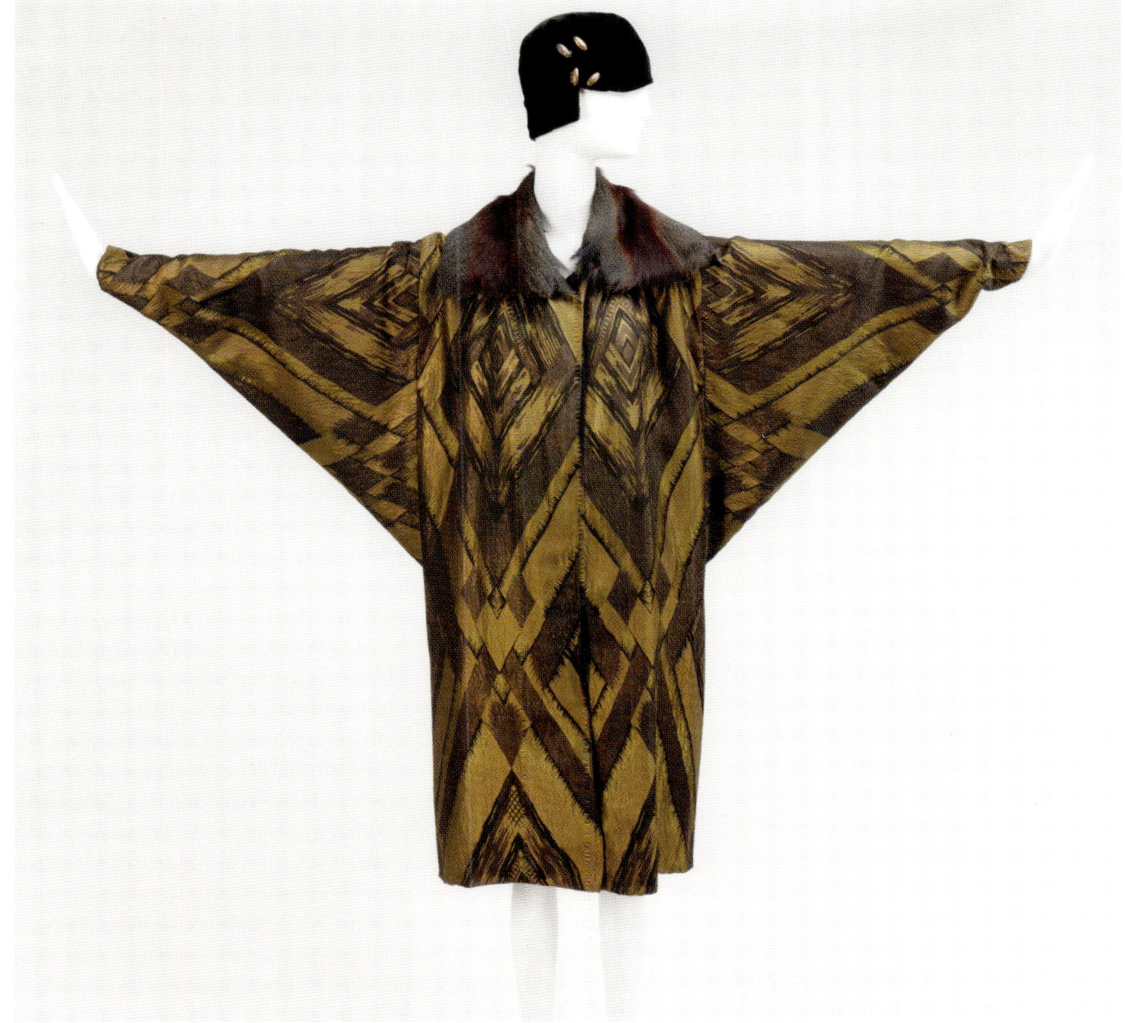

FIG. 57
René Buthaud, French, 1886–1986; *Vase*, c.1934; glazed stoneware; 14 × 7 in.; Saint Louis Art Museum, Richard Brumbaugh Trust in memory of Richard Irving Brumbaugh and Grace Lischer Brumbaugh 83:2000

FIG. 58
Paul Léon, French, 1874–1962; printed by Librairie Larousse, French, founded 1850s; "Limousine à Conduite Intérieure," in Ministère du Commerce, de l'Industrie, des Postes et des Télégraphes, *Exposition internationale des arts décoratifs et industriels modernes, Paris 1925*, 1927–32

FIG. 59
Cocoon Coat, c.1929; silk brocade, silk charmeuse, and monkey fur; Courtesy of the Missouri Historical Society, St. Louis

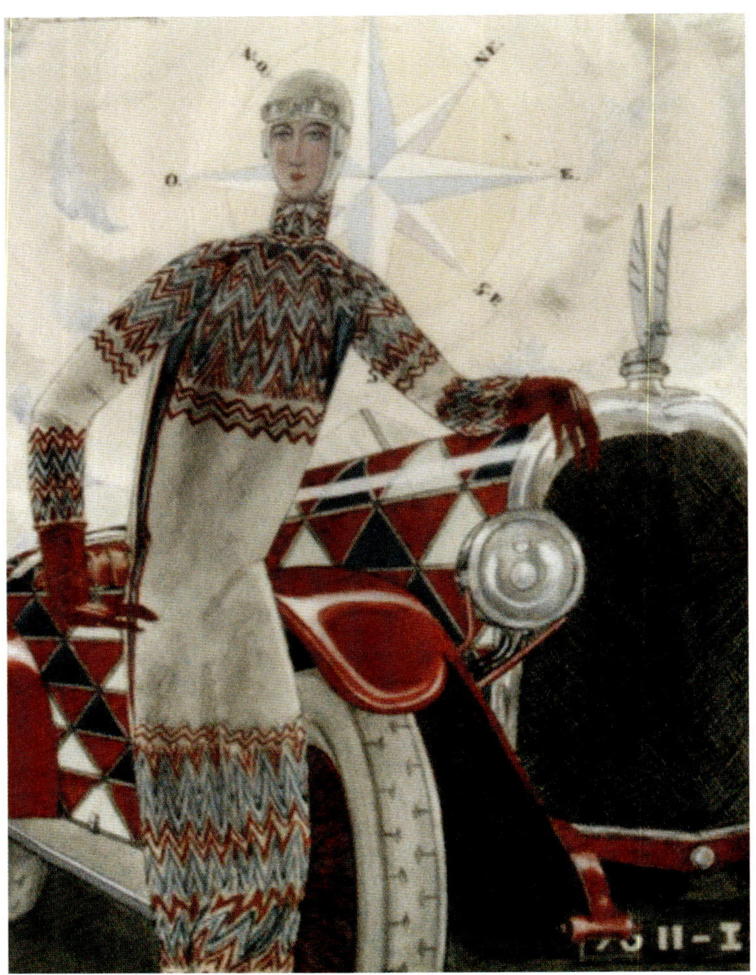

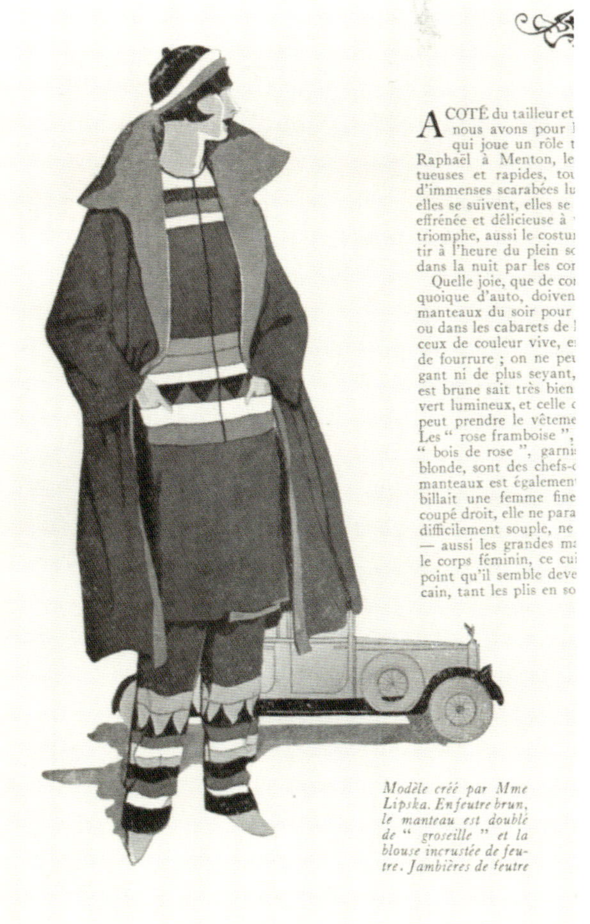

A COTÉ du tailleur et
nous avons pour
qui joue un rôle
Raphaël à Menton, le
tueuses et rapides, to
d'immenses scarabées l
elles se suivent, elles se
effrénée et délicieuse à
triomphe, aussi le costu
tir à l'heure du plein s
dans la nuit par les co
Quelle joie, que de co
quoique d'auto, doiven
manteaux du soir pour
ou dans les cabarets de
ceux de couleur vive, e
de fourrure ; on ne pe
gant ni de plus seyant,
est brune sait très bien
vert lumineux, et celle
peut prendre le vêteme
Les " rose framboise ",
" bois de rose ", garni
blonde, sont des chefs-
manteaux est égalemen
billait une femme fine
coupé droit, elle ne para
difficilement souple, ne
— aussi les grandes m
le corps féminin, ce cu
point qu'il semble deve
cain, tant les plis en so

Modèle créé par Mme Lipska. En feutre brun, le manteau est doublé de " groseille " et la blouse incrustée de feutre. Jambières de feutre

the time, cars were *habillées,* or "dressed," by coachbuilders, just as women were clothed by leading designers. While they rarely achieved the same cultural currency as couturiers like Poiret, Jeanne Lanvin, and Coco Chanel, their orbits intersected. Saoutchik's brother was a tailor at Poiret's workshop, and his longtime mistress Raymonde Moreau was one of Poiret's models.[15] Henri-Labourdette's wife, Georgette, was frequently featured in fashion publications wearing Suzanne Talbot gowns. Couturiers and coachbuilders closely collaborated to create coordinated ensembles at the popular *concours d'élégance*, car and fashion shows co-sponsored by major French magazines like *L'Auto* and *L'Officiel de la couture et de la mode*. They also courted the same clientele, luring celebrities like Josephine Baker, Claude May, and Mistinguett to promote their brands.

Women's fashion was closely linked with the development of coachwork in France. In *Un siècle de carrosserie française (A Century of French Coachwork)*, Henri-Labourdette proposed that coachbuilders widened the doors of automobiles to accommodate the large hats women wore before World War I. This adjustment initiated a cascade of changes to the modern car body.[16] As more and more women became drivers, coachbuilders offered adjustable seats and armrests. At the same time, manufacturers introduced new technologies like electric starters and more sensitive brakes. These gradual improvements made automobiles "elegant, softer, more pleasant," advantages that, although advertised to women, also appealed to men.[17]

Rather than focusing on the car's silhouette, the fair's participating coachbuilders explored surfaces, outfitting the interiors with colorful fabrics and leather, complex wood veneers, and lacquer and the exteriors with creative, colorful paint treatments. For the finish of a Carrosserie Nouvelle limousine by M. H. Lévy, Maurice Dufrêne devised a "lozenge" pattern, its jagged lines gradually thickening as they ascended from the angular rear mudguard (FIG. 58).[18]

Dufrêne's dynamic design followed a trend in textiles and fashion. In 1925, *L'Art et la mode* declared the lozenge the "single geometric figure" that most characterized modern feminine elegance.[19] The fragmented planes and strong diagonals of Cubist and Futurist paintings and sculp-

FIG. 60
Georges Lepape, French, 1887–1971; cover illustration for *Vogue Paris*, November 1924

FIG. 61
Sarah Lipska, French (born Poland), 1882–1973; ensemble advertised in "L'Auto Encore, L'Auto Ouvert," *Vogue Paris*, January 1925

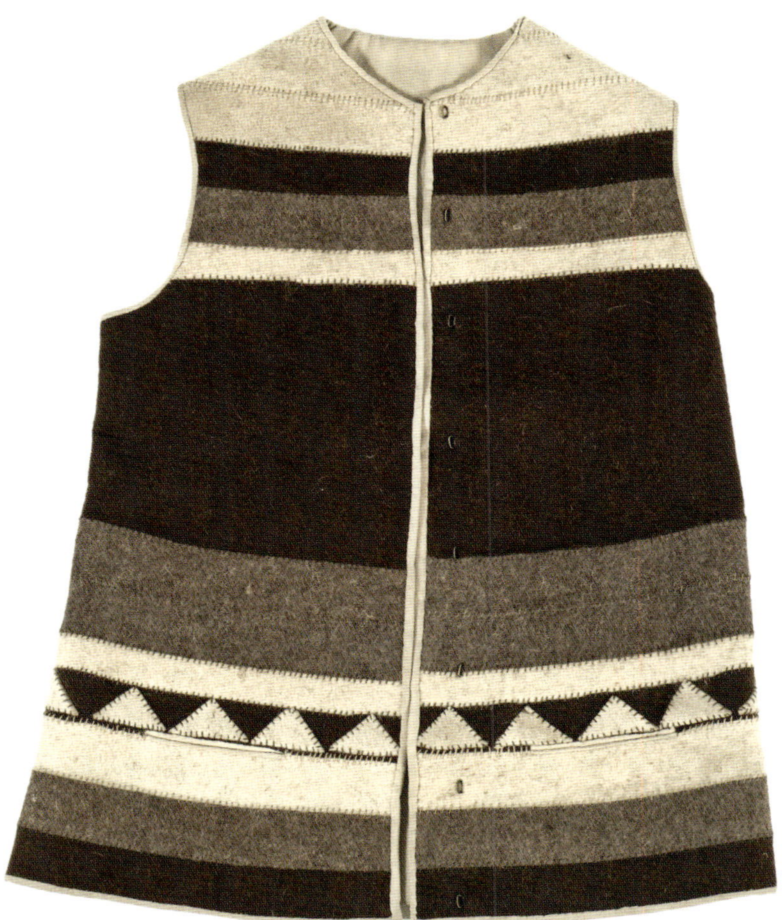

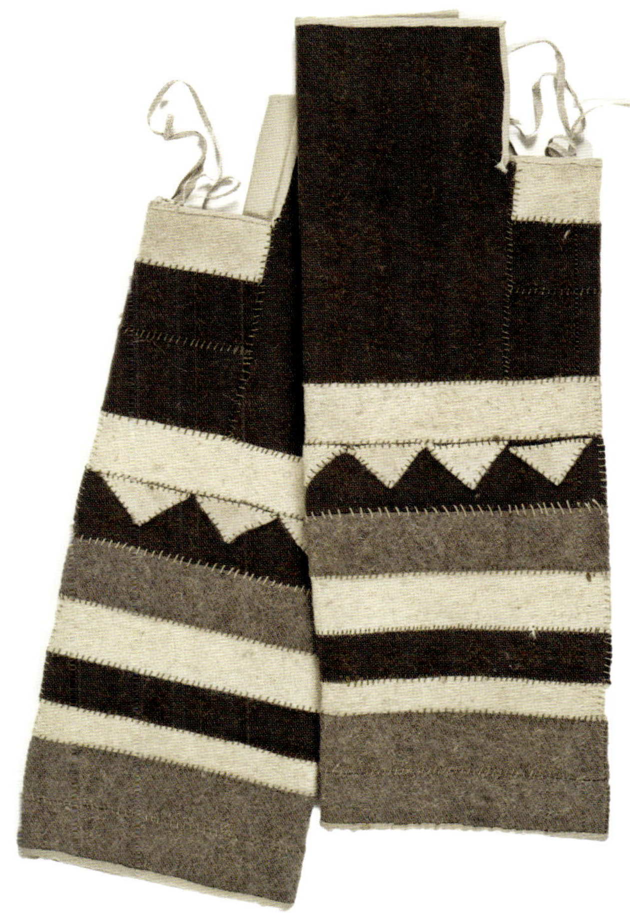

FIG. 62A, B
Sarah Lipska, French (born Poland), 1882–1973; *Winter Sports Outfit, Vest with Leg Warmers*, 1925; wool felt and twill with braided ribbons; Musées de Poitiers

tures informed, in part, this new design vocabulary, which was considered ideal for describing the vigor and velocity of modern life. Outerwear, especially for driving, frequently incorporated chevrons, diamonds, and triangles (FIG. 59). Lepape's cover for the November 1924 issue of *Vogue* featured a racer and her Voisin automobile "dressed" in coordinating patterns of red, white, and navy-blue diamonds and zigzag stripes (FIG. 60). The next year in *Vogue*, the Polish-born artist Sarah Lipska proposed a modern driving and winter sport ensemble consisting of a thick felt vest and leg warmers with triangle appliqués for bracing drives in open-top automobiles (FIGS. 61; 62A, B).[20]

A designer of textiles, furniture, ceramics, and glass, Dufrêne, an *ensemblier* like Ruhlmann, directed La Maîtrise, the interiors studio at the leading French department store, Galeries Lafayette. Dufrêne was a self-described "convert" to industrial manufacture and understood the challenges of scaling production. In 1921, he acknowledged, "We desire to work for everyone, but—for such an enterprise we must have big factories, an assured output, industrial organization and considerable capital."[21] Dufrêne's "modern silk" patterns for Cornille Frères from about 1921 and the increasing number of factory-made products sold at La Maîtrise during his tenure suggested he was inching toward his goal (PAGES i, ii). At the fair, Dufrêne oversaw the La Maîtrise pavilion. Sheathed in veined marble, the shop was a remarkably opulent venue for the fair's more accessible products.[22] An acknowledged expert in modern display and merchandising, Dufrêne also designed the row of temporary shops for the fair on the Pont Alexandre III, which included Sonia Delaunay and Jacques Heim's Boutique Simultané.

Coachbuilders lavished even more attention on automobile interiors, which were conceived like compact mobile rooms. Binder enlisted the Swiss-French artist Jean Dunand to embellish the cab of a Saint-Didier convertible in black lacquer meticulously embedded with minuscule fragments of crushed eggshell in a "geometric ornament of a very happy design" (FIG. 64).[23] The same motif was applied to the upholstery, possibly representing Dunand's spray-lacquered textiles. Dunand devised a second *laque de Chine* interior for a Binder limousine "constructed entirely of sheet metal," with "folding seats, hinges, and canteens"

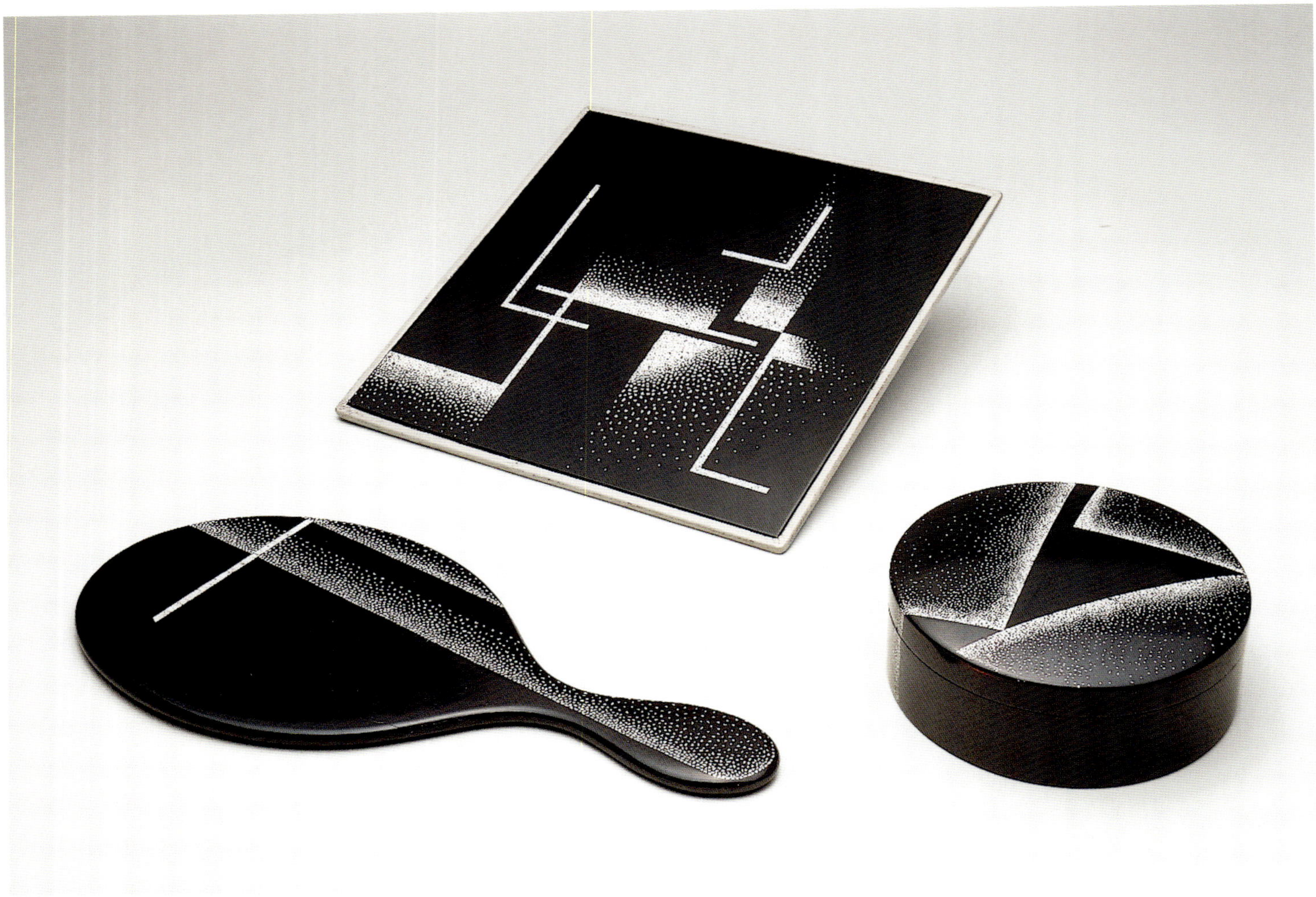

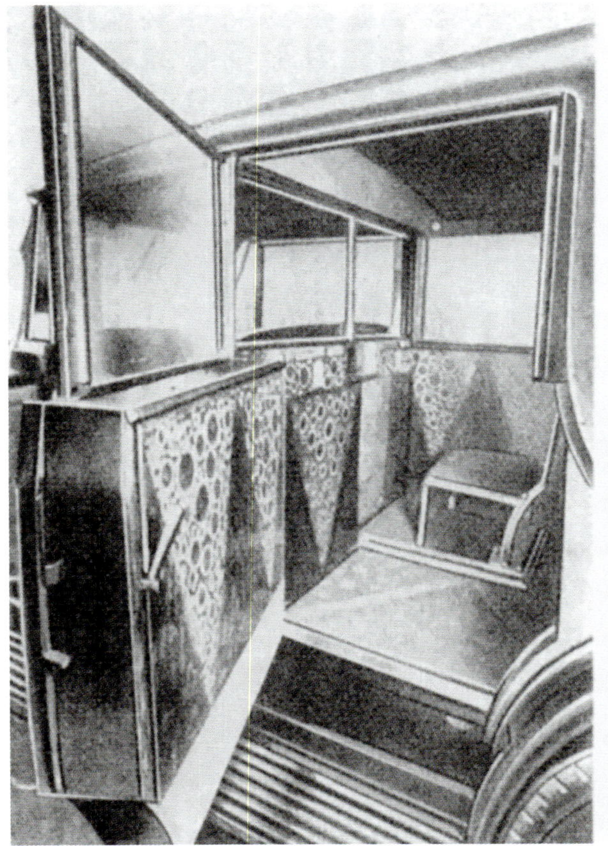

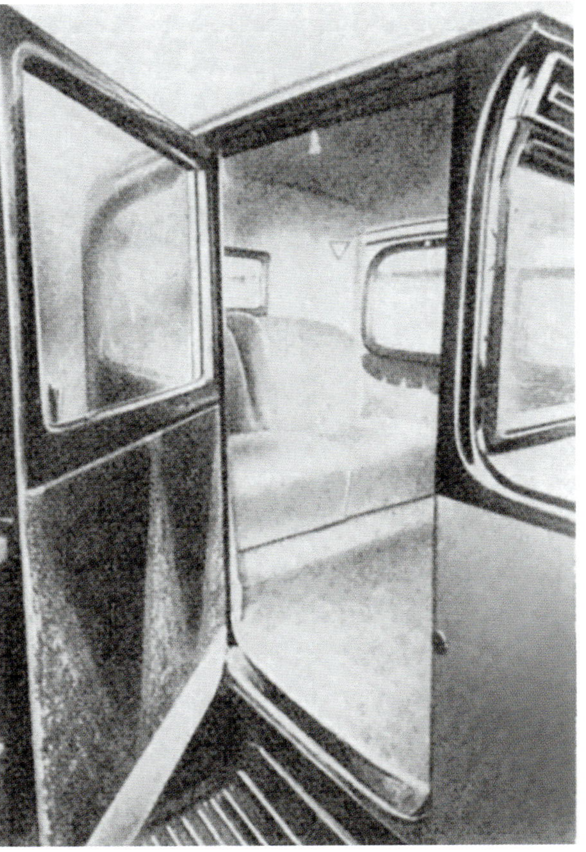

FIG. 63
Jean Dunand, French (born Switzerland), 1877–1942; *Dresser Set*, 1925–30; lacquer on copper, lacquer on wood, and crushed eggshell; tray: 10 ¾ × 10 ¾ in., covered box: 2 × 6 in., mirror: 13 ¾ × 6 ¼ in.; Minneapolis Institute of Art, Gift of Norwest Bank Minnesota

FIG. 64
Paul Léon, French, 1874–1962; printed by Librairie Larousse, French, founded 1850s; illustrations of a Voiture Transformable "Saint-Didier" and Limousine-Boule by coachbuilder Henri Binder, with lacquer interior decoration by Jean Dunand, in Ministère du Commerce, de l'Industrie, des Postes et des Télégraphes, *Exposition internationale des arts décoratifs et industriels modernes, Paris 1925*, 1927–32

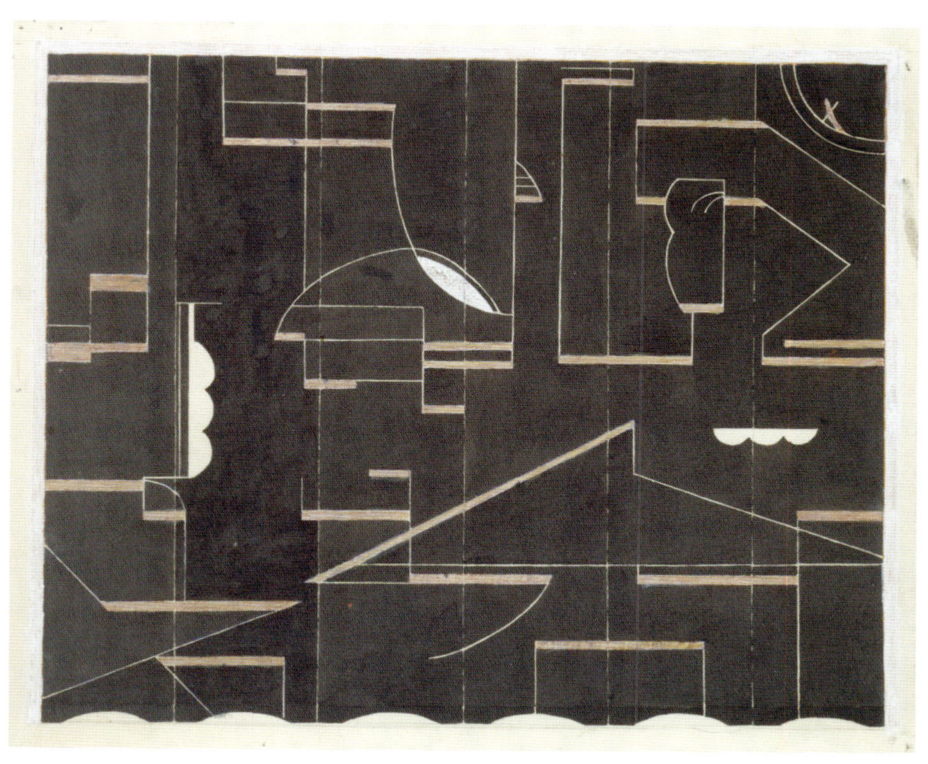

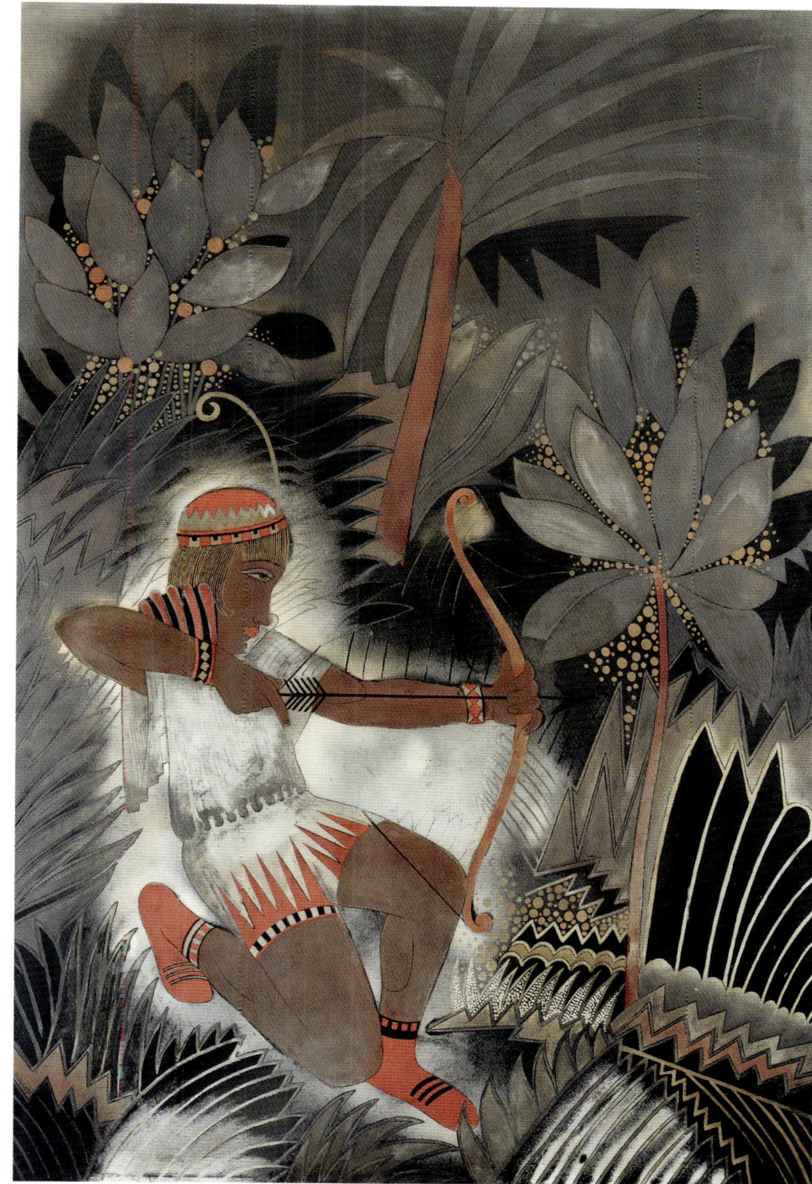

FIG. 65
Eileen Gray, Irish, 1878–1976; *Design*, early 1920s; pencil, chalk, India ink, and Chinese white; 9 13/16 × 11 7/8 in.; Victoria and Albert Museum, London

This design illustrates an incised six-panel lacquer screen similar to one purchased by Georgette Henri-Labourdette from Eileen Gray's Galerie Jean Désert.

FIG. 66
Jean Dunand, French (born Switzerland), 1877–1942; *Jeune Archer*, 1926; wood panel with colored lacquer and eggshell; 70 7/8 × 48 1/16 in.; Private collection

FIG. 67
Salon de Madame J. Henri Labourdette-Debacker, c.1927; published in "Jean Dunand," *L'Art d'aujourd'hui* 13, spring 1927

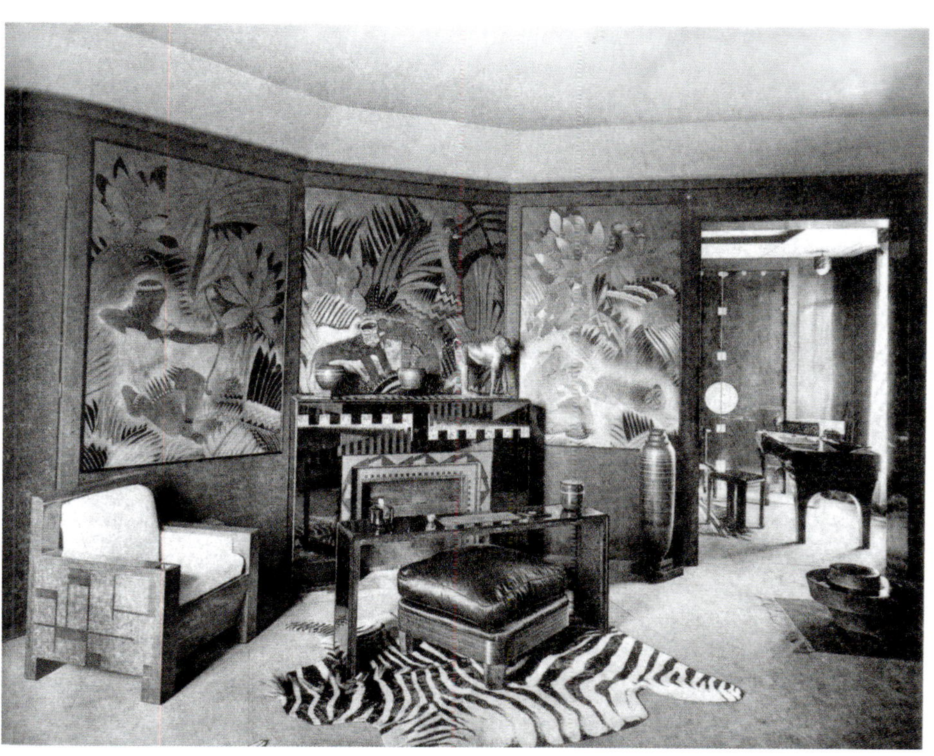

that retracted and receded to create an unobstructed and efficient design.[24]

Dunand first experimented with natural lacquer, a by-product of the sap from lacquer trees native to Asia, to finish and seal hand-hammered copper and brass metal vessels called *dinanderie*. Lessons with the Japanese lacquer master Seizo Sugawara in 1912 gave Dunand the tools and recipes to further explore the notoriously difficult material. By the early 1920s, he was producing a diverse range of lacquer objects, from small-scale dresser sets (FIG. 63), like those sold by the fashion designer and milliner Madame Agnès, to encrusted furniture and screens.[25]

Like Dufrêne's, Dunand's contributions to the transport section were modest compared to his many other projects for the fair. Four large metal and lacquer vases marked the corners of La Cour des Métiers (The court of trades), while small vessels intermingled with ceramics by René Buthaud at Devambez, another boutique on the Pont Alexander III (FIG. 57). Dunand's work reached epic proportions in the Société des Artistes Décorateurs's Pavillon de l'Ambassade Française, where he encased an entire room in lacquer panels inlaid with silver-leaf patterns of zigzags, polka dots, and concentric circles.

In 1926, Henri-Labourdette and his wife, Georgette, privately commissioned Dunand to create wall panels and an elaborate fireplace mantel for the salon of their Paris apartment.[26] Expressive of the French taste for exoticized classism, the triptych depicts a hunting scene set in a dense tropical forest, its flora rendered in a panoply of geometric patterns.[27] A young archer dressed in a tunic, shorts, and shoes, and wearing a feathered cap, all decorated in chevron patterns, pulls back his bow, targeting a lion in the adjoining panel (FIGS. 66, 67). Although generalized, the figure's coiffure and headpiece recall representations of ancient Nubian archers whose fame was increasing because of decades of archaeological excavations in the region. Georgette was an important client of Jean Désert, the Paris showroom of Irish designer-architect Eileen Gray (FIG. 65).[28] A photograph of the lacquer-paneled salon featured in the spring 1927 issue of *L'Art d'aujourd'hui* shows a large, scorched pine vase, commissioned from Gray by Henri-Labourdette in about 1920, resting on a small, fringed carpet.[29] A zebra-skin rug completed the exoticized interior that broadly drew its patterns and forms from Africa.

Materials and technologies traveled between craft and industry, following the designers and many artisans who responded to shifting consumer demands and economic opportunities. While a marker of luxury, lacquer's impermeability made it ideal for certain industrial applications. During World War I, Dunand was involved in experiments coating airplane propellers with natural

FIG. 68
Designed by René Lalique, French, 1860–1945, and Suzanne Lalique-Haviland, French, 1892–1989; made by Lalique et Cie, Wingen-sur-Moder, France; *Tourbillons Vase*, c.1925; press-molded glass and enamel; 7 7/8 × 6 in.; Saint Louis Art Museum, Museum Purchase 63:1930

FIG. 69
Designed by René André Coulon, French, 1908–1997; made by Saint-Gobain, Courbevoie, France, founded 1665; *Dressing Stool*, c.1930; glass, iron, and oilcloth upholstery; 24 1/2 × 24 3/4 × 15 1/4 in.; Saint Louis Art Museum, Funds given by donors to the 1985 Art Enrichment Fund 86:1989

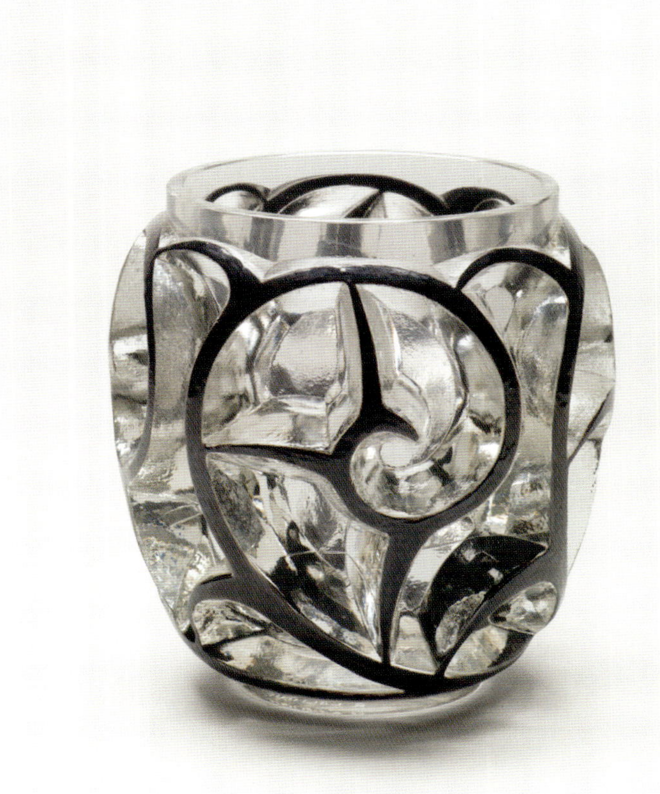

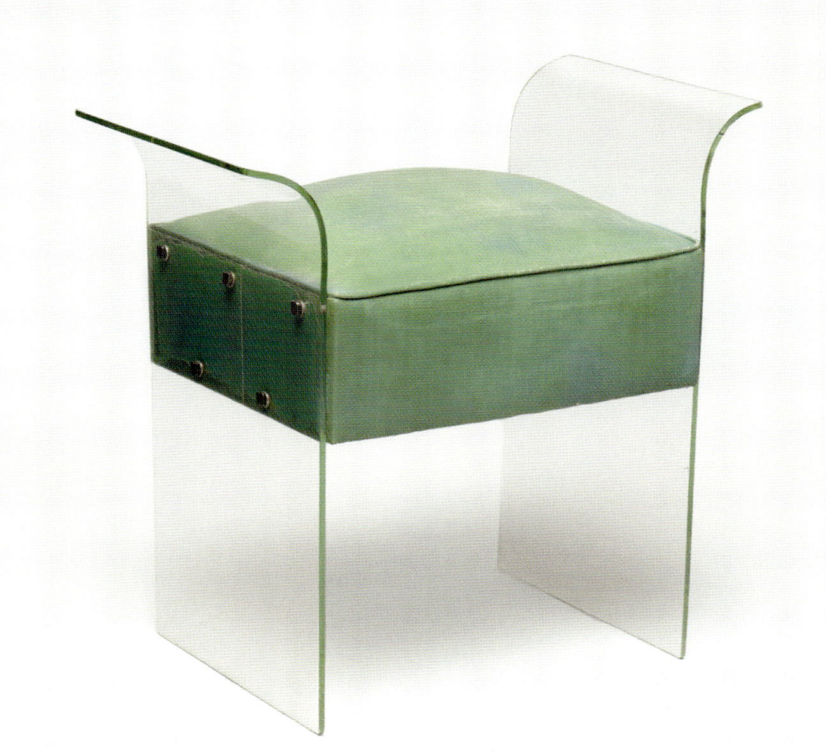

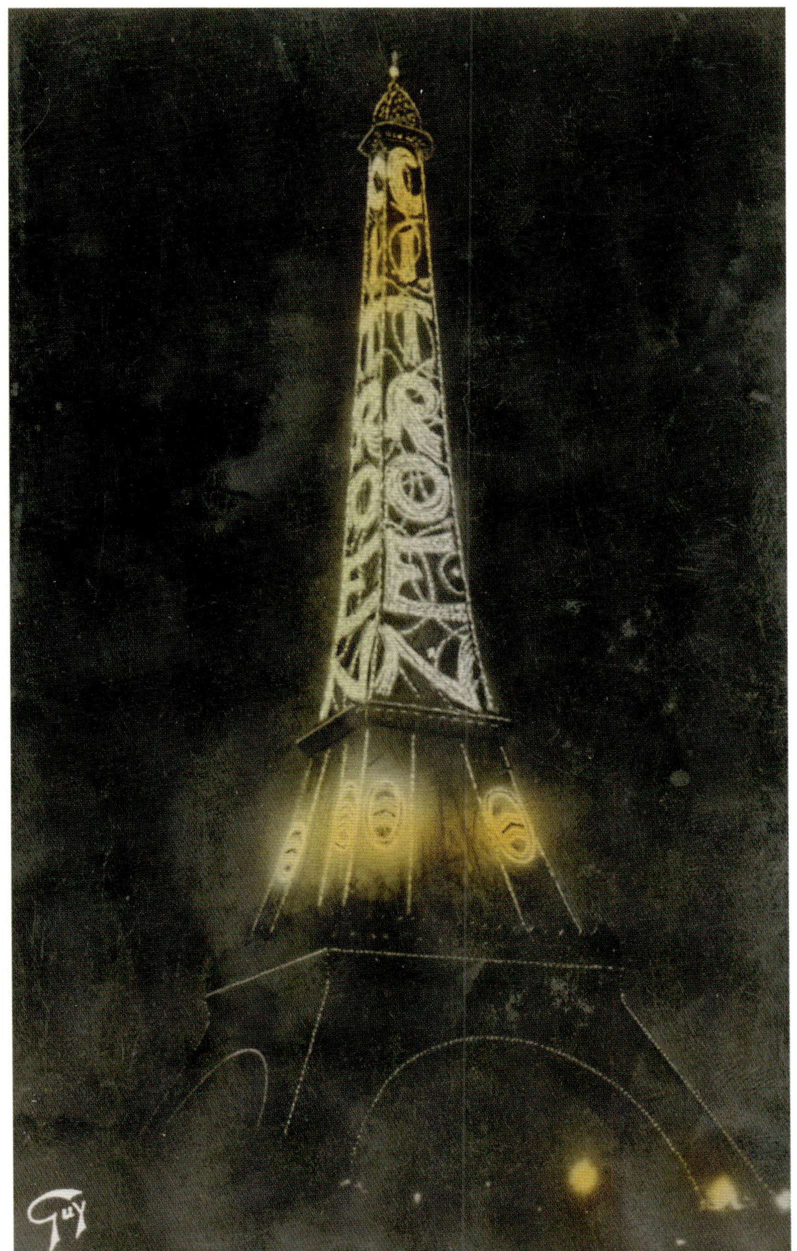

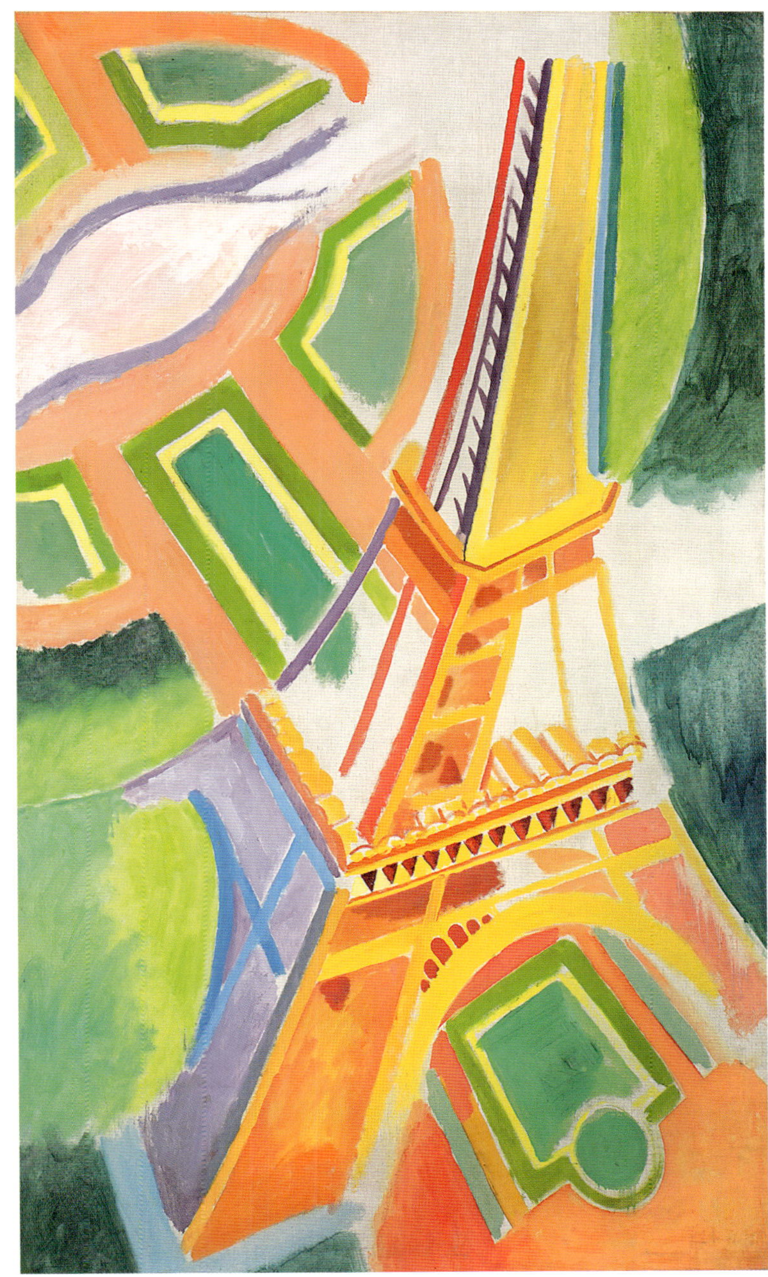

FIG. 70
Eiffel Tower with Citroën advertisement by lighting designer Fernand Jacopozzi, c.1925; Éditions d'Art "GUY," Citroën Promotion on Eiffel Tower from "Paris La Nuit," hand-tinted postcard; 5 ½ × 3 ¾ in.; Private collection

FIG. 71
Robert Delaunay, French, 1885–1941; *Eiffel Tower*, 1924; oil on canvas; 63 ⅝ × 38 ⅛ in.; Saint Louis Art Museum, Gift of Mr. and Mrs. Morton D. May 536:1956

lacquer to protect against deterioration.[30] Early success prompted the establishment in 1917 of the Société des Laques Indochinoises, which specialized in lacquering not only for the aviation industry but also for the automobile sector. Its workforce was largely recruited (reportedly under exploitive contracts) from France's colonies in Southeast Asia, which comprised parts of contemporary Cambodia, Laos, and Vietnam.[31] After the war, Southeast Asian lacquer artists based in Paris's Fourteenth Arrondissement supplied French department stores and jewelers with "high luxury" goods like lacquer screens and bricks, compacts, and lipstick and cigarette cases.[32]

Polymaths thrived in the freewheeling climate of entrepreneurship and innovation of early twentieth-century France. Édouard Bénédictus, whose colorful textiles and carpets featured prominently at the fair (FIG. 72), began his career as a chemist. While in the laboratory, he observed that a glass bottle coated with a nitrocellulose solution did not shatter when dropped.[33] Recognizing the potential of laminated glass in the automobile industry, Bénédictus filed a patent for Triplex Glass in 1909. Three years later, he founded the Société du Verre Triplex. Bénédictus devoted himself to decorative arts after the war but remained engaged in applications of new materials. His textile *Les Jets d'Eau* covered the walls of a grand reception room in the Pavilion of the French Embassy (FIGS. 73, 74). Its stylized streams of water—chains of squares and triangles and waving rivulets—shimmered thanks to the inclusion of rayon, a semisynthetic fiber made from regenerated cellulose.

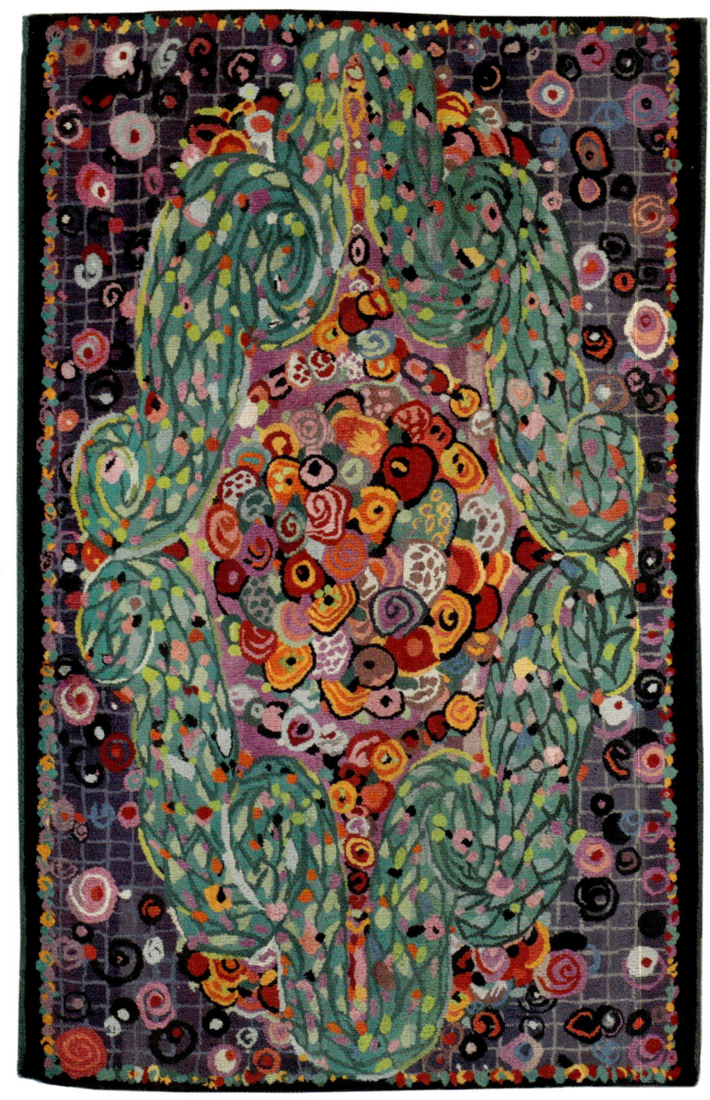

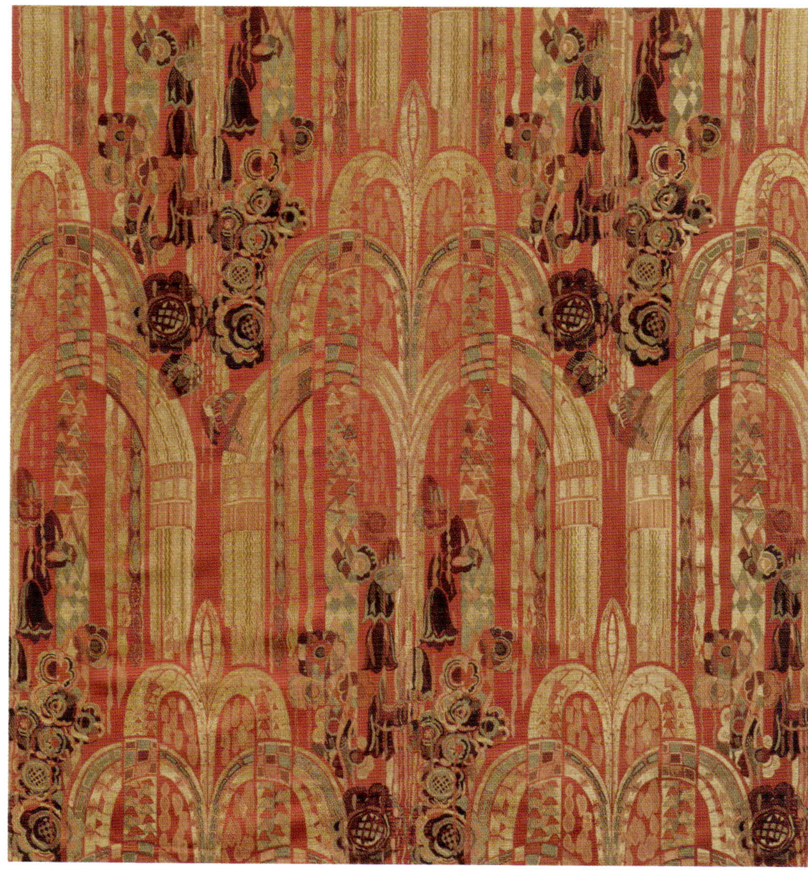

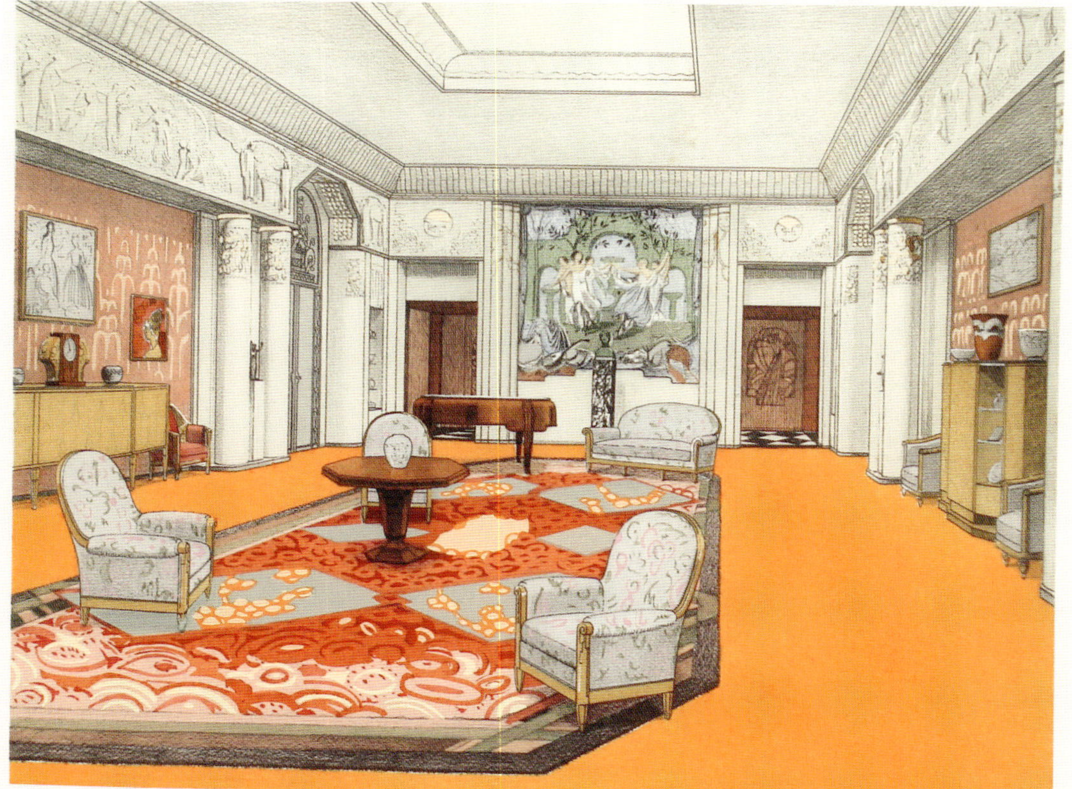

FIG. 72
Édouard Bénédictus, French, 1878–1930; *Rug*, c.1925; wool, plain weave with symmetrical knots; 121 × 79 in.; Lent by the Minneapolis Institute of Art, Gift of Ruth and Bruce Dayton and the Putnam Dana McMillan Fund

FIG. 73
Designed by Édouard Bénédictus, French, 1878–1930; made by Brunet Meunié et Cie, Paris, founded 1815; *Fountains (Les Jets d'Eau) Textile*, 1925; cotton and rayon; 53 ¼ × 49 ¾ in.; Saint Louis Art Museum, Funds given by The Lea Thi Ta Study Group 464:2018

FIG. 74
Designed by Henri Rapin, French, 1873–1939; and Pierre Selmersheim, French, 1869–1941; Grand Salon, Pavilion of the French Embassy at the Exposition Internationale des Arts Décoratifs et Industriels Modernes, Paris, 1925

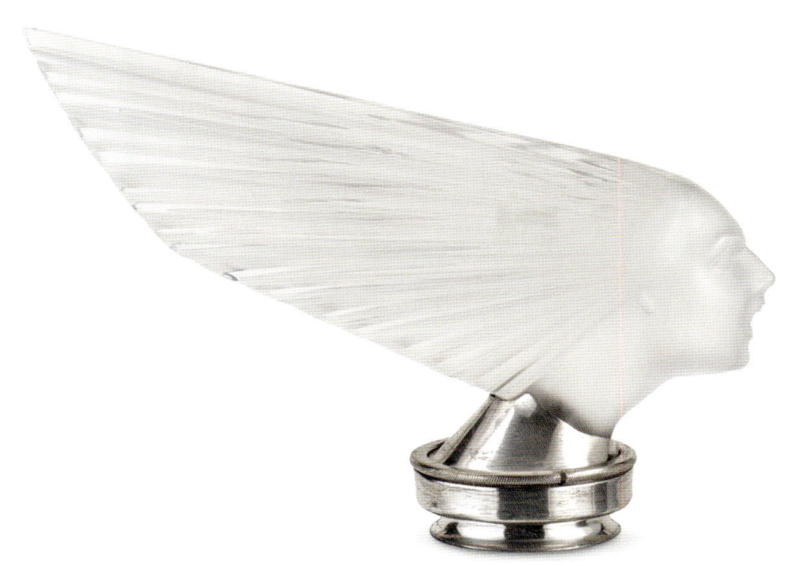

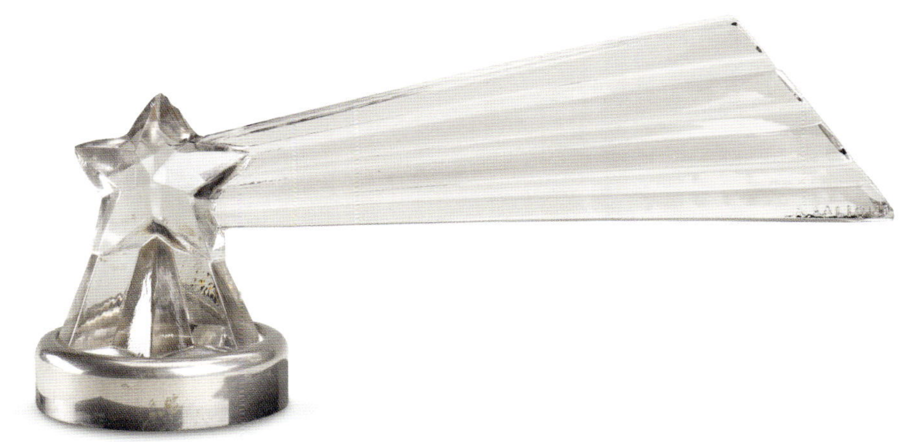

FIG. 75
Designed by René Lalique, French, 1860–1945; made by Lalique et Cie, Wingen-sur-Moder, France; *Victoire (Spirit of the Wind)*, designed 1928; glass, sterling silver, silver-plated copper, and granite; 11 ½ × 3 ⅞ × 8 ½ in.; The Baltimore Museum of Art: Gift of Dr. and Mrs. Edward F. Lewison, Baltimore, in Memory of their Son, Richard Jay Lewison (1953–1996); BMA 1997.454

FIG. 76
Designed by René Lalique, French, 1860–1945; made by Lalique et Cie, Wingen-sur-Moder, France; *Comète (Comet)*, designed 1925; glass, Carrara glass, and chrome; 4 ⅛ × 4 × 7 ⅞ in.; The Baltimore Museum of Art

FIG. 77
Designed by René Lalique, French, 1860–1945; made by Lalique et Cie, Wingen-sur-Moder, France; *Cinq Chevaux (Five Horses)*, designed 1925; glass; 5 ⅞ × 5 × 7 ⅛ in.; The Baltimore Museum of Art

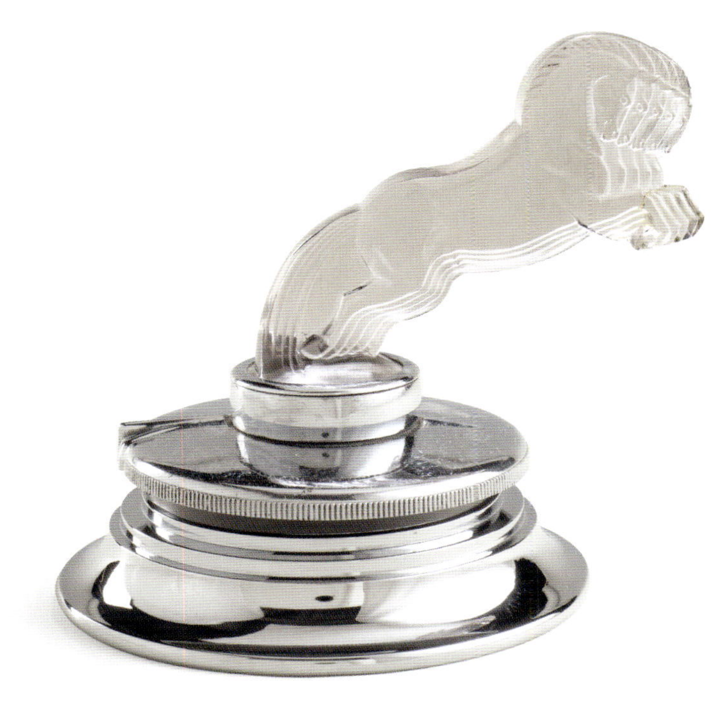

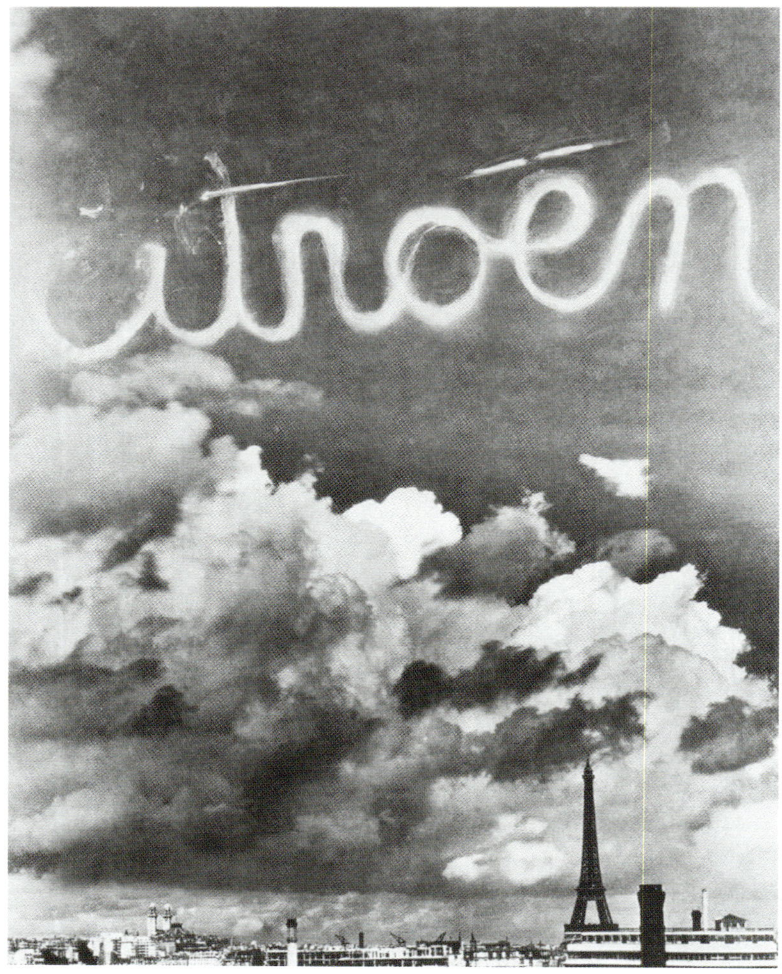

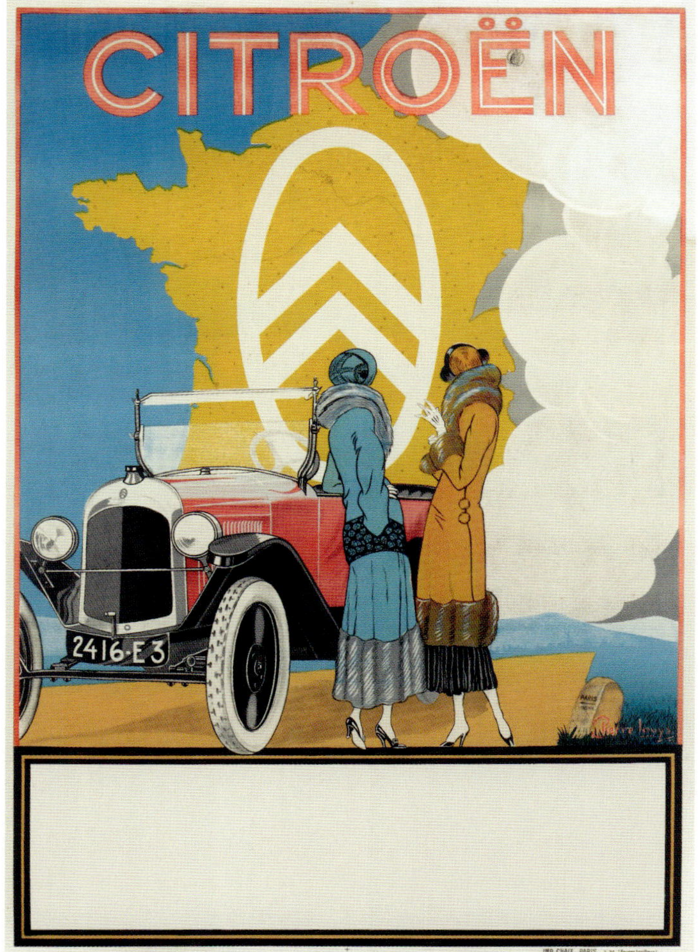

In 1927, the storied glass manufacturer Compagnie de Saint-Gobain acquired Bénédictus's Société du Verre Triplex and with it the technology to mass-produce laminated glass. By 1930, 28 percent of the company's profits derived from automotive safety glass.[34] The French carmaker Citroën used security glass in all its cars by 1931, and its competitor Renault made Triplex windshields a standard feature in its luxury Stella model in 1932. With fellow designer and architect Jacques Adnet, René-André Coulon created an extraordinary pavilion for Saint-Gobain at the 1937 International Exposition of Art and Technology in Modern Life (Exposition Internationale des Arts et Techniques dans la Vie Moderne) in Paris filled with his translucent furniture made in curved and tempered glass (FIG. 69).

Automobiles at the Edges

Though the latest models of Citroën, Renault, Delage, and Delahaye were conspicuously absent from the fair's many pavilions, the unofficial presence of the automobile was pervasive.[35] Two months after the inauguration of the exposition, the supremacy of its "fairyland of lights" was challenged by a novel treatment of Paris's Eiffel Tower.[36] Leading up to the fair, the Société de la Tour Eiffel had sought proposals for illuminating the monument.[37] The Italian-born artist and electrical engineer Fernand Jacopozzi and the painter Italo Stalla won over the committee, but the high cost of their ambitious plan required alternative funding. With the committee's endorsement, Jacopozzi engaged the automobile industrialist André Citroën, successfully pitching the light show as a kinetic advertisement for his brand.

Citroën had established his factory on the Quai de Javel in 1914 to supply the French army with munitions, and after the war he hastily transitioned his production line to automobiles, finding success with his first model, the Type A. Citroën had a reputation as a visionary marketer. For the 1922 Paris Motor Show, he hired planes to write "Citroën" in the sky above the Grand Palais (FIG. 78). Two years later, with the backing of the French government, he launched a promotional expedition across Africa on the company's Autochenilles (auto caterpillars), efficient off-road vehicles fitted with rear-wheel tracks to navigate rugged terrain. The Russian painter Alexandre Jacovleff and a small film crew documented the eight-month journey from Algeria to Madagascar, with the goal of establishing a tourist route linking

FIG. 78
Photograph of the first advertisement in the sky by Citroën before the 17th Paris Auto Show at the Grand Palais in 1922, published in Jacques Séguéla, *100 Years of Citroën Advertising* (Paris: Flammarion, 2019), 37

FIG. 79
Pierre Louÿs, French, 1894–1976; *Citroën Poster*, 1923; lithograph; 62 × 45 ½ in.; Private collection

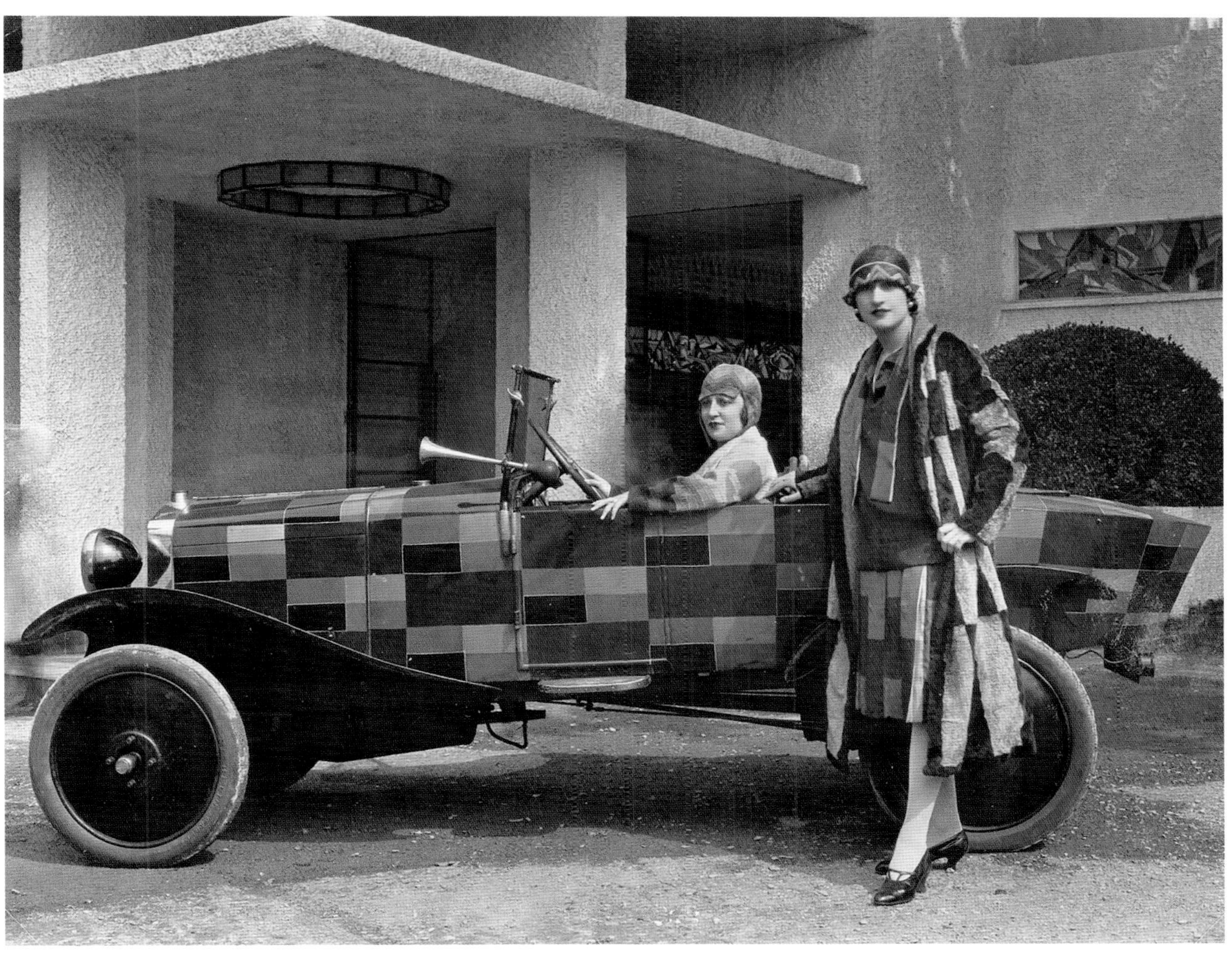

France's African colonies.[38] The resulting films, photographs, artworks, and books of *La Croisière noire* (The black crossing) were heavily promoted to the French public for years after the return.[39]

The illustrator and photographer Pierre Louÿs led the company's in-house "propaganda" department. A talented graphic artist and the husband of top Chanel designer Jeanne Morel, Louÿs launched a mass-advertising campaign, branding Citroën in colorful, customizable posters as an extension of French prosperity and elegance.[40] A 1923 poster features two women fashionably and practically dressed in cloche hats with ear warmers and fur-collared coats, their backs turned against the viewer and toward their open-top Type A and a map of France, framed by a plume of exhaust fumes (FIG. 79). A modern capitalist vision of the sublime, the points of Citroën's iconic chevron logo lead to Paris, proclaiming the marque's emerging centrality to the nation's and capital city's economy.

An enthusiast of Henry Ford's methods of mass manufacturing, Citroën largely produced low-priced automobiles with factory bodies, but it also catered to the growing taste for customization and small luxuries. In 1925, André commissioned the glass manufacturer René Lalique et Cie (FIG. 68) to create a cast-glass mascot, or radiator cap, for their 5 CV, a popular economy model with a jaunty, tapered tail. Lalique sculpted five overlapping horses—a literal evocation of the engine's units of power—their manes and tails rendered in crisp ridges, leaping forward in a frozen frame of collective momentum. *Cinq Chevaux* (Five Horses) is among the first of three mascots Lalique designed (FIG. 77). In August 1925, Lalique also created *Falcon*, a more conventional mascot adapted from an existing sculpture, and *Comète* (Comet), probably inspired by Jacopozzi's celestial designs for the Eiffel Tower unveiled a month earlier (FIG. 76).[41] Three years later, he celebrated the tenth anniversary of the 1918 armistice agreement that ended World War I with the now iconic *Victoire* (FIG. 75). A Nike for the automobile age, this victory goddess, hair stiffened by the wind, was propelled by the power of a roaring engine.

Jacopozzi's kinetic illumination was a daring undertaking. Citroën paid 600,000 francs for the design and installation, 350,000 francs for an annual rental fee, and 300,000 francs in taxes to the Paris city government. For about 40 seconds, fiery motifs and markers of the Citroën brand flashed in and out in a sparkling cinematic advertisement (FIG. 70):

FIG. 80
Coats designed by Sonia Delaunay and Jacques Heim with an Ariès Torpédo, in front of the Pavillon du Tourisme designed by Robert Mallet-Stevens, Paris, 1925; Bibliothèque nationale de France, Paris

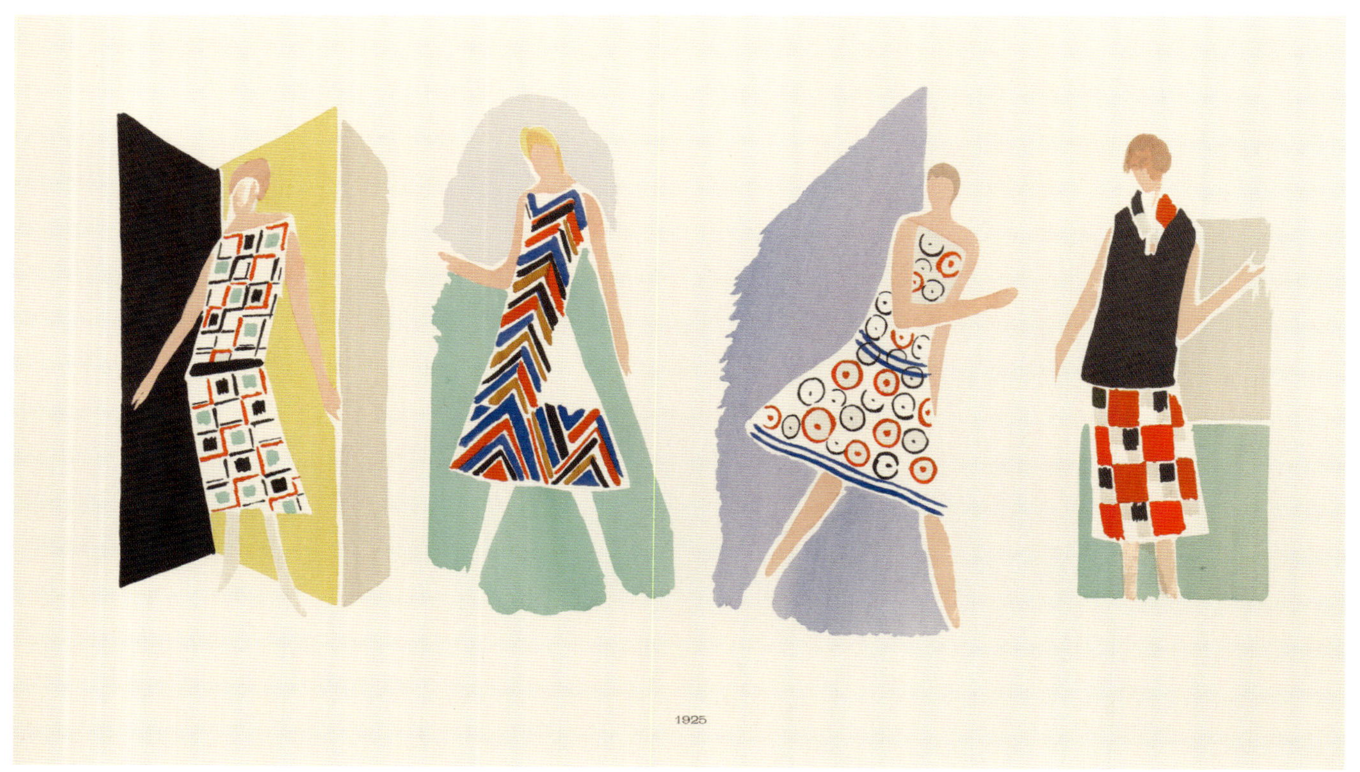

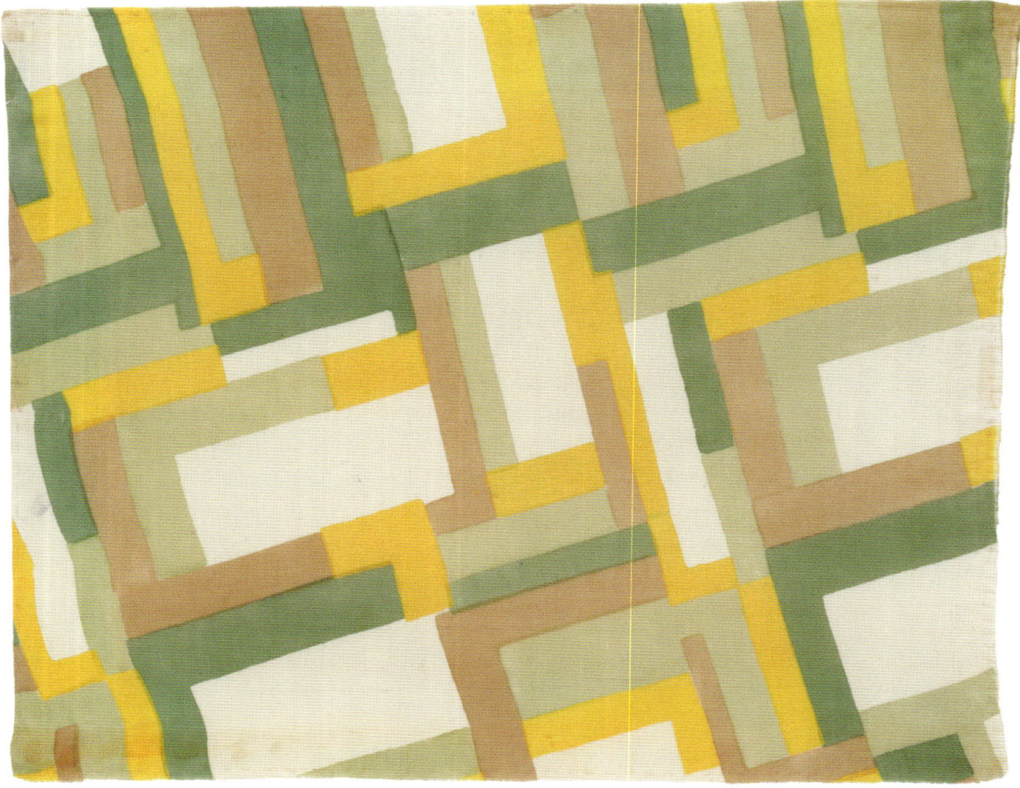

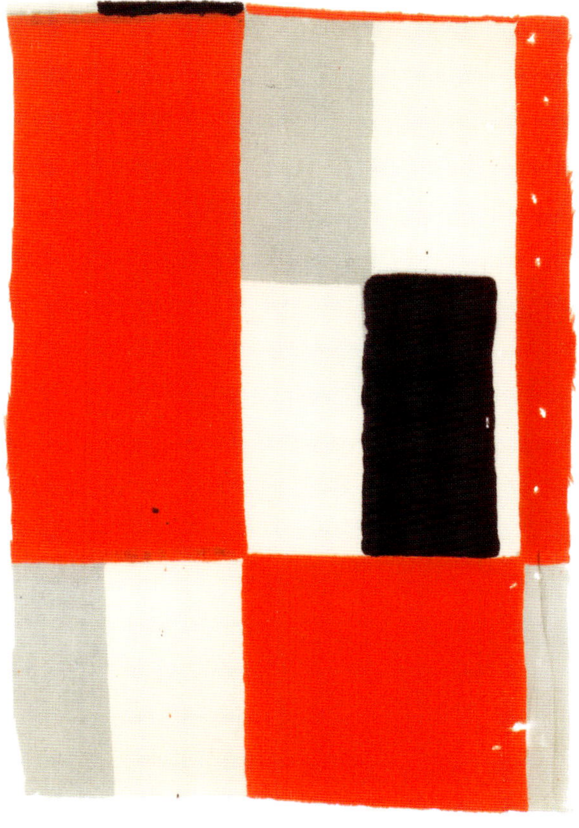

FIG. 81
Designed by Sonia Delaunay, French (born Ukraine), 1885–1979; published by Librairie des Arts Décoratifs, French; Color illustration from *Sonia Delaunay: Ses peintures, ses objets, ses tissus simultanés, ses modes*, c.1925; pochoir and relief process; 23 × 16 in. each; Missouri State University Libraries, Springfield, Missouri

FIG. 82
Designed by Sonia Delaunay, French (born Ukraine), 1885–1979; made by Ferret Frères et Cie, Saint-Denis, France; *"Tissu simultané" n° 1*, 1924; printed silk; 14 7⁄8 × 19 1⁄2 in.; Musée des Tissus et des Arts décoratifs de Lyon

FIG. 83
Designed by Sonia Delaunay, French (born Ukraine), 1885–1979; made by Ferret Frères et Cie, Saint-Denis, France; *"Tissu simultané" n° 35*, 1923–24; printed silk; 9 1⁄16 × 6 1⁄2 in.; Musée des Tissus et des Arts décoratifs de Lyon

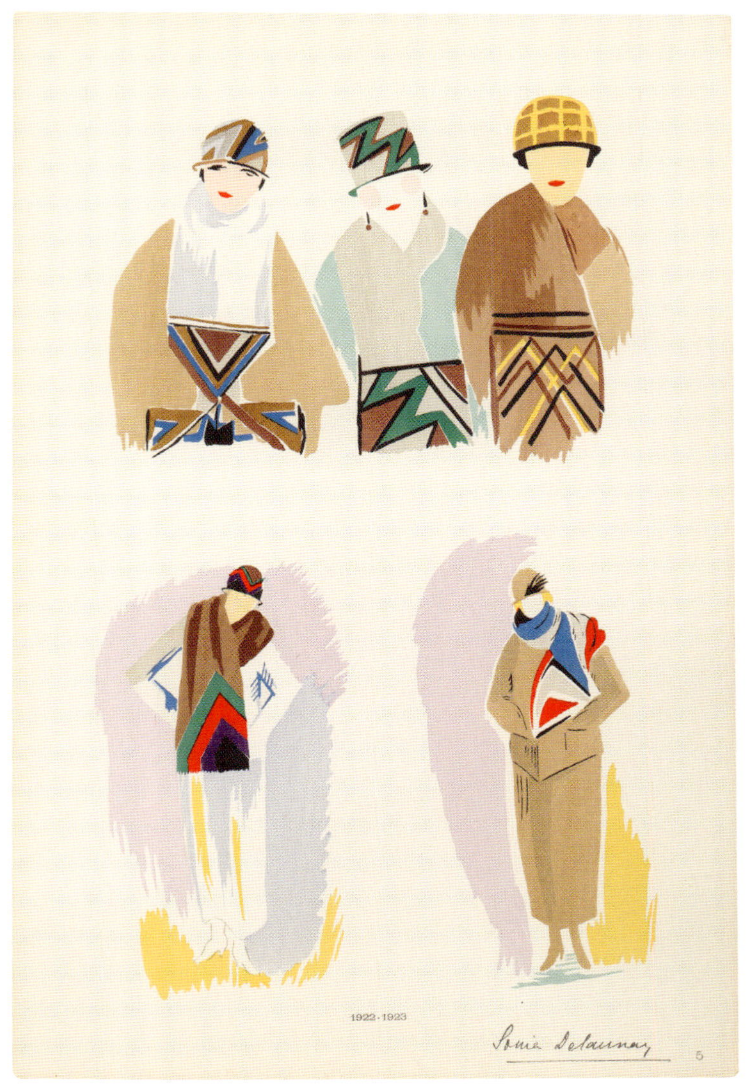

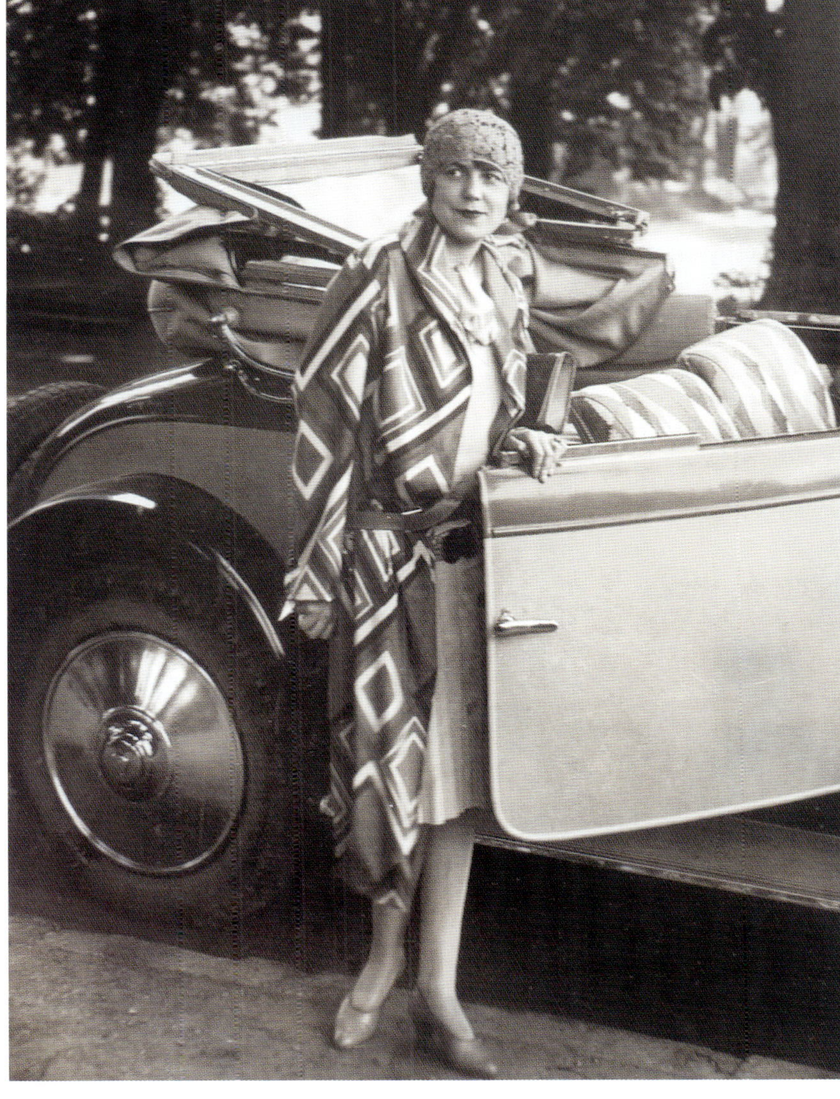

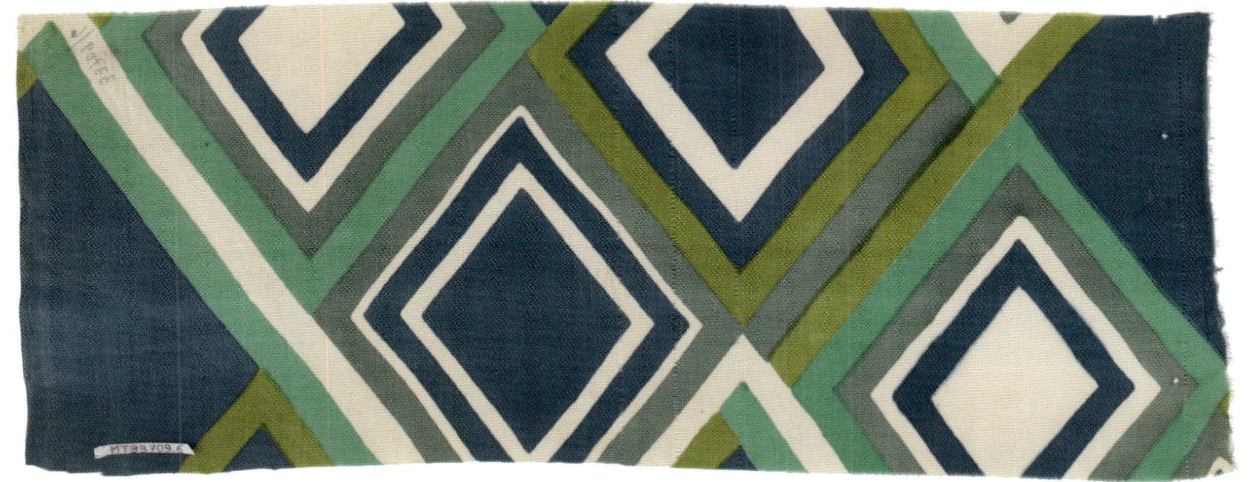

FIG. 84
Designed by Sonia Delaunay, French (born Ukraine), 1885–1979; published by Librairie des Arts Décoratifs, French; Color illustration from *Sonia Delaunay: Ses peintures, ses objets, ses tissus simultanés, ses modes*, c.1925; each: pochoir and relief process; 23 × 16 in.; Missouri State University Libraries, Springfield, Missouri

FIG. 85
Model wearing coat designed by Sonia Delaunay in front of a Talbot automobile, c.1926–27

FIG. 86
Designed by Sonia Delaunay, French (born Ukraine), 1885–1979; made by Ferret Frères et Cie, Saint-Denis, France; *"Tissu simultané" n° 186, color 4*, 1926; printed silk; 7 ½ × 19 5⁄16 in.; Musée des Tissus et des Arts décoratifs de Lyon

> There are nine different combinations of lights which shift and change continuously. The first motif shows the simple outline of the tower in white light. Then a shower of stars falls from the top, followed by huge arabesques in the signs of the zodiac. A great ruby flame now rises from the top of the tower while, lower down, in fiery escutcheons, appear the dates 1889–1925. The design again changes, and enormous white stars composed of 600-candle power globes flash out along the length of the tower; and these stars presently become comets with golden tails. Then the final display. Writhing strands of light suddenly turn into letters, and the enraptured city spells out, between the second and third platforms, the word C-I-T-R-O-Ë-N, while, in place of the numerals, appears the double chevron trademark of the firm.[42]

The display, intended to run until 1926, marred Paris's night sky, as many critics bemoaned, but adaptations continued for nearly a decade.[43]

Citroën's commercial capture of the Eiffel Tower coincided with the rehabilitation of its reputation among artists as a symbol of the modern, industrial age. The Swiss architect Le Corbusier (Charles-Édouard Jeanneret) wryly reported in *The Decorative Art of Today*: "The Eiffel Tower has been accepted as architecture. In 1889, it was seen as the aggressive expression of mathematical calculation. In 1900, the aesthetes wanted to demolish it. In 1925, it dominated the Exhibition of Modern Decorative Arts. Above the plaster palaces writhing with decoration, it stood out pure as crystal."[44] The facets of the conspicuous "crystal" were an especially compelling subject for the artist Robert Delaunay. Robert and his wife Sonia founded "Orphic" Cubism, a label assigned by the poet Guillaume Apollinaire to their distinctive visual language in which color became both an expressive and structural tool.[45] Delaunay first painted the Eiffel Tower in 1910 and returned to the subject in 1922. In this later iteration, which included a monumental work for the 1925 fair, the fragmentation of the earlier series gave way to bright saturated colors—orange, sunny yellow, lavender, peach, and chartreuse—juxtaposed to convey the tower's prismatic monumentality (FIG. 71).

Robert Delaunay's keen interest in automobiles was a natural extension of his obsession with modern technology. As Sonia wrote in her autobiography, "I close my eyes and imagine Robert. I see him painting while Apollinaire sleeps. No, he's not in his studio. So? So, I see him driving a torpedo. Even to get a pack of cigarettes, he took his car. The car, it was modernity. But also, an atmosphere that allowed him [Robert] to dream alone. At that

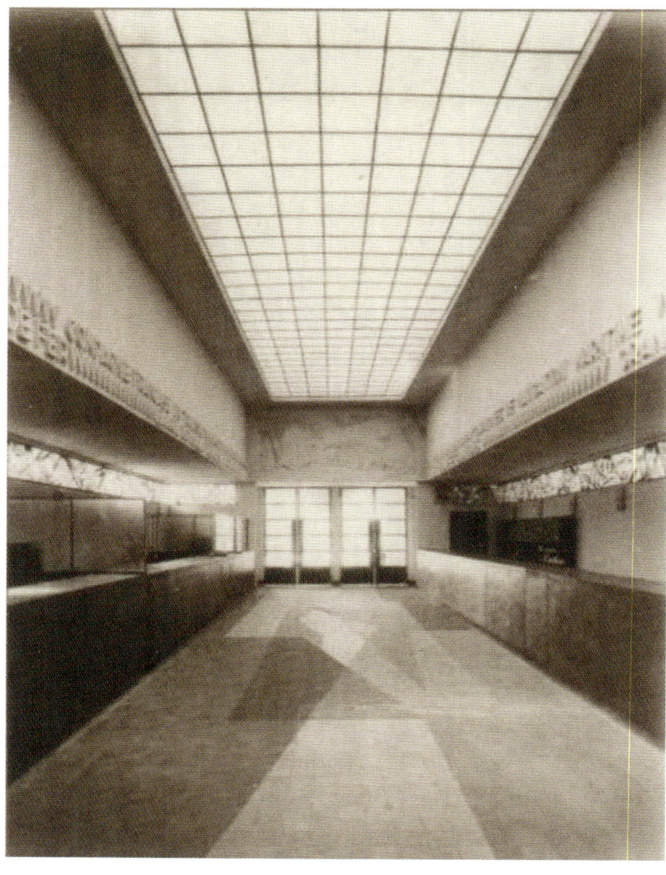

FIG. 87
Pavillon du Tourisme featuring stained glass by the artist Louis Barillet at the Exposition Internationale des Arts Décoratifs et Industriels Modernes, Paris, 1925

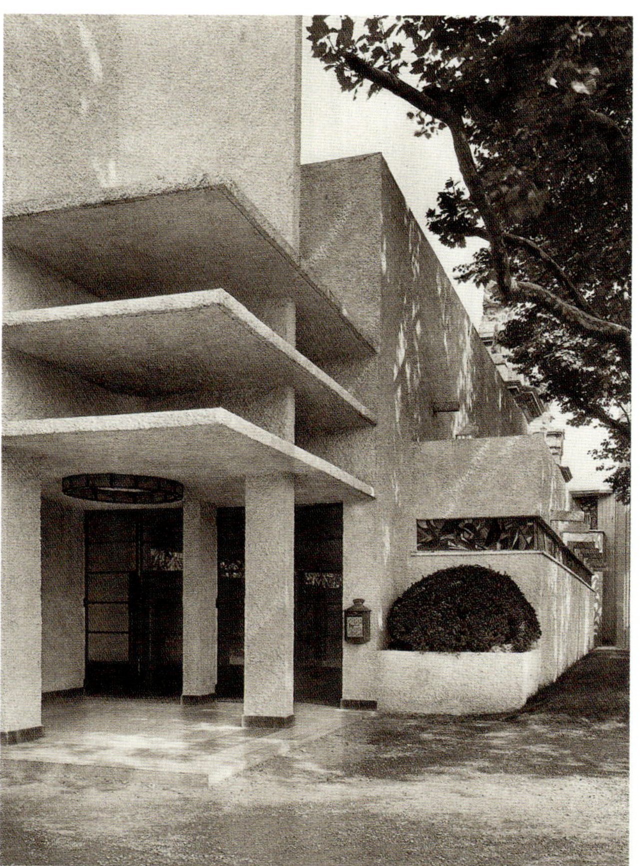

FIG. 88
Designed by Le Corbusier, Swiss (active France), 1887–1965; and Pierre Jeanneret, Swiss, 1896–1967; printed by A. Lévy; *Pavillon du Tourisme (Exterior) at the 1925 Exposition Internationale des Arts Décoratifs et Industriels Modernes, Paris*, in Michel Roux-Spitz, *Bâtiments et jardins, cent planches en héliogravure*, 1925

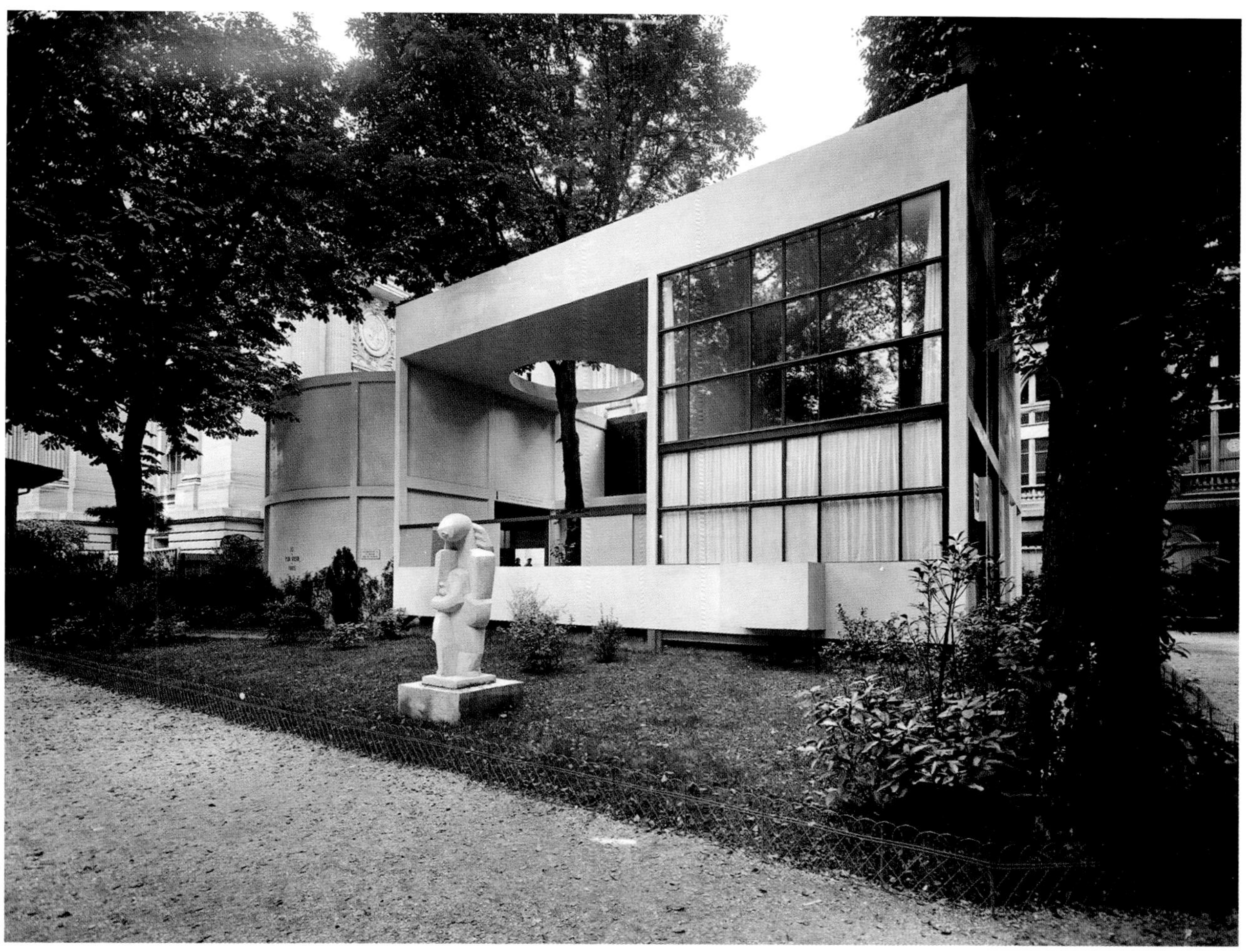

FIG. 89
Designed by Le Corbusier, Swiss (active France), 1887–1965; and Pierre Jeanneret, Swiss, 1896–1967; printed by A. Lévy; *(Exterior) Pavillon de l'Esprit nouveau at the 1925 Exposition internationale des arts décoratifs et industriels modernes, Paris,* in Michel Roux-Spitz, *Bâtiments et jardins, cent planches en héliogravure,* 1925

time, one could drive while dreaming. Ah, Delaunay and his machines!"[46] The Delaunays bought their first car in 1922 and were not without one again during their lifetimes.

Despite Robert's infatuation, it was Sonia who most famously engaged the car as an object worthy of her professional attention. At the 1925 fair, she and the couturier Jacques Heim dressed two models in her fashions—patchwork and embroidered dresses, jackets, hats, and caps—and placed them in front of a coordinating car for a photograph that circulated worldwide (FIG. 80). Delaunay custom-painted the Ariès Torpédo in a geometric pattern of black, green, and gray squares at the invitation of its owner, the journalist Maurice Kaplan.[47] The inventive paint treatment, echoed in the automobile bodies at the transport section, vividly incarnated the flexibility of her simultaneous color theory. Drawing on the physicist Michel-Eugène Chevreul's 1838 text *On the Law of Simultaneous Contrasts of Color*, which showed that the optical perception of color is relative and changing, the Delaunays developed a visual language of pure abstraction that harnessed the dynamism of color contrasts. Of his wife's designs, Robert Delaunay mused, "They are responsive to the painting, to the architecture of modern life, to the bodies of cars, to the beautiful and original forms of airplanes—in short, to the aspirations of this active, modern age, which has forged a style intimately related to its incredibly fast and intense life."[48] Delaunay would later pose models wearing simultaneous fashions with the couple's luxurious Talbot upholstered in coordinating fabrics (FIG. 85). While few of her garments survive, textile samples and albums of Sonia's fashion illustrations attest to her studied color juxtapositions that captured the syncopated rhythm of interwar Paris (FIGS. 81–84, 86).

Delaunay's open-top car was presented as a fashion accessory and an artistic canvas, but also a definitive statement on the power of a modern woman taking the wheel. The models' position in front of the fair's Pavillon du Tourisme, a temporary structure designed by the architect Robert Mallet-Stevens in reinforced concrete, served to accentuate both the visual synthesis and imagined bliss of self-directed travel taken in comfort and style. The Torpédo's aerodynamic sloping tail and windscreen-mounted bulb horn hint at both the flow and friction of car trips marred by traffic and poor roads. The driver's racing-capped head is framed like a modernist halo by a distant panel of stained glass by the artist Louis Barillet, a mélange of France's

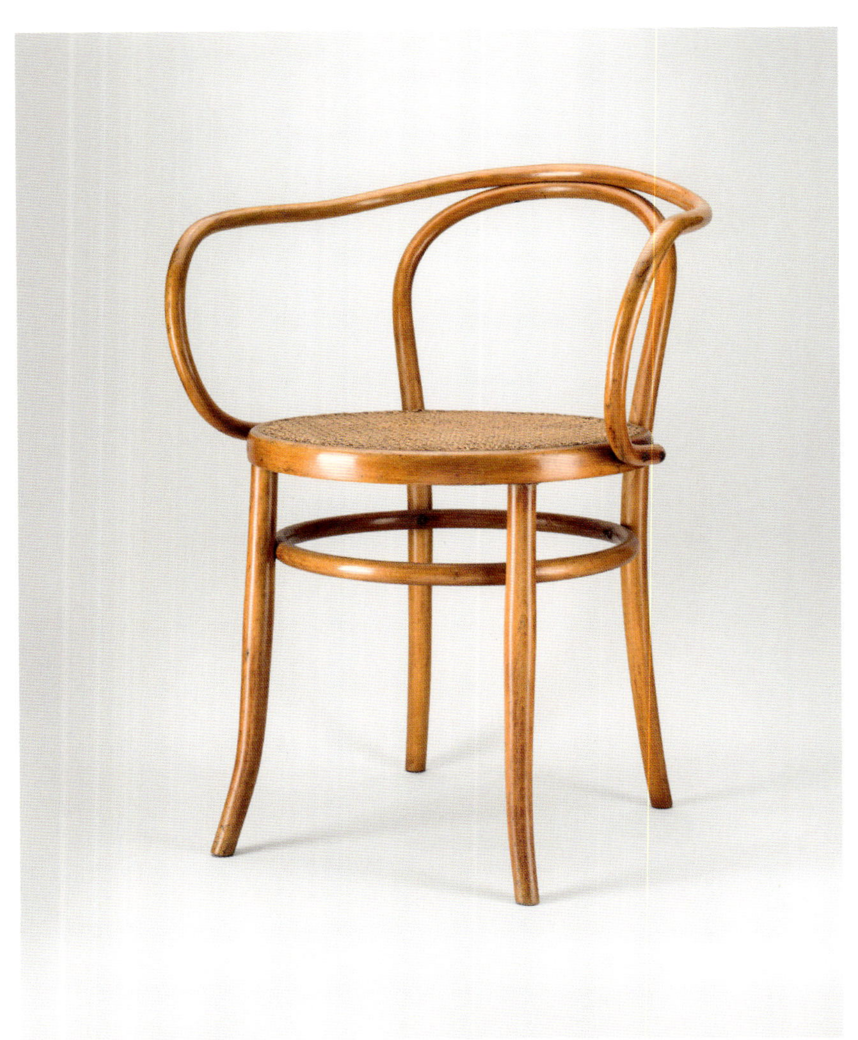

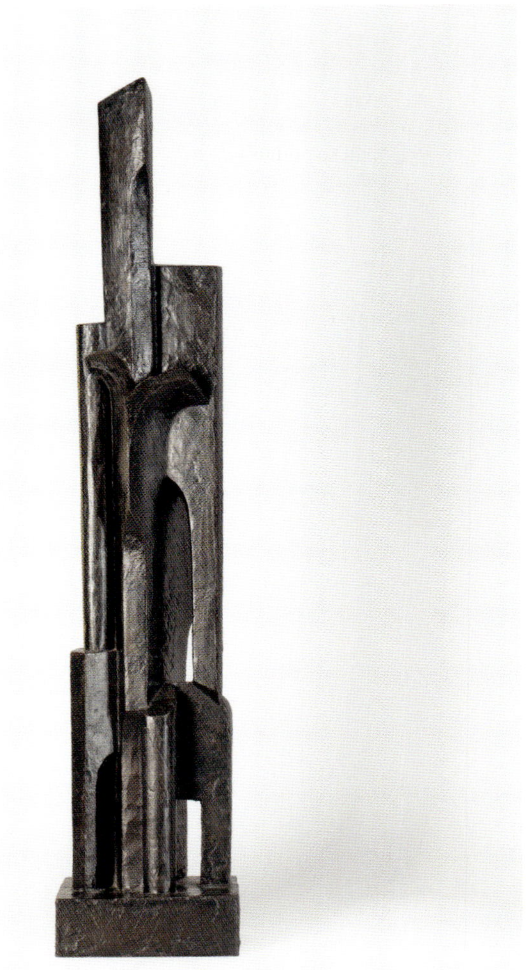

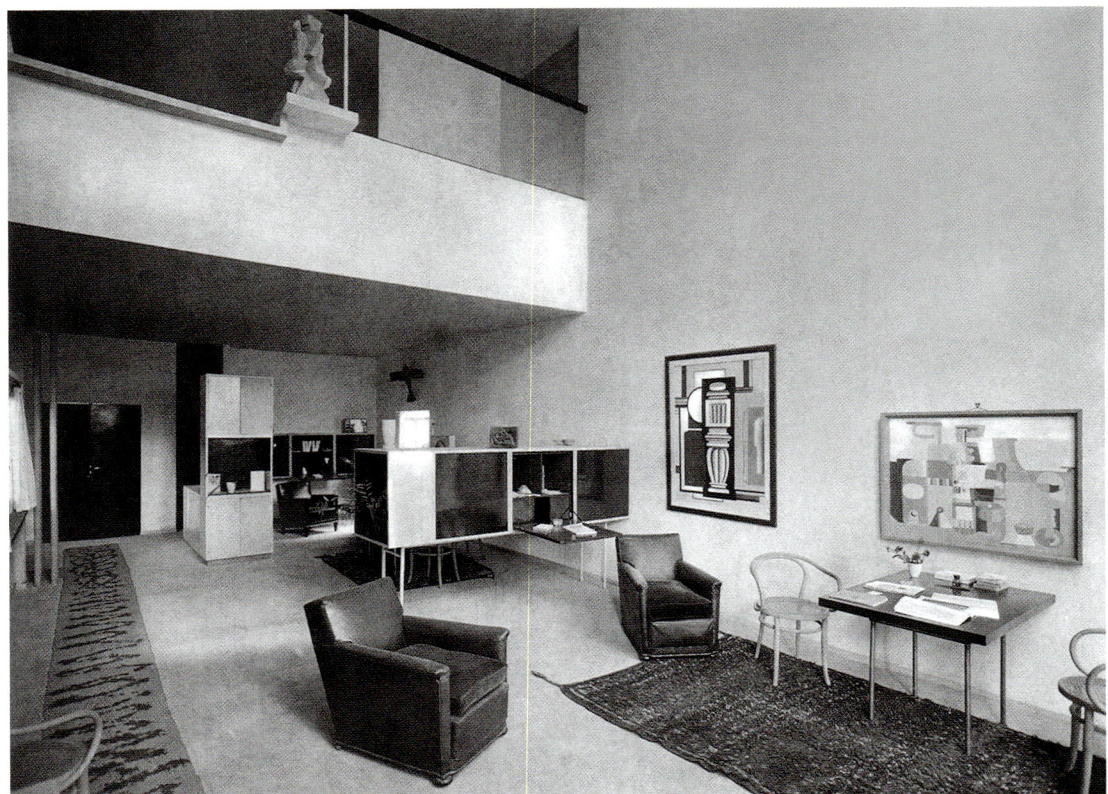

FIG. 90
Gebrüder Thonet, Vienna, Austria, founded 1853; *Armchair (Model No. 9)*, c.1904; beechwood and cane; 30 ½ × 23 ½ × 21 in.; Saint Louis Art Museum, Richard Brumbaugh Trust in memory of Richard Irving Brumbaugh and in honor of Grace Lischer Brumbaugh 250:1992

FIG. 91
Jacques Lipchitz, French (born Lithuania), 1891–1973; *The Standing Personage*, 1916; bronze; height: 41 ¼ in.; Saint Louis Art Museum, Gift of Mr. and Mrs. Joseph Pulitzer Jr. 150:1973

FIG. 92
Designed by Le Corbusier, Swiss (active France), 1887–1965; and Pierre Jeanneret, Swiss, 1896–1967; printed by A. Lévy; *(Interior) Pavillon de l'Esprit nouveau at the 1925 Exposition Internationale des Arts Décoratifs et Industriels Modernes, Paris*, in Michel Roux-Spitz, *Bâtiments et jardins, cent planches en héliogravure*, 1925

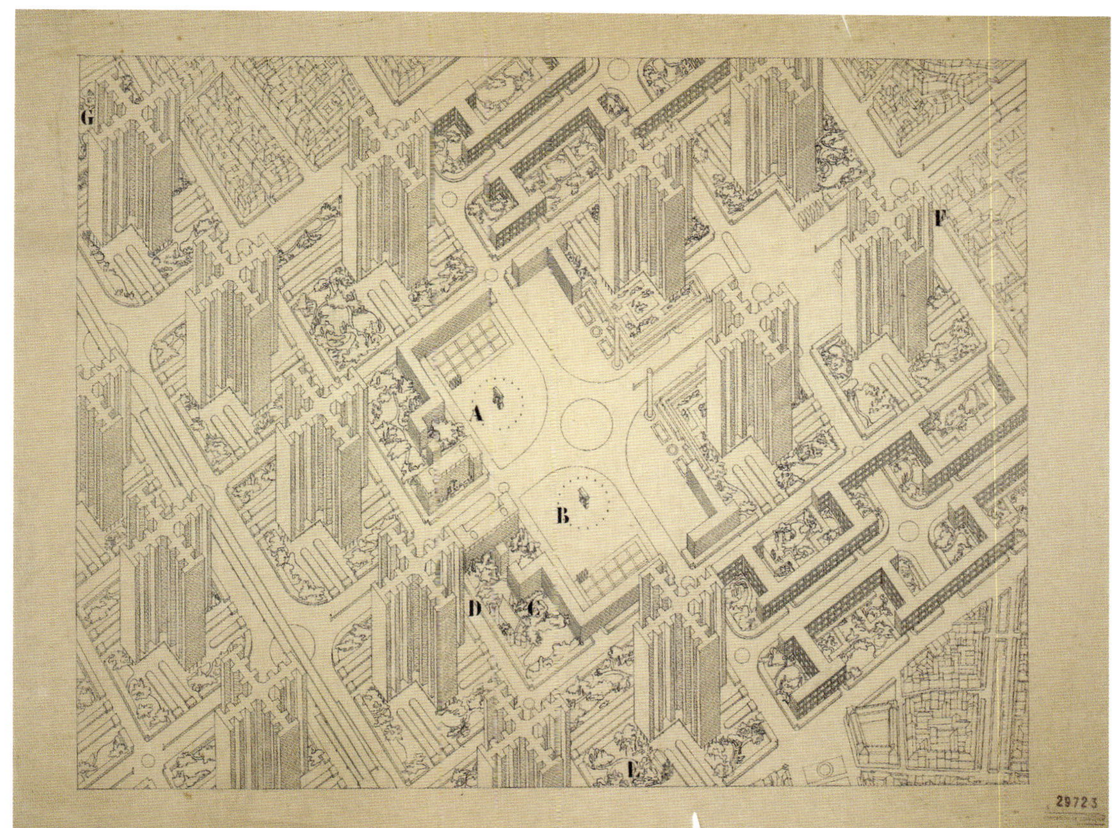

FIG. 93
Le Corbusier, Swiss (active France), 1887–1965; *Le Plan Voisin, Paris, 1925*, 1925; India ink on medium tracing paper; 29 1/8 × 40 3/16 in.; Fondation Le Corbusier, Paris

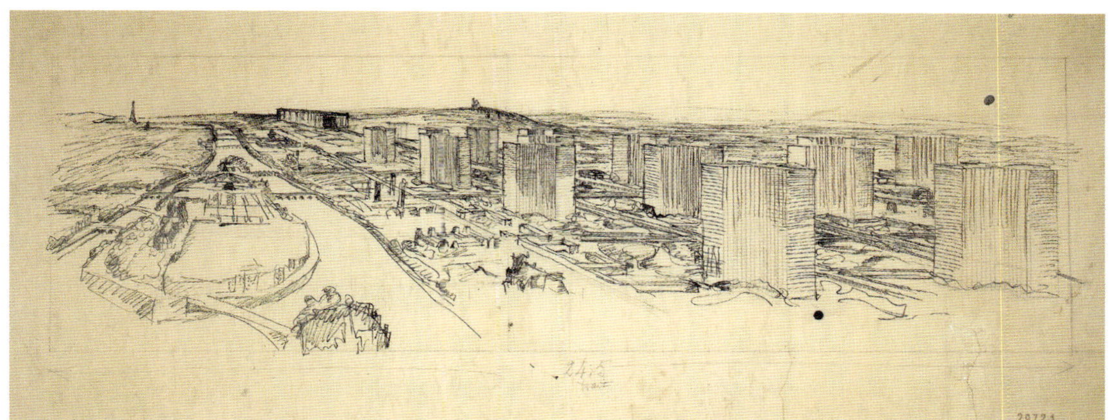

FIG. 94
Le Corbusier, Swiss (active France), 1887–1965; *Le Plan Voisin, Paris, 1925*, 1925; black pencil and India ink on tracing paper; 23 1/16 × 44 7/8 in.; Fondation Le Corbusier, Paris

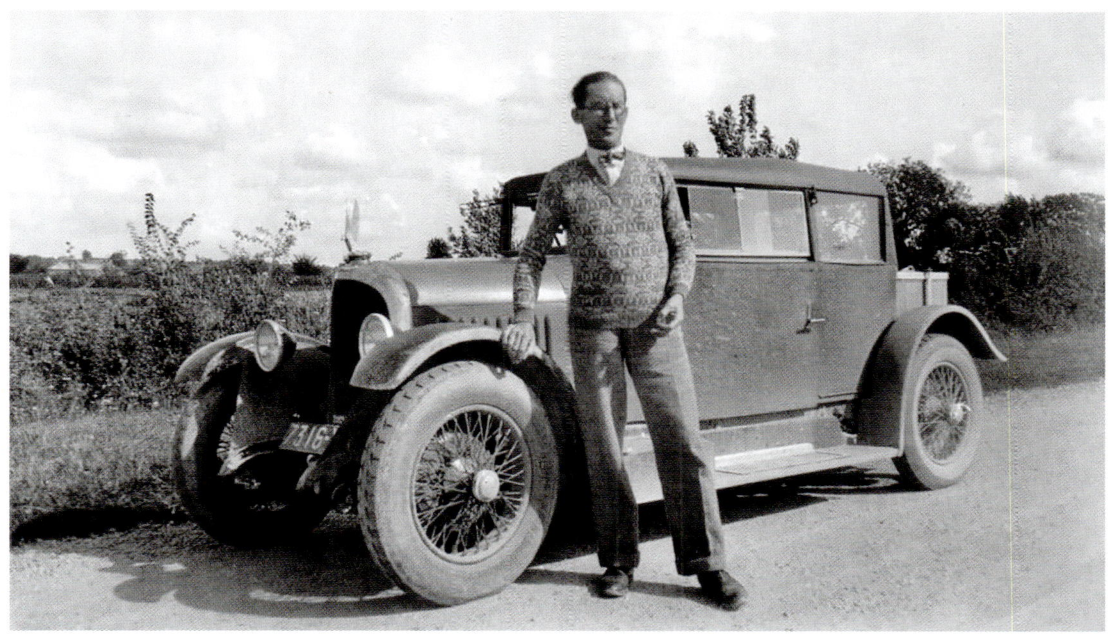

FIG. 95
Le Corbusier with his 1927 Voisin C7; Norman Foster Foundation Archive

national monuments and picturesque towns rendered in "nervous, angular lead lines and black and white 'print' glasses" (FIGS. 87, 88).[49] This seamless presentation, a symbiosis of art, craft, and engineering par excellence, embodied to a cinematic degree the "cubist dream city . . . arisen overnight in the heart of Paris," described by American critics.[50]

Nearby, in a deliberately obscured wooded lot, another vision of modern Paris, transformed to accommodate the automobile, jolted visitors. Designed by the Swiss architects Le Corbusier and his cousin Pierre Jeanneret, the Pavillon de l'Esprit nouveau was composed of two distinct components: a two-story home and a rotunda built to house a pair of provocative panoramas painted by Le Corbusier.[51] Adopting its name from the magazine established by Le Corbusier, the painter Amédée Ozenfant, and the poet Paul Dermée in 1920, the pavilion embodied a central tenet of Purism. The same methods of standardization and mass production that naturally refined and perfected industrial products, especially modern machines like automobiles, could (and should) be applied to domestic architecture and urban planning.[52] Le Corbusier famously exhorted, "If houses were constructed by industrial mass-production, like chassis, unexpected but sane and defensible forms would soon appear, and a new aesthetic would be formulated with astonishing precision."[53] Furnished with freestanding and built-in storage units, laboratory glassware, and mass-produced furniture (including bentwood chairs by the Austrian firm Gebrüder Thonet), the model house was conceived as a modular unit to be repeated in a neat and ordered grid across a reimagined city center (FIGS. 89, 92). Free from the exuberance of the *ensembliers*, the plain plaster walls were hung with paintings by Le Corbusier and Fernand Léger. Sculptures by Jacques Lipchitz punctuated the interior and garden (FIG. 91). Mounted on the kitchen wall, a model airplane, an exemplar of the intersection of strength and material economy, paid quiet homage to the pavilion's partial benefactor, the aircraft and automobile manufacturer Gabriel Voisin.

A much louder tribute occupied the pavilion's rotunda. Of the two panoramas circling its walls, *Le Plan Voisin* was the most incendiary (FIGS. 93, 94). Stretching down the banks of the Seine, the design for the urban renewal of Paris proposed flattening the city's right bank and repopulating it with skyscrapers and highways—wide, straight arteries that seamlessly wove above and below parklands and plazas. Le Corbusier's solicitation of financial support from the automobile industry

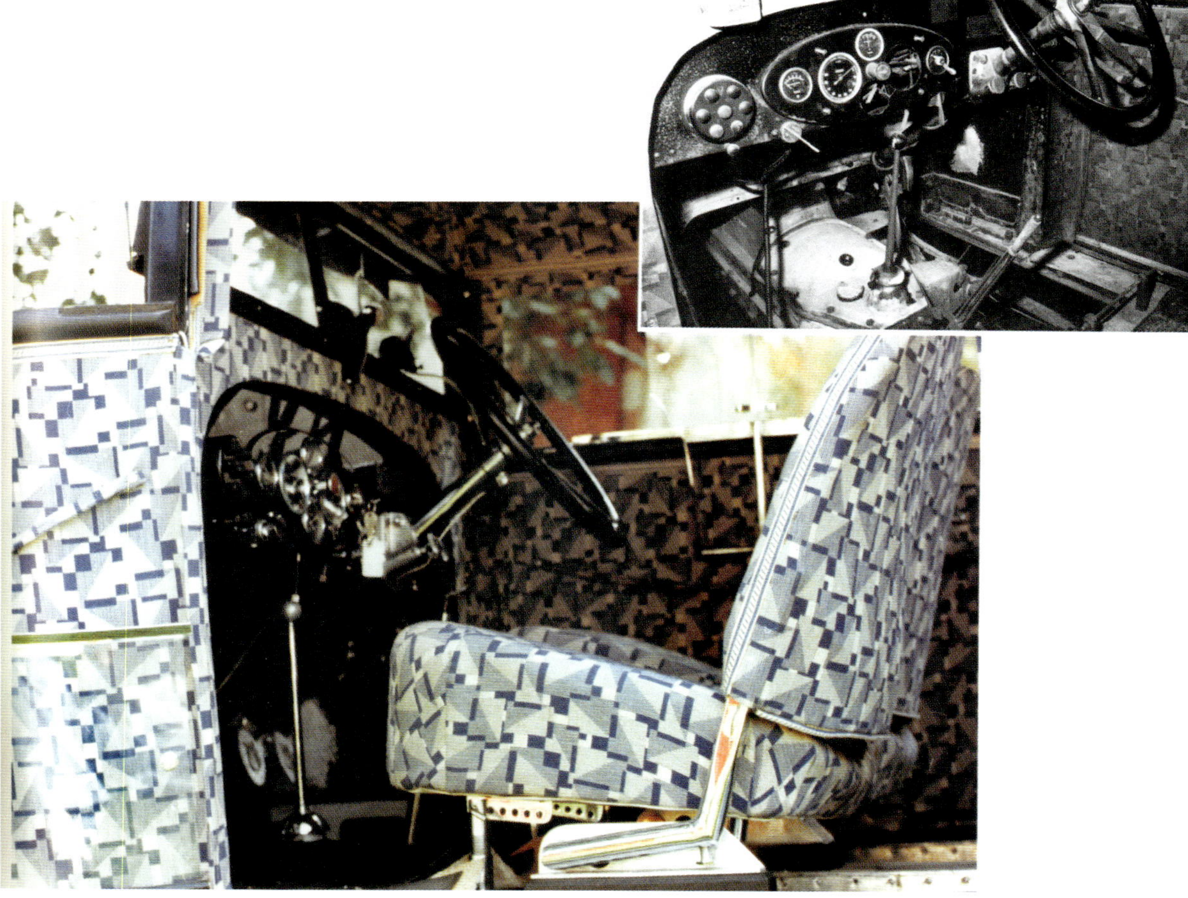

FIG. 96A, B
Original and reproduction Voisin interior fabric for Voisin C11, c.1927–29, from Pascal Courteault's *Automobiles Voisin 1919–1958* (London: White Mouse, 1991), 219

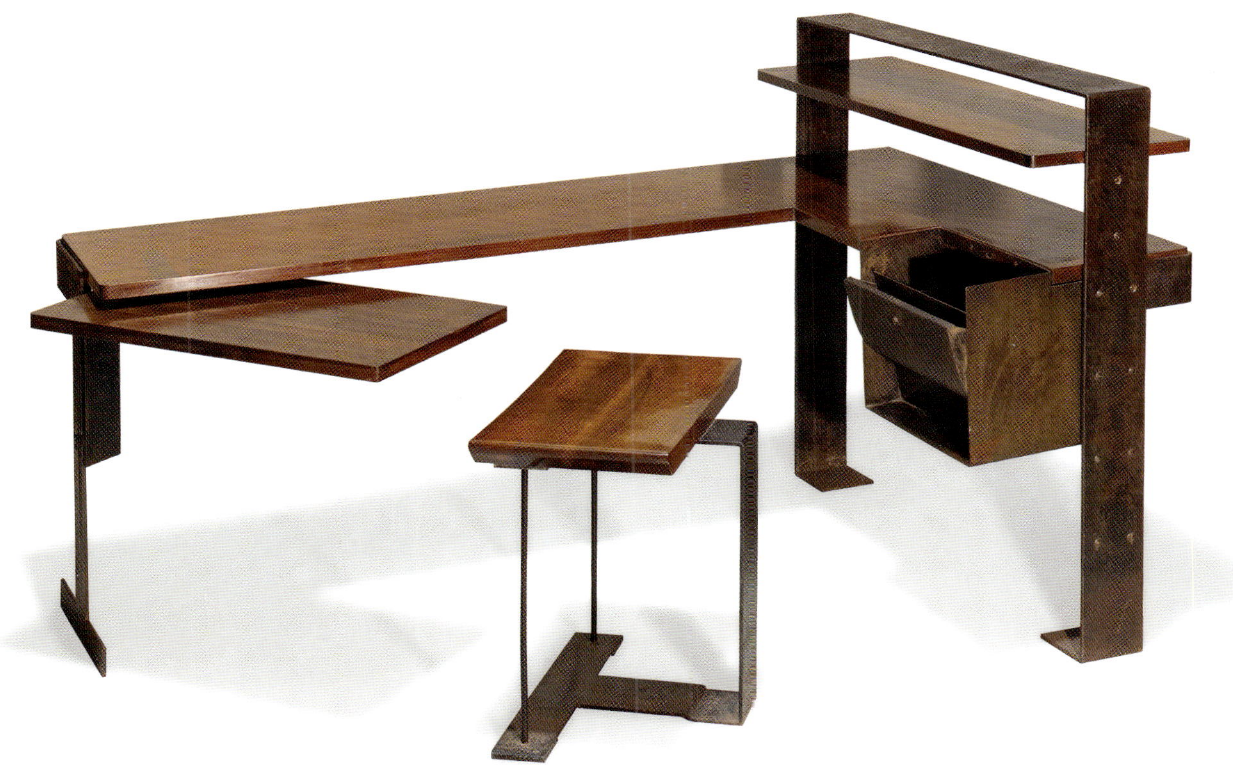

FIG. 97
Pierre Chareau, French, 1883–1950; *Desk and Stool*, c.1927; wrought iron and palisander; desk: 37 × 63 × 40 in., stool: 14 3/8 × 19 11/16 × 15 3/16 in.; National Capital Bank, Courtesy of the Geoffrey Diner Gallery, Washington, DC

was strategic. The name "Voisin" served to emphasize the automobile's impact on Le Corbusier's vision of the modern city "made for speed" and thus "made for success."[54]

With only the begrudging approval of the exposition's planning committee, securing financial backing for the avant-garde pavilion was not easy. Le Corbusier approached both André Citroën and Louis Renault without success before securing 25,000 francs from Gabriel Voisin. The two men were connected through Voisin's factory manager, Eugène Mongermon, who had invited Le Corbusier to design his Paris townhouse in 1922.[55] Ultimately, Mongermon abandoned the project but compensated Le Corbusier for his exploratory work with a discount on a Voisin car and an advertising contract from his employer in the publication *L'Esprit nouveau*.[56]

This convergence of editorial and advertising interests complicates Le Corbusier's frequent citation of Voisin automobiles in his publications and images of his architectural projects. In anticipation of the fair, he published a quartet of polemical books compiled from *L'Esprit nouveau* articles—*L'Art décoratif d'aujourd'hui*, *Vers une architecture*, *Urbanisme*, and *La Peinture moderne*—bringing his most salient theories and criticisms to a larger audience. In *L'Art décoratif d'aujourd'hui*, Le Corbusier declared, "Modern decorative art is not decorated,"[57] a disparagement of the handcrafted luxury goods presented at his colleagues' pavilions but best represented by standardized, mass-manufactured products, such as cars. The scholar Tim Benton has noted Le Corbusier illustrated his many provocations not with factory-bodied Citroëns, turned out by the thousand, but with expensive cars, especially Voisins.[58]

Voisin may have derided the coachbuilder's "deformed, hunchbacked, varnished monster, covered with the most baroque ornaments," but his company's own designs were hardly understated.[59] Le Corbusier famously owned a Voisin C7, a boxy sedan nicknamed the "lumineuse," or luminous, for its unusually large windows (FIG. 95). While its powerful engine and spring suspension reflected the refinements of engineers, the sumptuous coachwork with coordinating luggage offered in dazzling interior fabrics was designed by fellow architect André Noël-Noël Telmont and executed by the firm's craftsmen (FIG. 96A, B). The scholar Tag Gronberg suggested Le Corbusier's choice of a Voisin was an attempt to appropriate luxury vehicles to his "cause of standardization (and masculine identity)."[60] It is also possible his arrangement with Mongermon helped cultivate an early taste for Voisin's deluxe automobiles or that his financial relationship with the brand motivated his elevation of a car that, like most luxury vehicles, was an imperfect modernist paragon.

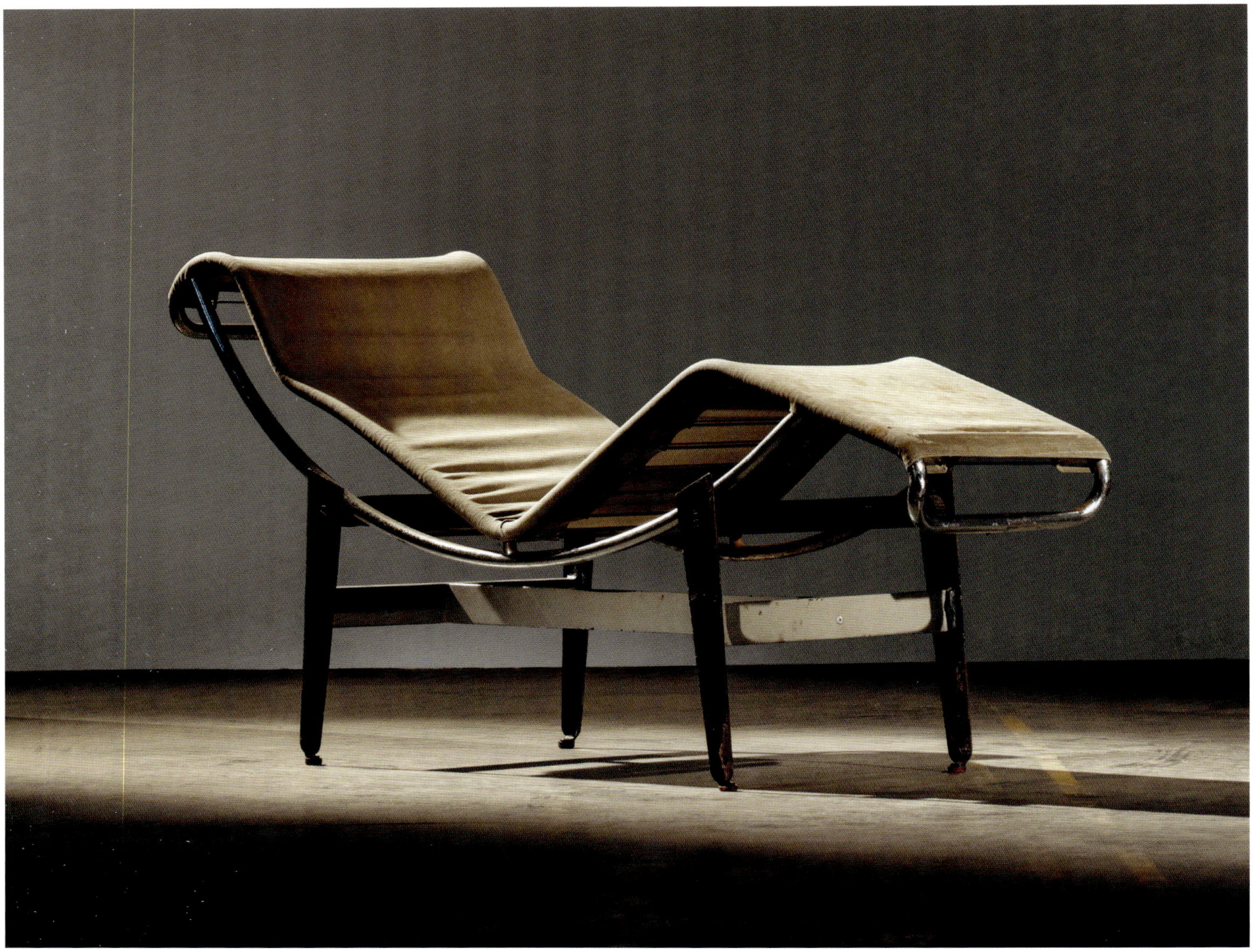

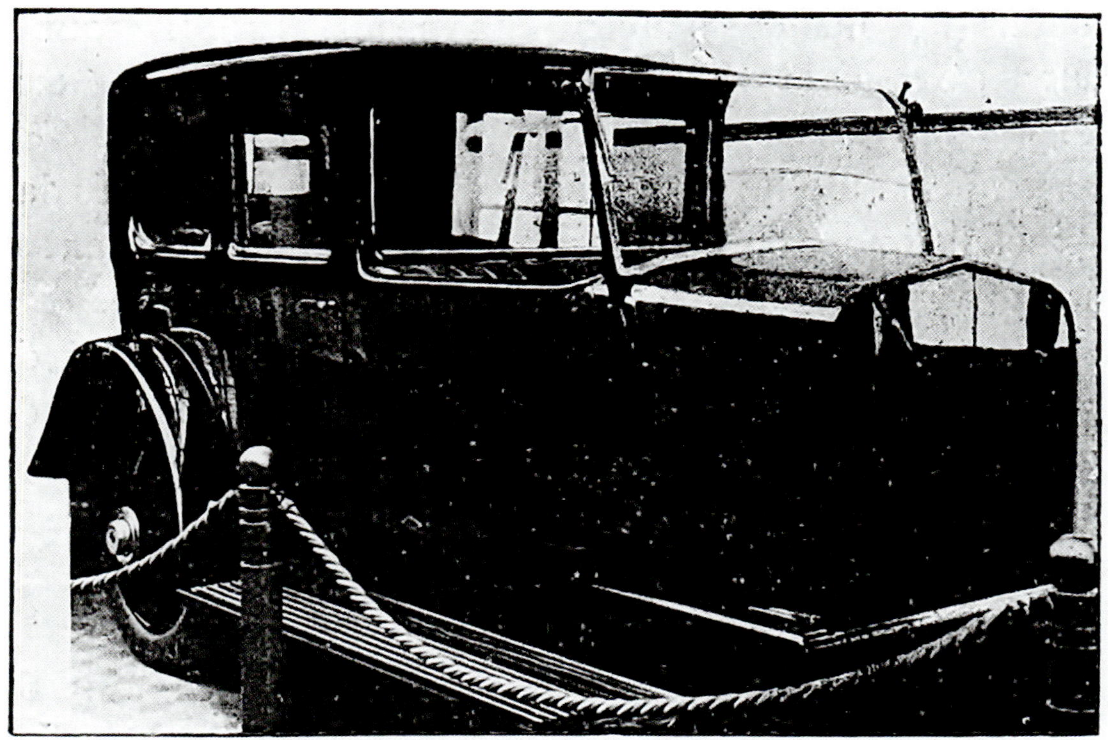

FIG. 98
Designed by Charlotte Perriand, French, 1903–1999, Pierre Jeanneret, Swiss, 1896–1967, and Le Corbusier, Swiss (active France), 1887–1965; *Chaise Longue*, c.1930; chrome-plated tubular steel, painted sheet metal, metal springs, rubber, and fabric; 27 9/16 × 62 5/8 × 18 7/8 in.; Laffanour Galerie Downtown, Paris

FIG. 99
Example of an engineless car from the Exposition Internationale des Arts Décoratifs et Industriels Modernes, Paris, 1925; photograph in *Omnia, revue pratique de locomotion*, June 1, 1925

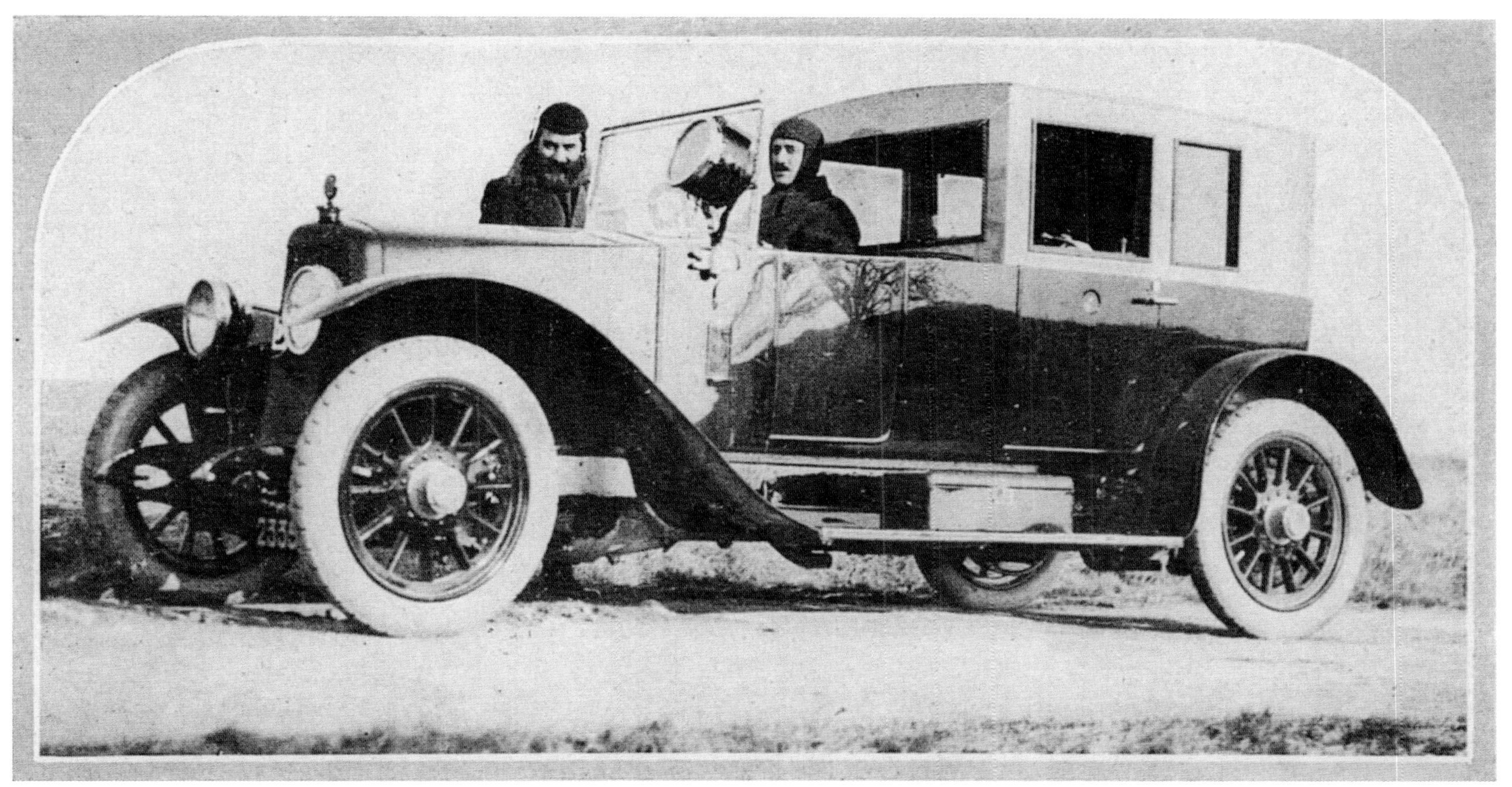

FIG. 100
Designed by Émile-Jacques Ruhlmann, French, 1879–1933; published by Guillaume Janneau, French, 1887–1981; *Panhard et Levassor Coupé de ville*, c.1920; illustrated in "Le Mouvement moderne," *La Renaissance de l'art française et des industries de luxe*, January 1, 1921

From Opulence, Efficiency

Despite its undeniable public success, the exhibition's failure to meaningfully engage the pressing issues of modern life contributed to its complicated legacy. Significant resources were poured into the construction of extravagant structures that were dismantled at the fair's end. As Gabriel Mourey argued in his 1925 review in *L'Amour de l'art*, architects and designers at the fair ignored "the three principles of economy that govern contemporary life: saving money, saving space, saving materials."[61] With their emphasis on surface ornamentation and celebration of handcraft, the immobile shells of Binder and Henri-Labourdette, exempt from engine grease and exhaust, were veritable microcosms of the fair's plaster show houses (FIG. 99). Nevertheless, they also reflected the possibilities of modern space planning, new materials, and principles of aerodynamics. Transformable furniture was on full display in the transport section. So, too, were hidden hinges, synthetic leather, and ingenious door handles. Le Corbusier, Pierre Jeanneret, Sonia Delaunay, and Robert Mallet-Stevens were already beginning to articulate the impact of automobiles on the fields of design and architecture at the Pavillon du Tourisme and Pavillon de l'Esprit nouveau. After lauding the fair's transport section, Gaston Varenne reflected that even the furniture of Ruhlmann, at its most stripped-down, showed signs of this new artistic path (FIG. 48).[62] Before long, the Paris-based designers Eileen Gray, Pierre Chareau, and Charlotte Perriand would fully harness these "principles of economy" to create flexible, lightweight, articulating furniture that "borrowed more and more frequently from the automobile" (FIGS. 97, 98).[63]

Citroën and Delaunay-Belleville understood implicitly that the automobile industry would not flourish on the backs of engineers alone, even if many modernists suggested otherwise. Manufacturers needed artists and designers to endlessly reimagine the automobile of the future and capture the attention of easily distracted consumers in an increasingly competitive marketplace. Born of technological innovation and experimentation and accelerated by the military economy, French automobiles proliferated thanks to the soft power of fashion, advertising, spectacle, and craft. Although the *ensemblier* Émile-Jacques Ruhlmann's name is hardly synonymous with advanced technology, he adored automobiles, from his first purchase of a speedy De Dion-Bouton in 1908. Indeed, he engaged with its production long before Le Corbusier sketched his idea for *Le Plan Voisin* or the *Voiture minimum* (PAGE 104). In 1921, he designed the coachwork for his own Panhard et Levassor *Coupé de ville*—a low, two-tone, closed-body car that bore his initials on the doors (FIG. 100).[64] Ruhlmann affectionately nicknamed the car "The Escape."[65] Slow work had a place in fast times.

1 Robert Forrest Wilson, *Paris on Parade* (Indianapolis: Bobbs-Merrill, 1925), 5–6.

2 For further discussion of the origins of the fair, see Charlotte Benton, "The International Exhibition," in *Art Deco 1910–1939*, ed. Charlotte Benton, Tim Benton, and Ghislaine Wood (Boston: Bulfinch Press, 2003), 141–55.

3 Helen Appleton Read, "International Exposition of Decorative Arts in Paris Has Practical Background for Display of Bizarre and Exotic Atmosphere of Luxury," *The Brooklyn Daily Eagle*, August 23, 1925, 16.

4 Gaston Varenne, "L'Exposition des Arts Décoratifs," *Art et décoration*, July 1, 1925, 15.

5 Guillaume Janneau, "Introduction à l'Exposition des Arts Décoratifs," *Art et décoration*, May 1925, 129.

6 *Delaunay-Belleville Portfolio with Carrosserie Designs by Benito, Lelong, Lepape, Martin, and Ruhlmann* (Paris: P. Draeger, 1924). The publication of the portfolio predates the fair. It is not clear if the designs or portfolios were exhibited, but Janneau used images of the "sketches" in two articles about the fair. Guillaume Janneau, "L'Exposition," *Le Bulletin de la vie artistique*, May 1, 1925, 185–88.

7 Benton, "International Exhibition," 146.

8 For more information on the evolving role of the *ensemblier* in early twentieth-century France, see Stéphane Laurent, "The Artist-Decorator," in Benton, Benton, and Wood, *Art Deco 1910–1939,* 165–71.

9 *St. Louis Post-Dispatch,* May 2, 1925, 13.

10 Ministère du Commerce, de l'Industrie, des Postes et des Télégraphes, *Exposition internationale des arts décoratifs et industriels modernes, Paris 1925: Rapport général; Section artistique et technique,* vol. 7: *Jouets, appareils scientifiques, instruments de musique, moyens de transport (Classes 16 à 19)* (Paris: Librairie Larousse, 1928), 78.

11 E. de Saint-Rémy, "Pourquoi nous n'aurons pas de Salon de l'Automobile en 1925," *La Vie automobile*, March 10, 1925, 102–3.

12 André Fréchet, "L'Art de la carrosserie et l'automobile de luxe," *Art et décoration*, 1921, 57.

13 "La carrosserie automobile a L'Exposition des arts décoratifs," *Omnia*, June 1, 1925, n.p.

14 Guillaume Janneau, "Le Mouvement moderne," *La Renaissance de l'art française et des industries de luxe*, January 1, 1921, 536.

15 Peter Larsen and Ben Erickson, *Jacques Saoutchik: Maître carrossier* (Deerfield, IL: Dalton Watson Fine Books, 2014), 145. Marie-Anne Raymonde Blanche Alphonsine Moreau was introduced to Jacques Saoutchik by his brother Georges, who also worked for Poiret.

16 Jean Henri-Labourdette, *Un siècle de carrosserie française* (Lausanne: Edita, 1971), 34.

17 Henri Petit, "Comment l'automobile est venue à la femme," *Art, goût, beauté*, October 1931, n.p.

18 P. Morel, "La Carrosserie française aux arts décoratifs," *L'Industrie automobile et aéronautique* (1925): 8.

19 Pierre de Trévières, "L'Age du losange," *L'Art et la mode*, April 1925, n.p.

20 J. R. F., "L'Auto encore, L'auto ouvert," *Vogue*, January 1925, 23.

21 Marcel Valotaire, "La Maîtrise, A Creative Force in Decorative Art," *The Studio* 96 (1928): 325–26. This article quotes Dufrêne from a 1921 article in *The Studio*.

22 Stéphane Laurent, "The Artist-Decorator," in Benton, Benton, and Wood, *Art Deco 1910–1939,* 167–70.

23 Ministère du Commerce et al., *Exposition internationale,* 8:78.

24 Morel, "La Carrosserie française," 9.

25 Jared Goss, *French Art Deco* (New York: Metropolitan Museum of Art, 2014), 73–79. Dunand's workshop, which numbered some 100 artisans, required such an enormous quantity of quality eggshells that Dunand kept his own flock of chickens.

26 Liliane Sarcey, "Une visite à l'atelier de M. Jean Dunand, 3.12.1925," *Conferencia, Journal de l'Université des Annales* 9 (1926): 438–45.

27 Félix Marcilhac and Amélie Marcilhac, *Jean Dunand* (Paris: Éditions Norma, 2020), 62.

28 Tim Benton, "Eileen Gray's *Jean Désert* showroom 217 Rue du Faubourg Saint-Honoré, Paris: Marketing Design in the 1920s," *Les Cahiers de la recherche architecturale urbaine et paysagère*, November 3, 2021, doi.org/10.4000/craup.8850.

29 "Jean Dunand," *L'Art d'aujourd'hui,* Spring 1927, 17–18.

30 Marcilhac and Marcilhac, *Jean Dunand*, 390–91.

31 La Société des Laques Indochinoises, "L'Exploitation des travailleurs coloniaux," *L'Humanité*, September 4, 1924, entreprises-coloniales.fr/inde-indochine/Laques_indochinoises.pdf, 3–4.

32 "Une industrie indochinoise qui a très bien réussi à Paris: Les ouvriers en laque," *L'Écho annamite*, January 28, 1929, entreprises-coloniales.fr/inde-indochine/Laques_indochinoises.pdf, 6–7.

33 Édouard Bénédictus, "Invention du Verre Triplex," *Glaces et verres* 18 (October 1930): 9–10.

34 "Grand Réalisations/Transports," Archives de Saint-Gobain, archives.saint-gobain.com/ressource/xxe/1932/renault-ne-jure-que-par-securit-et-triplex-1932.

35 Tag Gronberg, *Designs on Modernity: Exhibiting the City in 1920s Paris* (Manchester: Manchester University Press, 1998), 128.

36 *The Guardian*, Friday, July 3, 1925, 11.'

37 Several period press articles suggest Fernand Jacopozzi unsuccessfully approached the 1925 fair organizers with his plan for illuminating the tower before securing funding from Citroën. See Xavier Boissel, *Paris est un leurre: La véritable histoire du faux Paris* (Paris: Inculte, 2017), 51–63.

38 Jacques Séguéla, *100 Years of Citroën Advertising* (Paris: Flammarion, 2019), 59.

39 Citroën commissioned the sculptor François Bazin to create an automobile mascot based on one of the expedition's most famous photographs of Nobosudru, an aristocratic Mangbetu woman from the Congo.

40 Lance Cole, *Citroën: The Complete Story* (Ramsbury: Crowood Press, 2014), n.p.

41 Félix Marcilhac, *R. Lalique* (Paris: Éditions de l'Amateur, 2004), 496–98.

42 *L'Illustration Paris*, translated in "An 'Ad' on the Eiffel Tower," *Kansas City Star*, August 10, 1925, 11.

43 "Eiffel Tower Night Sign: A Flaming Disfigurement," *The Guardian*, July 3, 1925, 11.

44 Le Corbusier, *The Decorative Art of Today*, trans. James I. Dunnett (Cambridge, MA: MIT Press, 1987), XXV.

45 Simonetta Fraquelli, "Paris as Muse: Robert Delaunay's Paintings, 1909–38," in *Robert Delaunay and the City of Lights*, trans. Alexandra Cox and Caroline Schmidt (Heidelberg: Kehrer, 2018), 15.

46 Sonia Delaunay, Jacques Damase, and Patrick Raynaud, *Nous irons jusqu'au soleil* (Paris: R. Laffont, 1978), 65–66.

47 Dirk Van Oost, "Cars: Colors on the Move," in *Sonia Delaunay: Living Art* (New York: Bard Graduate Center, 2024), 198–99.

48 Robert Delaunay and Sonia Delaunay, *The New Art of Color: The Writings of Robert and Sonia Delaunay* (New York: Viking, 1978), 139.

49 Charles J. Connick, "Stained Glass, Too, Has Its Modernists," *Bulletin of the Stained Glass Association of America* 21, no. 2 (March 1926): 7.

50 Helen Appleton Reid, "The Exposition in Paris," *The Studio* 82 (November 1925): 96.

51 Richard Difford, "Infinite Horizons: Le Corbusier, the Pavillon de l'Esprit Nouveau Dioramas, and the Science of Visual Distance," *Journal of Architecture* 14, no. 3 (2009): 295–323.

52 For discussion of Le Corbusier's "engineer's aesthetic," see Tag Gronberg, "Making up the Modern City: Modernity on Display at the 1925 International Exposition," in *L'Esprit Nouveau: Purism in Paris, 1918–1925* (Los Angeles: Los Angeles County Museum of Art, 2001), 102–13.

53 Le Corbusier, "Eyes Which Do Not See: Automobiles," *Towards a New Architecture* (United States: Dover Publications, 2013), 133. Note he uses the term "chassis," industrially manufactured, rather than "automobile," to make his point.

54 Le Corbusier, *The City of Tomorrow and Its Planning*, trans. Frederick Etchells (Cambridge, MA: MIT Press, 1971), 179.

55 In a March 15, 1936, issue of the journal *Excelsior*, announcing Eugène Mongermon's marriage to Suzanne Palinski, his title is listed as director general of the Voisin Factories. *Excelsior: Journal illustré quotidien: informations, littérature, sciences, arts*, March 15, 1936, 2.

56 Pascal Courteault, *Automobiles Voisin 1919–1958* (London: White Mouse, 1991), 15.

57 Le Corbusier, *The Decorative Art of Today*, 84.

58 Tim Benton, "Dreams of Machines: Futurism and l'Esprit Nouveau," *Journal of Design History* 3, no. 1 (1990): 31–32.

59 Christian Dauvergne, "La Lutte contre l'air: Interview de M. Gabriel Voisin," *Art et industrie* (France: n.p., 1927), 56.

60 Gronberg, "Making up the Modern City," 112.

61 Gabriel Mourey, "L'Exposition des Art Décoratifs et Industriels de 1925," *L'Amour de l'art: revue mensuelle*, January 1, 1925, 286.

62 Varenne, "L'Exposition des Arts Décoratifs," 15.

63 Ernest Tisserand, "Feu Le Salon de Réception," *L'Art vivant* 25–26 (1926): 341.

64 Janneau, "Le Mouvement moderne," 561–63.

65 Florence Camard, *Ruhlmann*, trans. Elizabeth G. Heard (New York: Rizzoli, 2011). Camard cites Ruhlmann's design for Delaunay-Belleville reproduced in the 1925 issue of *Art et décoration*. This car, however, was not likely built, and it is more likely that "La Fuite" instead refers to the very similar-looking Panhard et Levassor coupe designed by Ruhlmann and pictured in *La Renaissance de l'art française et des industries de luxe*. She quotes Jules Deroubaix: "the Boss's car that was *La Fuite* [the Escape]. . . . What a beautiful sight! With the initials 'JER' in tiny 10-centimeter letters on the door" (pp. 49, 506).

1931 BUGATTI TYPE 41 "ROYALE" WEINBERGER CABRIOLET

KEN GROSS

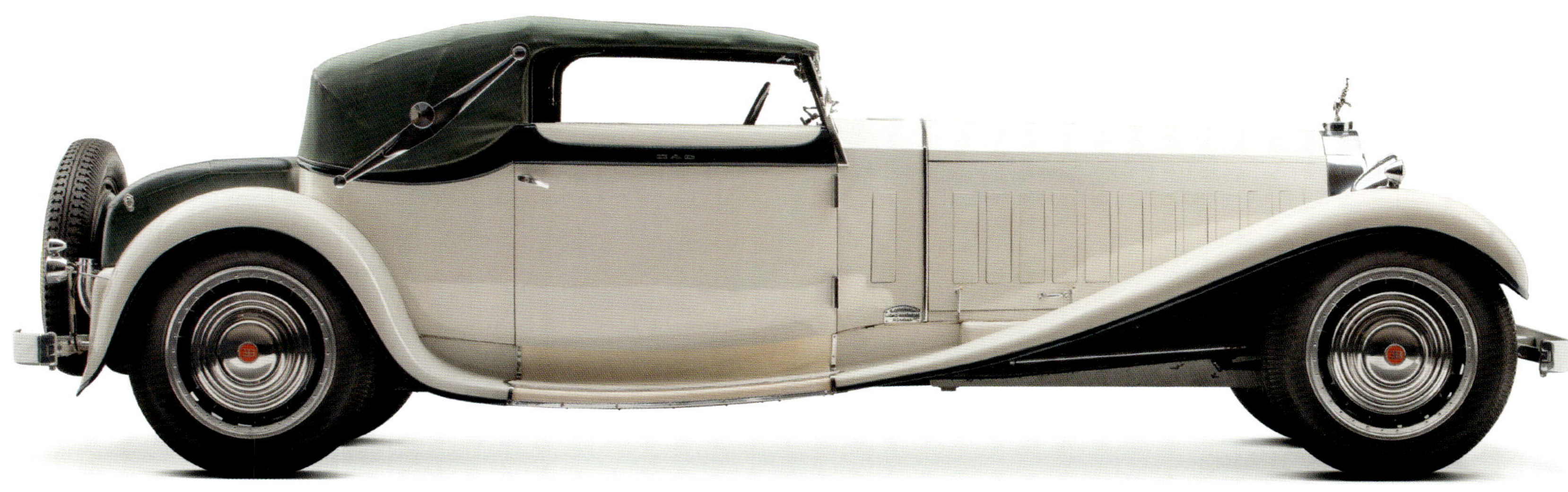

Ettore Bugatti, French (born Italy), 1881–1947; Automobiles Ettore Bugatti, Molsheim, France, active 1909–63; *Type 41 Royale Convertible*, 1931; 62 ½ × 233 × 82 ½ in.; From the Collections of The Henry Ford, Dearborn, Michigan

At a posh dinner in 1927, a British woman reportedly remarked to Ettore Bugatti (1881–1947), "Your cars are fast and beautiful, but for true elegance, one must turn to Rolls-Royce or Bentley."[1] Somewhat miffed, "Le Patron" immediately began developing a luxury car that he had been considering since 1913. It would rival Rolls-Royce and Hispano-Suiza and be enormous in scale, utterly smooth, and whisper-quiet, with a huge 12.7-liter, 300 bhp, inline, single overhead camshaft straight eight. Cast as a single block, the engine had an integral cylinder head, making it very expensive and complex to produce and equally more so to service. Twenty-five examples were planned. Bugatti had royal clients in mind, and one car was reputed to be slated for King Michael of Romania, but that sale never happened. Few Bugattis, the early Brescias being an exception, had model names. Bugattis all had type numbers, but from the outset, this luxury behemoth was known as "La Royale."

Its enormous chassis followed standard Bugatti practice. A three-speed transaxle with the top gear as an overdrive ratio ensured power was smoothly transferred. A touring car body from a Packard was initially fitted so the prototype could be tested extensively. Ettore liked the car and drove it frequently as he refined many details. Just six Type 41 chassis were built. Testing accidents meant that over time, more than six bodies were completed. Each Type 41 was ordered for wealthy clients, and all were built by prominent European coachbuilders. The magnificent proportions of the 21-foot-long car enticed Jean Bugatti (1909–1939), who worked with Joseph Walter on the design of several bodies.

The onset of the Depression meant the market for expensive luxury cars contracted exponentially. Ever innovative, Ettore Bugatti responded to a French government request for powerplants for a new high-speed passenger train. Whether in pairs or in quad powerplant installations, modified Royale engines were used to drive what the French called "Automotrices," or self-propelled railcars. Jean Bugatti tested one of these *wagons rapides* at more than 100 miles per hour and in the process blew out all the glass windows of a train station.[2]

In 1930, Dr. Joseph Fuchs, of Nuremberg, Germany, placed an order for a Royale chassis. He wanted a roadster to be bodied by his usual coachbuilder, Ludwig Weinberger of Munich. Delivered in 1931, the handsome cabriolet featured a prominent folding top, flanked by landau irons. The body was painted black with a distinctive yellow stripe. The rise of Nazi Germany precluded Fuchs from enjoying his new car. He fled

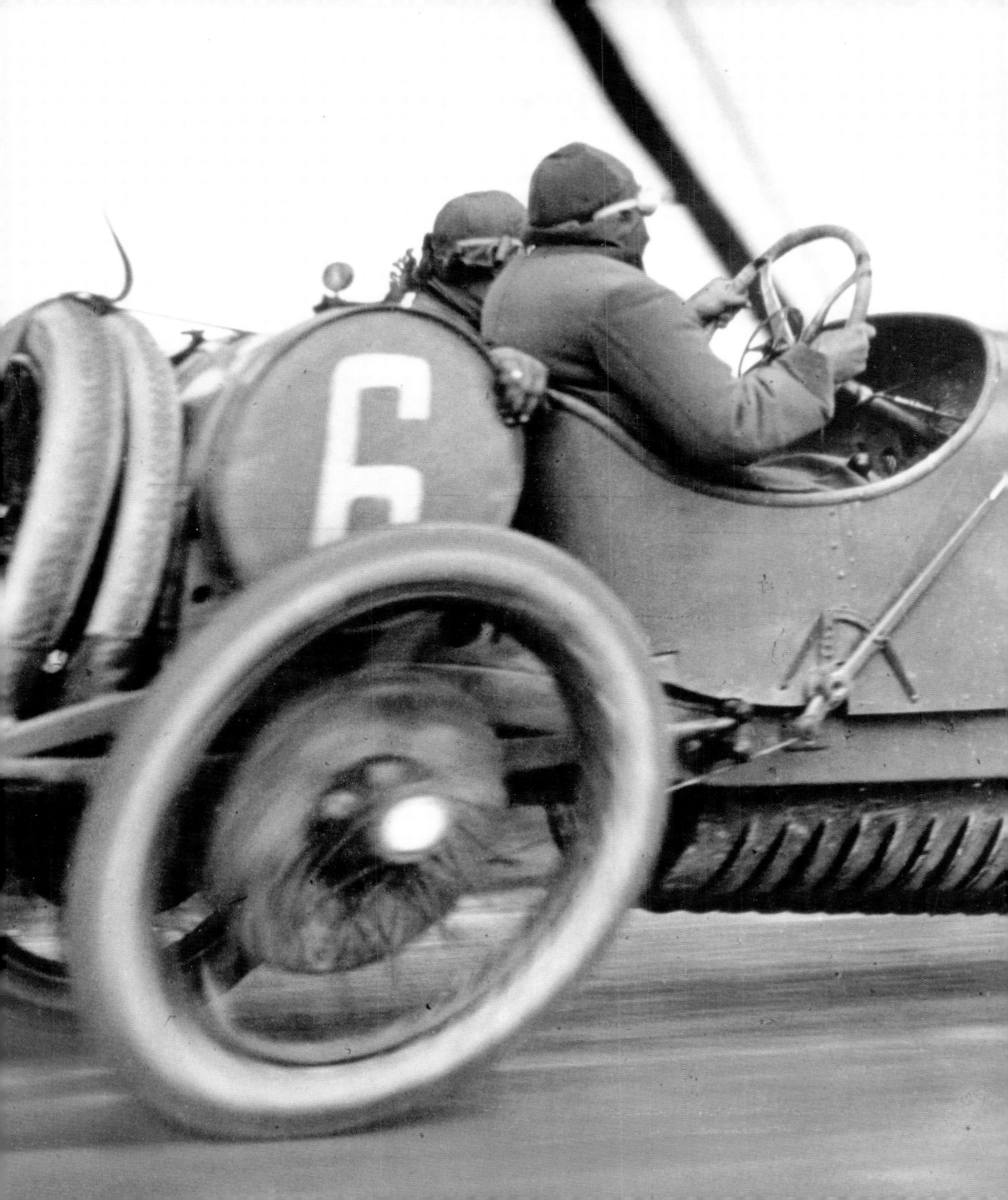
6

CUSTOM COACH-BUILDING IN INTERWAR FRANCE

KEN GROSS

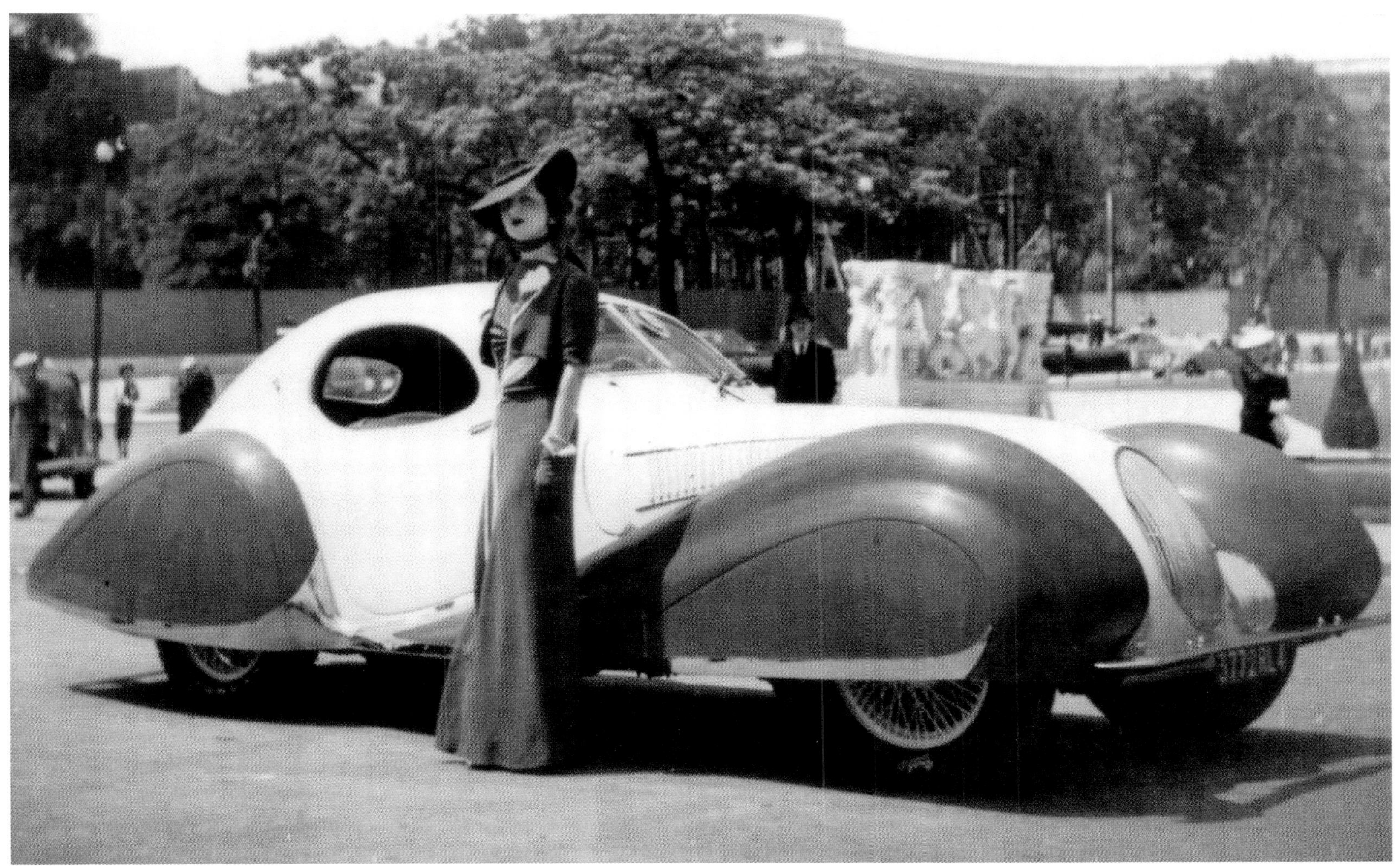

FIG. 101
Stella Mudge, Princess of Kapurthala, wearing an Elise Menneret ensemble, with her 1937 Talbot-Lago by Figoni et Falaschi, at the Concours d'Élégance Féminine at the Trocadero, Paris, June 24, 1938

For decades, classic-car enthusiasts have flocked to posh outdoor events known as *concours d'élégance*, essentially juried fashion shows on wheels. At these gatherings, luxurious, coach-built automobiles are arranged on a magnificent lawn, while beautifully dressed owners, models, and presenters parade past a panel of judges who decide which car and which lady represent the finest pairing on display.

The definitive portrait of this genre is arguably that of Princess Stella (Narinder Kaur) de Kapurthala, posing beside her 1937 Talbot-Lago T150C-SS coupe in a color-coordinated skirt, jacket, and wide-brimmed hat (FIG. 101). (Born in England as Astella Alice Mudge, the former dancer at the Folies Bergère had married an Indian maharajah.) The setting is the Concours d'Élégance Féminine in Paris, and the car's handcrafted coachwork is by the acclaimed Parisian *carrossiers* Figoni et Falaschi (FIG. 102). The image is unforgettable, and it speaks eloquently to the subject of this exhibition.

The *concours d'élégance* originated in the era of the horse-drawn carriage. Those who could afford a bespoke conveyance sought out a coachbuilder to execute a body design to their wishes and specifications. The coachbuilding trade originated long before mechanical engineers invented and perfected internal combustion engines. Less expensive production carriage bodies and even commercial wagons were available, but the best coaches were meticulously handcrafted, hand-painted, and trimmed and upholstered with the finest materials. The result was the ultimate in personalized land transportation, and the term "carriage trade" became a euphemism for wealthy clientele.

The carriage tradition carried over into the automobile industry. Why settle for a mass-produced car body when you can have one custom crafted to your exact taste and requirements? Many of the resulting body styles and their nomenclature emanated from the carriage era. Traditional coach names like phaeton, landaulette, sedanca de ville, cabriolet, shooting brake, coupé de ville, and brougham evolved into popular custom and later even some mass-produced body styles. Writing in *The Beaulieu Encyclopedia of the Automobile*, Brian Sewell noted:

> Once the horseless carriage period was over, [the coachbuilder] was the craftsman

who could make a car, if not go faster, certainly make it look as though it could. He could lower and lengthen bonnets, fair the wings, incorporate the boot, split and rake the windscreen, dispense with running boards, camouflage bulk with parti-colors and the hand-drawn coachline, enclose the front wheels and spat [skirt] the rear and with the deliberate use of line and balance, create an impression of performance, deceptive but often very beautiful.[1]

The transition from carriage building to custom coachwork for cars took place at the dawn of the automotive age. Fledgling automakers who had been engaged as bicycle manufacturers, in locomotive works, as machine-tool suppliers, and in many other businesses were able to build engines and chassis, and even assemble vehicles, and the carriage makers were already in the business of providing wood-framed bodywork. As the demand for horse-drawn carriages receded, the carriage makers were able to turn their operations quickly to satisfy the new orders for automobiles.

In the coachbuilding era, specialist companies in the United States, the United Kingdom, and Europe were engaged in crafting fully bespoke and semicustom production bodies. With the advent of unit-body construction, this practice came to an end. At the same time, the taste for an expensive, bespoke custom body, purpose-built for a flashy new roadster or dignified limousine, went out of fashion.

In postwar Italy, *carrozzerias* like Pininfarina, Ghia, Vignale, Zagato, and Boano continued to produce custom bodies for more exclusive marques like Ferrari and Maserati. Pininfarina and Bertone made production-run bodies for Alfa Romeo and others. In France, Chapron, Saoutchik, Figoni et Falaschi, and Letourneur et Marchand continued to operate in the immediate postwar period, but restrictive tax policies on luxury goods doomed automakers like Delahaye, Delage, and Bugatti, and unless a coachbuilder could produce more commercial work, such as truck bodies, they closed their doors.

For the first decade after 1900, most early automobile bodies were open styles, some with folding tops. The framework was constructed from hardwood, like kiln-dried ash, and the bodywork consisted of fabric or metal panels, or a combination of the two, attached to it. As aircraft construction quickly evolved from fabric to metal material, and shapes transitioned from boxy silhouettes to curves, automobile bodies followed suit. Windshields soon appeared. Wheels progressed from wooden to wire spokes, and then were crafted of steel or aluminum. Doors, which had been an option on carriages, became more commonplace on cars. Closed bodies, with glass windows to protect passengers from the elements, began to supplant open styles. Cloth upholstery, in addition to the traditional leather or leatherette, also began to be used for interiors. Coach painting, a term for a finish meticulously applied with a paintbrush, gave way to superior new coatings that were sprayed on. The noted automobile restorer David Cooper wrote, "When you look at the finest prewar classic cars, you see only the art of the coachbuilder. Everything visible and tactile, the custom handmade body and the interior, is the work of the coachbuilder."[2]

FIG. 102
Joseph Figoni (middle) celebrates the 1933 Le Mans win of the Alfa Romeo 8C 2300, which he bodied, with drivers Tazio Nuvolari (left) and Raymond Sommer (right)

FIG. 103
The Figoni et Falaschi workshop with Claude Figoni in the center, 1939

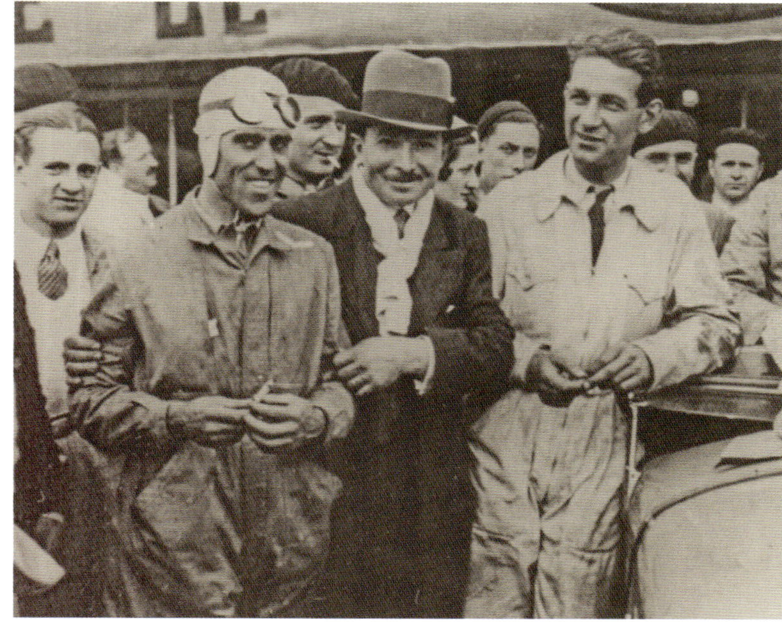

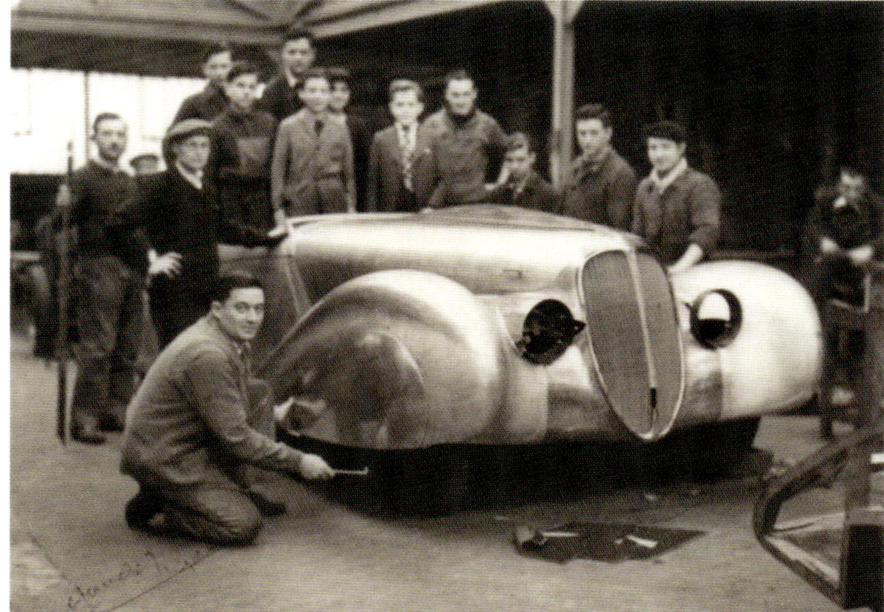

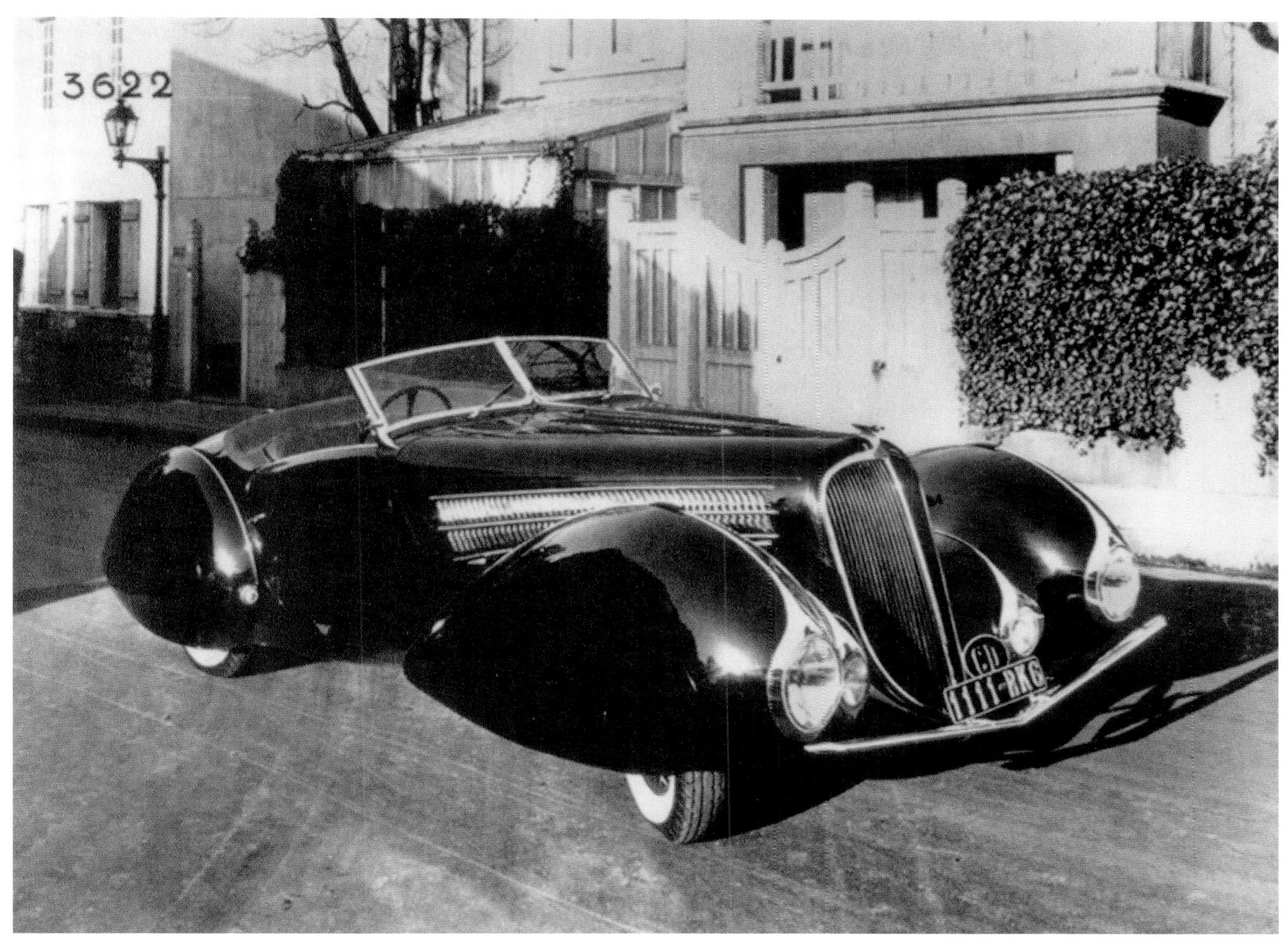

In the early days, very few auto manufacturers built the bodies for their cars. They completed a rolling chassis, with the engine and drivetrain, then shipped it to a coachbuilder for completion. The automaker's efforts were hidden under the sheet metal or the fabric, in the case of a Weymann patent or similar leatherette body. "The coachbuilder's work," Cooper explains, "expresses the style, elegance and beauty of a fine automobile, much as a couturier's dress adorns and presents a beautiful woman. In essence, each of these cars was built by two companies. You *see* the work of the coachbuilder, and you experience and *feel* the work of the manufacturer as you drive the car."[3] According to Ovidio Falaschi, "We really were true couturiers of automotive coachwork, dressing and undressing a chassis one, two, three times and even more before arriving at the definitive line that we wanted to give to a specific chassis-coachwork ensemble" (FIG. 103).[4]

The creation of a custom design usually began with a visit to a coachbuilder or, in rare cases, a high-end dealer. Wealthy patrons could request a custom body that accorded with their specifications and individual taste. Alternatively, they could order a catalogue body—one that was already designed—from the coachbuilder and have selected elements altered. In either case, the process took time, as long as four to six months. If the work was to be personalized and completely customized, the clients might be shown sketches or color renderings. They would work with the coachbuilder to refine the design until they were satisfied. In the case of a catalogue body, upholstery options and exterior paint choices could be selected, not unlike the process for ordering a bespoke suit or gown from a tailor or couturier. Coachbuilders often prepared a wooden model or miniature car that could be painted, allowing a client to imagine the car in their color choice. Some of these lavish renderings have survived today, and they are very artistic (and very valuable).

The principal mechanical constraint was the specific chassis chosen. A proposed design had to fit the manufacturer's chassis exactly. To that

FIG. 104
Delahaye 135MS roadster featured at the Paris Auto Salon in 1936, illustrated in Richard Adatto and Diana Meredith's *Figoni on Delahaye* (Deerfield, IL; Dalton Watson Fine Books, 2023)

end, the critical fixed points on the chassis—the radiator location, its angle and height, the firewall, the wheel openings, et cetera—were predetermined. The designer then worked within those dimensions to render the hood, fenders, body style, and specific two- or four-door configuration. A few luxury carmakers, like Duesenberg, sold most of their automobiles as a complete running but bare chassis, with the factory radiator and imposing grille, hood, cowl, fenders, running boards, bumpers, and even some accessories, and the coachbuilder worked within those parameters. Rolls-Royce, Mercedes-Benz, and many others preferred this approach. With the car's basic design decided, a draftsman would then render full-scale front, side, and top elevations. In the classic era, long before the use of modeling clay became prevalent, the coachbuilder's skilled team would fashion a full-sized, 1:1 scale, wire framework (called a maquette) by hand, which allowed the artisans to envision the car in three dimensions before building it. That procedure helped work out any design details that could not be resolved in two dimensions on paper.

E. PFISTER, **51, Avenue de Colombes, GENNEVILLIERS**
Constructeur **(Seine)**
Reg. Com. SEINE 159.119 **Tél. : GRÉsillons 15-81**

La MACHINE UNIVERSELLE
INDISPENSABLE pour le TRAVAIL des métaux en feuilles

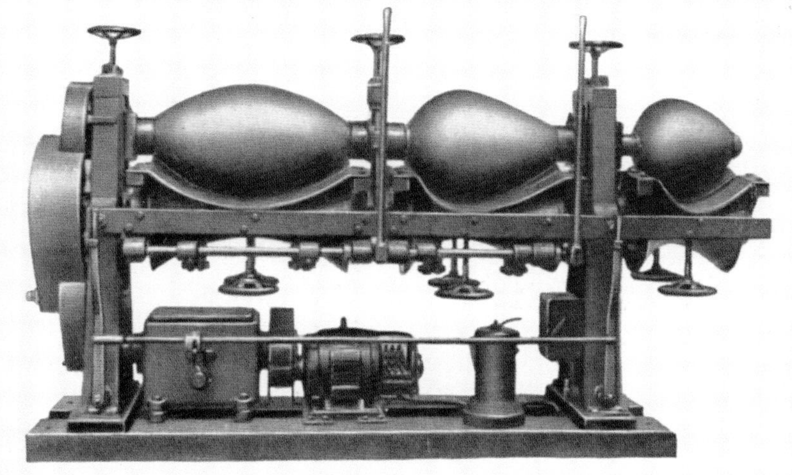

CARROSSERIES
TOLERIES
AUTOMOBILES
AVIATION
AUTOCARS
AUTOMOTRICES

Cette machine munie de 3 jeux de molettes de différents rayons permet de former et cintrer **LES PIÈCES LES PLUS DIVERSES** de la carrosserie automobile, sans changement de molettes.

MEILLEURES et Nombreuses Références.
Prix sur demande.

FIG. 105
Three Olive Machine advertisement

Coachbuilding craftsmen would first construct a wooden skeleton in the shape of the body. Once assembled, this framework served as a permanent structure over which the metal panels of the actual body were attached. No wood was visible, except perhaps on an instrument panel, door trim, or a steering wheel where surfaces might be laminated. The process of building the wooden body framework involved skilled carpentry. Dried wood could either be steam-bent, cut down from a larger piece of wood, fabricated from several smaller pieces of wood, spliced with finger joints or dovetails, or built up from several overlapping pieces. Often, the framing components were made from multiple pieces that were glued together. The largest wooden components were usually the solid door posts; they had to support a heavy door and the stress from it being repeatedly opened and closed. Coachbuilders used a variety of approaches to build the structure, and the quality of the wooden skeleton varied from one atelier to another. Two different teams worked to complete this process: iron workers fabricated structural supports and the many brackets needed to hold the body panels, while sheet-metal specialists formed the curved panels.

Cooper notes, "The coachbuilder's art is to fit a complex curved sheet metal skin snugly over the wood skeleton. The larger the sheet metal panels that make up the body, the less welding and joining is needed, enabling faster production."[5] To save time, one group of carpenters would work on the structural wood, while others used the maquette as a guide to build a solid-wood body buck. The metalworkers then used that carefully formed and smoothed buck as a template to ensure the panels

aluminum. In function, the English wheel is the most effective in forming smaller body panels. The device is shaped like a large, closed letter C. At its ends are two small wheels: an upper flat rolling wheel and a lower domed anvil wheel. A single skilled operator holds a sheet of metal, either aluminum or steel, and manipulates it as it is run back and forth to form compound (double) curves. The depth of the C frame is called the throat, and the larger the throat, the larger the metal sheet that can be formed. The design of this device has changed very little since the nineteenth century. Different-

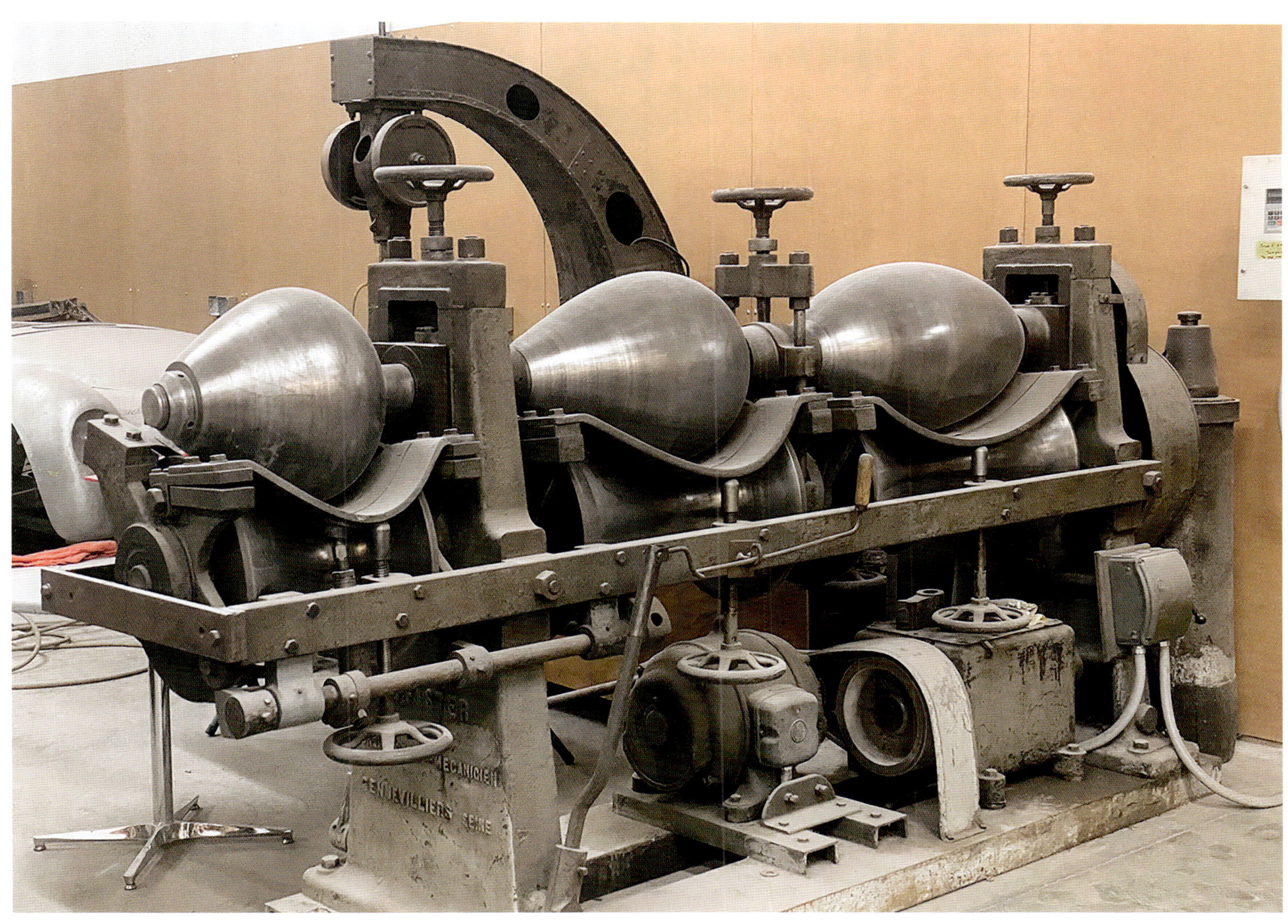

FIG. 106
Three Olive Machine at Cooper Technica Restorations, Wisconsin, 2024

were hand-formed to match the shape of the car's new body. Craftsmen in Italy, specifically those in the Emilia-Romagna region, were known for their metalworking skills, which dated back to the armorers of the Middle Ages. They used sandbags and even sections of tree stumps as hard surfaces on which to hand-hammer and smooth the sheets of aluminum alloy that became the body panels.

In England and North America, many shops used a device called an English wheel (or wheeling machine) to form body panels from sheet

sized anvil wheels can be used to achieve the desired curve or crown. The English wheel is more effective and quicker than the traditional (and somewhat primitive) hammer and dolly method of shaping panels.

When the sheet metal is passed between the wheels, the metal is stretched and it becomes thinner. As the alloy panel stretches, a convex (curved) surface is formed. To achieve panel accuracy, the operator must continually reference the new panel to a forming buck or template. A great

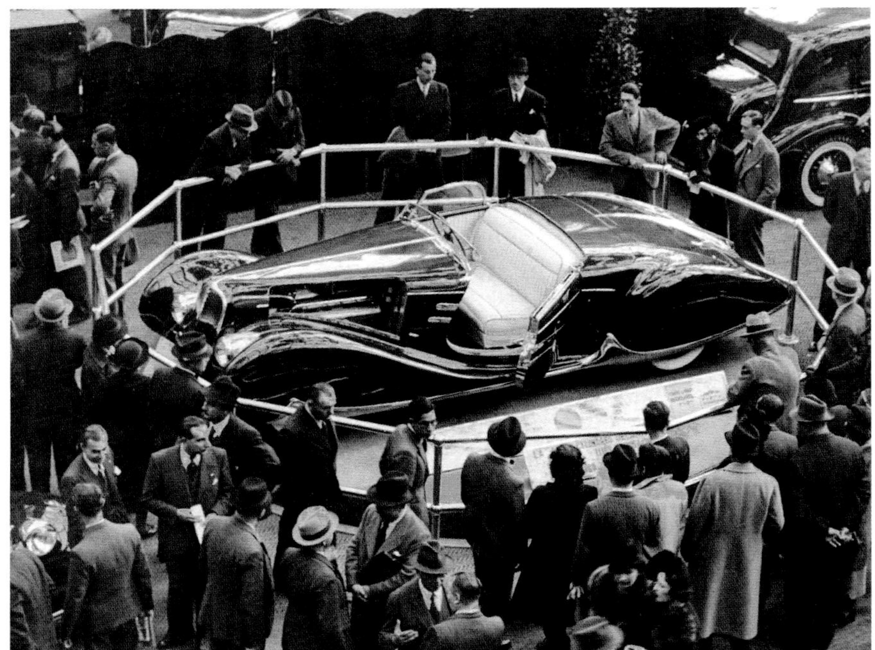

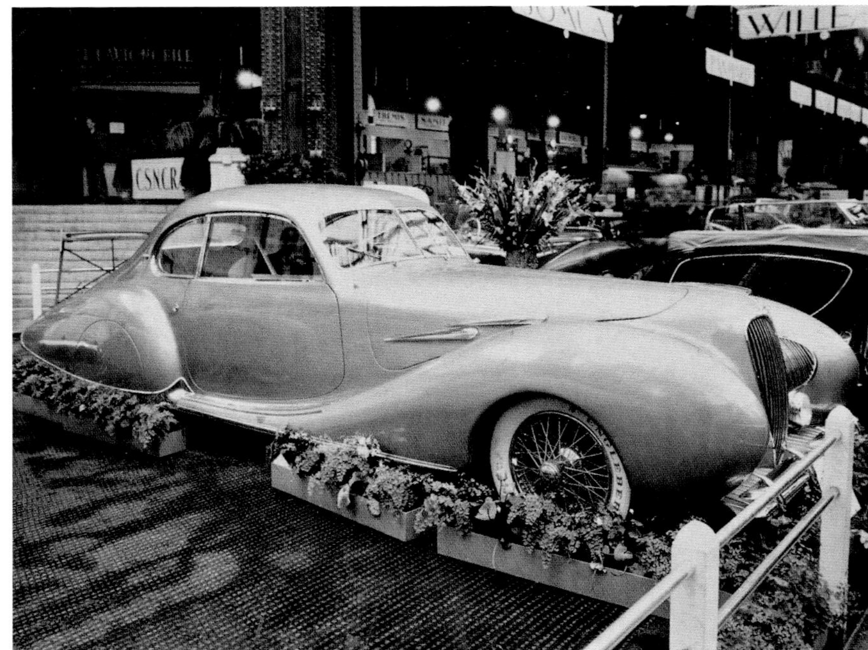

deal of skill (and patience) is required to ensure the flat metal panel is formed in the desired shape. Large panels are difficult to form and are often finished by welding the completed pieces together, then smoothing and filling the separation. Large, low crown panels may require two operators working together to move and manipulate the sheet metal. In some cases, the metal may need to be annealed or carefully heated above its recrystallization temperature and then cooled to increase ductility (softness) and reduce hardness.

In France, a very different crown-forming method was used. The French *carrossiers* used a huge device called a Three Olive machine that was capable of forming very large, curved panels (FIG. 105). The machine, which weighed more than 9,000 pounds and was driven by an 8-horsepower electric motor, required two men to operate. They would stand on either side of the machine and feed the panel back and forth between one of three wide, curved rollers, each shaped differently. As the rollers slowly turned and the alloy panel was manipulated, a curved shape gradually formed. After the operators determined the primary curve—the area of the metal that must be stretched the most—they selected the roller that matched the shape. They then slid the sheet metal back and forth through the Three Olive. The receiving technician turned and twisted the metal, checking the panel against the forming buck repeatedly to ensure a match.

After the shape was determined to be correct, the technician needed to shrink the edges using a power hammer. The panel was fed back through the Three Olive machine for planishing or smoothing. The difference between forming panels with a Three Olive versus an English wheel is considerable. With an English wheel, operators must make many small panels and weld them together. The Three Olive machine's rollers were available in six sizes. Cooper points out, "a well-equipped French coachbuilder would have one or two Three Olive machines, an Eckold shrinking machine, an English wheel, a power hammer and other sheet metal forming tools."[6] Finally, after considerable test fitting, the panels were butt welded together by hand, at low heat, to avoid distortion. The result was a beautiful, continuously curved surface. French *carrossiers* designed cars with voluminous sweeping curves. The Three Olive machine ensured the designers could specify these curvaceous bodies and the work could be done quickly and efficiently.

The process of building a complete body was time-consuming. The French coachwork authority Richard Adatto says that the wooden mockup required about 110 hours to complete. The ironworkers and panel beaters needed between 600 and 700 hours; the painters needed 150 hours; the detailing team responsible for the instrument panel, chrome trim, and glass needed 400 hours; and the upholsterers required another 150 hours. A fully custom body required about 2,200 hours to complete.[7]

Fine automobiles of the 1930s reflected the tastes of the countries that produced them. American luxury brands manufactured large, powerful, multicylinder cars, with long hoods and sweeping fender lines, thus ensuring the magnificent proportions that thrilled designers and coachbuilders

FIG. 107
Delahaye Type 165 at the 1938 Paris Auto Salon, illustrated in Richard Adatto and Diana Meredith's *Figoni on Delahaye* (Deerfield, IL; Dalton Watson Fine Books, 2023)

FIG. 108
Delahaye 135M by Figoni et Falaschi at the 1938 Paris Auto Salon, illustrated in Richard Adatto and Diana Meredith's *Figoni on Delahaye* (Deerfield, IL; Dalton Watson Fine Books, 2023)

from coast to coast. Although there were exceptions, British styling tended to be staid, upright, razor-edged, and even more formal. Italian *carrozzerias*, before the war, began to experiment with gentle streamlining. In Germany, a worship of the Baroque and a Brutalist style that reflected the Fascist government dictated the shape of many luxury vehicles. High-end French cars, especially the dreamy work of Figoni, Saoutchik, Pourtout, Vanvooren, and Letourneur, exuded a palpable joie de vivre (FIG. 110).

When World War I ended, companies like E. I. du Pont de Nemours and other large producers of munitions were left with vast quantities of cordite, a mixture of nitrocellulose and nitroglycerine. Even before the war ended, Du Pont was researching the commercial application of these chemicals in peacetime. Through a fortunate accident, the laboratory engineers discovered that a cellulose nitrate solution, with pigments added, could become a durable, high-gloss, quick-drying finish for automobiles. The traditional oil-based automobile paint of that era required a long time to dry, and the resulting finish was neither ideal nor long-lasting. This new paint sped up the production process—bodies no longer had to dry for weeks—and led to the "garageless car," which could withstand harsh weather conditions.[8]

The new paint also vastly expanded the range of color choices. Firms like Figoni introduced dazzling color combinations, often in pairs and even trios, resulting in bold new looks. Sonia Delaunay and others designed new surface treatments using bright colors in patterns and geometric shapes. This practice did not catch on with exteriors, but innovative automakers like Voisin applied the patterned look in vivid colors to interior fabrics. There were no rules as to what could be used, and in the infancy of the automobile, considerable experimentation took place.

With varying creative influences and a wide range of client input, the leading French *carrossiers* had markedly different styles. Figoni et Falaschi, arguably the best, most creative, and influential of these firms, specialized in streamlining. Giuseppe Figoni lauded and celebrated the teardrop, thought to be the perfect aerodynamic shape, and his talented metalworkers created impossibly curvaceous bodies that were almost fanciful (FIG. 109). Some of his clever features, like a folding windscreen that lowered into the cowl, and wheels that turned under enclosed front fenders, required engineering patents to execute. A fully skirted Delahaye 135MS roadster (FIG. 104), like the Aga Khan's Salon car, could be termed "a Paris gown on wheels."

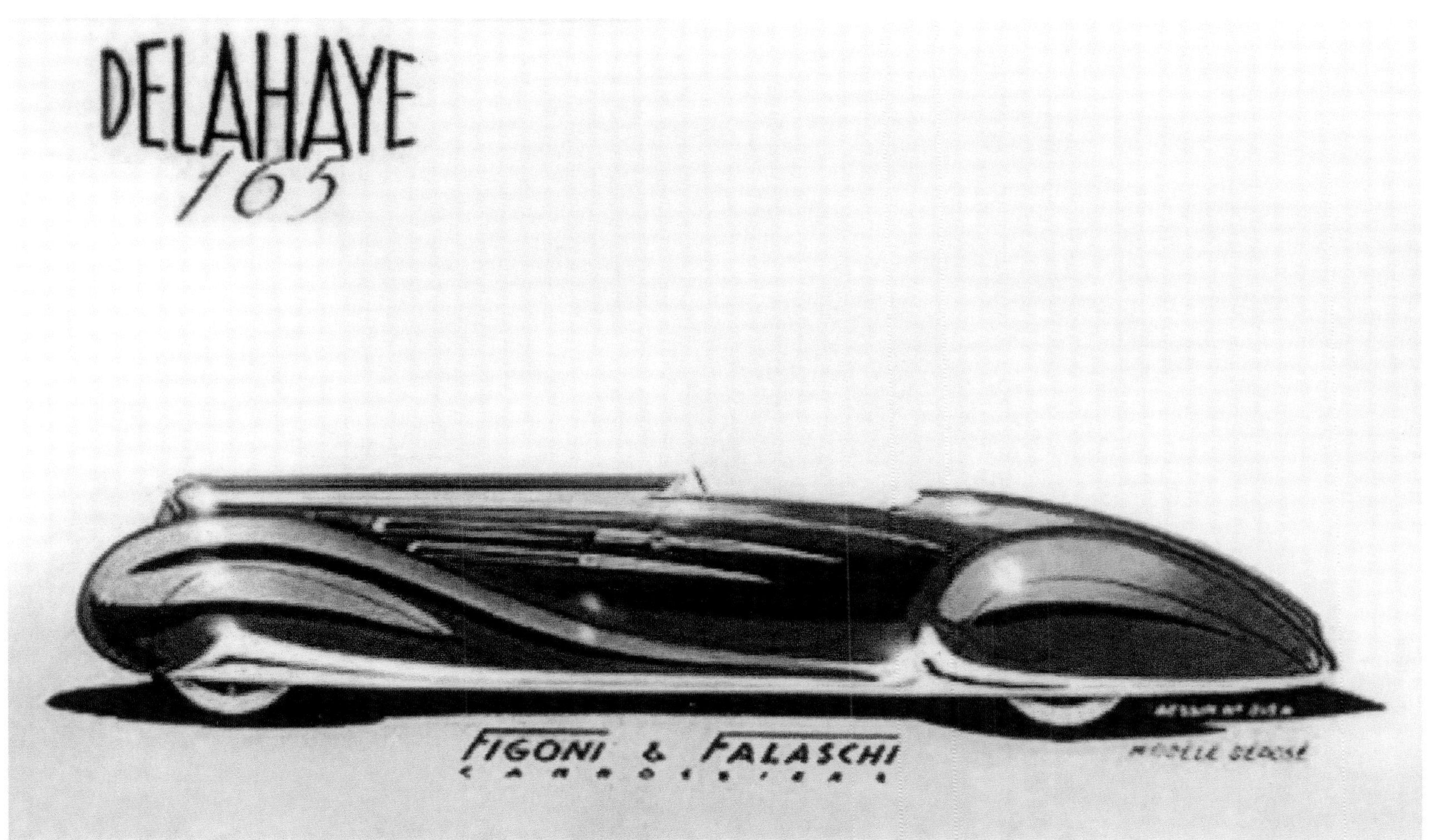

FIG. 109
Advertisement for a Delahaye 165 by Figoni et Falaschi

Saoutchik's designs also displayed very dramatic shapes, and he used a variety of chrome accents, almost to an extreme. Marcel Pourtout's cars, aided with considerable input from the brilliant dental technician-turned-designer Georges Paulin, were somewhat more subdued than Figoni and Saoutchik, but the extended overall lines of his cars implied speed, even while they were standing still. Chapron and Letourneur created beautiful, if less flamboyant, automobiles. The understated Chapron Delage D8-120 Aérosport, built in limited numbers, epitomized the elegant conveyance for a sophisticated lady or gentleman who had wealth and taste but no need to flaunt it.

Vanvooren could execute almost anything, as he did when Figoni was too busy to make the Bugatti 57C for the Shah of Iran (PAGE 176). "Build us a car like Figoni," he was supposedly told on an impossibly short timetable. Recognizing the publicity that would follow from such an assignment, Vanvooren complied. Carrosserie de Villars will forever be known for a sweeping one-off cabriolet that won Best of Show at the Pebble Beach Concours d'Elegance in 1996. Monsieur de Villars's demanding and flashy clientele included Prince Aly Khan and Prince Gourielli, the husband of the cosmetics magnate Helena Rubinstein. Jacques Kellner's work was dignified, formal, and sophisticated. The leading *carrossiers* all affixed discrete signature plates to their cars, usually mounted under the doors, so that they could be read by passersby when parked.

The concept of streamlining has fascinated the auto industry for generations. Beginning in the 1930s, and continuing until the outbreak of World War II, the confluence of developments in aircraft design; the sleek shapes of fast railroad locomotives; advanced highways like the German Autobahns, the Italian Autostradas, and the Pennsylvania Turnpike; along with epoch-changing global events like the 1939 New York City World's Fair, encouraged automotive designers and engineers to imagine, style, and build streamlined cars that were functionally aerodynamic, fast, and increasingly fuel-efficient.

From 1930 to 1942, automobile designs were often organic, emulating the classic teardrop shape that was thought to be perfect for cheating the wind (FIG. 110). The results were brought to life in cars with startling shapes that looked as though they were ready to be embraced and caressed. Even if they were not noticeably faster than their predecessors, they *looked* fast. In a few cases, the conservative public balked. In the United States, sales of well-known brands, like Chrysler, slipped and then recovered as consumers tentatively embraced and then accepted this brave new look.

The influence of streamlining was felt far beyond automotive styling. The popular school of design called Streamline Moderne had an undeniable effect on the shape of radios, appliances, transport trucks, locomotives, and speedboats, along with such household items as table flatware, water pitchers, toasters, pencil sharpeners, and cocktail shakers.

Automotive streamlining, when it first appeared, was equated with modernity as well as efficient aerodynamics. The automobile, a child of the twentieth century that was rapidly changing and evolving mechanically during the 1930s, became the perfect metal canvas for streamlined design. These cars on display, presented as kinetic art, are indeed rolling sculpture, yet they are eminently capable of dynamic function.

The cars in this exhibition were designed without the myriad safety and crash-absorbing features that affect the look and shape of the modern automobile. The operative charge was that they be sleek and streamlined. Arguably the sleek designs from Figoni et Falaschi, appearing on Delahaye and Talbot-Lago chassis, epitomized the ultimate adaptation of streamlined principles to road-going automobiles. The fact that these cars were breathtakingly beautiful was a bonus.

The annual Paris Auto Salon, with its Art Nouveau signage (FIG. 108); the glittering Earl's Court exhibition in London; and the long-running New York Auto Show, with its myriad of automakers and dedicated stands, along with many other contemporary exhibitions in major cities worldwide, were the catalyst for coachbuilders and the general public to view the latest designs (FIG. 107). Bugatti launched its startling Type 57 Aérolithe coupe in London and Paris in 1934. A stunning tour de force, it stopped showgoers in their tracks. Streamlined and svelte with a totally modern shape, it did not resemble any of its still square-rigged competitors, and it was the perfect foil to announce that Ettore and Jean Bugatti had created a bold new platform that could suit many body styles. Coachbuilders debuted new approaches and commissions at the Salon, and wealthy socialites like the Aga Khan often bought the new creations directly from the show stand. Despite the gathering war clouds in Europe in the late 1930s, these lavish auto shows persisted nearly until the outbreak of hostilities.

New coachwork designs were also previewed at *concours d'élégance* in Paris and in the South of France, paired with the work of preeminent designers like Coco Chanel, Nina Ricci, and Jeanne Lanvin. These events received extensive

FIG. 110
Geo Ham cover for *L'Illustration* automobile and tourism issue, Paris, October 3, 1936

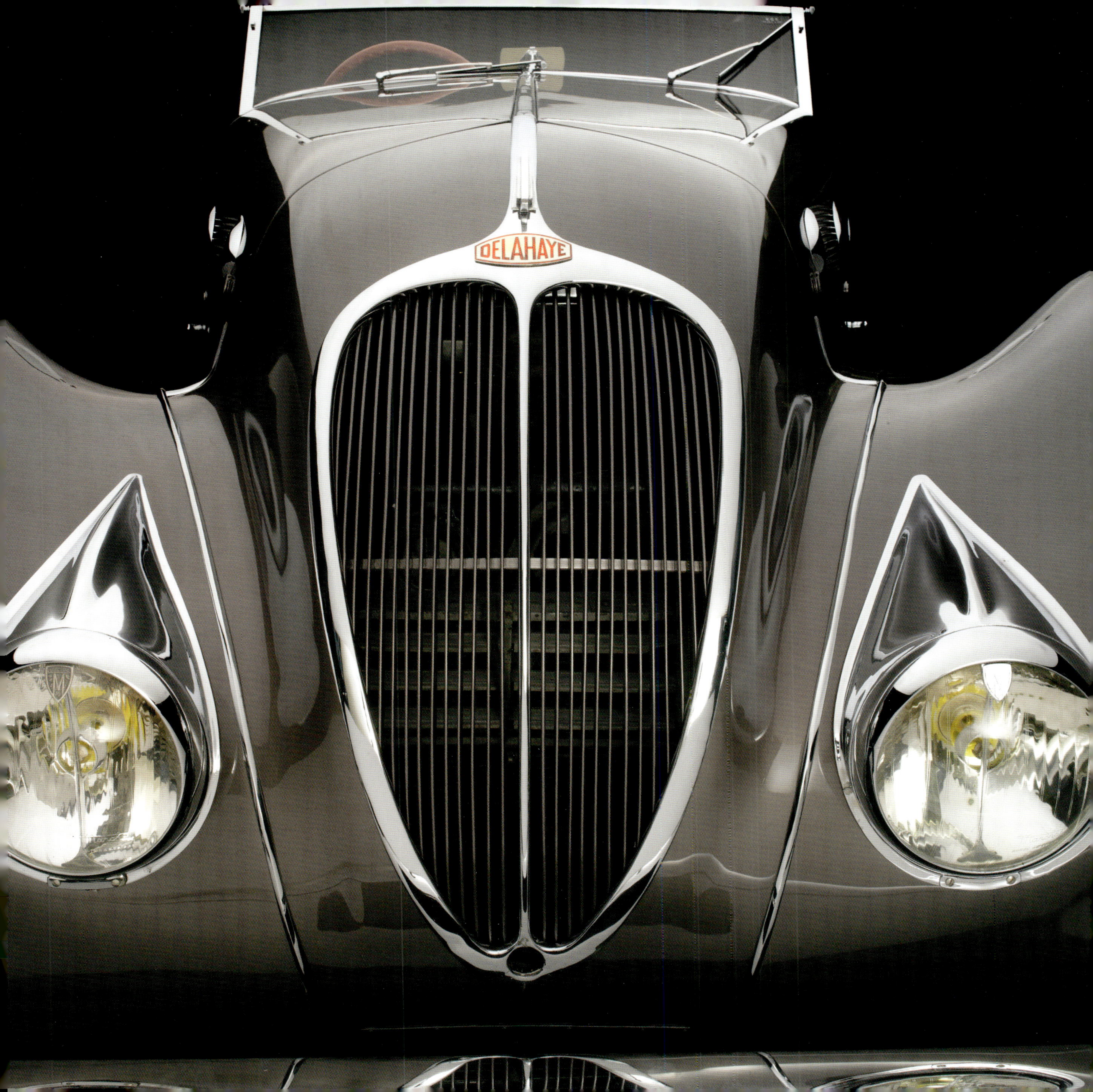
DELAHAYE

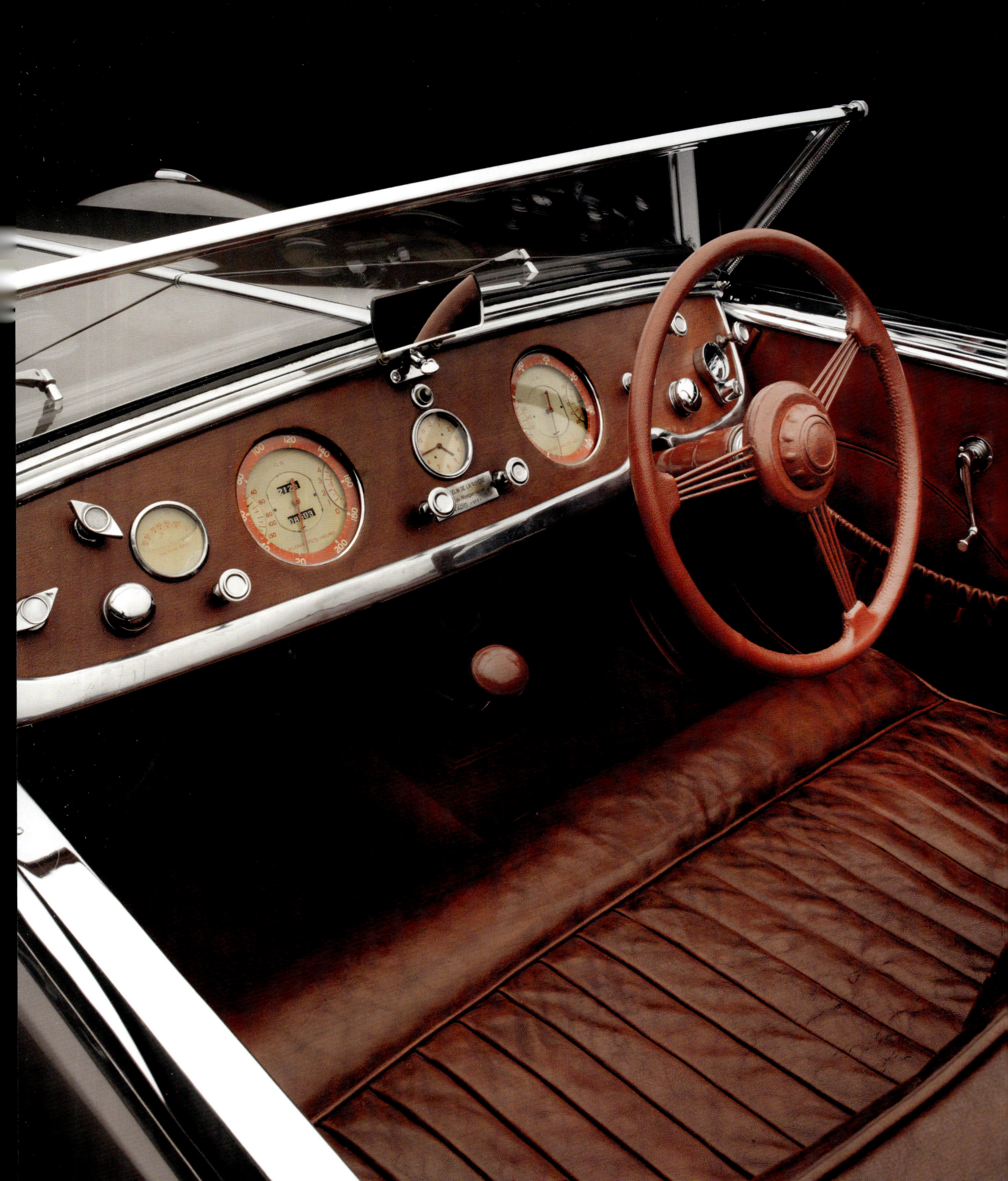

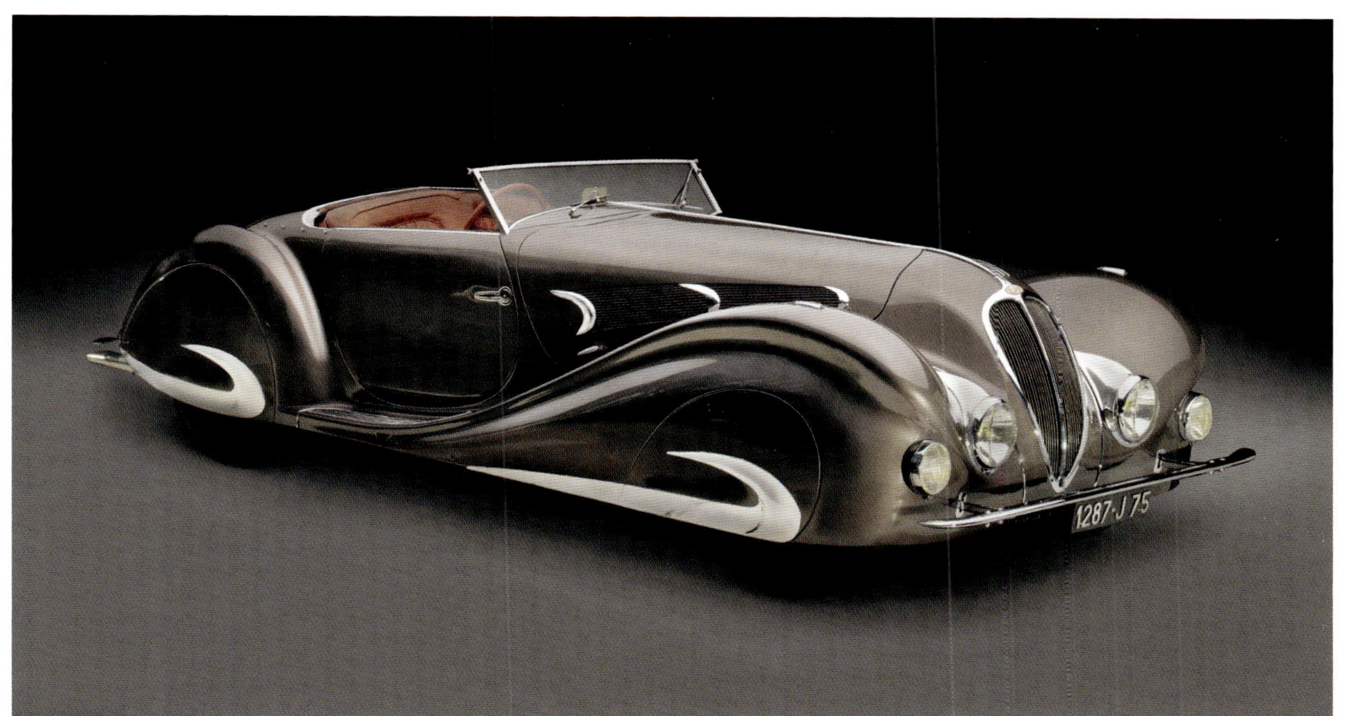

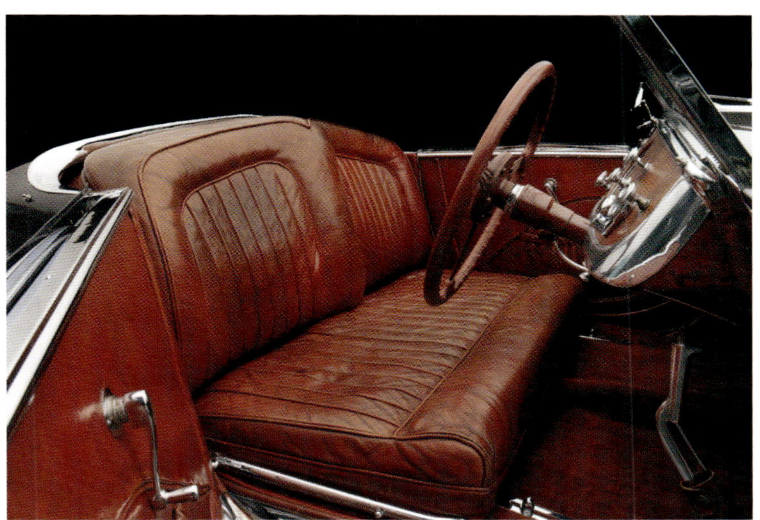

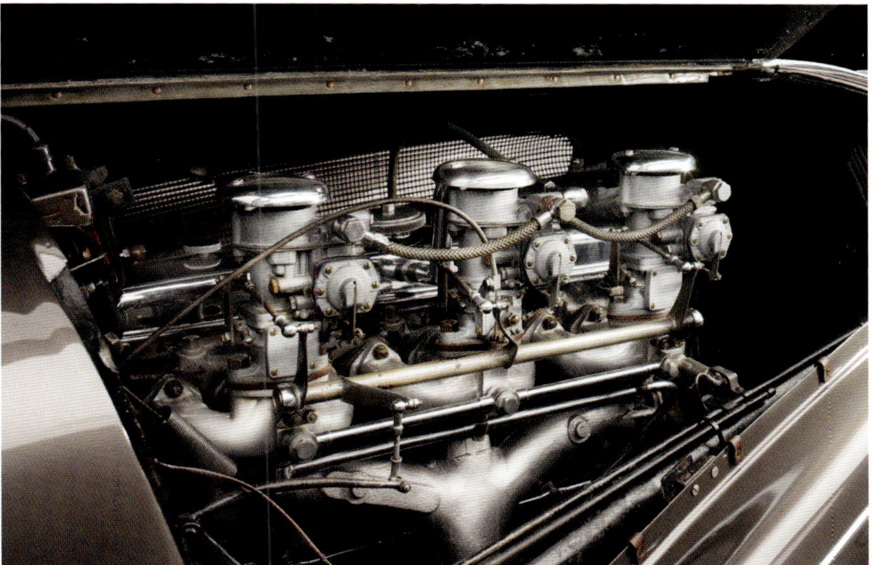

French authorities impounded the car for nearly a year while the correct ownership was determined. The car's owner was able to restore it completely at the Figoni workshop, with assistance from the Delahaye factory. The carburetion system was changed from three up-draft to three down-draft carburetors. Finishing trim touches were applied by the Parisian firm Hermès, which reupholstered the seats and side panels in red leather. The original leather interior, still nicely preserved, has never been restored.[2]

In 1949, chassis no. 48563 was sold to a Mr. Hanselin, who registered it in Paris and repainted it in Bugatti blue. When he sold the car to Jean-François Charton, only 5,200 kilometers had accumulated on the odometer. Charton repainted the roadster ivory in 1978 and drove it very carefully until October 2001, when he sold it to Miles Collier; even then, it had been driven a mere 8,030 kilometers (fewer than 5,000 miles). Collier rebuilt the engine, restored the car, and repainted the Delahaye yet again, this time in a lovely gray-silver. Following its restoration, chassis no. 48563 was shown at the Pebble Beach Concours d'Elegance and again in the exhibition *Rolling Sculpture* at the Vero Beach Museum of Art in 2023.

Loaned by the Miles Collier Collection at the Revs Institute for Automotive Research, Naples, Florida

1 Richard Adatto, *From Passion to Perfection: The Story of French Streamlined Styling* (Paris: Éditions SPE Barthélémy, 2002), 17–19.

2 Richard Adatto and Diana Meredith, *Delahaye Styling and Design* (Deerfield, IL: Dalton Watson Fine Books, 2006), 65–70.

GABRIEL VOISIN: HOMES, HIDEAWAYS, AND A HEAD IN THE CLOUDS

GENEVIEVE CORTINOVIS

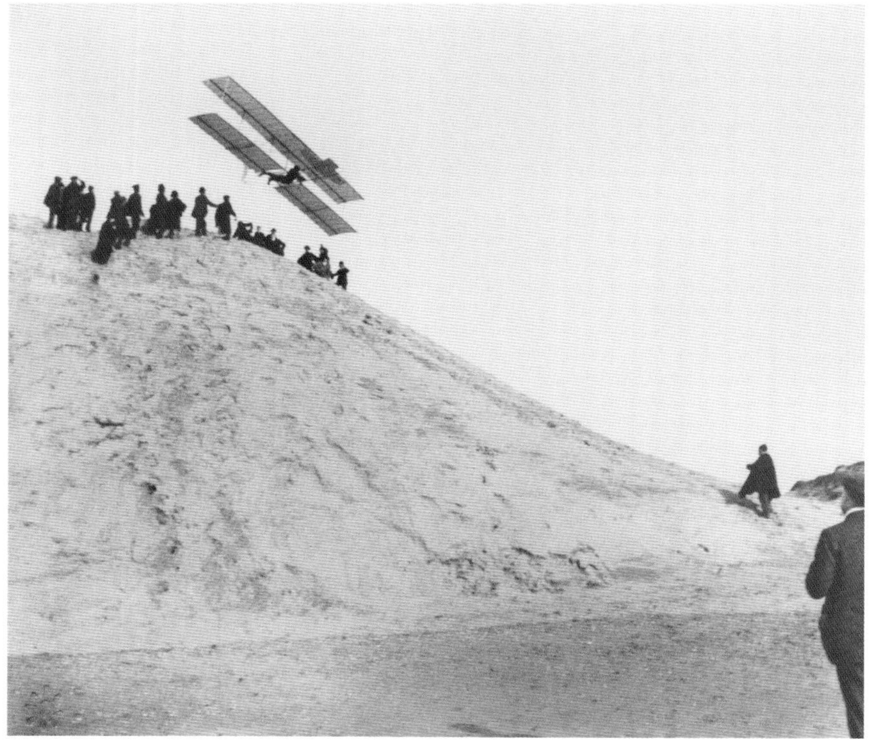

FIG. 112
Jacques-Henri Lartigue, French, 1894–1986; *Merlimont. First Flight of Gabriel Voisin in the Archdeacon Glider*, from "The Lartigue Portfolio," 1904, printed 1978; gelatin silver print; 7 ⅜ × 8 ⅜ in.; Saint Louis Art Museum, Gift of Frederick P. Currier 305:1995.2

Aviation pioneer and trailblazing automobile manufacturer Gabriel Voisin began his career building gliders for Ernest Archdeacon, a French lawyer, balloonist, and aviation booster. In 1904, the photographer Jacques-Henri Lartigue captured Gabriel's first flight at Merlimont on the northern coast of France (FIG. 112). The daring aviator hovers over a small crowd of spectators perched high on a sand dune as he takes off on what would prove to be a short journey. Two years later, Gabriel and his younger brother Charles founded Appareils d'Aviation Les Frères Voisin, the first industrial aeronautical producer in France. From 1912, the company, led by Gabriel after Charles's tragic death in a car accident, primarily manufactured planes for the French military and, at the close of World War I, produced some sixty airplanes a week. Having amassed a considerable fortune, Gabriel was nonetheless at a crossroads at the end of the war. Under pressure to convert his factories to a peacetime economy, he explored commercial aviation, automobiles, and architecture as possible paths forward.[1]

Recognizing the devastation of France's Western Front, Gabriel turned his innovative, if peripatetic, mind to housing. In 1918, he enlisted the help of his longtime friend and former schoolmate André Noël-Noël Telmont and his architectural partner Pierre Patout to design a prefabricated home that could be delivered to its new residents by truck. Steel-framed, the exterior walls and roof of the resulting Maison en Trois Jours, or

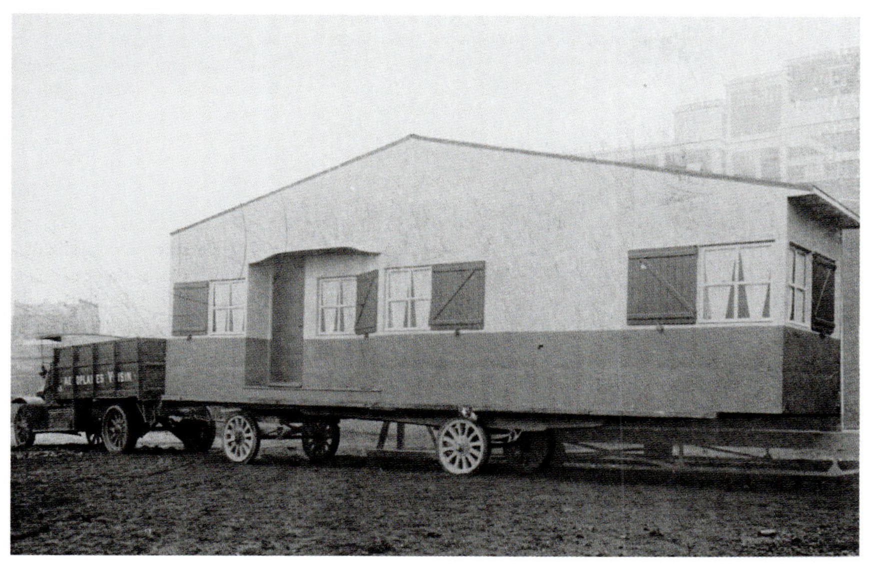

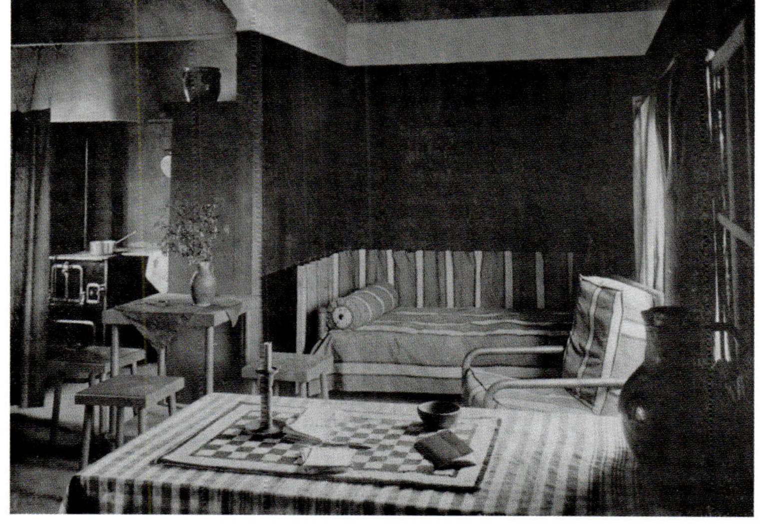

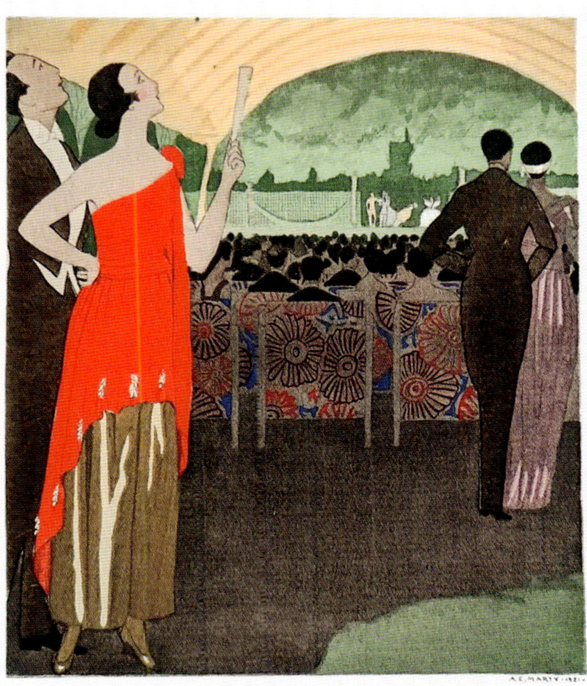

A L'OASIS

OU

LA VOUTE PNEUMATIQUE

ROBE DU SOIR, DE PAUL POIRET

House in Three Days, were constructed of sheet metal that could be impressed with surface decoration (FIGS. 113A, B). Inside, plywood walls, lined with cork for insulation, provided a warm substrate for the simple furniture and crisp striped textiles offered in the firm's furnished examples.[2] Compact but comfortable, the house combined the efficiency and standardization of industrial production with a modern but familiar design, equal parts airplane cockpit and summer cottage. Although lauded as "ingenious" by contemporaries like the modernist architect Le Corbusier, who admired their Fordian construction, the venture was ultimately unsuccessful.[3] Following André Citroën's example, Gabriel pursued automobile production full-time, "retaining the [home's] best technical ideas for reuse in the coachwork" of Voisin automobiles.[4]

Both Telmont and Patout remained key figures in Voisin's personal and professional life. The former became the company's in-house auto-body designer, responsible for many of Voisin's iconic silhouettes, light and lean in the imprint of the firm's first airplanes. The latter went on to design not one but two freestanding homes for Gabriel and his wife, Adrienne-Lola Bernet, in Boulogne-Billancourt, an automobile and airplane manufacturing center at the western edge of Paris. Built between 1921 and 1923, the imposing Hôtel Voisin was framed by large trees on a wooded lot between the boulevard d'Auteuil and the allée des Pins (FIG. 118). Compared to an "ancient theatre" by

FIG. 113A, B
Designed by Pierre Patout, French, 1879–1965; André Noël-Noël Telmont; and Gabriel Voisin, French, 1880–1973; *Maison en Trois Jours*, photograph in *Art et Décoration*, 1921

FIG. 114
André-Edouard Marty, *A l'Oasis, ou, La voûte pneumatique: Robe du soir, de Paul Poiret* illustrated in *Gazette du Bon Ton* 7 (1921): plate 53

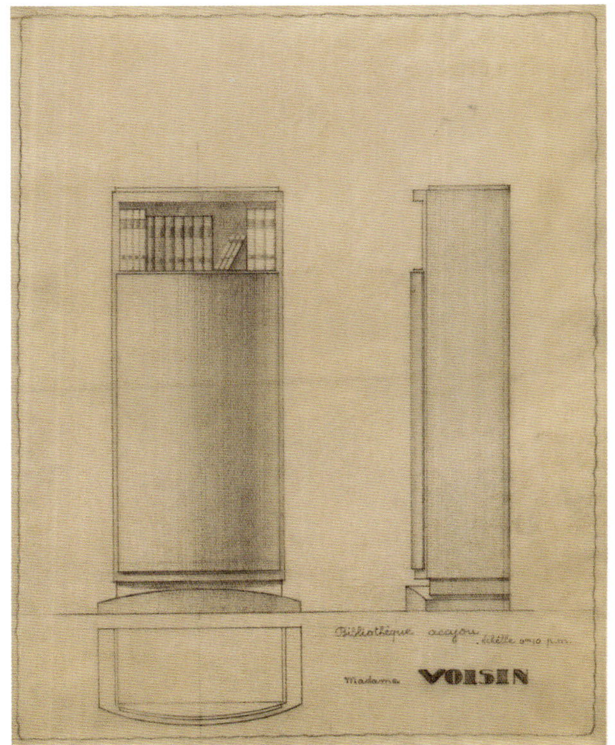

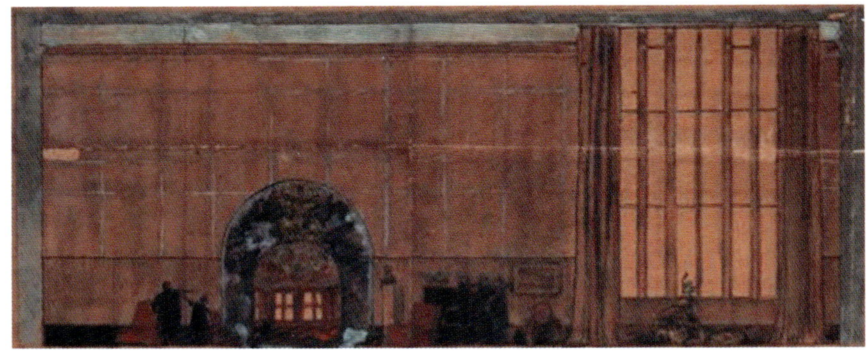

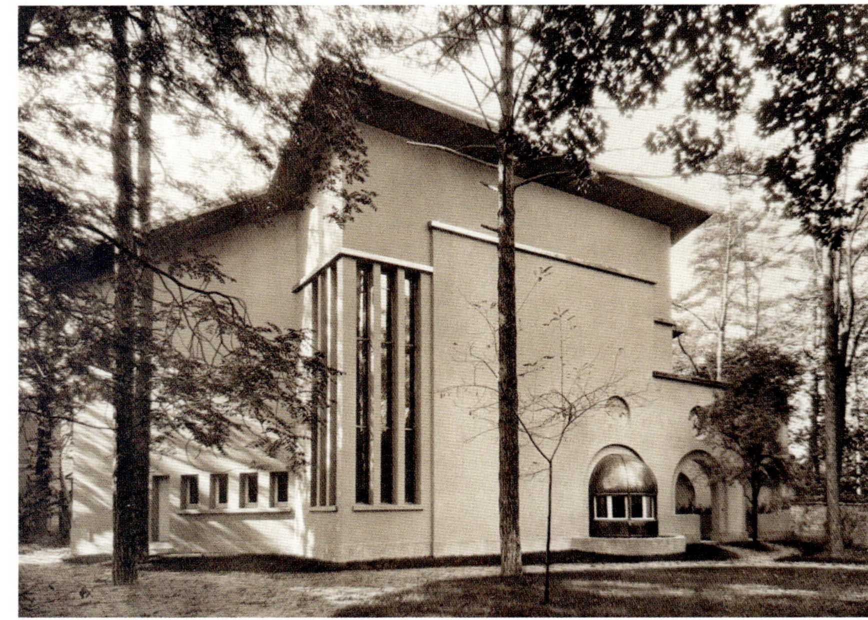

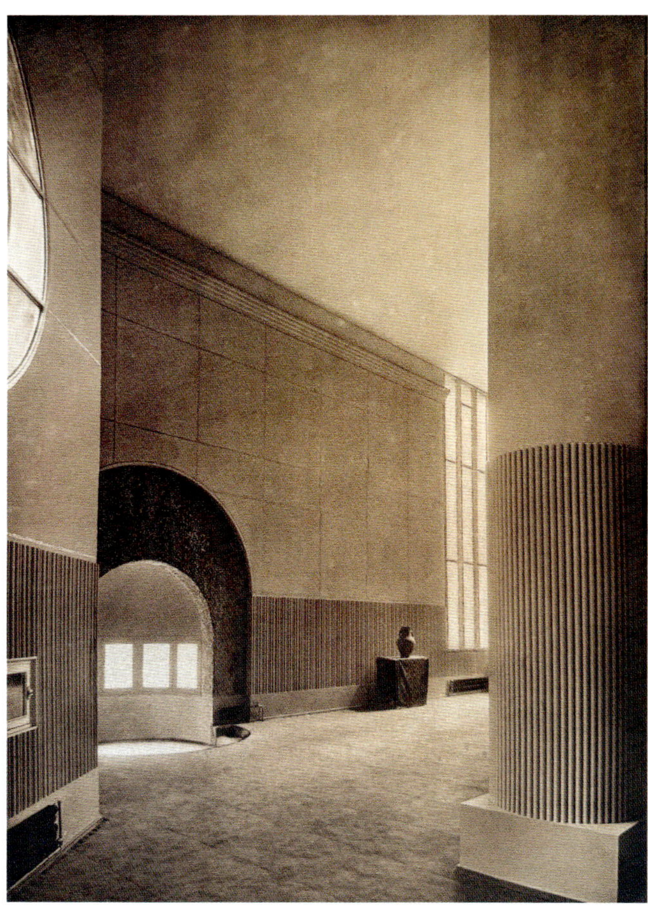

FIG. 115
Émile-Jacques Ruhlmann, *Villa Voisin (Boulogne/Seine)*, design for a bookcase, 1923–25; Archives Ruhlmann, Musée des Années 30, 1990.1.718.7

FIG. 116
Villa for Gabriel Voisin, boulevard d'Auteuil, Boulogne-Billancourt: Elevation of the hall on the side of the semicircular bow window (detail), 1923–26; ink and gouache on paper; 17 ¼ × 22 in.; Contemporary Architecture Archive Center, Paris 42 IFA 4

FIG. 117
Chevojon, Pierre Patout, Hôtel Voisin interior, Boulogne-Billancourt [incorrectly identified as Hôtel Particulier à Neuilly (Seine)], *L'Architecte* 1926, plate 24

FIG. 118
Chevojon, Pierre Patout, Hôtel Voisin exterior, Boulogne-Billancourt [incorrectly identified as Hôtel Particulier à Neuilly (Seine)], *L'Architecte* 1926, plate 22

FIG. 119
Lola Voisin in a Voisin C5, c.1925, as featured in *L'Époque des Carrossiers: The Art and Times of the French Coachbuilders* (Mullin Automotive Museum, 2018). The November 1923 issue of *Vanity Fair* credits couturier Paul Poiret with Voisin's "Scotch plaid" paint scheme.

FIG. 120
Cover of *Art, goût, beauté* 51, November 15, 1924

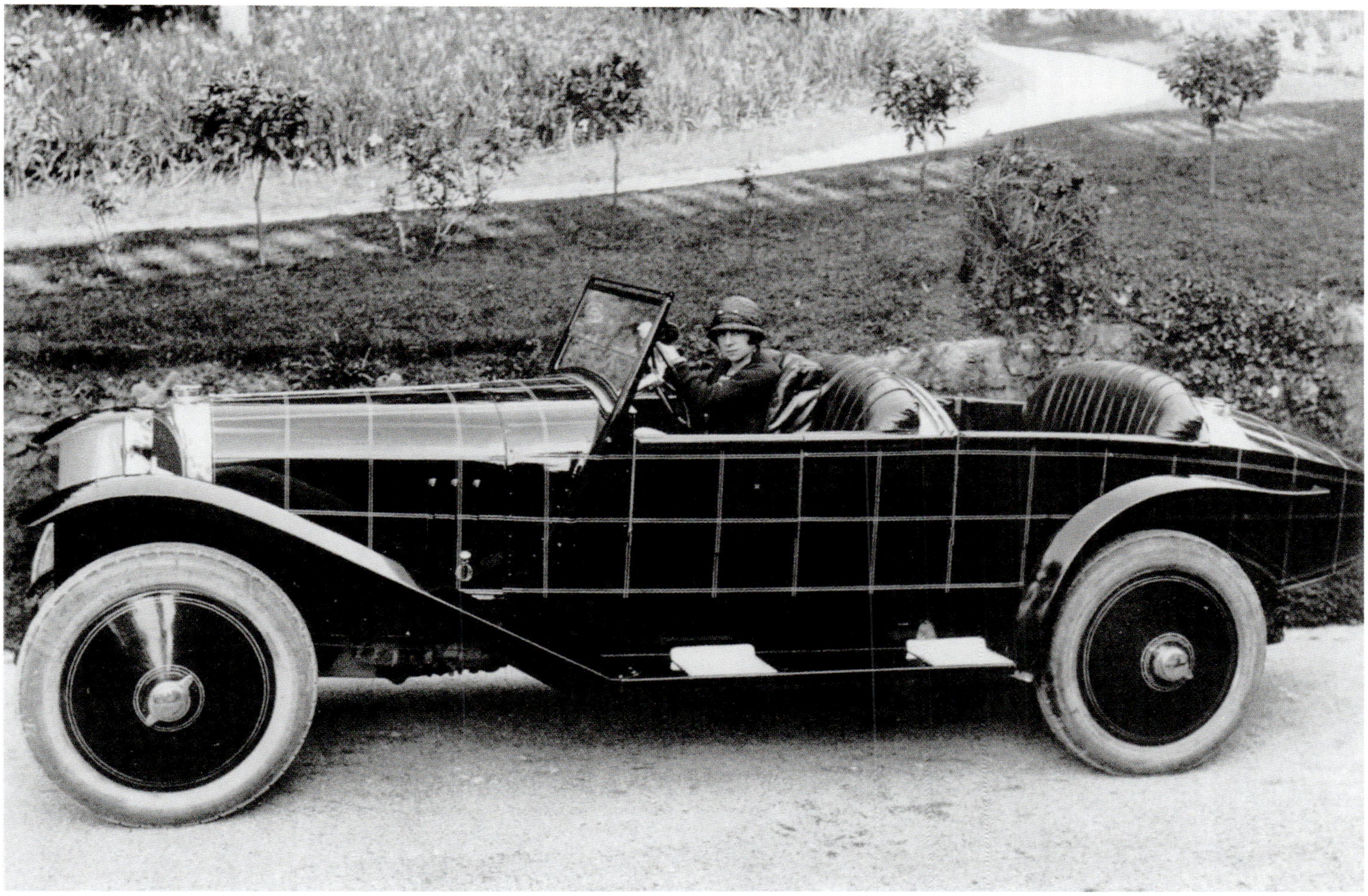

the contemporary critic J. E. Blanche, the building's towering, near-windowless facade covered by a corrugated iron roof was marked by sharp, irregular angles and a series of three arches surmounted by porthole windows, one with a projecting bay and the others leading to the mansion's entrance.[5] Inside, four enormous columns, topped by a lit atrium, served as a focal point of the massive soaring hall. Reeding, vertical below the chair rail and running horizontally as crown molding, and walls crossed with a simple grid were the few decorative applications in sparsely furnished rooms (FIG. 117).

Over time, Patout's longtime collaborator Émile-Jacques Ruhlmann contributed to the decoration of the house and the interiors of a second, smaller home built nearby in 1928. Sketches of a room with a figured marble fireplace and chimney and walls covered with Ruhlmann's typical interlaces and drawings for bookcases, beds, textiles, and a console table survive in the designer's archives (FIG. 115).[6] Patout's drawings, possibly realized in concert with Ruhlmann, envisioned a space considerably less austere than the black-and-white photographs published in *L'Architecte* and *Art et in-*

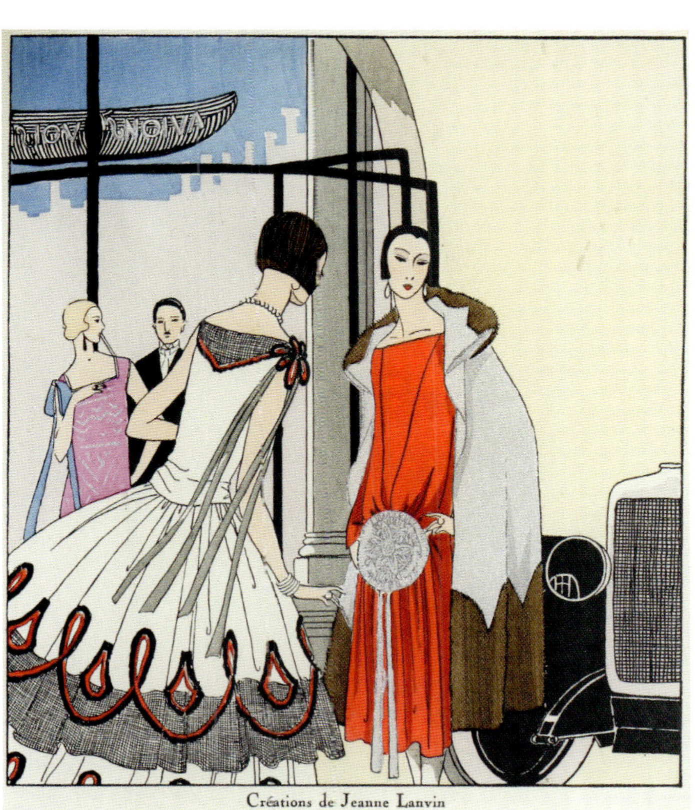
Créations de Jeanne Lanvin

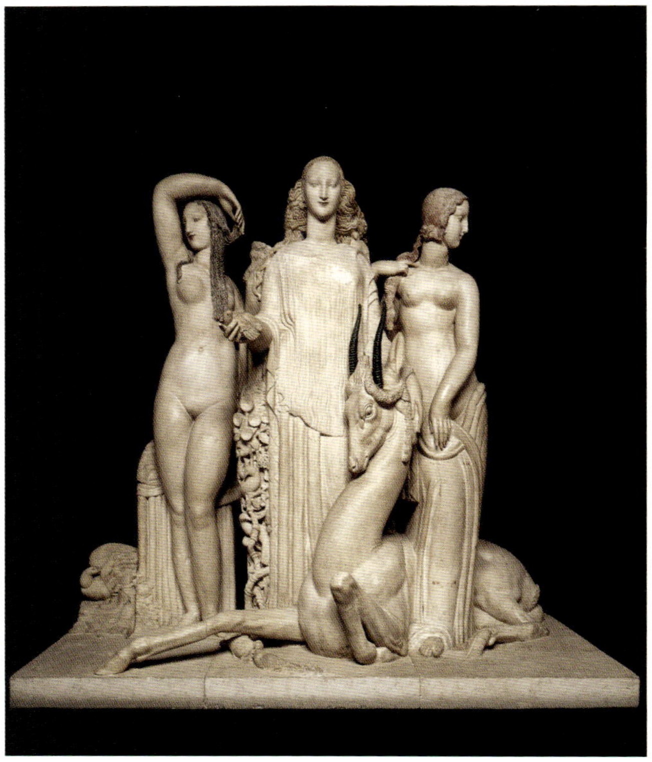

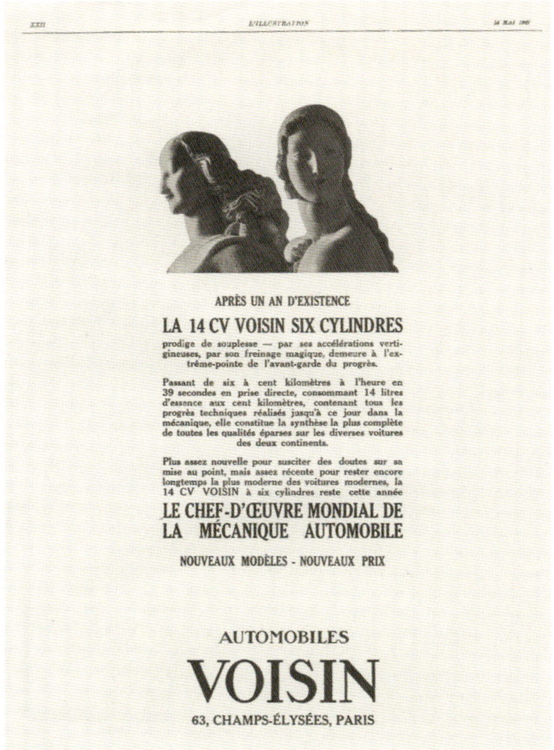

dustrie in 1926.[7] Soft furnishings and patterned surfaces transformed the semicircular alcove into a sensuous lounging nook, with paintings, sculptures, and upholstered chairs (FIG. 116).

Described by Blanche as "sumptuous and extremely sober," the mansion reflected Patout's use of contrasting masses and dramatic lighting, and the surprisingly grandiose tastes of its patrons.[8] Despite his supposed aversion to decoration for its own sake, citing Darwin's discoveries as proof of the natural laws of function dictating form, Voisin favored the same orientalizing opulence espoused by his social milieu.[9] His friends included the illustrator and designer Paul Iribe and fashion designer Paul Poiret, for whom Voisin designed a retractable pneumatic roof for his garden theater, the Oasis (FIG. 114). Voisin chose an Egyptian scarab as the logo for his company. Appearing as a delicate blue enamel badge on the hoods of his luxury cars, the large, winged beetle also hung from the firm's Patout-designed showroom on the Champs-Élysées (FIG. 120). His office and "hideaway" at 72 boulevard Exelmans in Paris, also the work of Patout and Ruhlmann, featured a hall-cum-theater and a "famous" blue mosaic-tiled swimming pool home to raucous costume parties.[10] His automobiles were offered with dazzling upholstery and surprising Art Deco flourishes, like Egyptian motifs and tartan paint schemes (FIG. 119).

Lola Bernet was the sister-in-law of the authors Victor and Paul Marguerite, with whom she lived during the couple's courtship. Victor wrote *La Garçonne,* a sensational 1922 novel that follows the young Monique, who, after learning of the affairs of her fiancé (incidentally, a motor-car manufacturer), embarks on a path of sexual and social liberation. The title, which translates as "tomboy," became synonymous with the modern French woman who cut her hair, drank, played sports, and drove "bigger, faster" cars.[11] Gabriel was a famous and self-confessed philanderer, taking mistresses throughout the couple's tumultuous marriage, which ended in divorce around 1928. Much less is known about Lola's personal life, but she is referenced as the sole patron on many of Patout and Ruhlmann's architectural plans. She also seemingly had an active role in their implementation after Gabriel's departure from their family home, possibly as early as 1924.

Although regularly flirting with bankruptcy, the Voisins purchased the colossal limestone sculptural group *Spring: Homage to Jean Goujon* by Alfred Auguste Janniot after its celebrated exhibition outside Patout and Ruhlmann's Pavillon du Collectionneur at the 1925 International Exhibition of Modern Decorative and Industrial Arts (FIG. 121).[12] The stylized face of the goddess Diana, flanked by two nymphs with luxuriant colorful hair, appeared in advertisements for Voisin automobiles in 1926 and 1927 (FIG. 123). The somewhat incongruent pairing of neo-archaic sculpture with text describing the six-cylinder 14 CV's "dizzying acceleration" and "magical braking"

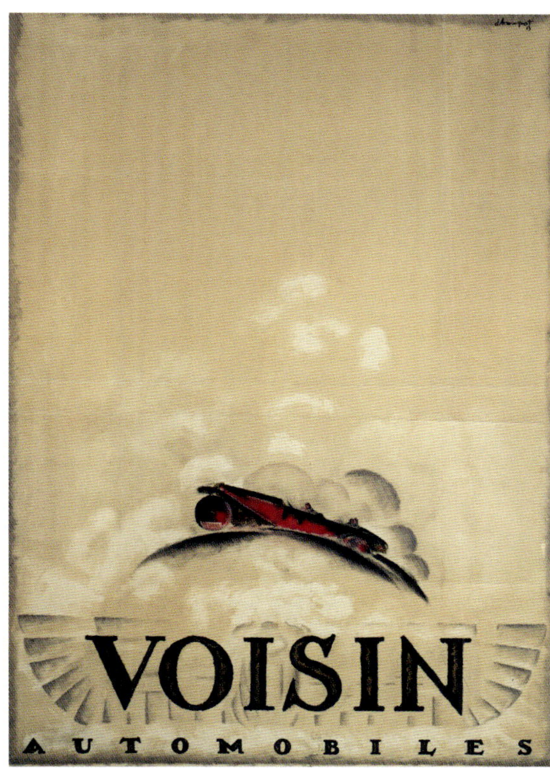

captures the idiosyncratic character of the brand, which courted courtiers, architects, actors, and artists. Madeleine Vionnet, Jeanne Lanvin, Le Corbusier, Maurice Chevalier, Arlette Dorgère, and Man Ray all drove Voisins.

The illustrator Charles Loupot designed Voisin's most celebrated advertisements. After training in lithography in Switzerland and absorbing the influences of German graphic design, Loupot "gradually evolved a very simple and striking style."[13] A 1923 poster printed by Devambez pictures a red Voisin torpedo roaring over an arched plane surrounded by billowing exhaust (FIG. 122). With more than half the composition left untouched but for wispy clouds, Loupot captures a dreamy, otherworldly setting. At any moment, the lightly shaded wings of the Voisin scarab might flap to life and set the sketchily rendered car aloft.

Loupot expresses the lightness and efficiency of Voisin automobiles and the effervescence of their unconventional maker. Chronically underfinanced and saddled with debts, Gabriel's protégés took up and perfected many of his best ideas. The engineer André Lefèbvre, who departed Voisin with Gabriel's blessing in 1933, went on to help realize Citroën's groundbreaking Traction Avant, the first mass-produced, front-wheel drive, monocoque-bodied car, and the iconic 2 CV, the Toute Petite Voiture (TPV), or very small car par excellence.[14]

FIG. 121
Alfred Auguste Janniot, French, 1889–1969; *Spring: Homage to Jean Goujon*, 1919–24; limestone (pietra di Roma), partial polychrome; 86 5/8 × 92 1/2 × 50 3/4 in.; Calouste Gulbenkian Foundation and Museum, Lisbon Inv. 2333

FIG. 123
Voisin advertisement, c.1925, *L'Illustration*, May 1927

FIG. 122
Designed by Charles Loupot, French, 1892–1960; printed by Devambez, French, founded 1826; lithograph in *Voisin Automobiles*, 1923; 64 × 47 3/4 in.; The Museum of Modern Art, Gift of The Lauder Foundation, Leonard and Evelyn Lauder Fund 159.1988

NOTES

1 Pascal Courteault, *Automobiles Voisin 1919–1958*, trans. Peter Hull (London: White Mouse, 1991), 40.

2 Henri Besnard, "Les Procédés modernes de construction rapide," *Art et décoration* (January–June 1920): 29–30.

3 L. C-S., "Les Maisons Voisin," *L'Esprit nouveau* 2 (1920): 215.

4 Gabriel Voisin, *My Thousand and One Cars* (Great Britain: Faustroll, 2012), 33. First published in 1962 as *Mes Milles et une voitures*.

5 J. E. Blanche, "Patout Architecte," *Art et industrie*, July 1926, 11.

6 Musée des Années 30, Boulogne-Billancourt, Fonds Ruhlmann, inv. nos. 1990.1.150.1–7, 1990.1.714.1-4, 1990.1.716.1-2, 1990.1.718.1-9. A 1939 auction catalogue lists mahogany and ivory bookcases by Ruhlmann, lots 100 and 101, and a sculptural group, *Spring: Homage to Jean Goujon*, by Alfred Auguste Janniot, lot 49, from the property of Lola Voisin. *Vente à Paris, Hôtel Drouot, 20 Janvier 1939. I. Objets d'Art d'Extrême-Orient … Appartement à Mme Lola Voisin* (Paris: Lahure, 1939).

7 Centre d'archives d'architecture contemporaine, Projet PATPI-B-22-3-Villa pour Gabriel Voisin, boulevard d'Auteuil, Boulogne-Billancourt (Hauts-de-Seine), 1922–28.

8 Blanche, "Patout Architecte," 12.

9 Christian Dauvergne, "La Lutte contre l'air: Interview de M. Gabriel Voisin," *Art et industrie* (France: n.p., 1927), 56.

10 Voisin, *My Thousand and One Cars*, 37, 41–42.

11 Victor Margueritte, *The Bachelor Girl* (New York: A. A. Knopf, 1923), 197.

12 Calouste Gulbenkian purchased *Spring: Homage to Jean Goujon* at the 1939 Drouot sale of the property of Lola Voisin. It is now in the collection of the Calouste Gulbenkian Museum, Lisbon, Portugal, inv. no. 2333.

13 John Harrison, "Posters & Publicity, Fine Printing and Design," in *Modern Publicity* (1927): 4.

14 Philippe Ladure, *Voisin: La différence* (Paris: Éditions du Chêne, 2014), XIV.

1937 VOISIN TYPE C28 AÉROSPORT COUPE

KEN GROSS

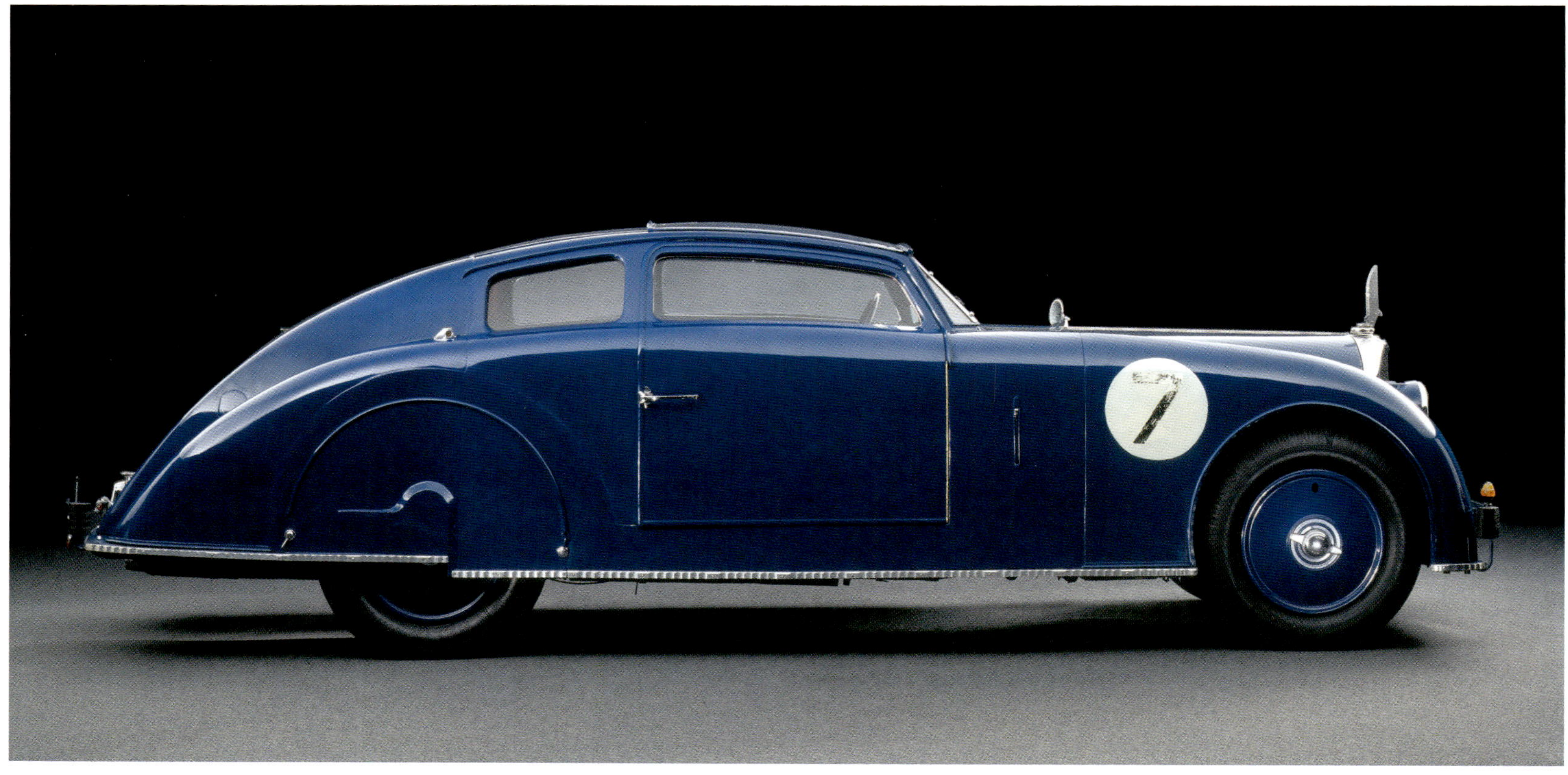

Avions Voisin, Issy-les-Moulineaux, France, 1905–46; *C28 Aérosport*, 1936; 65 × 194 × 58 in.; Keller Collection

The pioneering French aeronautical engineer Gabriel Voisin (1880–1973) was a gifted eccentric, whose profound knowledge of and skill in aircraft production contributed to the Allied victory in World War I. When the war ended, flush with profits, Voisin turned to automobile manufacturing, "sometimes with amazing results," in the words of the designer Robert Cumberford.[1]

The aircraft-like shape, integral construction, and styling of Voisin cars combined Gallic disregard for convention with a brilliant adaptation of aeronautical principles to ground transportation. Voisin's undeniably unique approaches to automobile design did not result in high sales, however. Richard Adatto, an authority on Voisin, wrote, "Voisins were relatively expensive and lacked broad appeal. Gabriel Voisin's solution, typical of the man, was not to follow the crowd."[2]

Streamlining polarized the world's automotive industry in the 1930s. Many automakers embraced it, for some to the detriment of sales, because conservative buyers were reluctant to move from more familiar, upright designs to more curvaceous cars. Voisin desperately needed a success. Overall company sales had fallen to just 150 units. He hoped that his new models C25 Aérodyne and C28 Aérosport would appeal to the luxury grand-touring market.[3]

Like so many early streamlined cars, the C28 retained its manufacturer's distinctive and prominent radiator grille, topped with Voisin's winged badge, and a tall Art Deco motif that resembled the stylized, sculpted wings of a giant bird. Like the four-door Aérodyne that preceded it, the two-door Aérosport's gracefully curved roofline arched like an aircraft wing into a tapered fastback motif.

The raked windscreen and low windows were just short of sinister. In lieu of separate fenders, the coupe's slab sides and skirted rear wheels were a portent of things to come. In his memoir, Voisin wrote: "I drew the car . . . in one fell swoop (and) built the first automotive pontoons the world had ever known."[4] There was a Jules Verne–like quality to the design. Inside, a multitude of switches, dials, and gauges mimicked the cockpit of an airplane.

The C28's 3.3-liter, six-cylinder, 103-horsepower sleeve-valve engine used sliding bands in lieu of conventional poppet valves. They were utterly silent in operation, but the tradeoff was that the sleeves required a great deal of lubrication, and the cars emitted a thin haze of blue smoke when underway. The transmission was a four-speed Voisin-Cotal preselector. The fastback coupe's superb aerodynamics permitted a top speed of 150 kilometers per hour (90 mph).

Although the C28 received a great deal of notice due to its startling shape, the buying public's response was not overwhelming. That did not dissuade Voisin, who returned to the Paris Salon in 1936 with an updated Aérosport. On the new car, the front fender lines were reshaped and the fenders were extended lower, but to no avail. Production ceased early in 1937.

Voisin was ahead of his time. His intent to adapt aircraft styling and advanced technology to automotive design was admirable, and it presaged General Motors' rocket-inspired Firebird series by twenty years.[5]

Loaned by the Keller Collection

1 Robert Cumberford, *Auto Legends: Classics of Style and Design* (London: Merrill, 2004), 121.

2 Richard Adatto in *Sensuous Steel: The Art Deco Automobile* (St. Paul, MN: Stance & Speed, 2013), 58.

3 Serge Bellu, Philipp Moch, and museum staff, *Vitesse-Élégance: French Expression of Flight and Motion* (Philadelphia: Coachbuilt Press, 2012), 100.

4 Richard Adatto, *From Passion to Perfection* (Paris: Éditions SPE Barthélémy, 2003), 257.

5 Philippe Ladure, Philipp Moch, Pierre Vanier, and Reg Winstone, *Voisin: La différence* (Paris: Éditions du Chêne—Hachette Livre, 2014), 150.

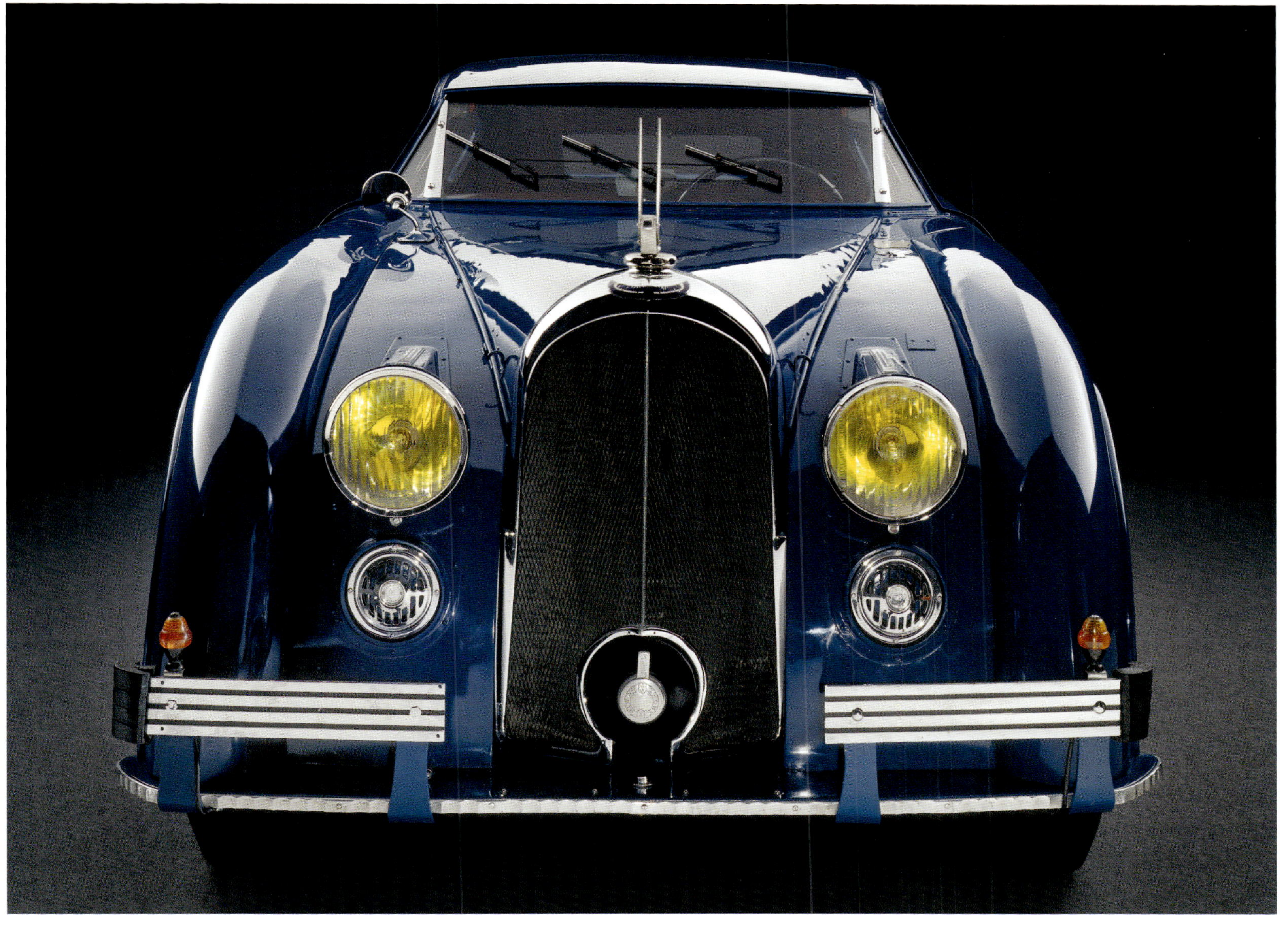

CONCOURS D'ÉLÉGANCE: JOSEPHINE BAKER, FASHION, AND THE AUTOMOBILE

JUSTICE HENDERSON

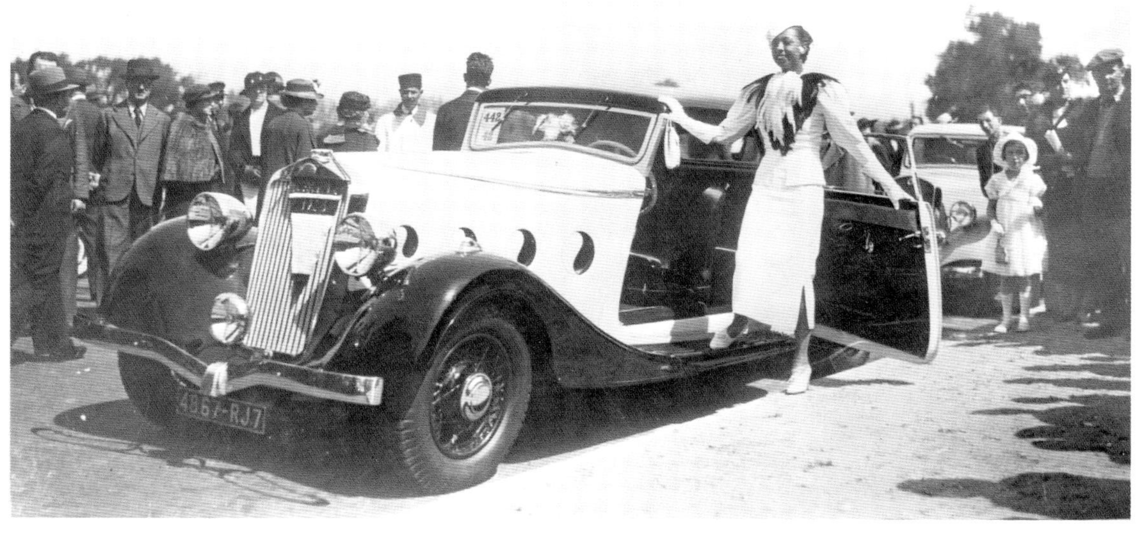

FIG. 124
Josephine Baker with her Delage D8-85, Paris, 1935; photograph in *L'Officiel*, July 1935

In this widely disseminated photograph, the actress Josephine Baker emerges from the dark interior of her coach-built Delage D8-85 in a glamorous *tailleur*, or woman's suit (FIG. 124). Her rayon *peau d'ange* (angel's skin) ensemble consists of a calf-length skirt and a puff-sleeve jacket, "trimmed with cock feathers in white and black."[1] With her matching gloves, purse, and hat, she exemplifies the spirit of the *concours d'élégance,* a juried gathering of private and company-owned cars. This photograph documents Baker during the *concours* at the Bois de Boulogne on June 7, 1935.[2]

Baker starred in the French film *Princesse Tam-Tam,* which includes footage of her at the event, one of the few historical recordings of the competition. It is unclear if Edmond T. Gréville, its director, incorporated existing press footage into the movie or if his crew was filming in the crowd. If the latter, the suit may have been made as a costume by a couture house, such as Philippe et Gaston. If the former, the outfit was likely by a designer Baker is known to have worked with—Jeanne Lanvin, Paul Poiret, or Georges et Janin, for example—and it may have been made specifically for her to wear at the *concours d'élégance.*

Baker's participation in the *concours* was a reflection not only of her celebrity status but also her interest in automobiles and auto rallies. Her Delage D8-85, which she had recently purchased, seems to have been the last Delage body ever produced by coachbuilders Letourneur et Marchand before their acquisition by the rival manufacturer

Delahaye.[3] Baker also owned a factory-bodied Delage D6 and a Donnet upholstered in Alpina reptile skin.[4] A photograph of Baker happily brandishing her French driver's license was published in the June 8, 1927, issue of the newspaper *Excelsior* the day after she passed her exam.[5]

Baker's connections to the automobile industry reflect the growing trend of women behind the wheel in the 1920s, when, as explained in Daniel Marcus's essay in this catalogue, they began to influence automotive design. The fashion industry, too, began to prioritize flexibility in clothing to reflect the active lifestyle of the modern woman. Using lightweight fabrics and loose silhouettes, designers combined function and adornment. Baker's skirt, for example, features a slit that allows her to enter and exit the vehicle with ease. Like the automobile's sleek upholstery, sculptural fenders, and circular motifs, her jacket's two-tone feather collar mimics the color scheme of the car and conveys a sense of motion, with the lightweight material adding a playfulness to a classic shape.

A gouache, ink, and crayon maquette, likely for a poster by the French artist Émile Deschler,[6] depicts Baker in a similar feathered collar and white hat (FIG. 125). Her central placement, raised shoulders, and bright smile, rendered through gestural mark-making, black outlines, and simplified design, capture a sense of personality and vibrancy. In the painting, the role of the feather collar shifts from mere accessory to focal point. The feathers—and Baker's perhaps nude figure—recall her costumes of the 1920s and 1930s, such as the iconic banana skirt she wore in performances at the Folies Bergère or the peacock-inspired outfit at the Casino de Paris (FIG. 128). Although there

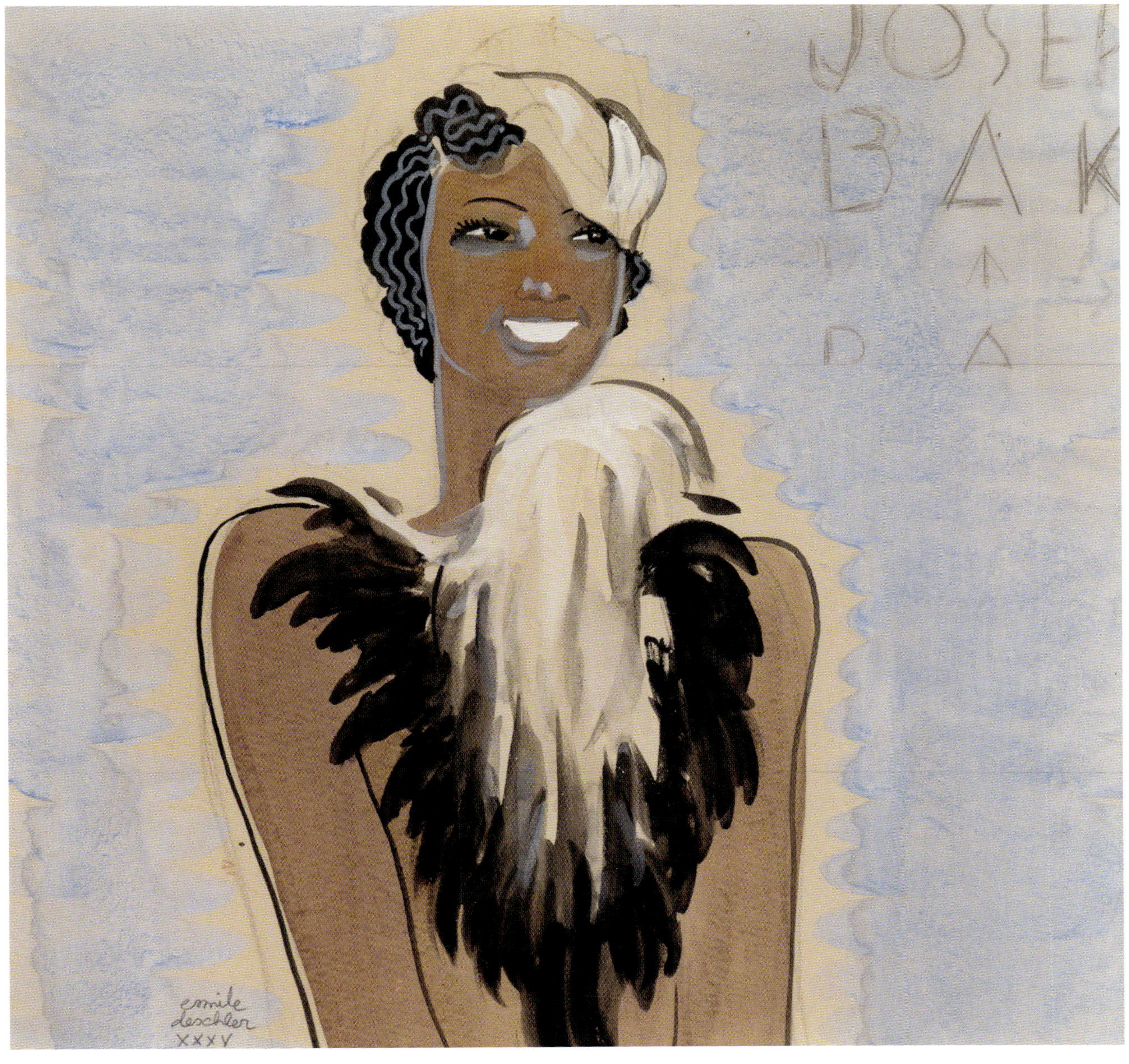

FIG. 125
Émile Deschler, French, 1910–1991; *Josephine Baker*, 1935; gouache, ink, and crayon maquette; 16 × 17 5/8 in.; Collection of Mary Strauss

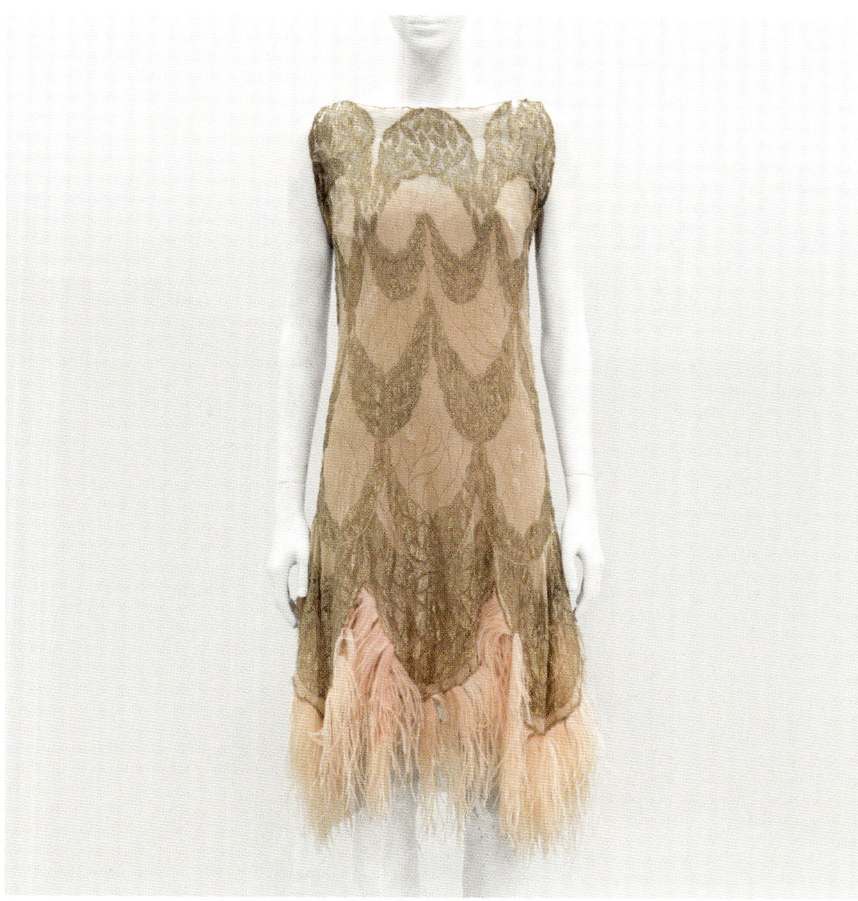

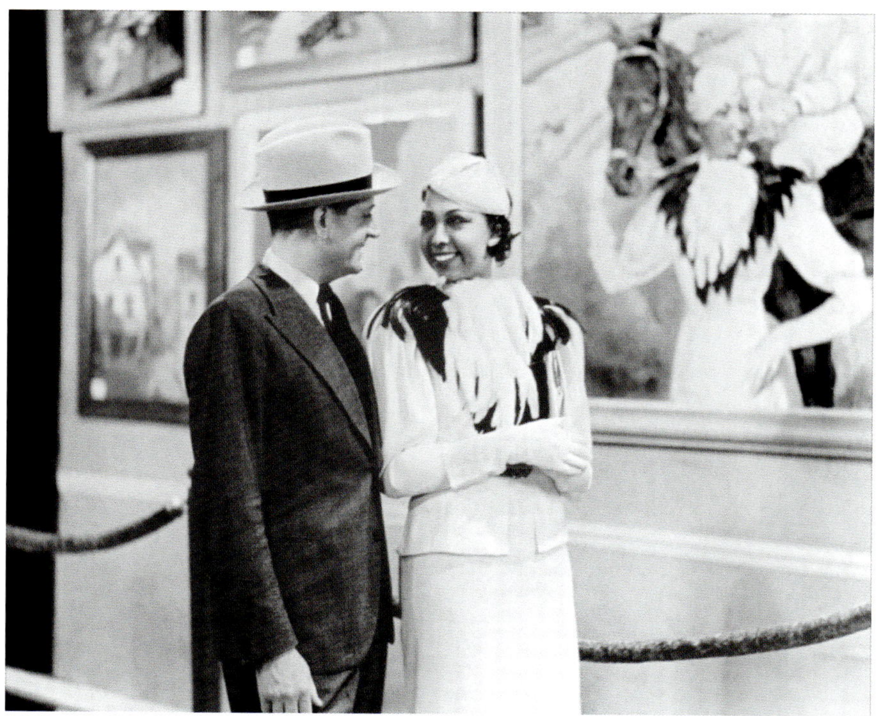

FIG. 126
Attributed to House of Chanel, Paris, founded 1910; *Evening Dress*, c.1932; metal and silk lace and ostrich feathers; Stephens College Costume Museum and Research Library, Columbia, Missouri

FIG. 127
Directed by Edmond T. Gréville, French, 1906–1966; produced by Arys Production, France; still from the film *Princesse Tam-Tam*, 1935

are similarities between these three depictions of Josephine Baker, the one at the *concours* stands out. The feathers hint at the spirit of her stage and screen persona, but her personal style begins to separate the characters she plays from the public image she is cultivating in Paris. Baker explained, "Since I personified the savage on the stage, I tried to be as civilized as possible in daily life."[7] Her style choices were a means of distinguishing herself from her fictional roles, and in so doing, she would later emerge as a fashion icon (FIGS. 126). As Olivia Lahs-Gonzales, the curator of the exhibition *Josephine Baker: Image and Icon*, observed: "Although she was frequently cast as the exotic in Pygmalion-like transformation myths on stage, Baker also undermined these recurring themes by presenting herself inside these characters as a sleek Art Deco modern with a smooth sculptured body and close-cropped hairstyle."[8]

Films like *ZouZou* and *Princesse Tam-Tam* relied on Baker not only as an actress but also as a choreographer.[9] The film historian Hannah Durkin explains that within *Princesse Tam-Tam*, "Baker's musical performances blur her stage image with her character, rupturing the theatrical illusion by calling attention to the performative nature of her role and encouraging audience identification even as they locate her as a racial Other."[10] The movie follows Alwina, a Bedouin woman who is brought into French society under the guise of being an Indian princess. During a film montage, Baker's character appears in her white suit from the *concours*, first in a portrait in an art gallery and later as she powders her face next to the Delage, signaling Alwina's Westernization (FIG. 127).[11] At the end of the film, however, she cannot resist joining a conga dance at a high-society event, and her lively personality and bountiful talents shine through and reveal the ruse. In some ways, Alwina's narrative mirrors Baker's own rise to fame. Born as Freda Josephine McDonald in St. Louis, Missouri, her skills and timing made her an international vaudeville sensation, and she became the first Black woman to star in a major motion picture with *Siren of the Tropics* in 1927.

As a fashion icon and car enthusiast, Josephine Baker exemplified the spirit of the *concours d'élégance*. The event allowed her to express her identity and exercise freedoms that would have been restricted in the United States. The *concours* provided a stage for Baker to demonstrate her personal style and automobile as embodiments of her agency, which would come to shape the image of the modern French woman.

FIG. 128
Louis Gaudin, French, 1900–1936; *Josephine Baker, La Grande Revue*, 1930; color lithograph; 63 ¾ × 31 ⅜ in.; Collection of Mary Strauss

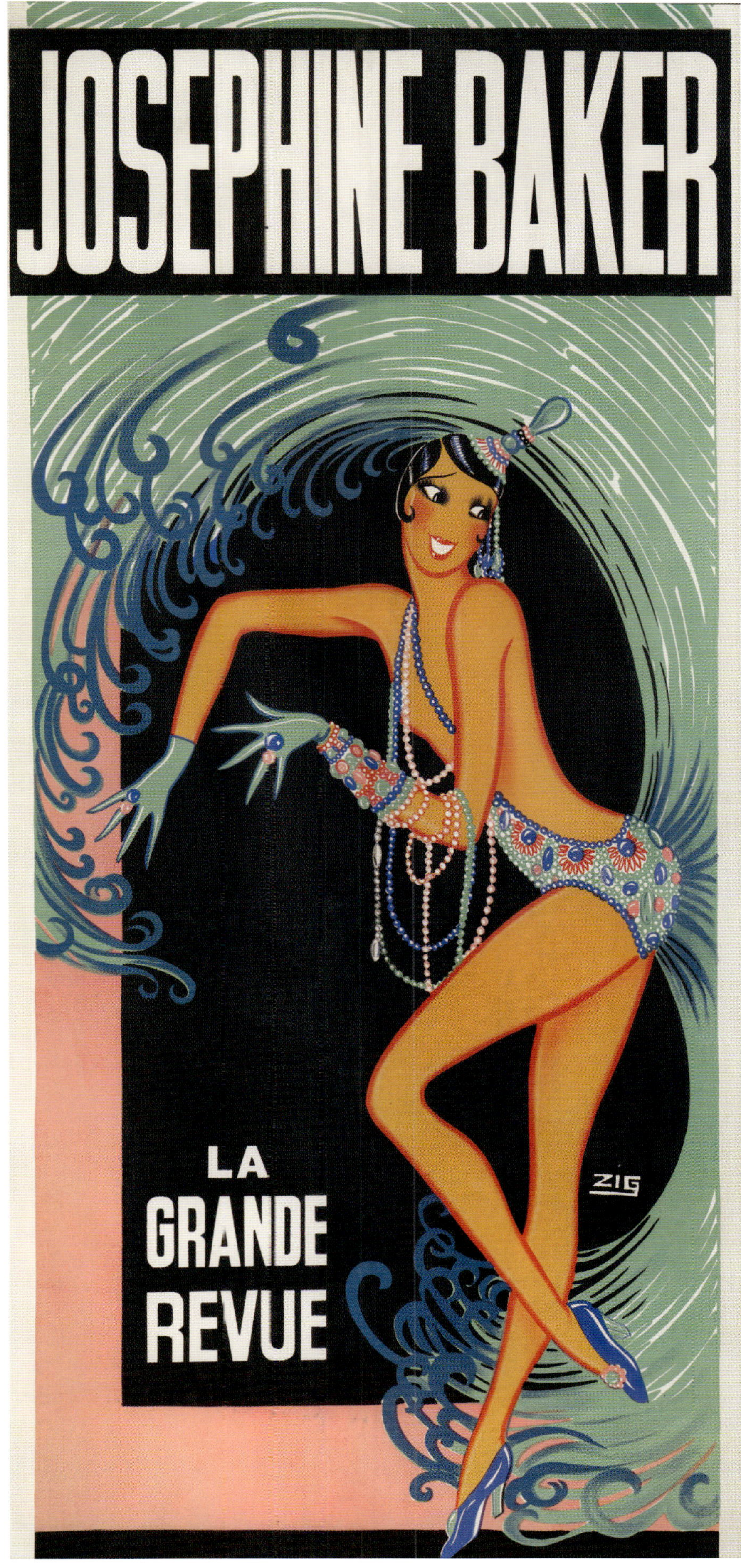

NOTES

1 "Bright Cars in Spotlight at Paris Fete," *Richmond Times-Dispatch*, August 4, 1935, 28. The article "Que de fleurs, que de plumes" in the July 28, 1935, issue of *La Femme de France* highlights the "Rooster feather lapels adopted by Joséphine Baker" at the 1935 *concours*, conceding, "but a music hall star can carry it all."

2 Paul Oliver, "Les élégances se sont donné rendez-vous au Bois," *L'Auto*, August 6, 1935, 3.

3 Daniel Cabart, Claude Rouxel, and Jacques Dorizon, *Delage: France's Finest Car* (Deerfield, IL: Dalton Watson Fine Books, 2007), 275.

4 Lysiane Bernhardt, "Le Salon de L'Automobile," *La Revue de La Femme*, November 1, 1927, 47.

5 Bennetta Jules-Rosette, "Josephine Baker: Inventing the Image and Preserving the Icon," in *Josephine Baker: Image and Icon*, ed. Olivia Lahs-Gonzales (St. Louis: Reedy Press, 2006), 18.

6 Kenneth Silver, *Paris Portraits: Artists, Friends, and Lovers* (New Haven: Yale University Press, 2008), 53.

7 Michael Borshuk, "An Intelligence of the Body: Disruptive Parody Through Dance in the Early Performances of Josephine Baker," in *The Josephine Baker Critical Reader: Selected Writings on the Entertainer and Activist*, ed. Mae Henderson and Charlene Regester (Jefferson, NC: McFarland, 2017), 130.

8 Olivia Lahs-Gonzales, "Josephine Baker: Modern Woman," in *Image and Icon*, 40.

9 Hannah Durkin, *Josephine Baker and Katherine Dunham: Dances in Literature and Cinema* (Urbana: University of Illinois Press, 2019), 106.

10 Durkin, *Josephine Baker and Katherine Dunham*, 110.

11 *Princesse Tam-Tam*, directed by Edmond T. Gréville, 1935, 49:28–49:42.

1938 DELAGE D8-120S CHAPRON CABRIOLET

KEN GROSS

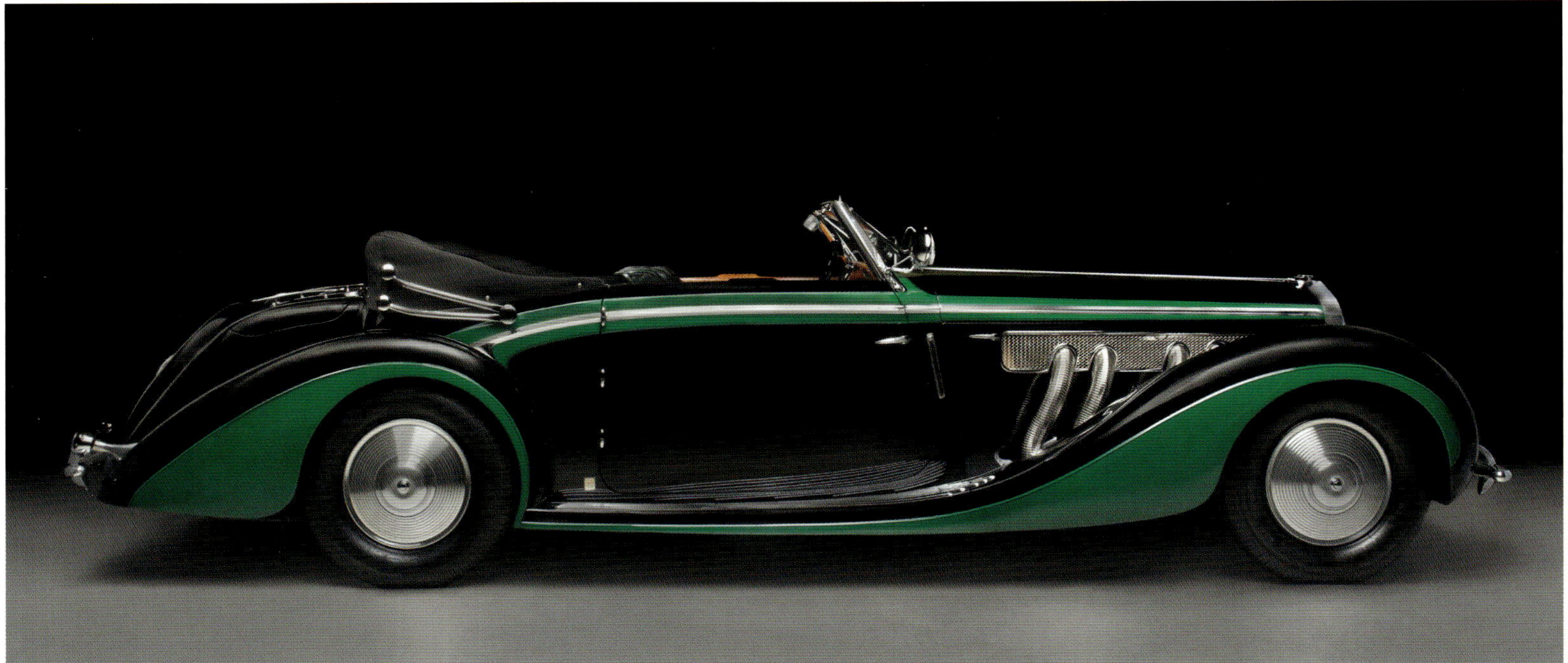

Henri Chapron, French, 1886–1978; Delage, Levallois-Perret, France, active 1905–53; *D8-120,* 1937; 65 ½ × 211 × 74 in.; Courtesy of Linda and Paul Gould

La Belle Voiture Française, "The Beautiful French Car," was a phrase coined to describe the automobiles created by Louis Delâge (1874–1947), and it became the slogan for one of France's oldest and most renowned automobile companies. Delage began production in 1905 with very simple models, then proceeded to build successful race cars that made the firm a household name in elite circles. René Thomas won the 1914 Indianapolis 500 in a Delage, averaging 82.47 miles per hour. Another Delage, driven by Albert Guyot, finished third in that race.

The Delage D8-120S, a new model for 1938, offered a lowered chassis ("S" stood for "surbaissé," or "lowered"), and the 4.7-liter overhead valve straight eight's output was increased to 120 bhp, with 190 lbs/ft of torque. The transmission was a four-speed Cotal electromagnetic preselector unit. Smooth shifts could be made with a fingertip. The brakes were large four-wheel hydraulic drums, capable of smooth stops from high speeds. The front suspension consisted of independent A-arms and semi-elliptic leaf springs, and a solid axle served the rear. The D8-120S's bare chassis could be purchased for 105,800 French francs. The fee for custom coachwork was an additional 43,000 to 45,000 francs, making the D8-120S one of France's most expensive luxury cars in the period. Fewer than one hundred were built.

The company founder Delâge liked expensive, handcrafted cars. Accordingly, renowned coachbuilders like Figoni et Falaschi, Fernandez et Darrin, Henri Chapron, Carrosserie Pourtout, Letourneur et Marchand, Franay, and Jacques Saoutchik favored the elegant Delage D8 chassis to showcase their designs, winning numerous *concours d'élégance*. Henri Chapron (1886–1978), whose atelier built this stunning convertible cabriolet, began in 1919 in Neuilly-sur-Seine, a suburb of Paris. Success allowed him to move to a new facility at Levallois-Perret in 1935, where some 350 artisans built 500 bodies annually for leading French luxury marques.

Henri Chapron's stylish coachwork enhanced this car's lovely proportions. An impossibly long hood, flanked by inset headlights faired into the fenders, stretches rearward to a subtly slanted windscreen flanked by a pair of spotlights. Four external exhaust pipes, shielded with chrome-plated covers, hint at a powerful engine beneath the hood. The radiator shell has a discreet curve that accentuates the car's flowing lines. Artillery-style spoked steel wheels, fitted with understated black wall tires, filled gracefully arched fenders. Inside, top-grain leather coddled four passengers. A Chapron coachbuilder's badge is prominently displayed on both sides of the car, just behind the long, suicide-style, front-opening doors. The

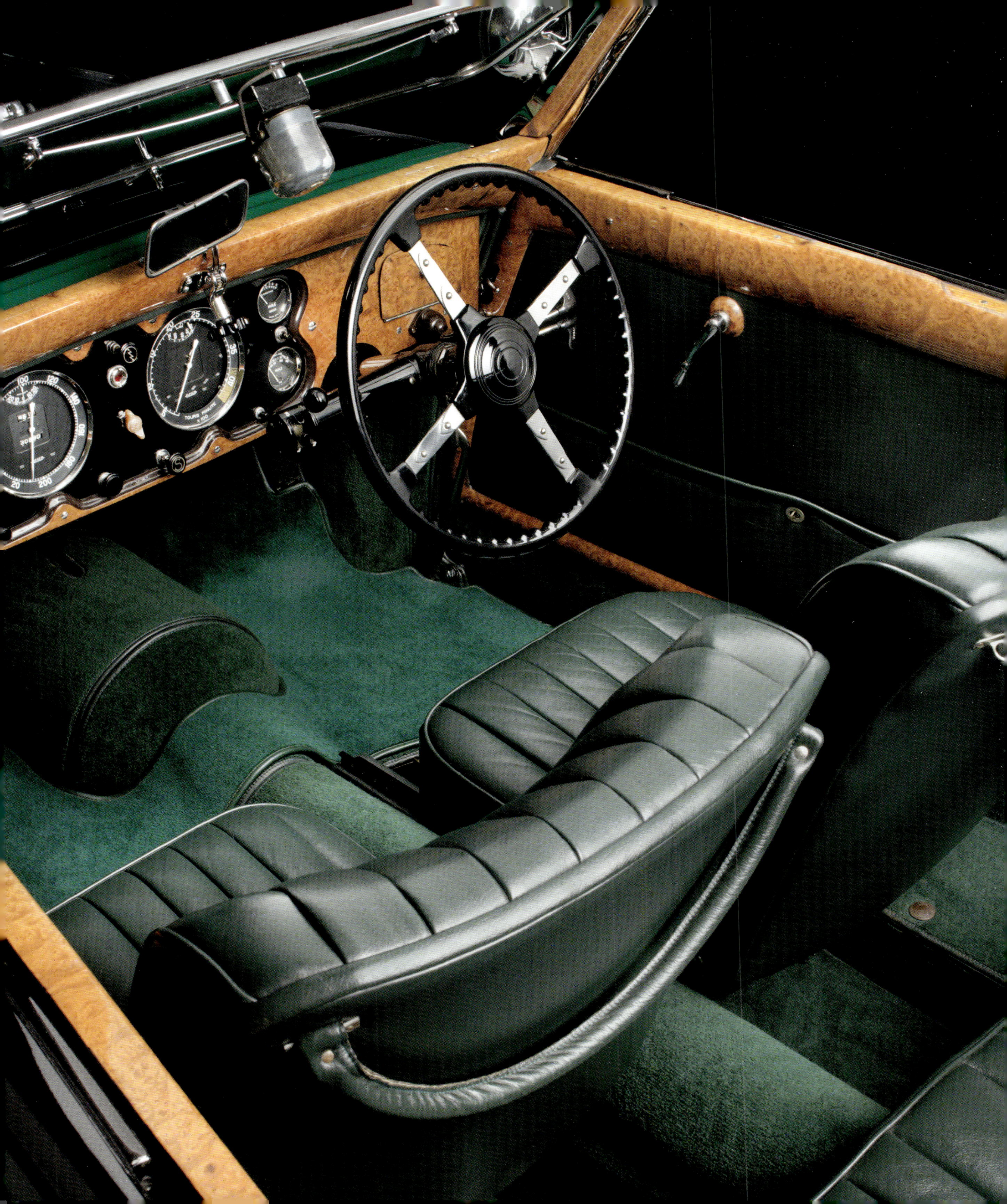

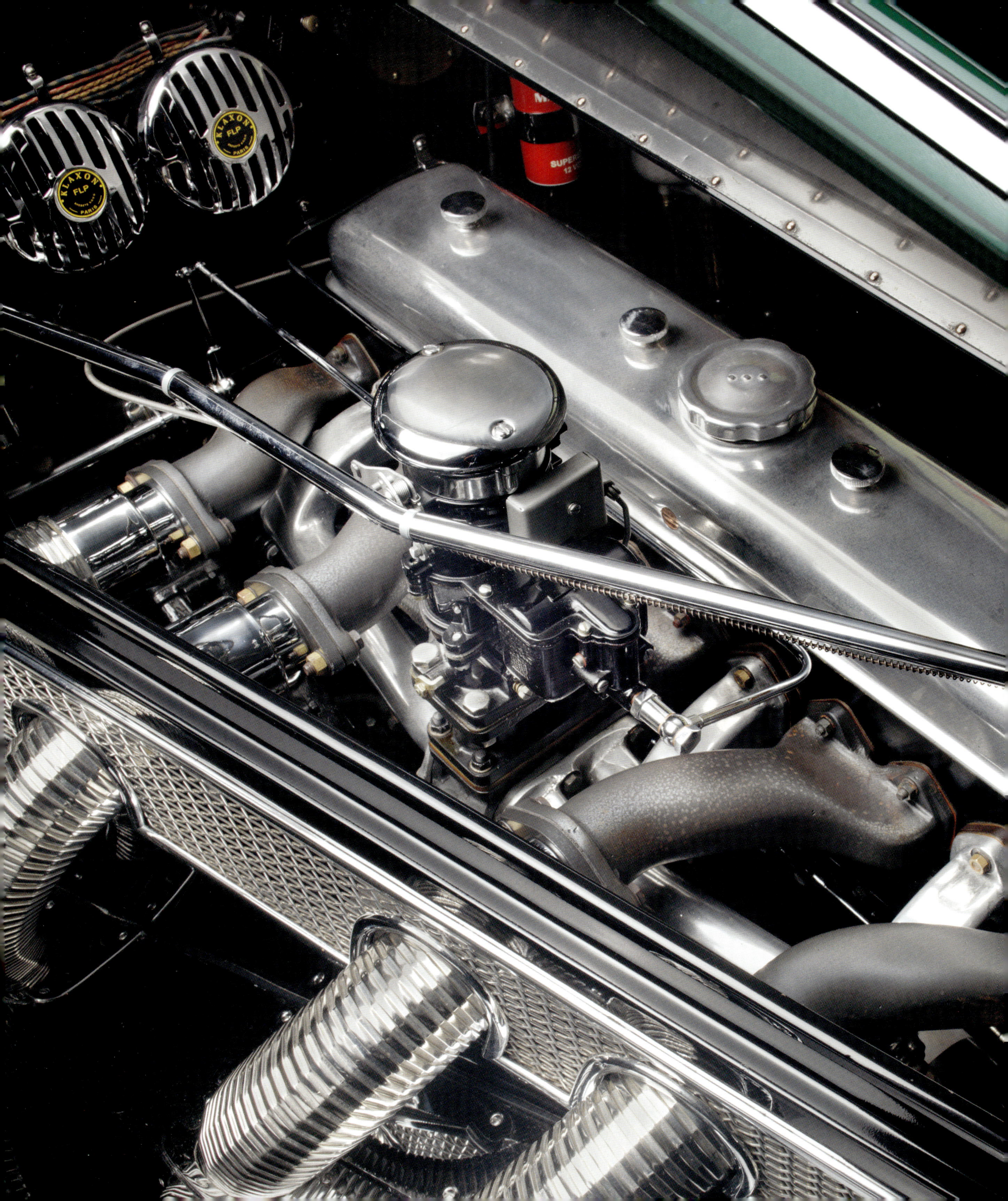
KLAXON
FLP
PARIS
KLAXON
FLP
PARIS

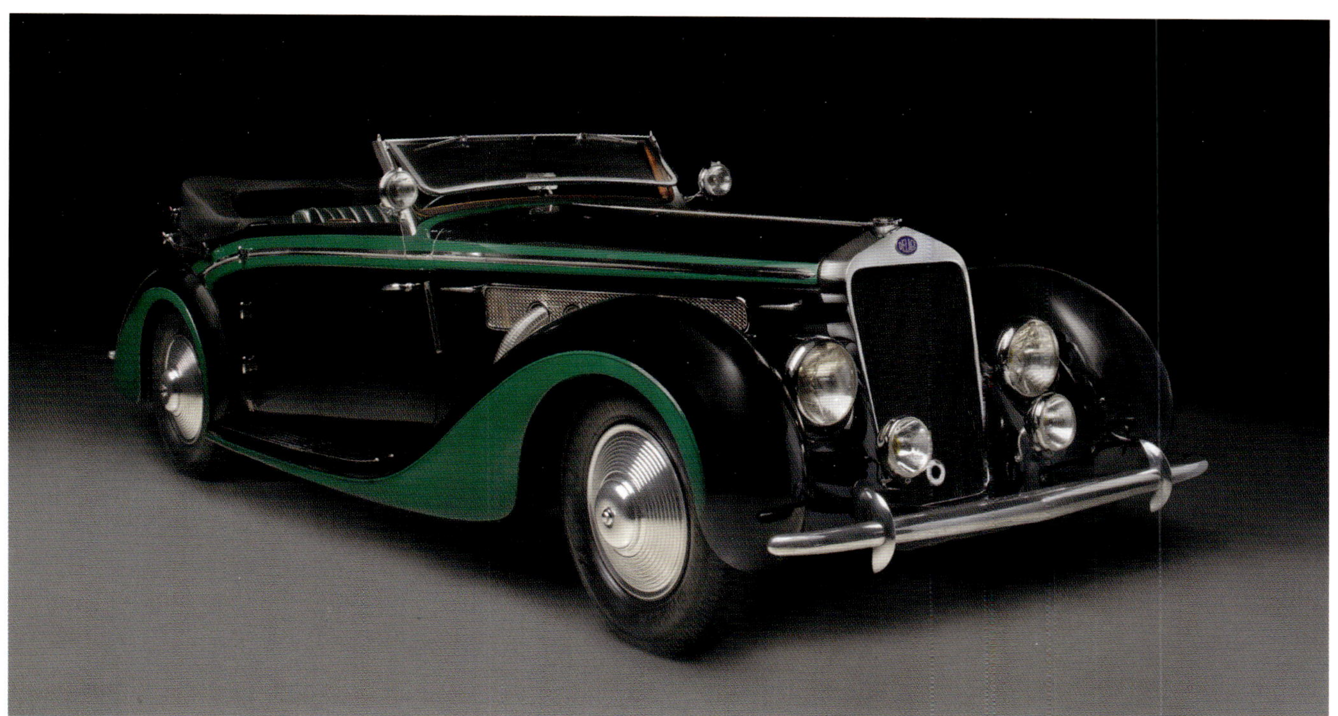

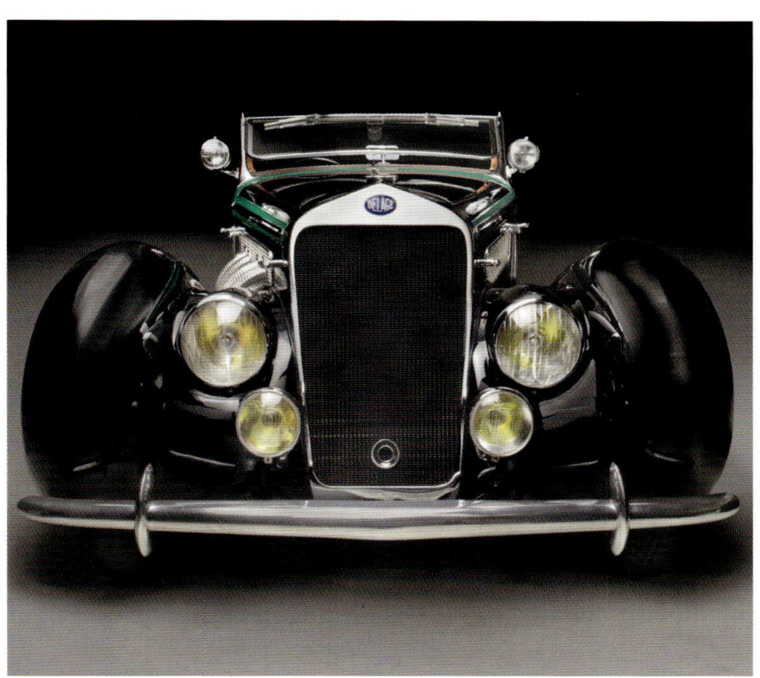

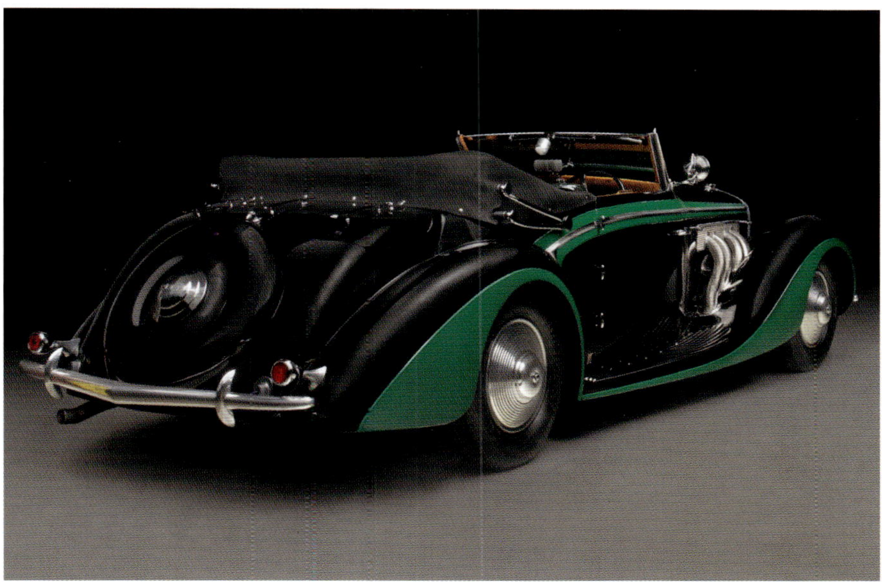

svelte cabriolet's canvas three-position soft top features plated, carriage era–style, landau irons. It can be opened halfway for a most elegant appearance.

Chapron's coachwork was always very elegant, if conservative and understated, compared to the curvaceous sweep of most Figoni designs. That aside, the gracious lines of the D8-120S Aérosport coupe were highly acclaimed. In 1930, Delage advertisements crowed that its cars received more *concours* awards than its rivals. The D8-120S was the last Delage model offered after the company merged with Delahaye in late 1935. Smart convertibles like this one are very desirable today.

Loaned by Linda and Paul Gould

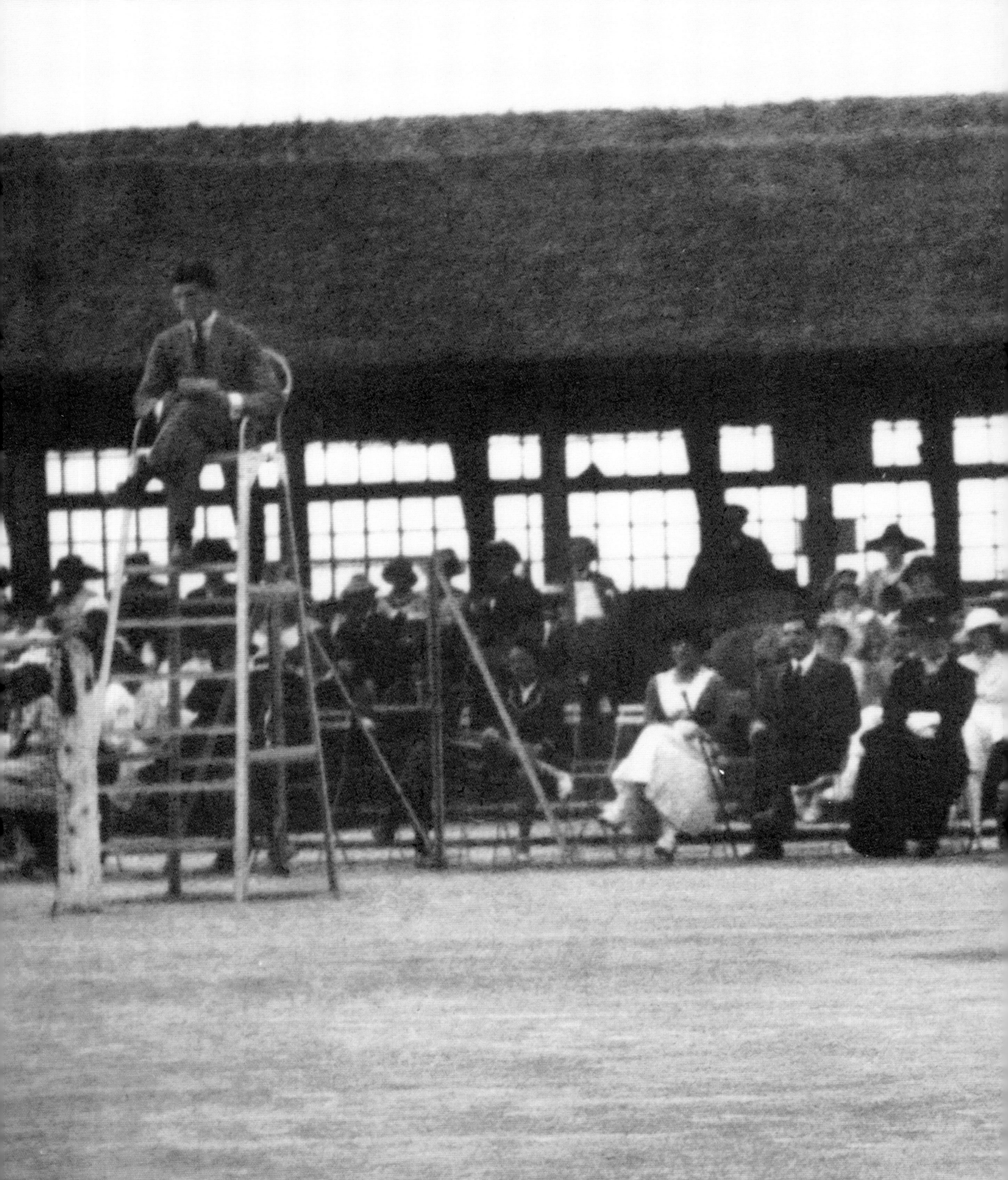

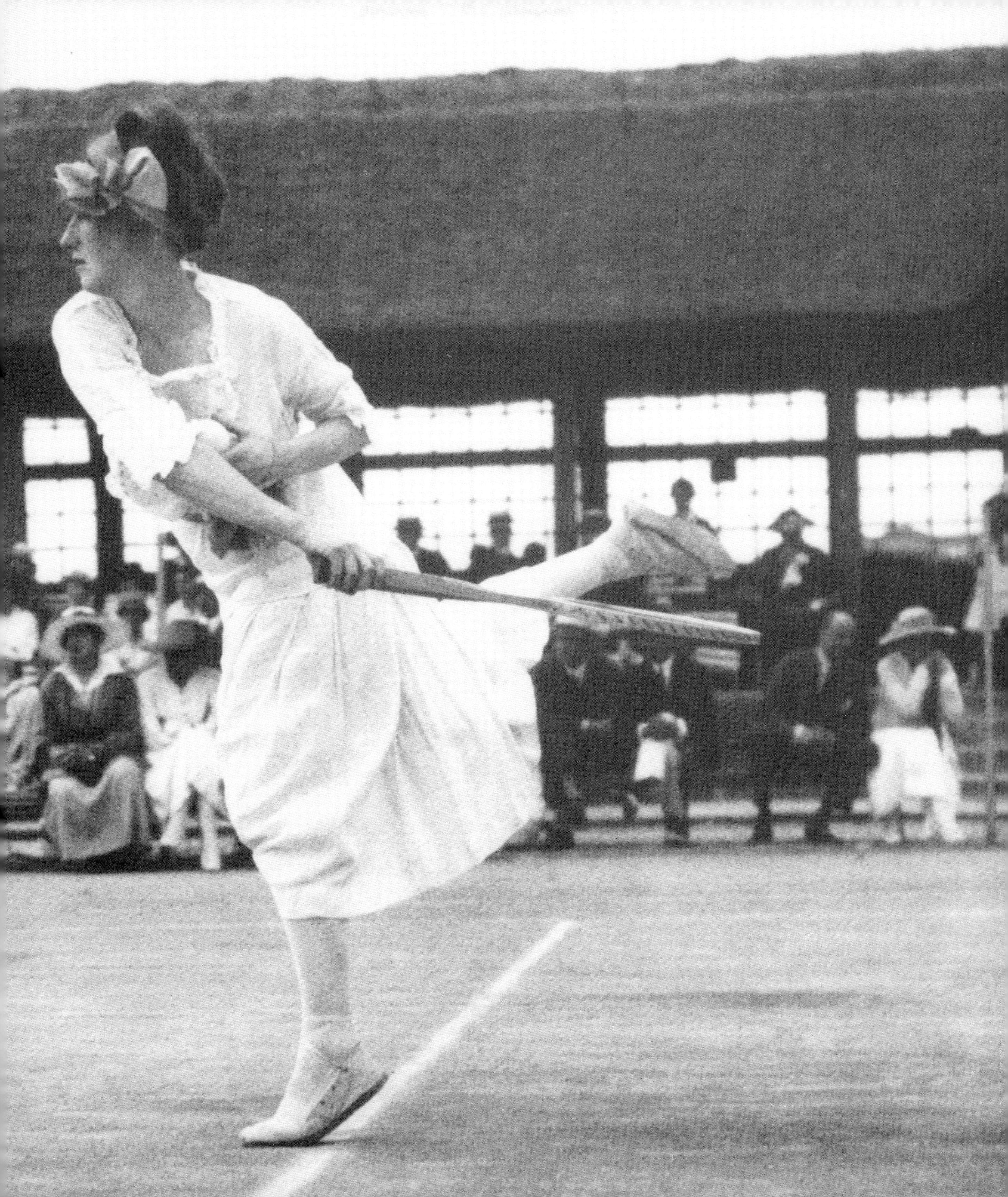

THE ELEGANT RACER IN INTERWAR FRANCE AND HER FASHION GLOW

PIERRE-JEAN DESEMERIE

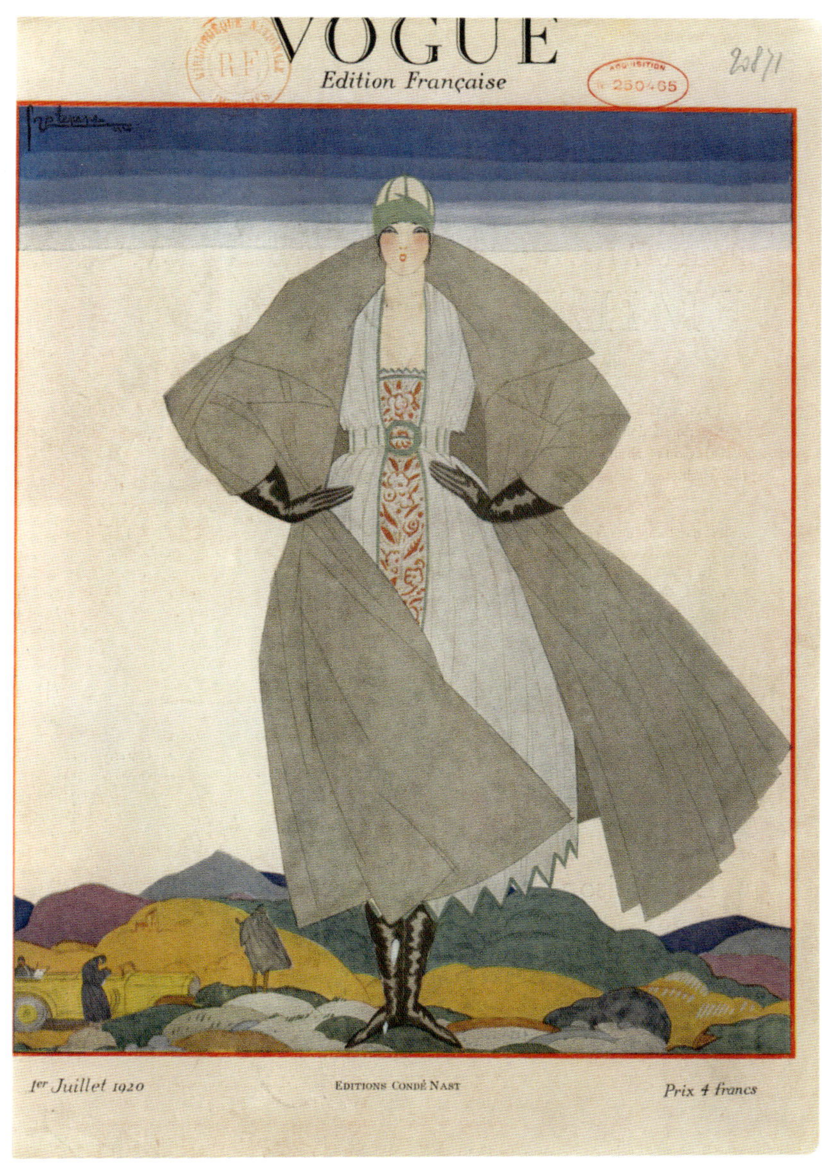

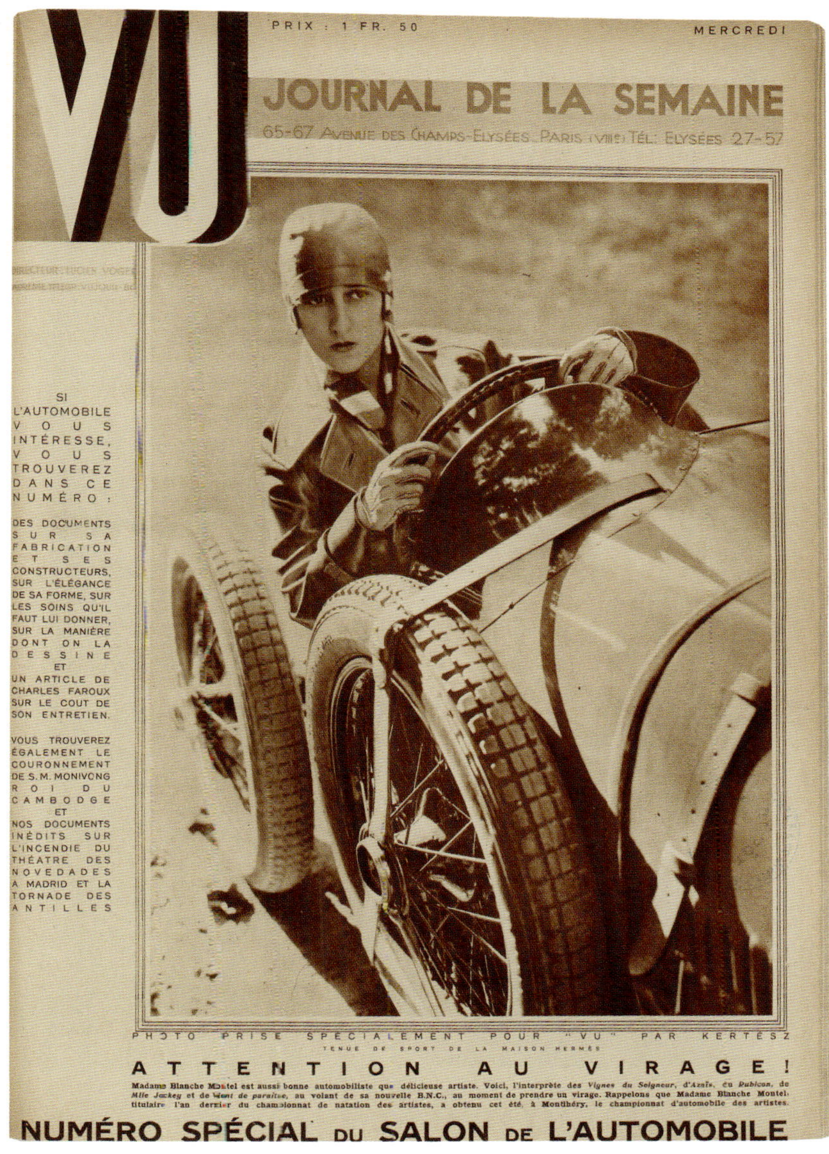

FIG. 129
Georges Lepape, French, 1887–1971; cover illustration for *Vogue Paris*, July 1, 1920

FIG. 130
André Kertész, French (born Hungary), 1894–1985; *Actress Blanche Montel wears the "Tenue de Sport" by Maison Hermès*, cover of *Vu: Journal de la Semaine*, October 3, 1928

July 1, 1920, early morning. The *élégante* Élaine Greffulhe, daughter of the fashion icon Comtesse Élisabeth Greffulhe, sorts through her mail and finds the second issue of French *Vogue* (FIG. 129).[1] On the cover is a woman dressed as a driver, wearing a long gray, wide-cut coat with large armholes and a high collar. When belted at—and emphasizing—the waist, the coat covers her delicate dress, shielding it from dust. "Underneath the wrap-around coat, the highly protected dress can be as elegant as you like," a friend of Élaine's would later report.[2] While flipping through the magazine, Élaine—among the few women who had earned a driver's license—would have seen numerous advertisements for cars and associated fashions, as well as advice on maintaining one's femininity even after driving hundreds of miles through the countryside.[3] With a hat, gloves, and boots to protect her silk stockings, the wealthy woman would be well-equipped for motoring at leisure, and with a spare pair of heels and gloves stashed in the compartment newly designed for such accessories, she would be ready for any occasion.[4] She could leave her outerwear in the car, change her accessories, and go to lunch without appearing "trop 'sport,'" that is, masculine and inappropriately sporty. Beginning with this issue, *Vogue* would show the world that the automobile was both fashionable *and* feminine.

The *Vogue* cover announced a new trio on the stage of the interwar period: fashion, elegance, and the automobile. The magazine's marketing strategies aimed at making the car a fashion accessory, and correspondents downplayed its more masculine aspects, presenting it as a modern and attractive object for the (wealthy) woman. Reinforcing the imperatives of femininity was also part of this strategy, tamping down gender anxiety about a woman's participation in a man's pastime.

A few years later, in 1926, Élaine joined the only women's driving club in France, the Automobile-Club Féminin de France (ACFF), as vice president. Her portrait was quickly published in the French press, presenting her as an elegant judge of automobile fashion.[5] But cars and driving were not simply trends that allowed for new clothes. They were also part of a new way of life, bringing new conceptions of the outdoors and perceptions of the body and its adornment (FIG. 130). Could the car body and the fashion body be united?

During the interwar period, cars and automotive sportswear emphasized movement and comfort. As driving became more common, the automobile inspired dreams of freedom and travel to other parts of the world. These ideas became pivotal to the politics of tourism, especially to colonies, at a moment when French workers received more paid vacations than they had before the war (FIGS. 9, 131). Visits to North Africa, specifically the Sahara, were now possible—Madame Citroën crossed that desert in the 1920s—and new clothing options were also available.

Though the automobile craze originated in the US, the trend was soon Frenchified, especially with the 1929 financial crisis prompting a focus on national production in France. The car industry quickly tried to increase ties with the French fashion industry, one of the country's most successful economic and cultural sectors, often presented as evidence of its cultural superiority. Driving—a man's sport at its inception—was soon transposed into the fashion world, where feminine elegance, beauty, and luxury became central in the making of the French "haute automobile," just as they were central to haute couture.

The Evolution of Car Design and Automobile Fashion

As early as 1923, the magazine *L'Auto* specified two ways to dress for driving: for a competitive sport or a leisure activity.[6] For a sport "that only a few years ago was reserved for men . . . an outfit close to men's clothing for the convenience of contact and action" was necessary, especially in the typical open-body car.[7] Women could wear a full-body jumpsuit, usually constructed with light-colored and durable, washable fabrics, with a long zipper so that it was easy to put on. Another possibility was a tweed ensemble consisting of a jacket and full-length trousers or plus fours. Protective accessories included leather gloves, a plain cap with

FIG. 131
Henri Cartier-Bresson, French, 1908–2004; *First paid vacations, along the Marne river, France, 1936*, 1936; gelatin silver print; 7 11/16 × 10 3/4 in.; Fondation Henri Cartier-Bresson, Paris

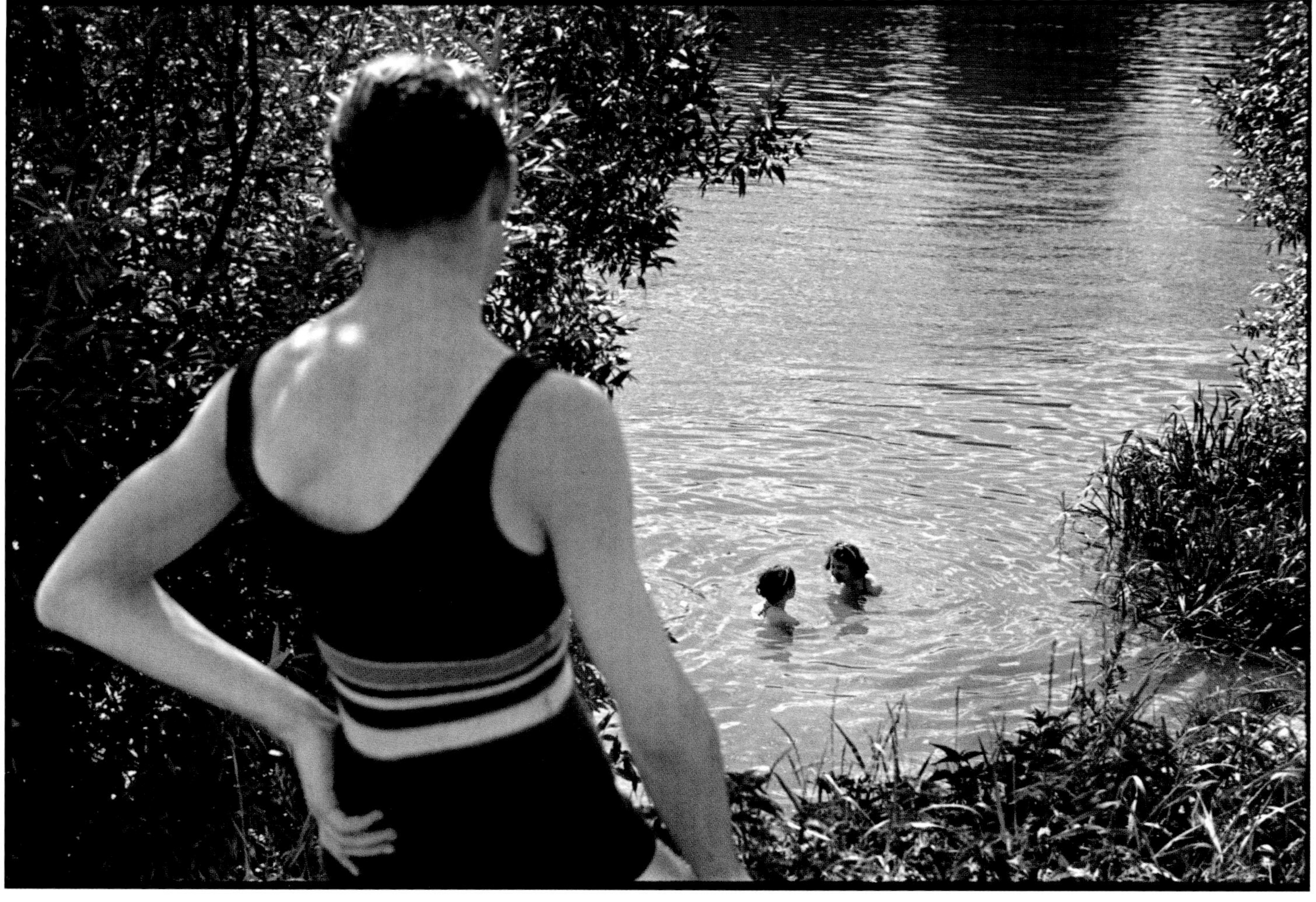

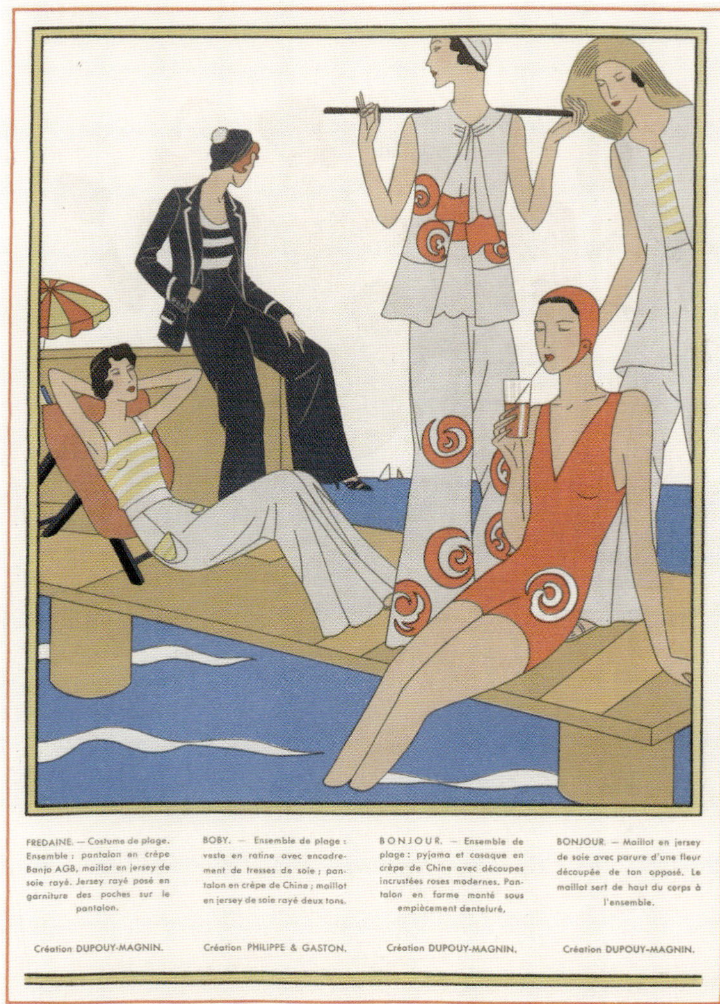

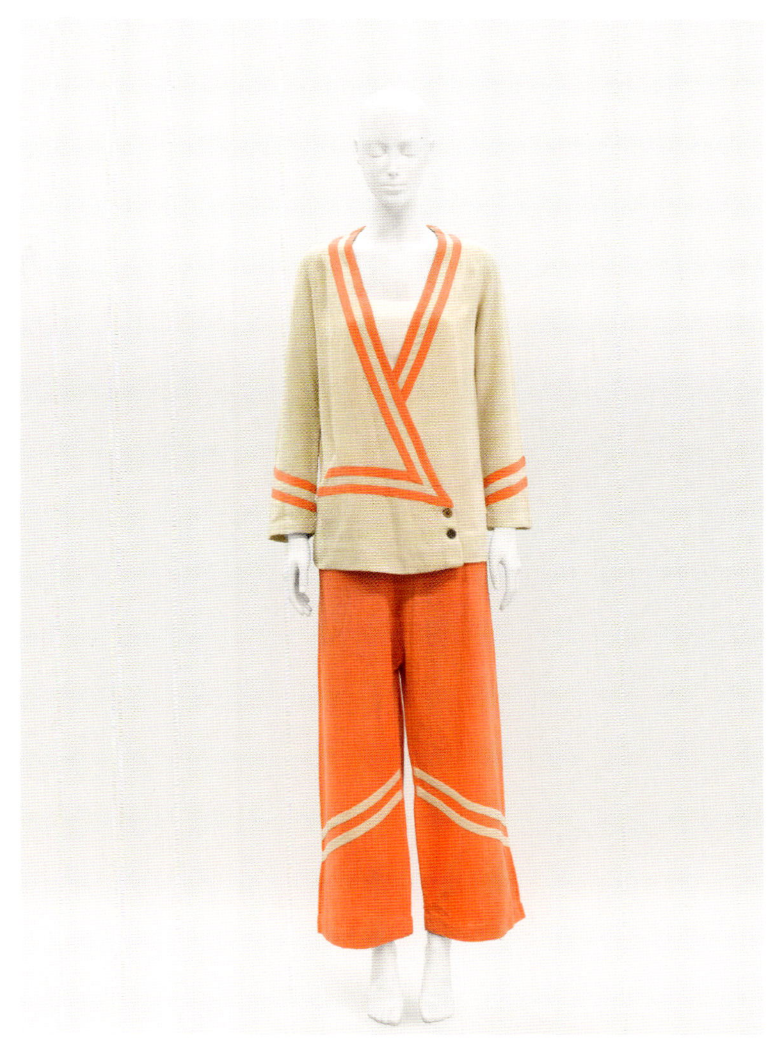

FIG. 132
Ensemble de plage designed by Dupouy-Magnin and Philippe et Gaston in *Art, goût, beauté,* August, 1931

FIG. 133
Jacket and Pants, c.1930; cotton plain weave and buttons; Stephens College Costume Museum and Research Library, Columbia, Missouri

"Whether she's driving or being driven, a woman needs to wear an appropriate costume . . . , until the blessed days of summer. . . . This August we've seen pajamas in the cabriolet, bathing suits in the torpedo, and bathrobes over 'nothing-else' in closed-cab cars." (Lysiane Bernhardt, *Revue de l'ACFF*, July 1933).

chin straps, and thick mica goggles. Except for the addition of a few technical advancements—lining or padding made of rubber foam, for example, to absorb shock—the sports outfit remained mostly unchanged during this period.[8] Some of these elements made their way into high fashion, while others, like the jumpsuit, were left behind.

With closed-body cars, less protective attire was needed, ending an era of thick fur driving coats with "amateur motorists dressed as polar explorers."[9] Before car heaters became common, the driving coat was needed to keep riders warm and protect their clothing, especially in a convertible or when the windows were open. Driving coats were designed to be wide enough to cover any outfit, with high collars for wind protection and large armholes with specific cuts to allow for raglan sleeves or sleeves with an underarm gusset (FIG. 136). The female driver could also wear a blouse with a removable collar under her coat or sweater; "nothing could be simpler once arrived than to bleach the collars we carry dozens of, which fit the blouses separately like men's collars," often secured with a tie (FIG. 134).[10]

The advancement of the automobile also opened the door to new accessories, and designers were bursting with inventive ideas. In the interwar period, cars typically had separate keys for the locks and ignition. Before long, as keys became smaller and lighter, Hermès launched a key ring that "allow[ed] the usually small key to be found in the bag or pocket."[11] Gloves, essential for driving, became increasingly practical and experimental. Crispin gloves, which featured a sewn cuff, or elbow-length styles were favored to protect sleeves from mud, dust, or grease, and some featured zippers for easy removal. Disposable paper gloves, easily stored in the glove box, were worn to avoid staining expensive leather gloves with oil.[12] Hermès designed a detachable pigskin cuff fitted with multiple inner pockets "for rouge, powder, change, and a handkerchief."[13] With advances in automotive technology that allowed for smoother steering, such as independent front wheels, thinner leather gloves were designed for better grip and maneuverability. This marked a shift from the thick, lined gloves used before World War I for driving in open-chassis cars. As automobiles

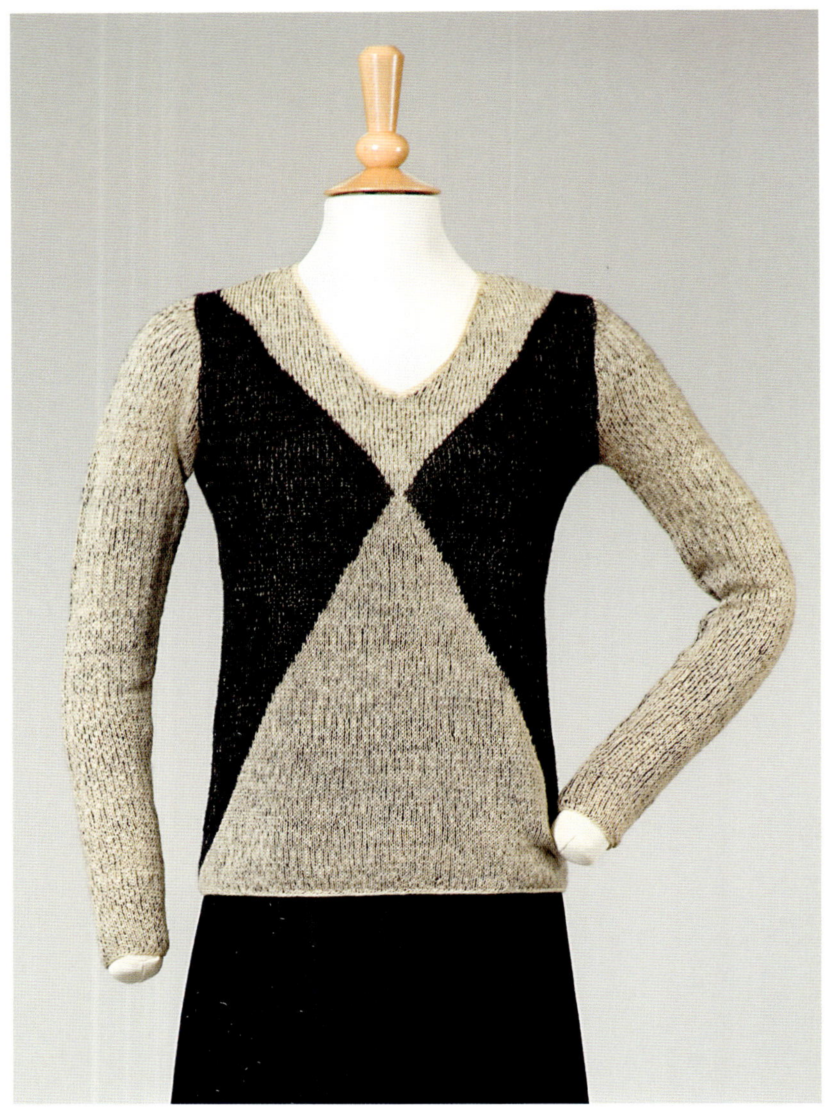

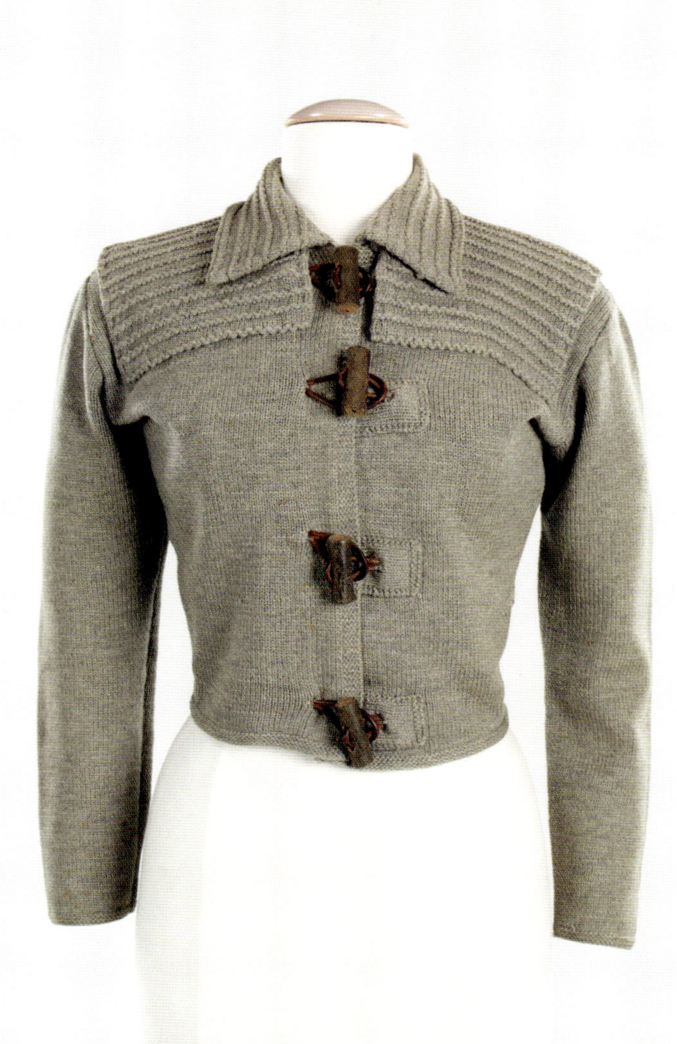

transitioned to closed bodywork with heaters, gloves with their own openwork designs and perforations were introduced to allow hands to breathe.

Materials also influenced the choice of motoring ensemble. Wool poplin, a tightly woven, finely ribbed broadcloth made of silk and wool, was suitable for driving attire, as it was easy to clean, crease-free, and lightweight. Designers used wool not only because it was common, but because its natural properties made it appropriate for automotive fashions. Two years after opening his Paris boutique, Cristóbal Balenciaga designed a raglan traveling coat made of Escorial wool.[14] Appreciated for its lightness and natural elasticity, such coats were less likely to wrinkle and recovered their original shape easily.

Among many designers interested in movement, a key feature in automotive design, one stands out: Lucien Lelong, a theoretician and technician of kineticism in fashion (FIGS. 140, 145). "What is kineticism? Quite simply, the theory of the figure in motion," said Lelong.[15] "[It] is the fashion for the woman on the move (FIGS. 135, 138); for the modern girl who drives, plays tennis, etc.... with a cut designed to allow even violent movements, without, as in the past, violating a sleeve or moving the waistline."[16] A brochure by Shell summarizes this codependent evolution of the automobile and attire:

> Our [age] is one of speed; we've made it the basis of a new aesthetic. . . . In 1904, . . . a narrow . . . and disproportionately high car body. It's true that they harmonize with the customs of the time: tight waists, leg of mutton sleeves, hats perched on top of the head. . . . We prefer now sleek, smooth, pure lines that, despite or thanks to the mechanical idea, meet our ideal of suppleness. . . . And that goes perfectly with soft collars, leather gloves, fancy sweaters, and also the short skirts and narrow helmets of our [female] companions. . . . Everything is logical and harmonious. . . . Handbag, scarf, matching the bodywork, why not? (FIGS. 139, 141)[17]

FIG. 134
Elsa Schiaparelli, Italian, 1890–1973; Schiaparelli, Paris, founded 1927; *Sweater*, c.1928; cashmere knit; Western Reserve Historical Society, Cleveland, Ohio

FIG. 135
Elsa Schiaparelli, Italian, 1890–1973; *Sweater*, c.1935; wool and leather; Brooklyn Museum Costume Collection at The Metropolitan Museum of Art, New York, Gift of the Brooklyn Museum, 2009; Gift of Arturo and Paul Peralta-Ramos, 1955

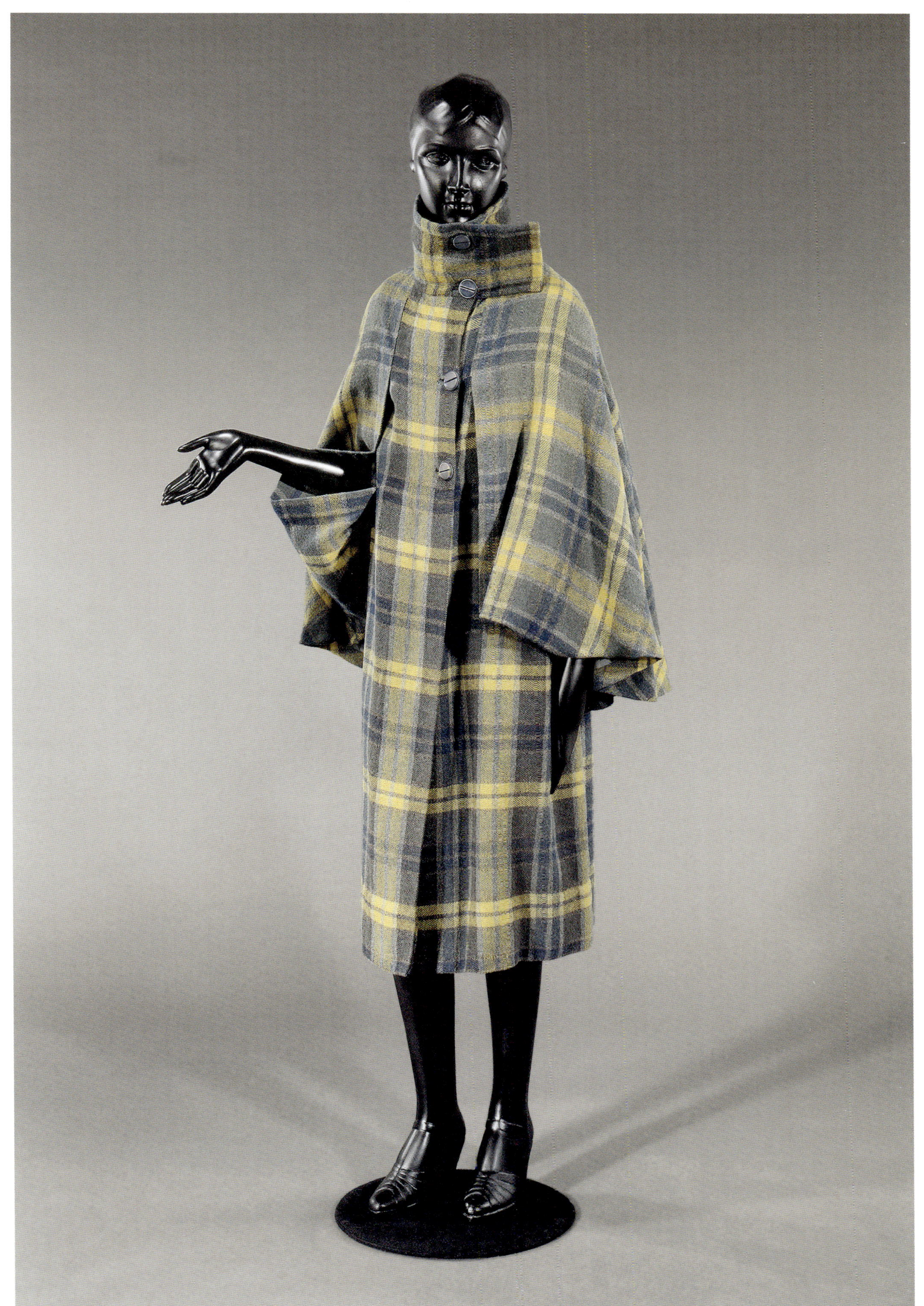

FIG. 136
Dornac, *"100 à l'heure" ("In the fast lane") Traveling Coat*, c.1923; Scottish wool twill; Palais Galliera, Musée de la Mode de la Ville de Paris, GAL1968.42.2

This coat, cut with practical, wide, open sleeves, reflects the appetite of a decade enamored with movement, speed, and frenzy—the same ideas promoted in car design. The name of this coat reflects this new lifestyle.

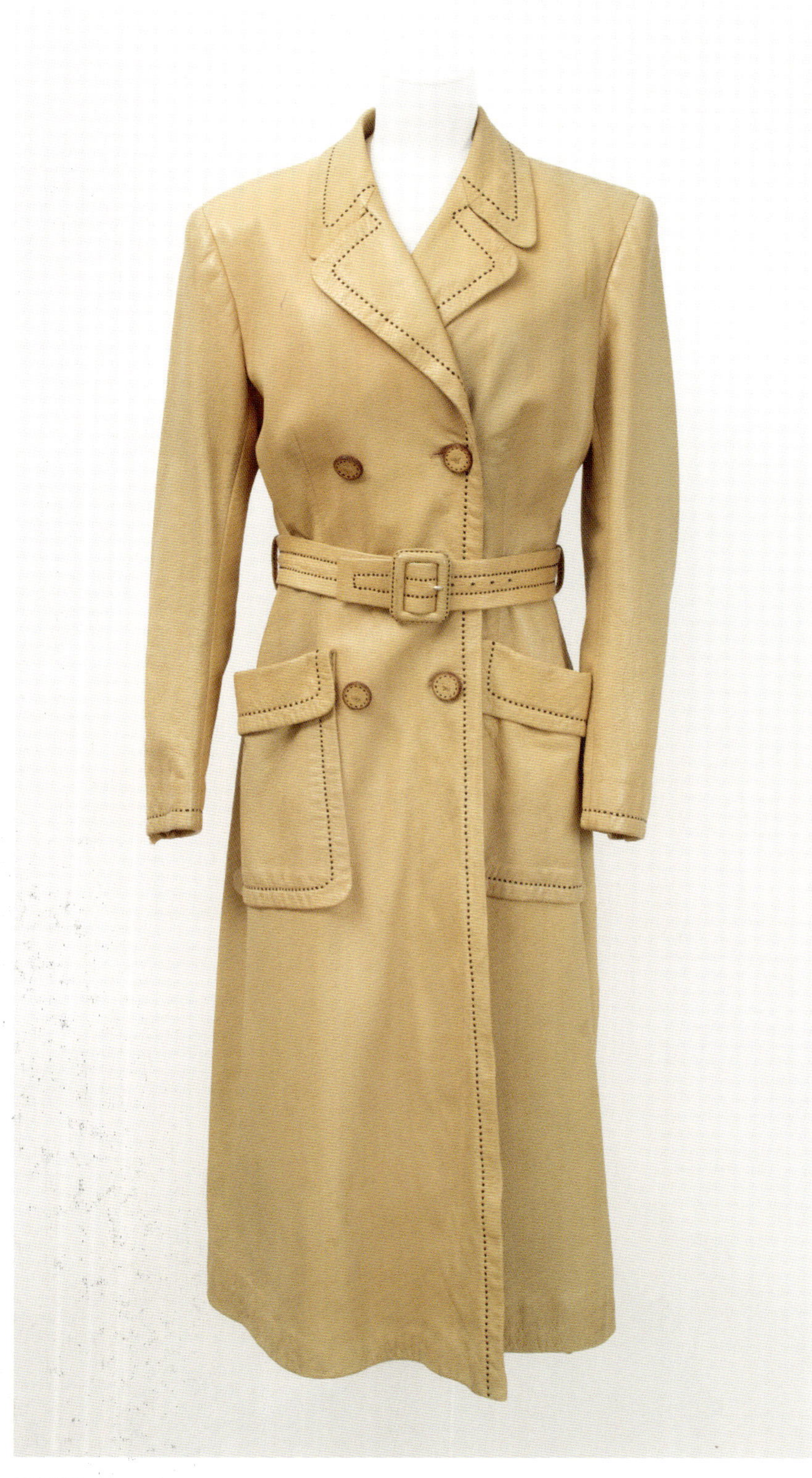

FIG. 137
Hermès, Paris, founded 1837; *Bespoke Coat Inspired by AVION Coat*, Collection Sport Autumn–Winter, 1935; stag leather; Conservatoire des Créations Hermès

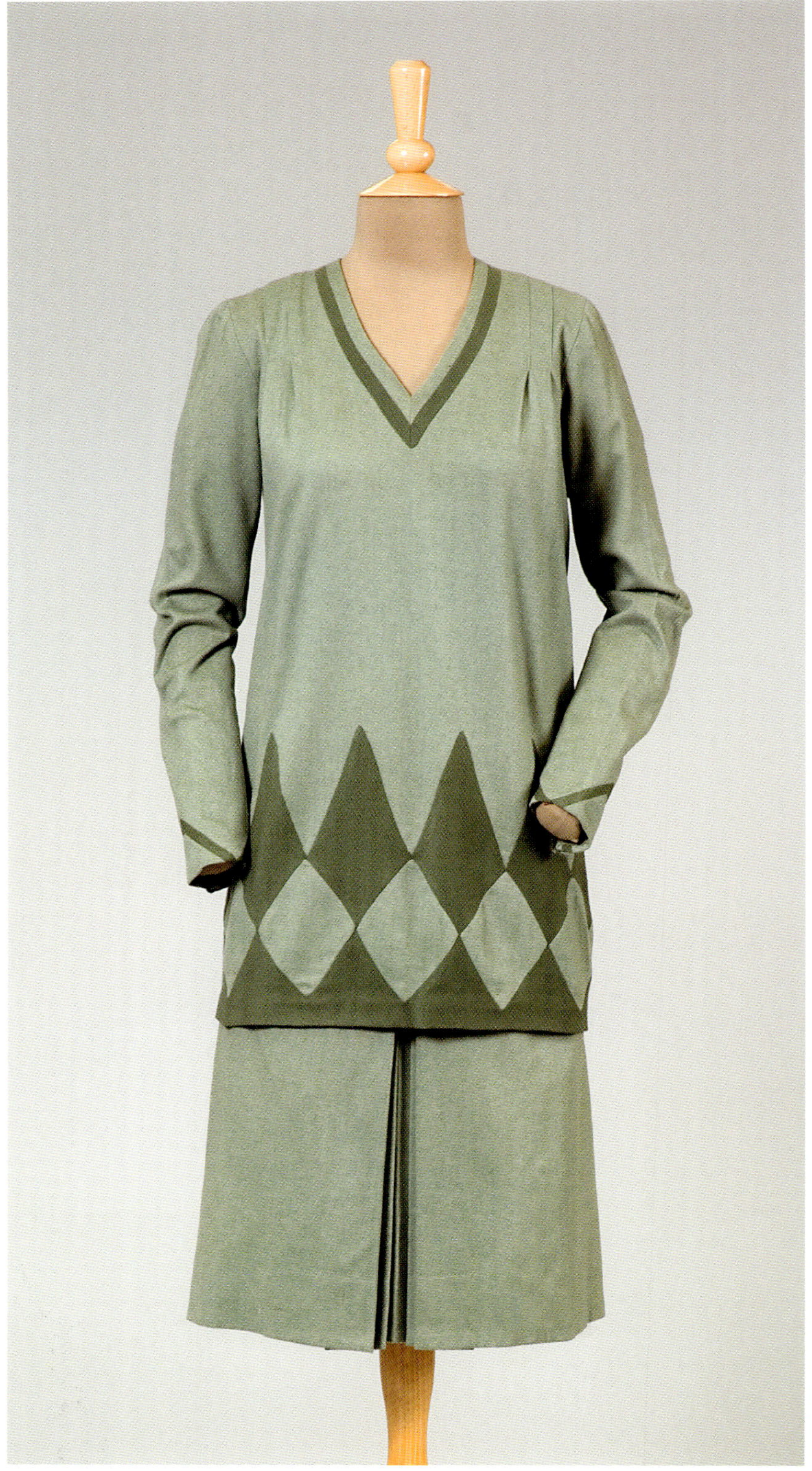

FIG. 138
Jeanne Laffitte, Paris, active c.1926–29; *Sport Suit*, c.1928; wool twill and silk; Western Reserve Historical Society, Cleveland, Ohio

The essential sportswear outfit—sweater, matching skirt, and sometimes an extra jacket—was used for driving. Some automotive versions feature wider sleeves but tight cuffs, or a buttoned, removable lining for year-round use. As for other sports, the modern woman used modular elements to adapt her attire for the activity.

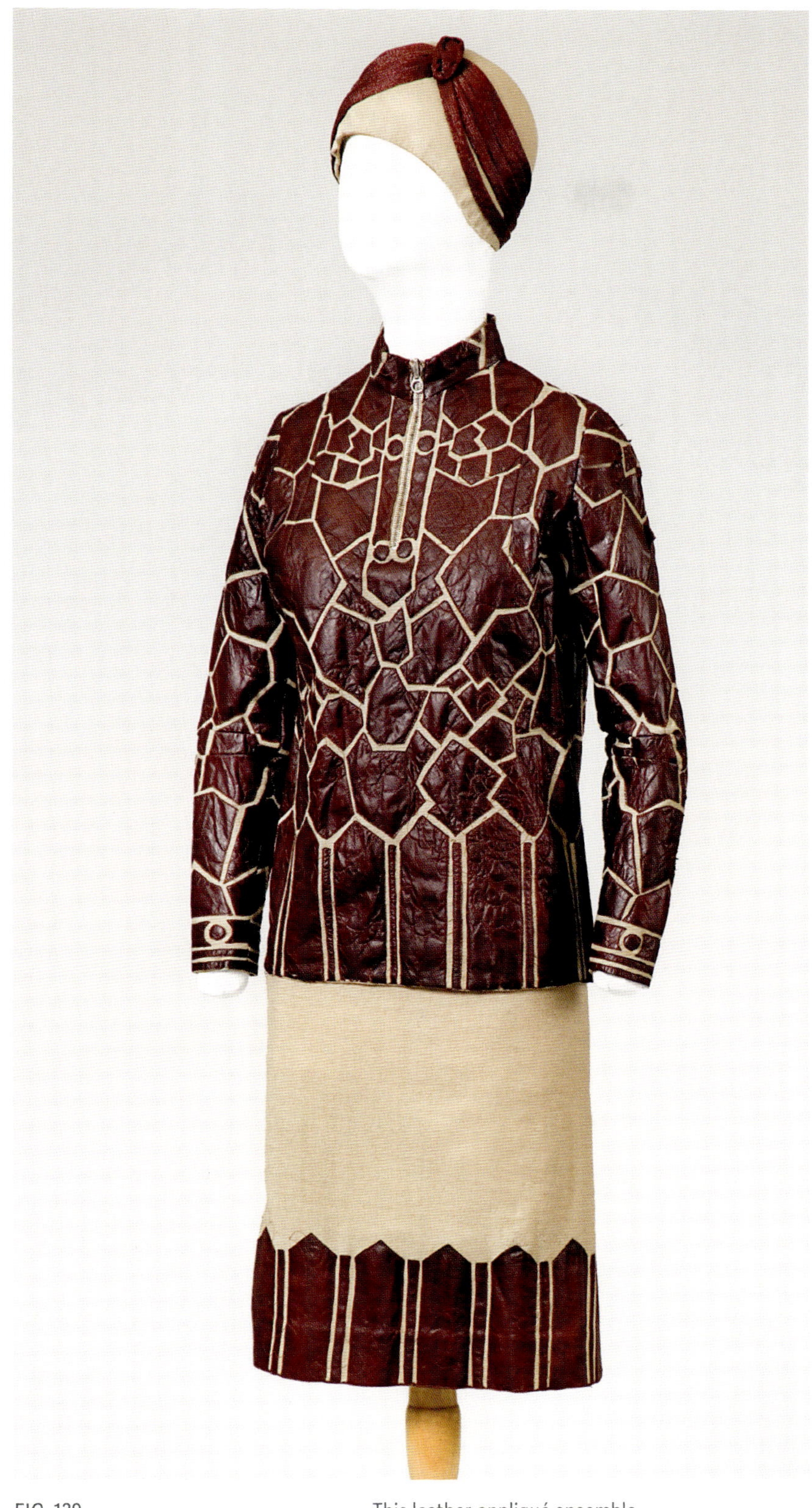

FIG. 139
French; *Ensemble*, c.1928; wool twill flannel with kid leather appliqués and topstitching; Western Reserve Historical Society, Cleveland, Ohio

This leather-appliqué ensemble was acquired in Paris as part of Maud Eells Corning's trousseau. Automobile fashion became so popular that it became part of wedding trousseaux or wedding gifts, as *Le Petit Écho de la Mode* wrote in 1927.

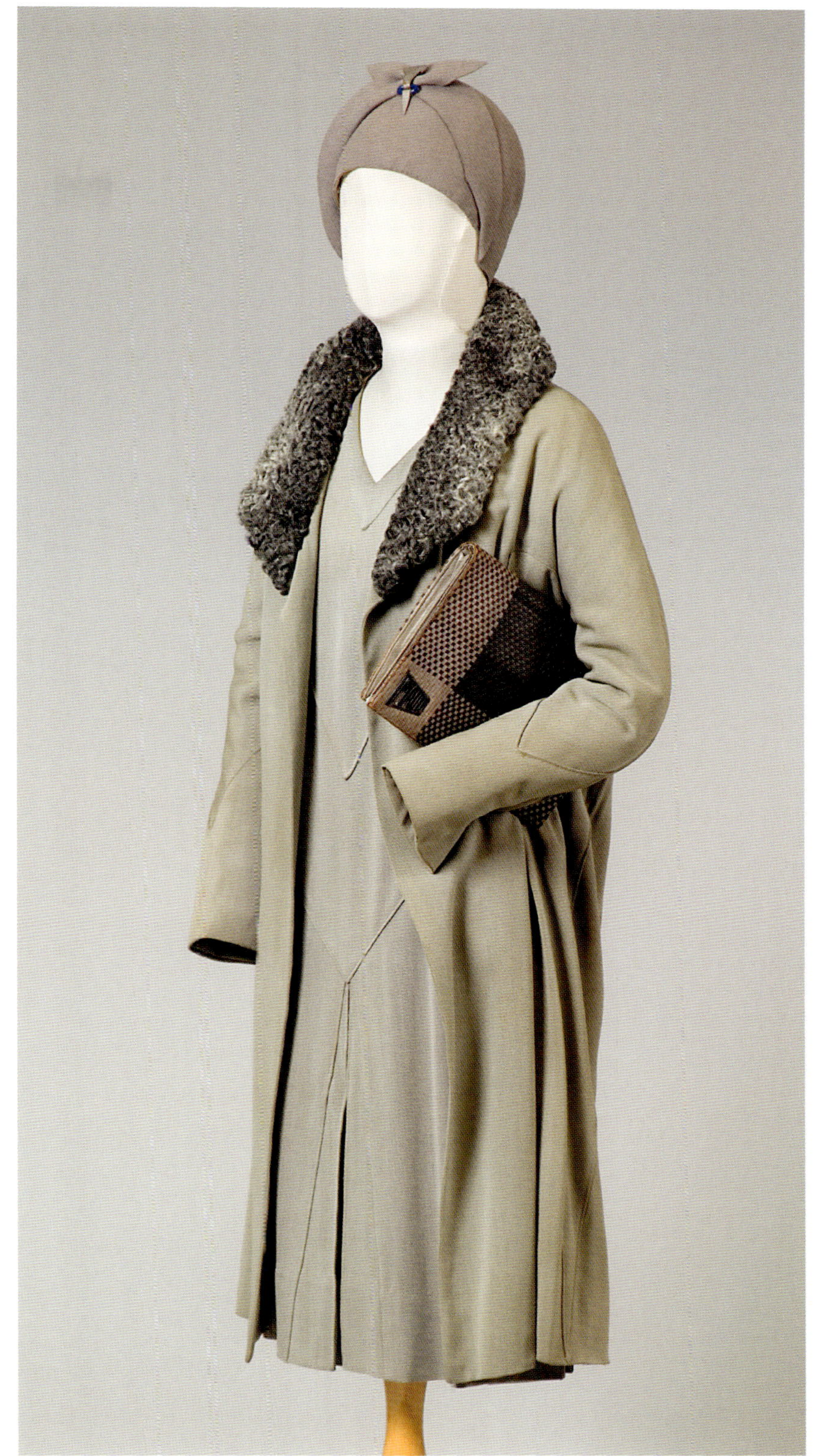

FIG. 140
Lucien Lelong, French, 1889–1958; House of Lelong, French, 1921–48; *Coat and Dress*, spring 1928; wool plain weave with karakul [Persian lamb fur] collar; *Clutch Purse*, 1928; woven leather; Cécile Marguerite, Paris; *Cloche*, wool felt with sterling and lapis brooch; Western Reserve Historical Society, Cleveland, Ohio

Fashionization, Feminization, and Gender Imperatives

In 1925, Parisian women were described as challenging female expectations: "These beings—without breasts, without hips, who smoke . . . who, during the night at the Bois de Boulogne . . . seek out savory and acrobatic pleasures on the plush seats of 5 horsepower Citroëns—these aren't young girls! . . . No more women either!"[18] The car, a means of traveling to the Bois de Boulogne, is not only here a symbol of free movement but also of sexuality, especially for women identified as tendentious *garçonnes*. Violette Morris was one of these controversial figures. A lesbian, athlete, and successful driver who often dressed as a man, she gained widespread attention by defying gender norms, notably through her driving performance (FIG. 142).

Lysiane Bernhardt, granddaughter of the actress Sarah Bernhardt, was also an actress, driver, and journalist, including for the ACFF. Though she evoked an impudent masculinity in her motoring fashions, she insisted it was only transitional: "Transvestism, Madame, must never be more than a state of chrysalis, allowing you to become even more feminine," she said. "You can still be a woman and handle a car. . . . No need to dress up as a mechanic."[19] The wealthy women in the ACFF were highly visible in the press, especially for their elegant sobriety, or as the popular newspaper *Le Gaulois* wrote, "*un port de toilette* that always reflected the refined appeal of the Frenchwoman, the Parisienne 'racial' side."[20]

Automobile fashion borrowed from men's wardrobes, and its essential piece—the wide coat—obscured the female body (FIG. 137). The interwar period in France is often perceived as the first golden age of sportswear, featuring a *garçonne* style. Concerns about women appearing too masculine, however, led to the feminization of sportswear (FIGS. 143, 144). Unlike what François Thomazeau calls the "quasi-unisex" attire offered to drivers before the Great War, the interwar era made automobile clothing fashionable and distinctly feminine, serving to reshape femininity and enforce gender norms.[21] Designers' strategies to maintain "real Chic"—the ability to "get out of the car after five hundred kilometers in an outfit that doesn't

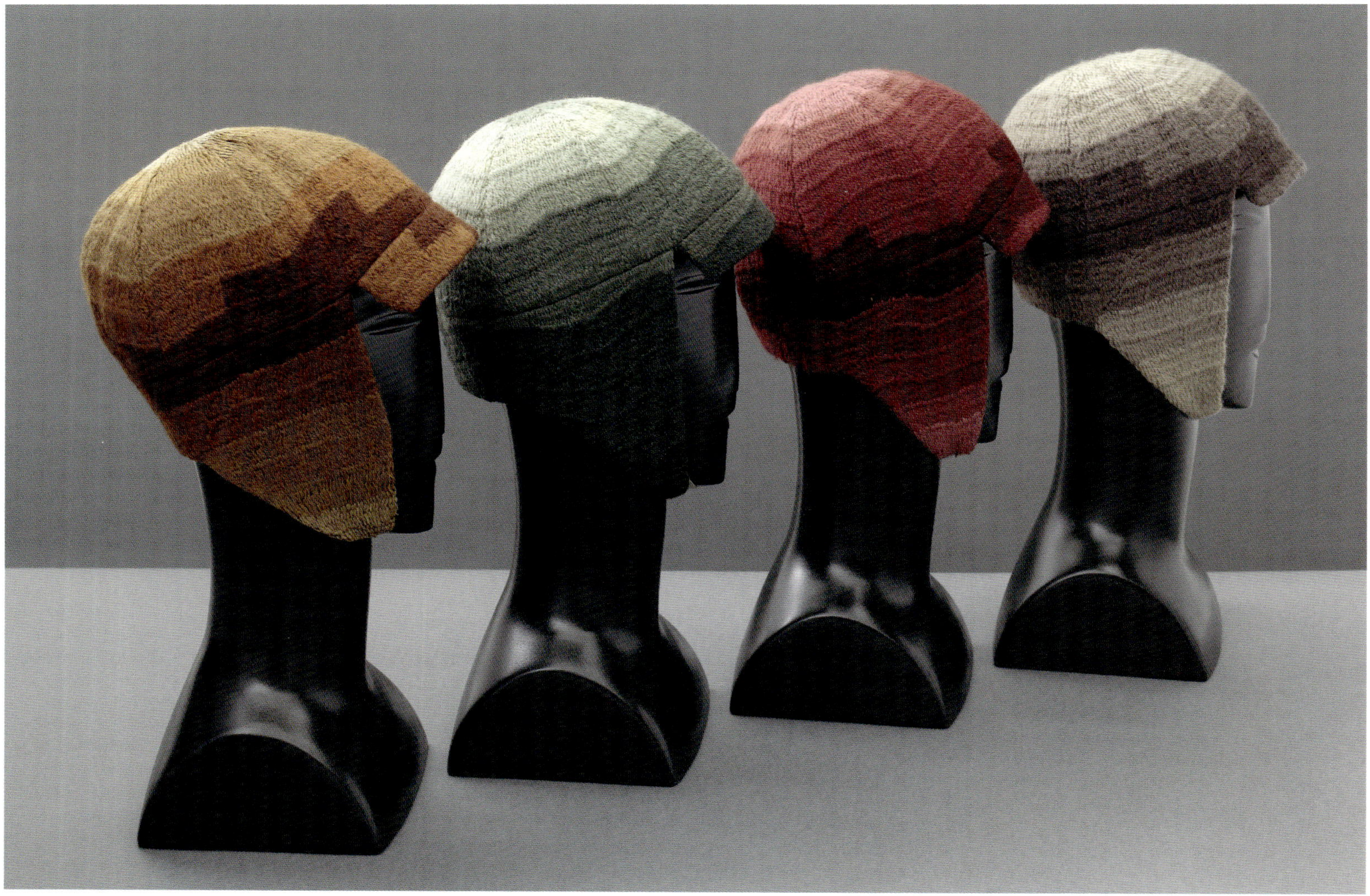

FIG. 141
Sonia Delaunay, French (born Ukraine), 1885–1979; *Driving Hoods*, 1924–28; embroidered polychrome wool with green damask rayon lining; Palais Galliera, Musée de la Mode de la Ville de Paris, GAL1971.24.3ABCD

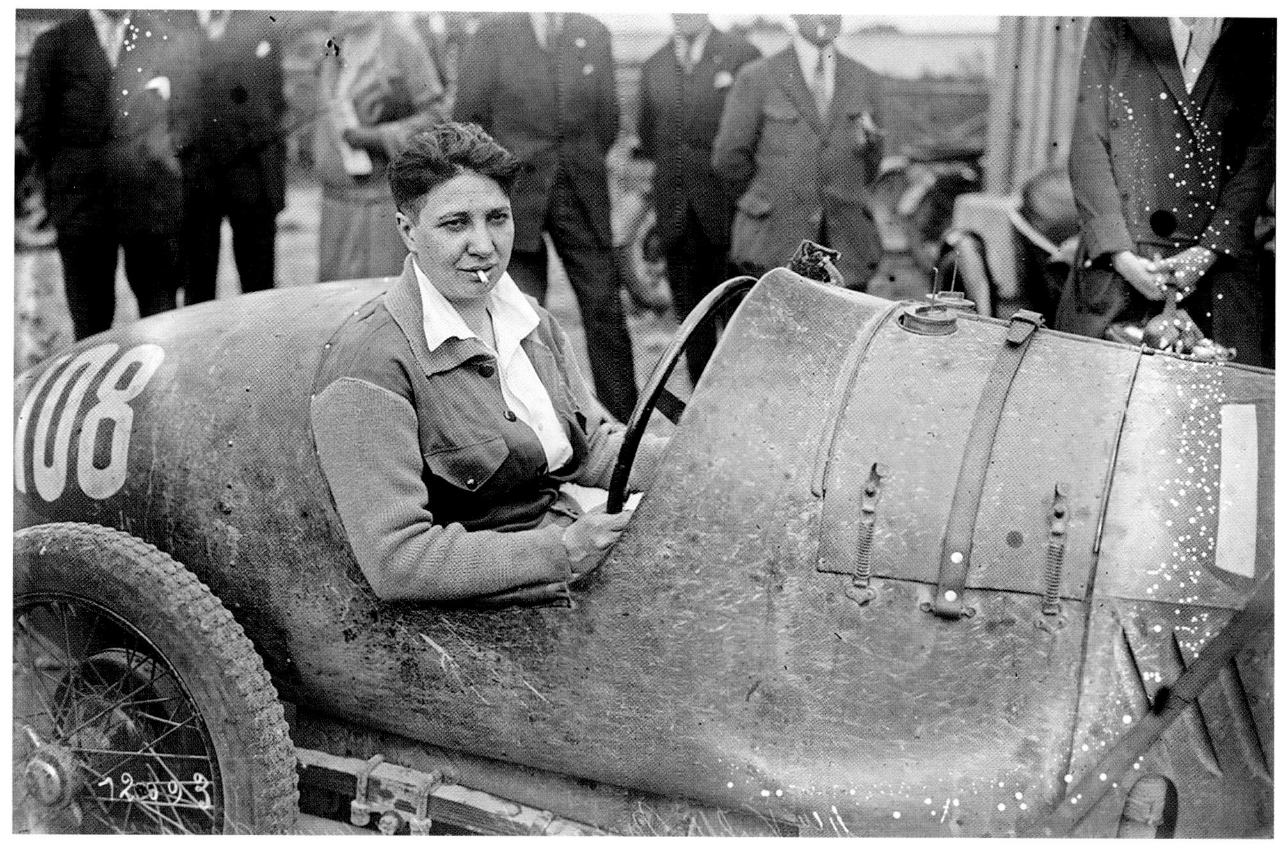

FIG. 142
Agence Rol, French, 1904–1937; *Mademoiselle Violette Morris, winner of the women's skill competition at the Montlhéry autodrome*, Paris, June 12, 1927; Bibliothèque nationale de France, Paris, département Estampes et photographie, EI-13 (1445)

Portrayed wearing a man's shirt under a jacket with practical, knitted sleeves and leather panels, Morris was an actual "being without breasts." She later had a mastectomy because the "two cumbersome machines—useless in sport—made it difficult to handle the steering wheel" (Fourchadière, *L'Oeuvre*, 1930).

evoke a Central Asian expedition"[22]—communicated the new imperatives of the *beau sexe* ("the fair sex" or literally "the beautiful sex"). Excessive fabric wrinkles, which appear while driving, could reveal a woman's various activities and imply the neglect of her appearance. The house Henry à la Pensée, which specialized in travel clothing, introduced a portable iron with a folding handle that could be easily stored.[23] Many wide coats, such as the reversible *tenue à transformation* (transformation outfit), could be easily converted into elegant attire after a drive. The textile manufacturer Rémond produced reversible woven material with the coarse grain of "sports fabrics" and a smooth, velvety lining. "Automobile girdles," in latex or rubber knit, were short enough to be more practical while one was sitting for a long time, while assuring a thin(ner) waist, especially when the wearer was standing out of the car.

Tamara de Lempicka's 1929 self-portrait embodies both modernity and femininity (FIG. 31). Her flawless makeup signals her gender. Cosmetic brands promised long-lasting wear, ensuring women could emerge from their cars "looking as fresh as when [they] got in."[24] Comte Frédéric de Janzé, the famous motorist, describes a 1929 automobile equipped with a wooden box, similar to one by Cartier, which opened at the touch of a button to reveal "mirror, powder, perfume, . . . the beauty necessities made each day more necessary."[25]

Women were cautioned against appearing unladylike after a drive. One tale tells of "a young woman whose engagement to a young man . . . ended because he saw her one day getting out of a car, with badly pulled stockings."[26] Capitalizing on such fears, the knitwear manufacturer André Gillier, known for his collaborations with René Lacoste, promoted his products with a similar story: "Madame, why did this badly torn stocking spoil all the pleasure of your last country ride [with a man]? For the car . . . JiL stockings are the perfect complement to your sportswear."[27] These imperatives spread to the attitude of the driver. École Vauban, a driving school for women in Lyon, reassured their students (and parents) that it was "a chic school for dames," where one could learn how to drive elegantly as a lady.[28]

The automobile, too, became deeply intertwined with fashion, to the extent that "when it comes to cars, fashions change as quickly as the Rue de la Paix."[29] After 1929, French *carrossiers* elevated their work, comparing it to haute couture:

> There has been a tendency to believe in the disappearance of "made-to-measure" bodywork . . . as if all automobiles will be clad in "ready-to-wear" bodies. The prophecy doesn't hold; even supposing it's true on the other side of the Atlantic, it would be a fiasco in Paris, a city of taste, elegance,

> creative center of fashion. Can you imagine the Paris couturiers disappearing under the onslaught of mass-produced clothing factories? Impossible.[30]

In 1935, *Vogue* proposed: "[If] in the past, a woman's personality was defined by her dress and her hat, now there's something even better: her car. Don't you think, Madame, that the one a coach builder dressed [*habilla*] with more studied lines and more harmonious colors is indeed a reflection of the woman who owns it?"[31] The article included photographs of women posing by their cars: "The camera's lens caught Countess Arnaud de Contâtes in a pale blue suit by Maggy Rouff, a navy blue straw hat, a dark blue and myotis blue coach Peugeot 601."[32] The matching car became a fashion accessory that could enhance a woman's elegance as much as a hat.

Automobile shows became social events, from the annual Salon de l'Automobile at the Grand Palais to the *concours d'élégance* (FIG. 151), not unlike Fashion Week.[33] The comparisons between what covers the body of a car and the body of a woman became a commonplace: "Cars go to their coachbuilders (*carrossiers*), women to their dressmakers (couturiers), there's only the beginning of the words to change. Cars waste as much time with those who dress them as our companions. . . . What could be prettier than a woman who has been able to have a car body made in harmony with her toilette?"[34]

Cars were described with phrases like *les toilettes* and *la silhouette des automobiles* or *habiller une automobile* with bodywork. "Lightness," "graceful feminine lines," "long silhouette," "elegance," "harmony," "charming," "class," "smart," "gracious," "slim," "thin," "slender," "svelte," "delicate," "refined," and "ravishing" were all used to describe the ideal car, which are not unlike characterizations and qualities expected from women and their clothes. An advertisement for Peugeot plays on these similarities: "I have a perfect friend. She's elegant, sober, lively, confident, punctual, economical. She's my 202 [name of the car model]."[35] All the qualities expected of an ideal 1930s young woman became qualities desired in a car. The advertisement shows the idealized 202 woman—elegant in a long lamé evening dress, lively while playing tennis, confident as well as faithful—ending with a picture of the car.

The Automobile: Modern Femininity Across the Empire?

In 1931, Élaine Greffulhe was invited by Madame Citroën to visit the Colonial Exhibition of 1931,

FIG. 143
Jenny Sacerdote, French, 1868–1962; Jenny, Paris, active 1909–1940; *Jacket*, c.1926; silk crepe, karakul [Persian lamb fur], silk braid, metallic thread, and silk plain weave; Courtesy of the Missouri Historical Society, St. Louis

FIG. 144
Sweater, c.1930; wool knit; Stephens College Costume Museum and Research Library, Columbia, Missouri

FIG. 145
Attributed to Lucien Lelong, French, 1889–1958; *Afternoon Dress*, c.1927; silk chiffon. Stephens College Costume Museum and Research Library, Columbia, Missouri

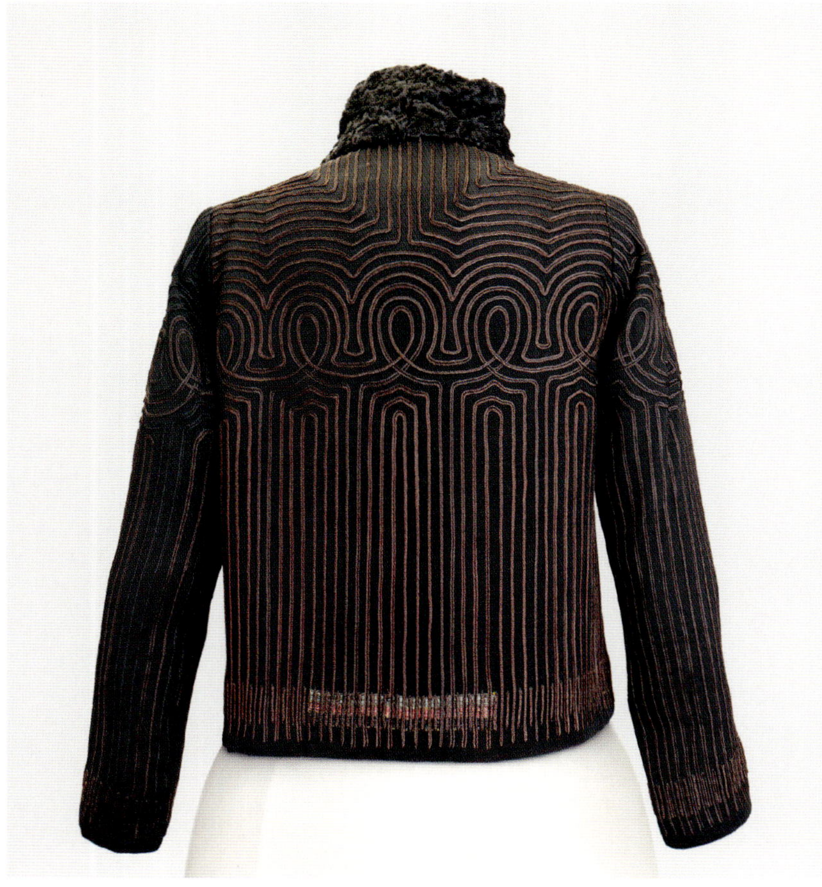

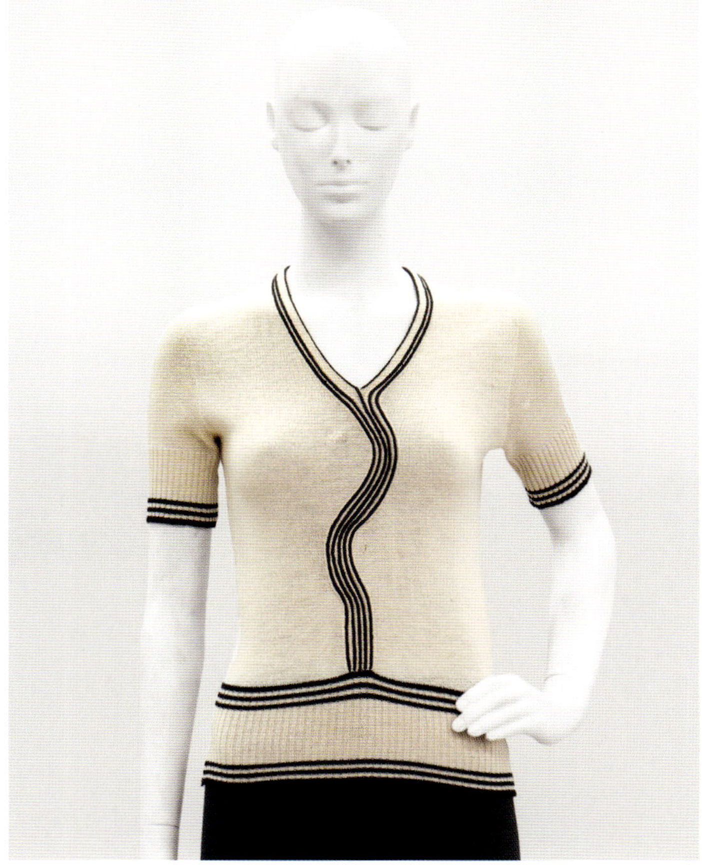

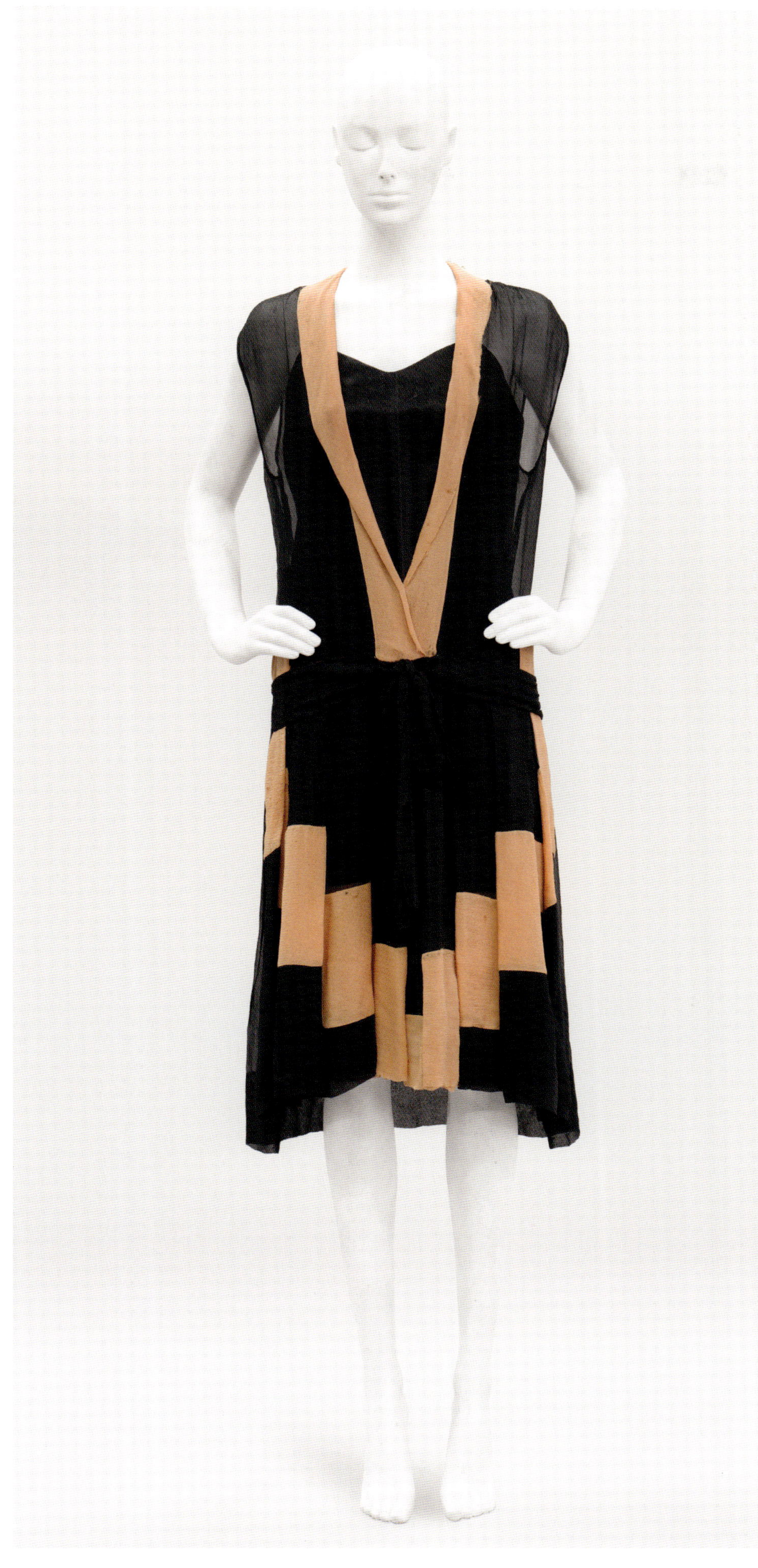

where cars were presented alongside a section promoting tourism in the French colonies, as "the automobile . . . could not fail to feature so prominently at this major event. . . . It has always provided and will continue to provide such excellent services to the colonies."[36] Élaine could have toured the exhibition in an electric car, driven by a chauffeur in colonial attire.

In North Africa, the settler world was drawn to the automobile—Renault launched in 1924 its 10 CV Coloniale with a heightened chassis. The automobile became a modern tool for settlers to discover and appropriate all the Algerian territories explored hitherto by the military or bourgeois *hiverneurs* (winterers). The use of the car was also part of the woman settler's mission: "Don't forget . . . that you, the Algéroise, are just like the Parisienne, the 'Frenchwoman' everywhere imitated, never equaled. That's why, as an Algéroise, I want you to be sporty, modern, ready to embrace all the conquests of science and use them to your advantage," stated the local women's periodical.[37] Citroën, which promoted its cars for the "elegant [settler] woman," opened a store on rue d'Isly, Algiers's "rue de la Paix." Describing rue d'Isly at a busy hour, a guidebook noted the presence of "light dull-skinned *colons'* sons, in too bright color clothes, jumping out of a red-leather convertible with bold nickel [plating]."[38] The settlers' sons are identified by their eye-catching cars, the bodywork of which reflects the light of the Algerian sun and their own wealth.

The automobile was a political engine that promoted tourism, especially in Algeria, the "North African California," as imagined by the colonial government. The author of the Algerian automobile Dunlop Guidebook dedicated it "to the Good French people, who have understood their duty . . . to explore North Africa."[39] The automobile played not only a symbolic role but also a practical one in this exploration, allowing French tourists to traverse the region with ease. Visitors to Algiers, often struck by its modernity ("there's hardly any violent sensation of having left Paris"),[40] could drive to natural parks, visit Roman archaeological sites, or venture into the desert or mountains where ski resorts had been established. Tourism groups tried to seduce French visitors, showing them the various environments that such a colony offered, all safely accessible with the modern car (FIG. 146). This was the aim of the guidebook, "published under the High Patronage of the Governor of Algeria": "No doubt your tours through these regions, so diverse but so rich in promise, will have inclined you to love them. . . . You will not refuse them your sons and daughters . . . in this land of

1er Septembre 51

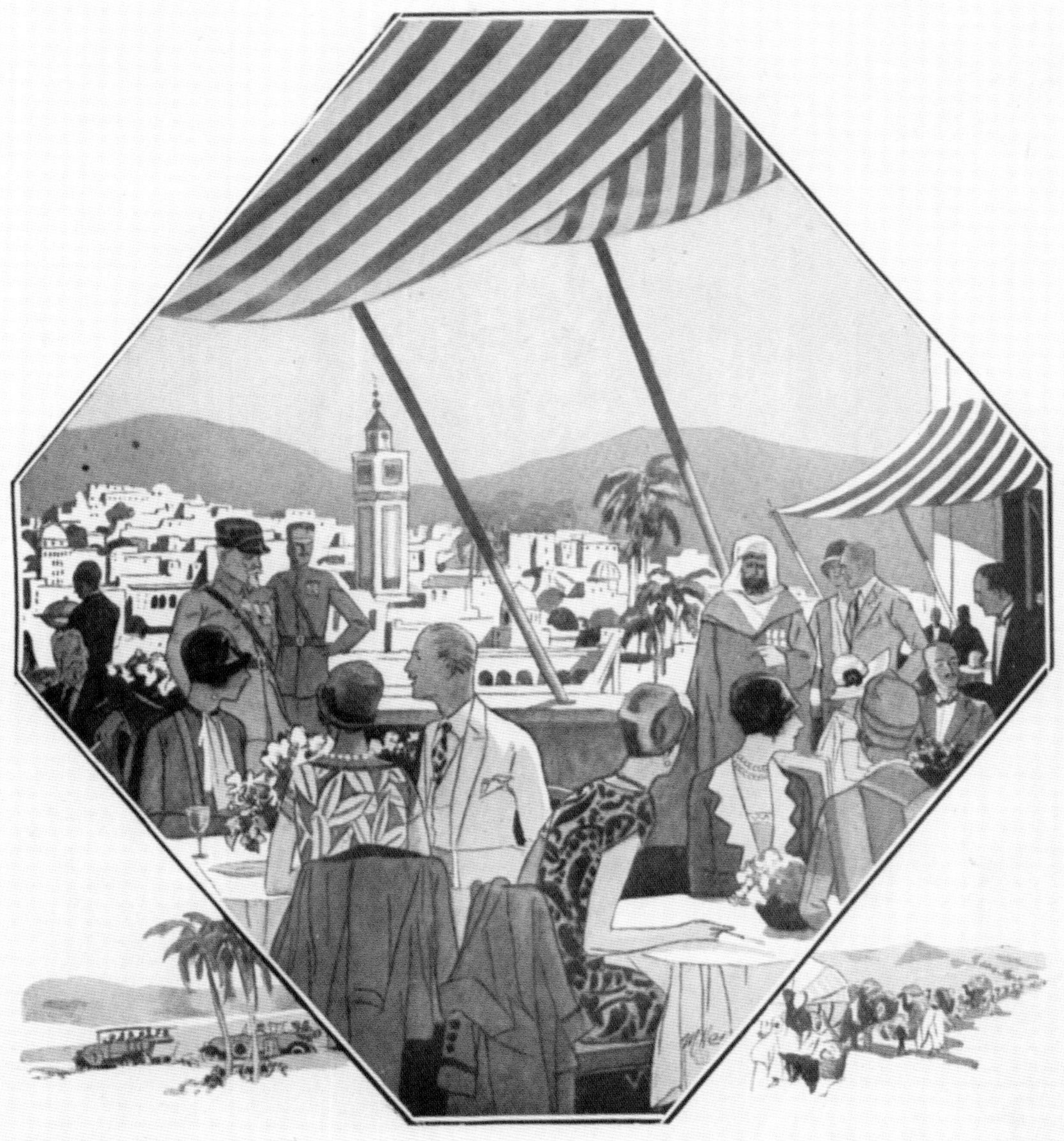

Passez les mauvais jours d'automne et d'hiver dans les pays du soleil
au Maroc — en Algérie — en Tunisie — dans le Sahara

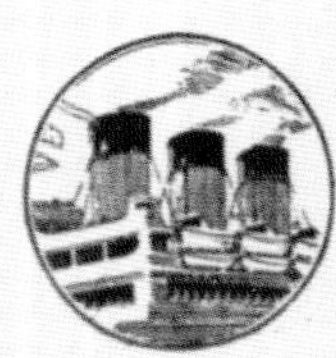

Le « Voyage à la Mode a décrété l'opinion universelle des touristes en parlant des « Auto-Circuits Nord-Africains ». Ce grand réseau automobile, dont la ligne principale — sur plus de 6.000 km, — va de l'oasis de Gabès jusqu'au pied de l'Atlas marocain s'impose comme la voie triomphale du tourisme africain. Non content de révéler toutes les beautés proches de la côte, il pousse maintenant d'importantes pointes vers les grands oasis du Sud et vers les hautes dunes du Sahara ou les émotions du touriste rejoignent presque celles de l'explorateur.

Le billet forfaitaire de la Société des Voyages et Hôtels Nord-Africains (service touristique de la Cie Gle Transatlantique) délivre de tout souci et de tout aléa. Il comporte tous les frais :

Traversées maritimes.
Parcours terrestres en automobile.
Séjour dans les 36 hôtels « transatlantique ».
Service des bagages.

Ces voyages en Afrique du Nord organisés comme ils le sont et pour lointains qu'ils paraissent, réalisent absolument cet idéal de repos dans le confort dont est friand notre monde civilisé.

Écrire à la STÉ DES VOYAGES & HOTELS NORD-AFRICAINS
6 *bis*, Rue Auber, PARIS

ou s'adresser :

AU SALON ARABE DE LA CIE GLE TRANSATLANTIQUE
6, Rue Auber, PARIS

et dans les Agences de la Compagnie :

12, Avenue de Verdun, NICE -- Villa Larralde, Rue Garderès, BIARRITZ, etc...

ou Compagnie Française du Tourisme, 30, Boulevard des Capucines, Paris.

FIG. 146
Advertisement for "Auto-Circuits Nord-Africains," published in *Vogue Paris*, September 1, 1926; Paris, Bibliothèque Nationale de France, Paris, département Littérature et art, FOL-V-5554 (BIS)

For such a trip, light-colored linen jersey—a crease-resistant fabric—or pure wool flannel was favored. The latter maintains warmth while also absorbing sweat and allowing it to evaporate slowly, a valuable quality for travel in the desert, where temperatures fluctuated.

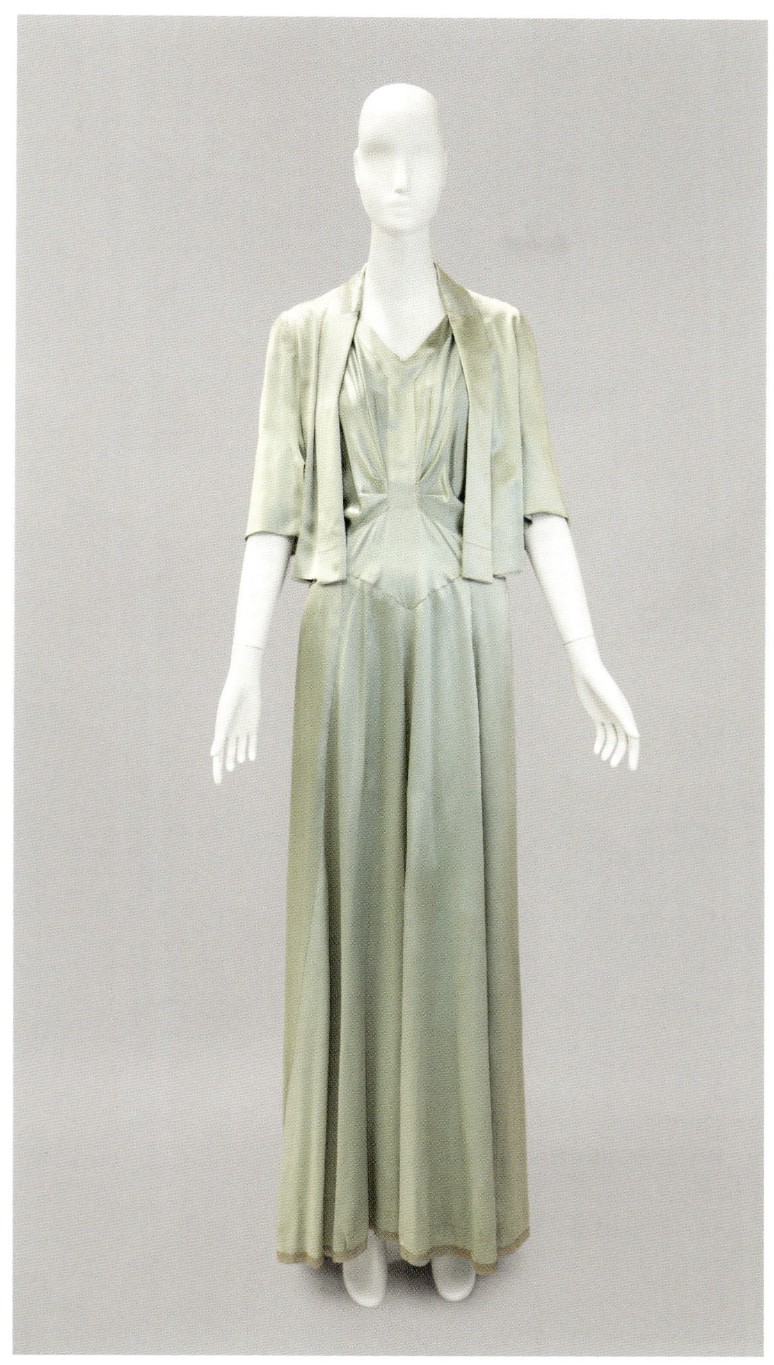

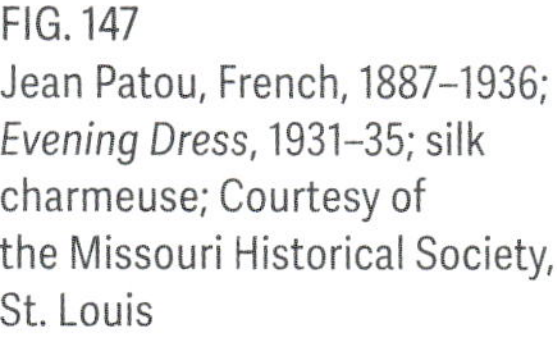

FIG. 147
Jean Patou, French, 1887–1936; *Evening Dress*, 1931–35; silk charmeuse; Courtesy of the Missouri Historical Society, St. Louis

Silk charmeuse is marked by a satin weave, a shiny and lustrous surface, and a matte finish on the reverse. This dress is constructed with many bias seams, highlighted with topstitching to create a slight ridge emphasizing the geometric shapes. The seams on the panels at the back accentuate the narrow waist.

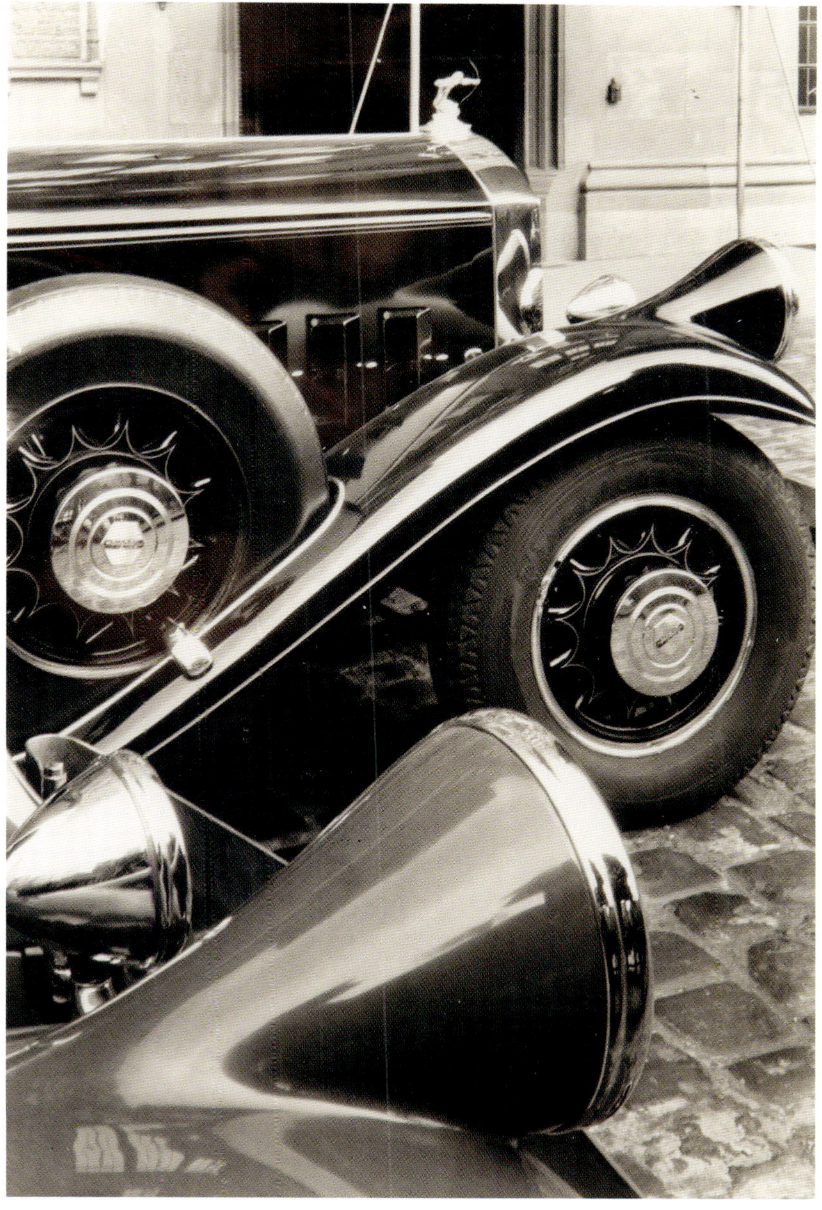

FIG. 148
Margaret Bourke-White, American, 1904–1971; *Pierce Arrow*, 1931; gelatin silver print; 10 × 8 in.; Estate of Margaret Bourke-White

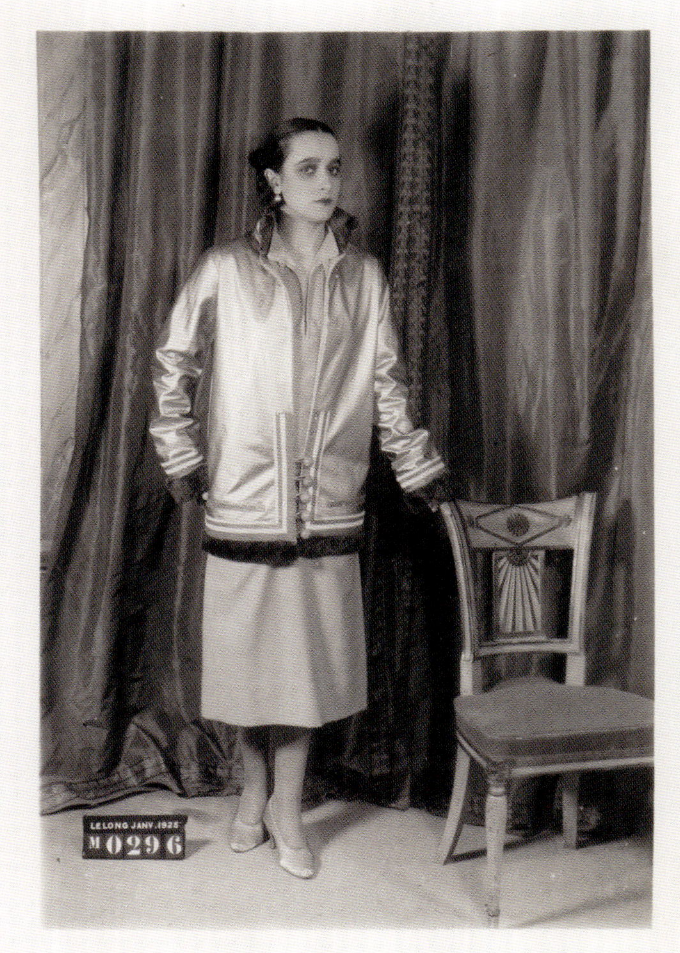

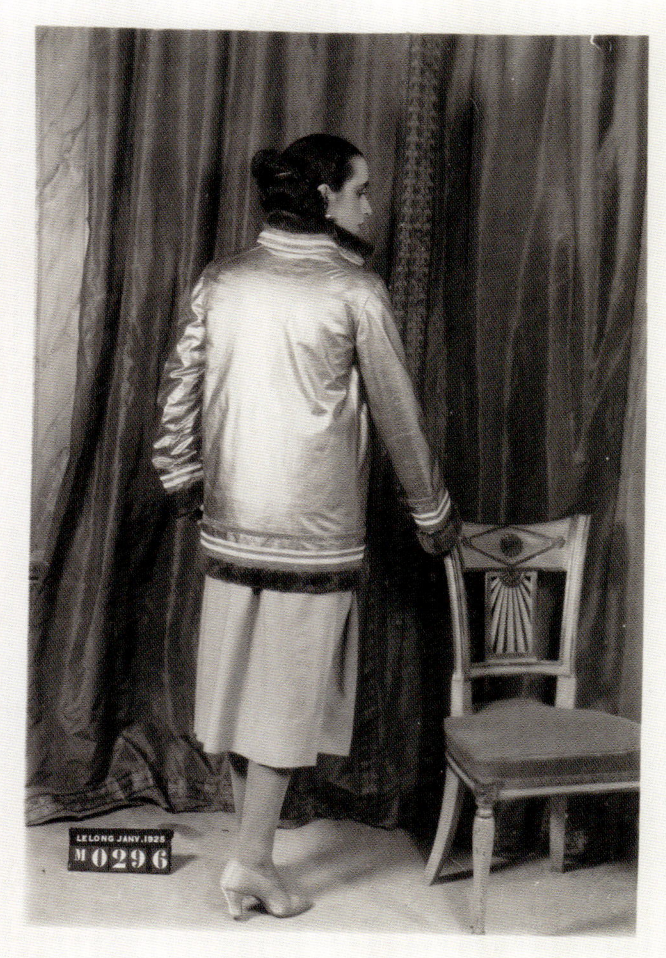

rejuvenation and fertility, for the renewal and broad blossoming of our race. . . . You are in France [and furthermore] you benefit from an excellent climate."[41]

For travel to the Sahara Desert, the ideal outfits sparked debate. An early photograph shows Madame Citroën dressed in practical, rather than elegant, attire: a "light and washable" duster, boots, and a colonial hat with a veil for "coping with the gray dusty air."[42] Guidebooks recommended summer *and* winter sportswear, along with the essentials: colonial helmet, veils, scarves, sandals, and tinted goggles, all storable in "Louis Vuitton . . . special, lightweight trunks that are absolutely impervious to dust and humidity."[43] Additionally, appropriating local garments like the veil *à la Marocaine* or the burnoose added an exotic appeal to the journey.

The colonization of the Sahara extended to turning its complex terrain into sites for festivities accessible by car. In 1932, the Automobile Club d'Alger considered hosting a "rock garden party" in the Hoggar Mountains after a rally.[44] Emmanuel Grévin recounts tales of tourists, including himself, traveling to the Hoggar, for which special garments were required: "Our clothes had to include both canvas and woolens. We carried sarouels, vast Saharan floating pants in pleated satinette. . . . As footwear, we wore canvas espadrilles with Basque-style rope soles, which we had to smear with 'gearbox' oil to make them last longer. . . . For sand, 'nails' (wide soles made of three layers of gazelle skin). For headgear, helmets and, above all, *chèche*."[45]

The materials used in automobile fashion can be traced back to the colonies.[46] Kapok, a natural fiber from places like French Indochina, was popular for quilting automotive attire and blankets in the 1930s. A valuable material, it was often counterfeited, leading to the official regulation and control of "fake kapok" by the French Foreign Affairs Ministry.[47] Driving from North Africa, viewed as "an extension of the Riviera," to colonial West Africa to hunt exotic animals also became popular.[48] According to her notes, the anthropologist the Comtesse Solange de Ganay gained an interest in the field through her 1930s hunting trips to French West Africa.[49] Photographs document her killing an antelope, wearing light colors, tight-laced espadrilles, sarouels, a thin shirt, and a colonial hat; another shows her family skinning a mamba,

FIG. 149
Designed by Lucien Lelong, French, 1889–1958; photograph of model wearing a sportswear dress and satin jacket with a metallic, imitation-lamé finish and ribbed knit edge at the waist, c.1925; Musée des Arts décoratifs, Paris, Fonds photographies Lelong, Licence—Dépôt de modèle N0296, 1925

As early as 1922, Lelong showed for day wear "woolen dresses suitable for sports, driving, or traveling, [which] paraded in a kaleidoscope of new tones, shimmering with silks and lamés intertwined" (*Excelsior*, February 2, 1922). The reflection of shiny materials brought a greater sense of movement.

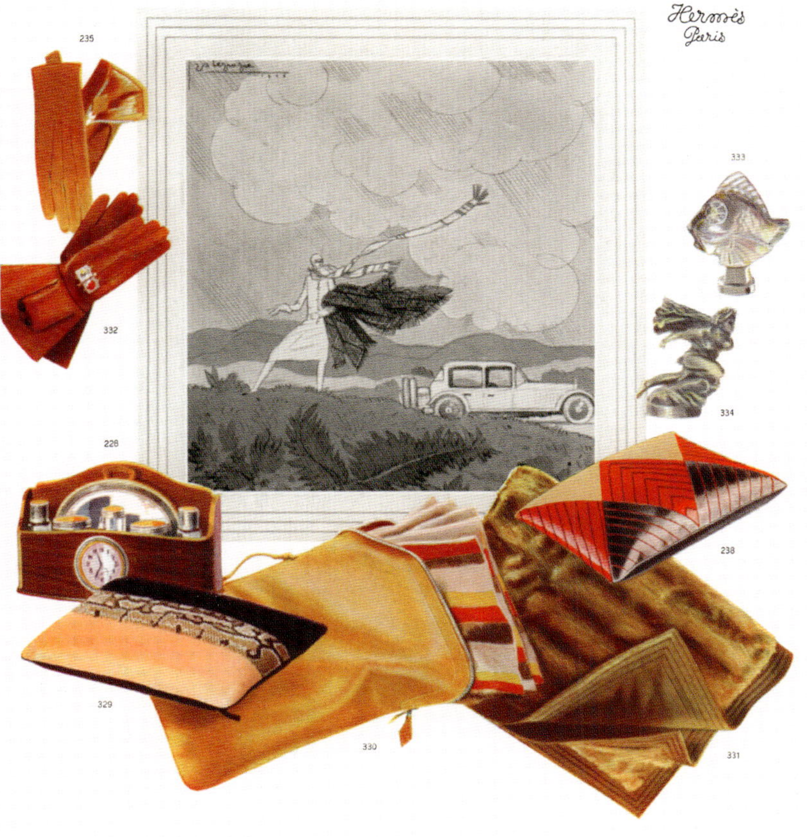

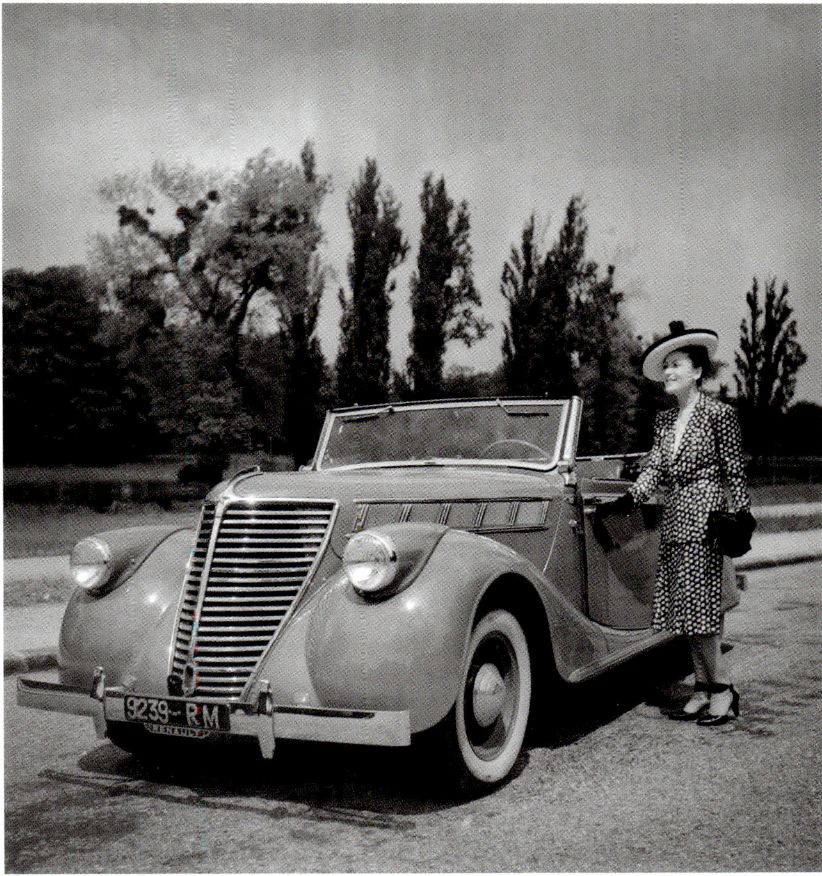

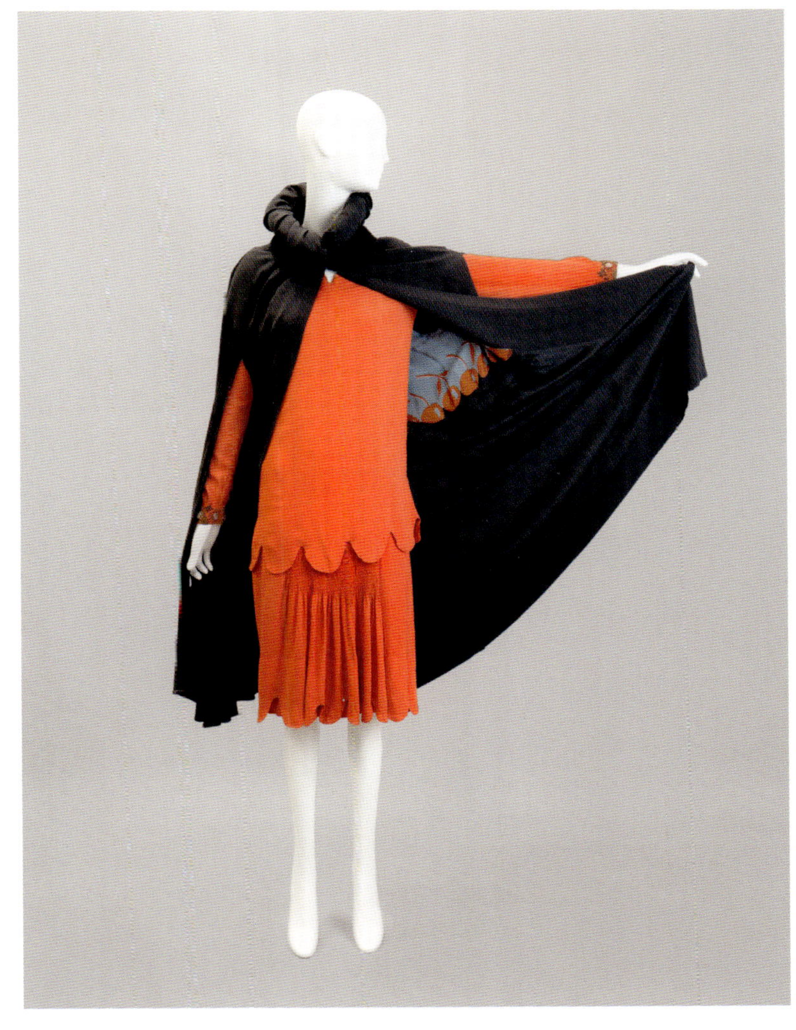

FIG. 150
Georges Lepape, French, 1887–1971; page from the Hermès Sellier catalogue *Maroquinerie, Voyage et Sport* (Leather goods, travel, and sport), 1926; Hermès Archives

FIG. 151
Model presenting a suit designed by Lanvin next to a Renault Viva Grand Sport at a *concours d'élégance d'automobile*, May 1939; Fonds Roger-Viollet, Paris

Events bringing couturiers and car manufacturers together became so popular that the 1928 Salon de l'Automobile was, in the words of the satirist Michel Herbert, "a true Parisian event," where people "do not go . . . to see automobiles [but] to launch a dress, to look trendy, to rub shoulders with personalities."

FIG. 152
Jean Patou, French, 1887–1936; *Cloak*, c.1926; silk crepe; Courtesy of the Missouri Historical Society, St. Louis

the same type of snakeskin that the designer Ronald Morrel used for a 1934 bodice.

The fascination with reptile hunting paralleled a growing trend for fashion made from their skins, including entire automotive ensembles.[50] Alpina, a supplier of reptile leather, promoted a complete look for French women with coats, hats, and bags, as well as car interiors, including doors, seats, and convertible roofs, in the material (since "the latest vogue, Madame, is your car body entirely covered in snakeskin").[51] The popularity of these materials, however, sparked concerns, with experts from the Muséum National d'Histoire Naturelle, like Paul Chabanaud and Jean Abel Gruvel, calling for the regulation of reptile hunting as early as 1925.[52] Despite the efforts of the National Permanent Committee for the Protection of Colonial Fauna, the capitalist demand for exotic skins prevailed, with some industrialists justifying the hunts to protect local populations from dangerous animals.[53]

The Car is the Woman, the Woman is the Car

In 1933, in a national Algerian publication from the Sidi Bel Abbès flying club, a journalist imagined what fashion might look like in an automotive world: "Fuel oil hair toque, aircraft canvas casaquin with avionine [paint or varnish used in aeronautics], plywood skirt varnished."[54] This humorous description evoked the potentiality of two worlds becoming one. Pauline Beery's 1930 book *Stuff* also highlighted the many uses for the new substances, especially one that could cover the body of the woman and the body of the car: "Cellulose solutions can be spun into textile fibers [artificial silk], forced into thin films, [and] painted on auto bodies."[55] As Renault promoted its 1937 cars as "thinner and [de facto] more elegant,"[56] these qualities informed a new conception of women's bodies: "In Baudelaire's time, women could only be compared to boats. Now we have cars and planes. This spring's woman resembles them; she's dynamic, even aerodynamic."[57] The aerodynamic silhouette in the 1930s introduced a new constraint: slimness.[58] Some of the automobile attire previously described was recommended for women "tall and thin," to follow the lines of the car.

Writers also played with this idea. Ann Bridge's short story *The Buick Saloon*, published in 1930, tells the story of a colonial diplomatic woman in Beijing who buys a blue limousine and hears a disembodied female voice speaking French in the back of her car. The automobile had become the receptacle of the French woman's soul, now sharing the same body—a kind of early fantasy of female human-machine symbiosis.

Technological driving accessories are also part of this story. Historians began to identify signs of "cyborg feelings" through a "magic unity with technology" achieved by those behind the wheel.[59] The bodies of the woman and the car could become one, and not only aesthetically. If we consider gloves a second skin, a pair produced by Hermès in about 1925 catches our attention: tan leather gloves fitted with two small electric lights protected by glass function as turn signals (FIG. 150). A particular device enables these lamps to light up with a press of two fingers whenever the driver's outstretched arm indicates that the car is about to turn. The woman's body appears here as a functional extension of the machine.

En Mettre Plein la Vue: The Fashion Glow

Recalling the 1928 Salon de l'Automobile, the Comte de Janzé tells us: "The Show is open . . . . Our eyes blur with sparks; a thousand lights are reflected on the gleaming panels and polished chassis, each more brilliant than the last."[60] A 1930 Citroën leaflet announcing the launch of the C6F indicates the new domination of "aesthetics preoccupations," a car having a purpose beyond the pleasure of driving. It has to honor its driver, reflecting their elegance and character. Citroën replied to these demands with "an all-steel bodywork [that] can offer such a clean, impeccable silhouette. The exclusive-use-of-metal result[s] . . . [in] slim, sleek cars with panels of spotless brilliance and unalterable shine."[61] A plain brilliance drove Citroën (and his competitors, with Peugeot launching the new, "very shiny" 401 in 1935) into the 1930s.

Commentators focused on advancements in automotive paint finishes and the reflective effect of the environment in both industrial and natural light (FIG. 148). A cover of *Le Chic Français de L'Automobile* used a drawing of a car in a diamond, with radiating lines, to express this aesthetic cornerstone.[62] One focus was on how the new bodywork interacted with light: "A vision of pure aesthetic value [is] in the context of today's city, . . . the nickel-plated car that shines in the sun and advances majestically . . . the most beautiful jewel that the modern woman can desire."[63]

At the same time, dazzling satin and lamé fabrics were elevated for the way they reflected light. The prioritization of radiance was embedded in their names: *Rayonne* for artificial silk. In his 1908 work *Sociology*, Georg Simmel wrote: "Adornment increases or enhances the impression of the personality, while it functions as its . . . radiation."[64] Both shiny surfaces (fabric and bodywork) could work as a radiant adornment, showing someone's

FIG. 153
Lanvin, French, founded 1889; drawing for Amilcar, a motoring/automobile ensemble, published in the album *Sports 1928*, 1928; Patrimoine Lanvin, Paris

The Lanvin drawing of Amilcar recalls the coat worn by Wanda Wulz in this portrait. When posing in her motorcycle outfit, wearing a hood with chin straps and mica and chenille wool goggles, the Surrealist photographer and driver chose a coat made with metallic threads. Inspiration goes both ways. If cars were promoted as fashion accessories, Lanvin produced designs named for car brands. When drawing the Lanvin Amilcar or Renault coats, the draftsman emphasized their radiant qualities, recalling the reflective bodywork of the automobile. Linear motifs, such as rays going in all directions, are part of this aesthetic of movement.

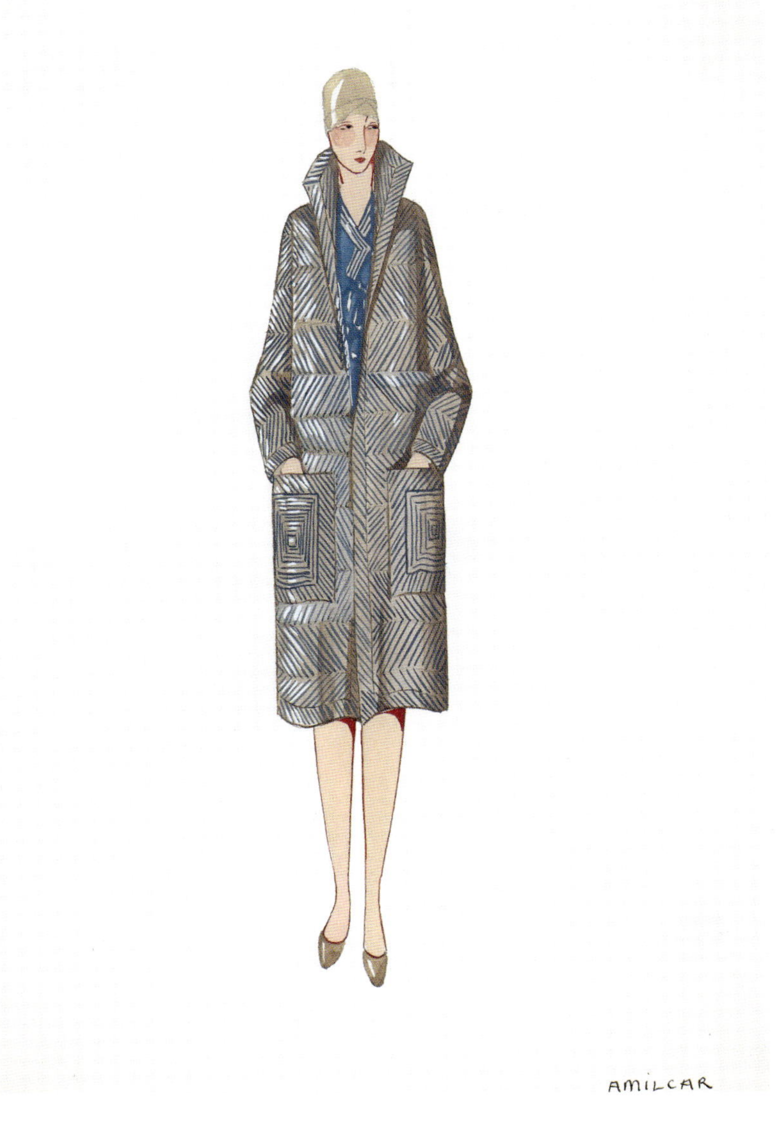

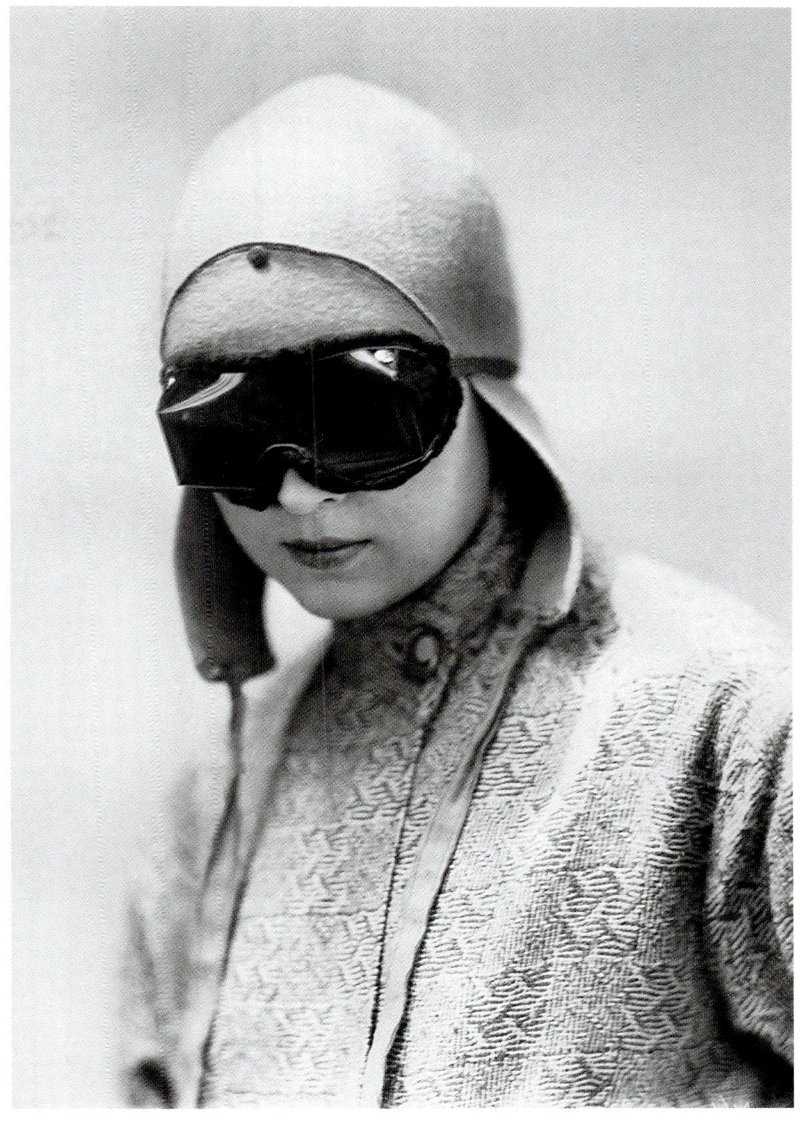

FIG. 154
Marion Wulz, Italian, 1905–1993, *Portrait of Wanda Wulz (1903–1984) in Motorcyclist's Gear,* c.1930–32; gelatin silver dry negative; 6 ½ × 4 ⅓ in.; Alinari Archives, Marion Wulz Archive, Florence, Italy, WMA-F-006884-0000

prestige. The *carrossier* Jean Henri-Labourdette drew this parallel: "If you think about it, you can draw a parallel with [fashion and] the car. The fronts of today's American cars, chrome plated, . . . make an impression; they *'tapent à l'œil'* [literally, "hit the eye"]. The owner can say to himself: 'I'm getting my money's worth.'"[65] These shiny surfaces flash, "tapent à l'œil," as a ray of light hits the eye in a display of wealth. It also shows this desire for visibility, especially for women, to whom social recognition had not yet been awarded.

Lamé and other shiny fabrics were valued for their exotic and luxurious qualities before the interwar period, but the 1920s and 1930s marked a shift in their fabrication and perception. Lamé became common for both evening and daywear, with its dazzling effect often imitated by satin, as seen in Lelong's sportswear jacket (FIG. 149).[66] Lelong deepened his understanding of light's impact on his creations, using it as "material, tool, artifice, or remedy" to add movement.[67] In his 1924 show, multiple hidden spotlights replicated day and evening light, with models parading on an illuminated glass floor.[68] Lamé also gained a new layer of meaning: Western modernity, reflected in its luminous surface. Promoting technical advances in shining fabrics was a way to update and Westernize these materials. Artificial viscose silk was appreciated for its more metallic sheen than natural silk (FIG. 152).[69] Bianchini's and Ducharne's 1927 collections showcased two perspectives: "heavy lamés" or damasks that "take us back to the sumptuousness of antique fabrics," evoking the silks of Venice, Angkor, or Versailles, versus "very modern suppleness" with items like "Mousse d'or" (golden foam), a plain lamé "almost unreal in its lightness,"[70] following the introduction of *laminette,* softer metallic threads. By the 1930s, the allure of shine had diminished, but "plain and fluid lamés . . . [were] everywhere" in collections by Jenny, Patou, Lanvin, Chanel, and Vionnet. Lamé, with its unembellished surface, mirrored the "contexture . . . in harmony

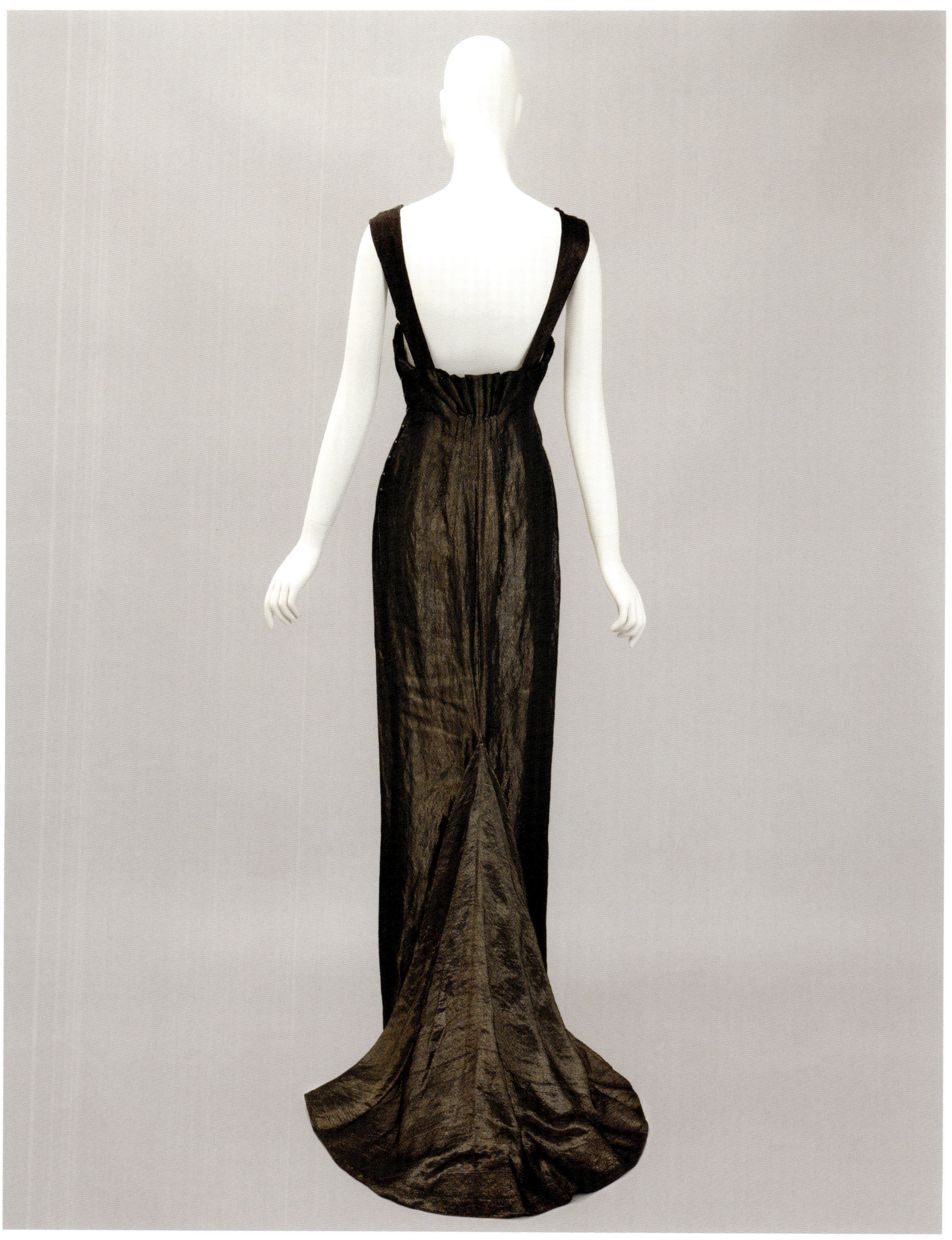

FIG. 155
Elsa Schiaparelli, Italian, 1890–1973; *Evening Dress*, winter 1934; lamé and metal buttons; Courtesy of the Missouri Historical Society, St. Louis

with . . . the bodywork of the automobile," becoming a Western reflecting/reflective surface (FIGS. 153, 154).[71]

In that sense, lamé and the *shinings* share a bond with coachwork construction. This period saw advancements in coachbuilding: new cellulosic paints and baked-on alkyd lacquers enhanced paint sheen, paralleling similar reflective qualities in cars and fashion (FIGS. 147, 148). André de Fouquières, an arbiter of elegance, appreciated at the Concours d'Élégance Automobile "the harmony there was between the color of the car, its varnish and the tone of the driver's toilette, the reflection of the silk," noting how the actress Rahna's purple-gray silk gown resembled "the steel of her carriage."[72] Shine became so central that some trendy 1930s fur driving coats were admired for their reflective properties: "Will we give in to the beautiful reflections of the golden otter, to the shimmering brilliance of the supple breitschwanz?"[73]

Today, mechanical noise, specifically the sound of cars, is almost inescapable in an urban setting, but in the 1930s, sonic and visual landscapes were changing. Early in the decade, Citroën promoted its new C6F by asserting, "elegant women . . . should be able to drive in evening attire."[74] Let us imagine a world in which cars are not as present as today, with the constant screech of their wheels on the road and roaring engines. A wealthy woman driving a Talbot convertible (the kind that had "great success with those who like to be seen; [since] the toilettes of elegant Parisiennes . . . are more easily admired")[75] arrives at a venue, announced by the sound of her streamlined car. She emerges in a long, slim Schiaparelli lamé (FIG. 155), her nails polished with shellac, her glossy hair lacquered and flawless, her car and herself shining in the electric glow of the party. She is ready to dance under artificial lights that will reflect off the shimmering metallic threads of her dress.[76] She is part of the economies of shine and glamour, from the moment she arrives to the moment she drives away.

1 All references to *Vogue* are from the French edition.
2 Francette, "L'Automobile et la Mode," *Revue de l'ACFF*, May 1926, 21.
3 In 1926, approximately 3% of license holders were women, which rose to 15% on the eve of World War II.
4 The National Motor Car and Vehicle Corporation in the US produced a National Sextet model specifically targeting women with "a series of compartments to store a bag, gloves, and all those unnecessary things a woman can't do without." *Vogue*, February 1, 1921, 14.
5 "L'Évolution de l'Automobile et ses Rapports avec la Mode," *Vogue*, July 1, 1923, 27.
6 "La Mode Sportive," *L'Auto*, April 20, 1923, 1.
7 J. R. F., "Les Fêtes dans le Jardin," *Vogue*, September 1, 1927, 11.
8 Archives INPI, Patent FR640745, 1927.
9 Maurice de Waleffe, "Histoire de la Carrosserie," *Le Journal*, October 13, 1926, 1.
10 J. R. F., "La Parisienne en Automobile n'oublie pas l'Elégance," *Vogue*, August 1, 1920, 12.
11 "A la découverte," *Vogue*, April 1, 1936, 92.
12 Archives INPI, Patent FR62182, 1927, Patent FR801361, 1936.
13 "Petits Riens de Grande Importance," *Vogue*, May 1, 1928, 28.
14 "Le Manteau de Voyage," *Vogue*, May 1, 1939, 74.
15 Lucien Lelong, interview in *Excelsior*, February 22, 1922, 2.
16 Pierre Bret, "Kinétisme," *L'Intransigeant*, March 8, 1926, 12; and "La Mode," *La Côte Basque*, August 15, 1926, 529.
17 Shell, *Dix personnalités de l'automobile nous disent* ... (Paris: SOC, ca. 1930), 9–10, Bibliothèque Forney, Paris, CC 3022 [1930] B.
18 Mary Louise Roberts, *Civilization without Sexes* (Chicago: University of Chicago Press, 2009), 20.
19 Lysiane Bernhardt, "Costumes de Sport," *L'Auto*, November 28, 1935, 7; and "L'Art de Se Bien Conduire," *Revue de ACFF*, May 1934, 37.
20 "ACFF chez la Duchesse d'Uzès," *Le Gaulois*, June 18, 1926; republished in *Revue de ACFF*, June 1926, 8.
21 Miren Arzalluz et al., *Paris, Mode, Sports* (Paris: Paris Musées, 2024), 39.
22 "Partir C'est Aussi Prévoir," *Vogue*, August 1, 1937, 91.
23 Another example is the fashion designer Lucile, who created a motorist's coat with intentional, densely gathered sleeves that masked minor wrinkles.
24 "Salons Kemolite," *Vogue*, April 1, 1928, 30.
25 Comte de Janzé, "Les Autos de 1929," *Vogue*, December 1, 1928, 41.
26 "Le Duel du Chic et de la Beauté," *Vogue*, October 1, 1920, 25.
27 "JiL," *Vogue*, April 1, 1930, 40.
28 Advertisement, "*Permis de Conduire: École Chic de Dames*," 1930s, Gérard Prévot private collection.
29 "La Buick 1929 est arrivée," *Vogue*, October 1, 1928, 71.
30 André Latour, "Nos Belles Carrosseries," *Art et industrie*, Summer 1934, 46.
31 Car photograph, *Vogue*, December 1, 1935, 19.
32 "Pour la Ville et pour la Route," *Vogue*, August 1, 1935, 25.
33 "Échos de la Grande Semaine," *Soierie de Lyon*, September 1, 1926, 643–44.
34 "Élégance en Automobile," *La Saison de Cannes*, February 12, 1928, 24–25.
35 Advertisement, Peugeot 202, *Vogue*, November 1, 1938, 1.
36 Prospect, "Un Peu de Tout," *Cycle et Automobile Industriels*, January 4, 1931, 9.
37 Parisis, "L'Avion Madame," *Elle: Revue de la Femme Nord-Africaine*, May 15, 1934, 13.
38 Emmanuel Grévin, *Rivages du Grand Erg* (Paris: Delamain et Boutelleau, 1938), 13.
39 Jean du Taillis, *Le Tourisme Automobile en Algérie-Tunisie* (Paris: Guides du tourisme automobile, 1923), 6.
40 Taillis, *Tourisme Automobile*, 57.
41 Taillis, *Tourisme Automobile*, 6.
42 Photograph in Taillis, *Tourisme Automobile*, 347. The quote comes from Y. de Lestrange, "Il y a une Saison Tunisienne," *Vogue*, September 1, 1927, 25.
43 Taillis, *Tourisme Automobile*, 36.
44 "Notes Sahariennes," *Le Pingouin: Organe du Club Aéronautique de Sidi-Bel-Abbes*, January 15, 1932, 1. For more information about the Algiers driving club, see Archives Nationales, Pierrefitte-sur-Seine, 20220558/17.
45 Emmanuel Grévin, *Voyage au Hoggar: Tourisme au Sahara* (Paris: Stock, Delamain et Boutelleau, 1936), 34.
46 White mica (from the Latin word *micare*, meaning "twinkle" or "glitter") is almost transparent and was used for motoring veils and goggles. It was sourced in the French colony of Madagascar, which saw increased extraction of the mineral during the interwar period.
47 Letter from Consul Général de France aux Indes Néerlandaises to Monsieur le Ministre des Affaires Étrangères, "Kapok et Faux Kapok," September 23, 1932, Ministères—Colonies, A 14-2, Archives Ministère Affaires Étrangères, Courneuve.
48 "Partir C'est Aussi Prévoir," 91.
49 Geneviève Calame-Griaule, "Solange de Ganay (1902–2003)," *Journal des Africanistes* 73, no. 2 (2003): 169.
50 The Compagnie Générale d'Outre-Mer, which invested in colonial businesses, evokes the chronic rise of reptile leather from the mid-1920s, used in luxury and semiluxury businesses. See also Dossier n. 1747, "Compagnie Générale d'Outre-Mer," 20040106/6, Archives Nationales, Pierrefitte-sur-Seine.
51 Snakeskin is flexible enough to be combined with any fabric or leather. The quote is from Lucie Neumeyer, "Details," *Art, goût, beauté,* September 1, 1928, n.p.
52 See *Bulletin de la Société Zoologique de France* 50 (1925): 169–71. See also Archives of the Committee: ARCH PC 23, no. 2 (1925–28), Muséum National d'Histoire Naturelle, Paris.
53 G. L., "Peau de Crocodile," *La Cordonnerie Française* 31, no. 357 (July 1927): 180.
54 "La Mode," *Pingouin*, January 15, 1933, 2.
55 Pauline G. Beery, *Stuff* (New York: D. Appleton, 1930), 280.
56 Renault Advertisement, *Vogue*, October 1, 1936, 20A.
57 "Ombres du Jour," *Vogue*, February 1, 1934, 11.
58 Fashion illustration of motoring coats for a "tall and slim woman," *Vogue*, February 1, 1921, 7; and "Le Soir, Lignes Longues Amincissantes," *Vogue*, January 1, 1931, 40, 43.
59 Gijs Mom, *Atlantic Automobilism: Emergence and Persistence* of the *Car, 1895–1940* (New York: Berghahn Books, 2014), 645.
60 Comté de Janzé, "Le Salon Automobile," *Vogue*, November 1928, 8.
61 *Citroën sous le signe de la C Six-F*, Médiathèque Louis Aragon, Le Mans, 2022-8291, Auto 4°4117, 629.209 44 cit.
62 *Le Chic Français de L'Automobile,* January 1927, cover.
63 Shell, *Dix personnalités*, 14.
64 Georg Simmel, *Sociology* (1908; Boston: Brill, 2009), 333, quoted in Antje Krause-Wahl et al., *Materials, Practices, and Politics of Shine in Modern Art and Popular Culture* (London: Bloomsbury Visual Arts, 2021), 4.
65 Jean Henri-Labourdette, "Quelques Impressions des États-Unis," *SIA* 21, no. 1 (January 1947): 3.
66 "Never so much gold had been seen as [in] this season, in both day- and evening wear." Rosine, "En Pleine Mode: Retour des Champs," *AGB*, November 15, 1924, n.p. Ten years later, textile industrialist Dognin "much appreciated by the couture world . . . presents for the day, weavings of gold, silver threads"; L. J., "Tissus," *Elle*, Christmas 1934, 15.

67 Eric Monin and Nathalie Simonnot, *L'Architecture lumineuse au XXe siècle* (Heule: Snoeck, 2012), 11.

68 Jacqueline Demornex, *Lucien Lelong, L'Intemporel* (Paris: Gallimard, 2007), 15.

69 Paul Luc, *Le Tissage de la soie artificielle* (Paris: L'Édition Textile, 1929), 35.

70 "La Collection de Bianchini" and "La Collection de Ducharne," *Vogue*, September 1, 1927, 46–48.

71 Myriane, "Éclatant succès de la soie," *La Mode Chic*, October 1, 1933, 9.

72 "Échos de la Grande Semaine," 644.

73 Martine Rénier, "Aimez-vous la fourrure?" *Fémina*, October 1, 1935, 14.

74 *Citroën sous le signe de la C Six-F.*

75 Janzé, "Salon de 1928," 52.

76 For more details on lamé, see Mei Mei Rado, "Fabric of Light, Surface of Displacement," in *Materials, Practices, and Politics of Shine*, 71–88.

1938 TALBOT-LAGO T150C SS FIGONI ET FALASCHI COUPE

KEN GROSS

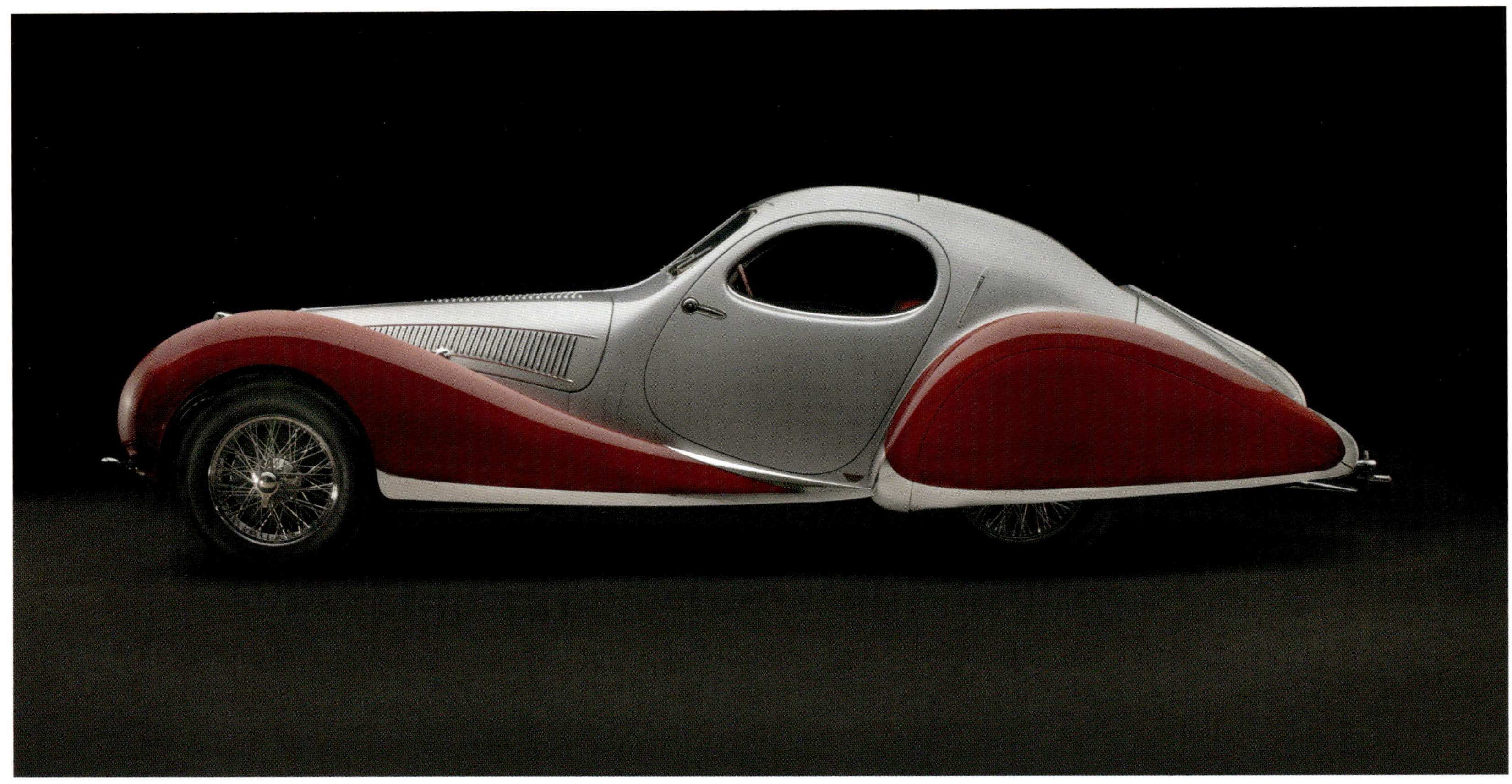

The sporting Talbot-Lago T150C chassis inspired open roadsters and closed cars, most notably a series of curvaceous custom coupes. Sensational in their heyday, they remain highly valued. Streamlined, sleek, and light enough to race competitively, they were called "Goutte d'Eau" (drop of water), and in English they quickly became known as the "Teardrop" Talbots.

Between 1937 and 1939, the famed Parisian *carrossiers* Figoni et Falaschi built twelve "New York"–style Talbot-Lago coupes, so called because the first was introduced at the 1937 New York Auto Show at the Grand Central Palace. Five more cars, built in a different notchback teardrop style, were named "Jeancart," after the wealthy French patron who commissioned the first example. Figoni et Falaschi craftsmen spent some 2,100 hours of painstaking handwork to complete each custom body. No two Teardrop coupes were exactly alike.

Antony Lago (1893–1960), Talbot's president, offered a top-of-the-line SS (Super Sport) version on the T150C's sturdy ladder frame, with independent wishbones in front and a live rear axle. For competition, a four-liter six-cylinder topped with a hemispherical combustion chamber head could be fitted with three carburetors for more than 170 bhp. Examples were optionally equipped with a Wilson four-speed preselector gearbox. A fingertip-actuated lever permitted instant shifts without the driver having to take a hand off the steering wheel. The T150C SS wasn't just beautiful; in 1938, a competition-prepared T150C SS Coupe finished third at the 24 Hours of Le Mans.

Chassis no. 90103, included here and the first of the "New York"–style Teardrops, is the car that Figoni et Falaschi registered to patent the model's aerodynamic shape. One of the three known versions with an alloy body, it was first owned by Freddie McEvoy (1907–1951), an Australian member of the

Figoni et Falaschi, Boulogne-sur-Seine, France, active 1935–50s; Talbot-Lago, Suresnes, France, active 1936–59; *T150C SS Teardrop Coupe*, 1938; steel chassis, aluminum alloy body; 50 × 174 × 64 in.; Collection of J.W. Marriott, Jr.

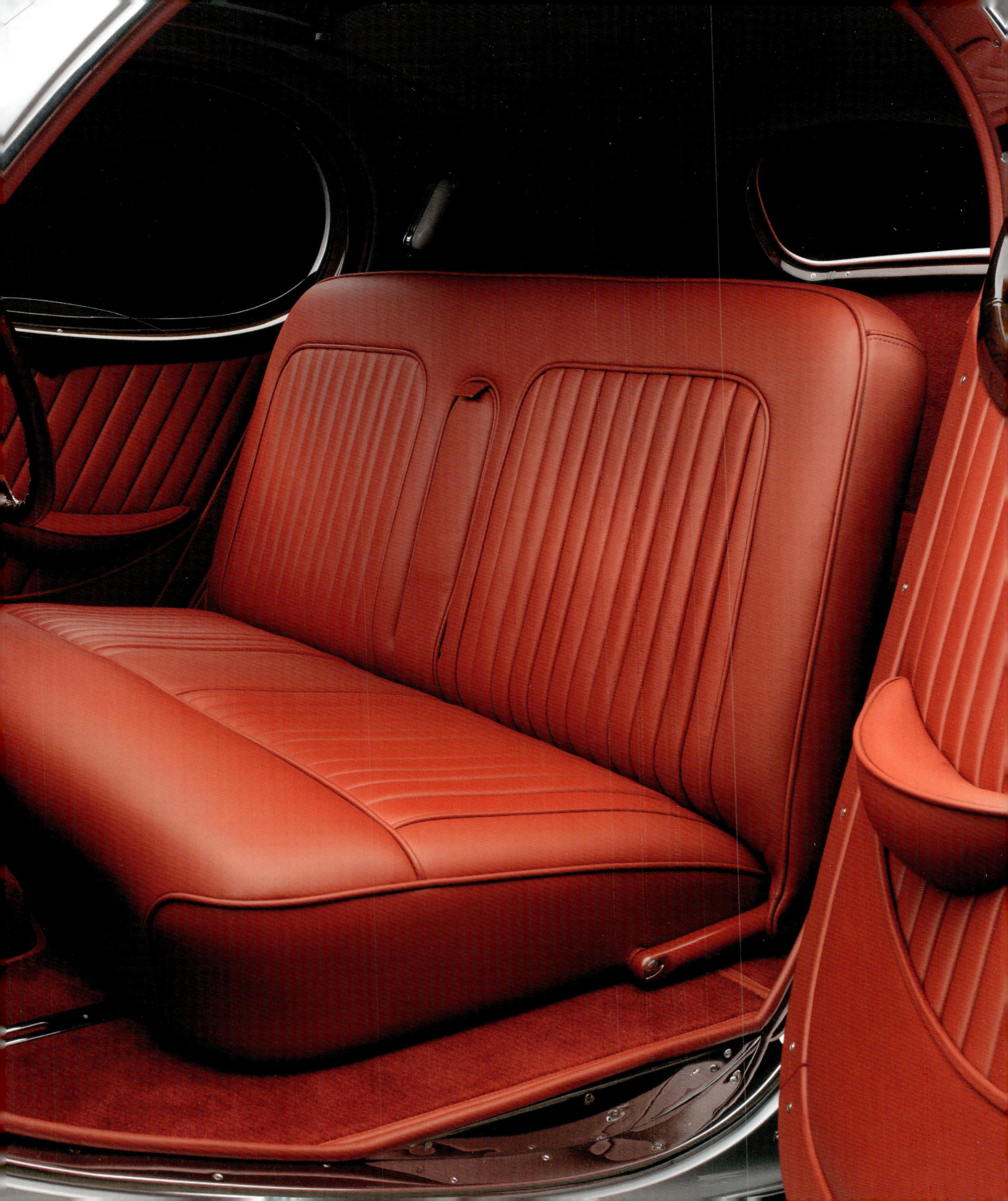

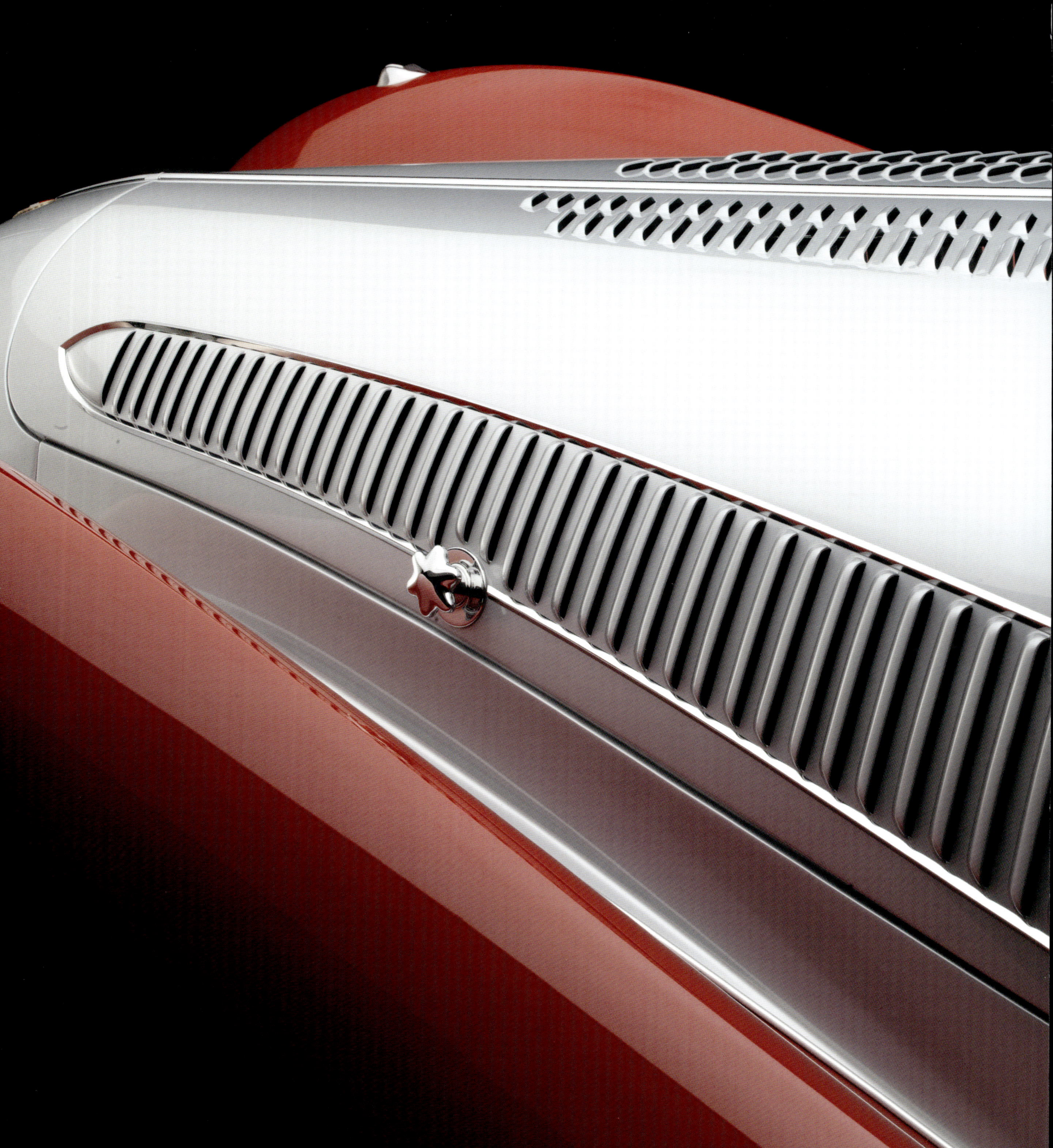

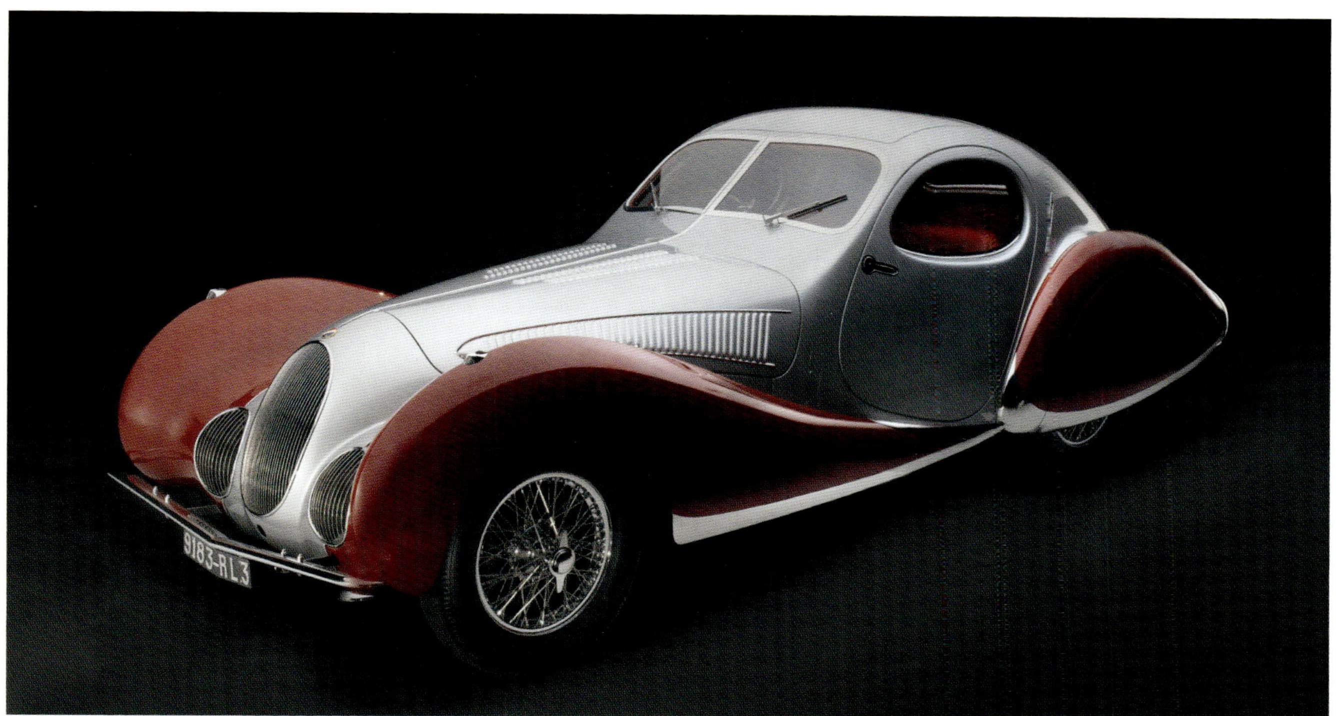

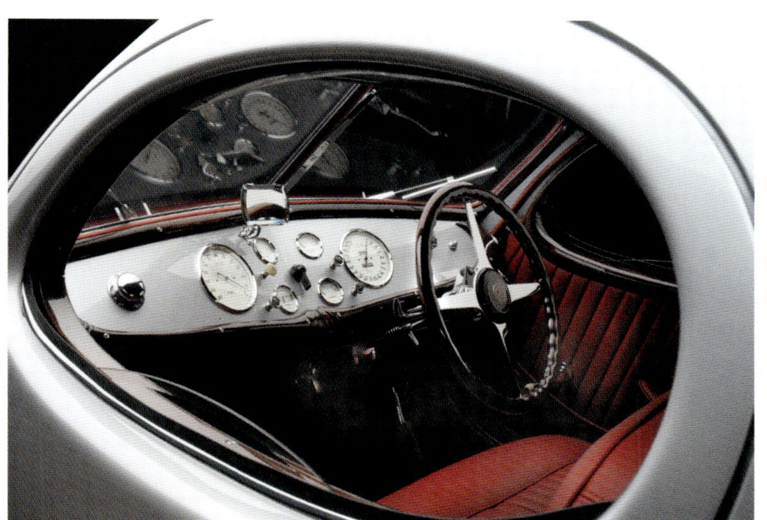

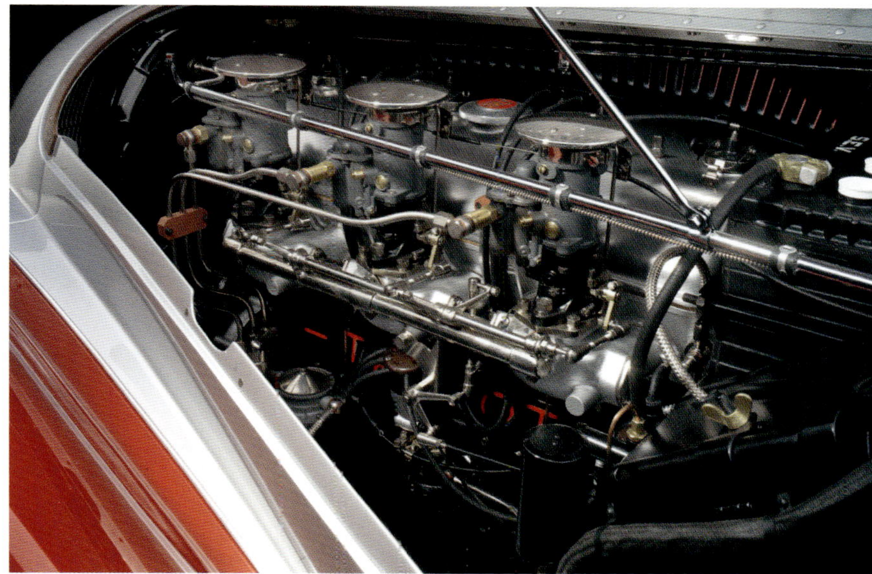

bronze medal–winning British bobsled team at the 1936 Winter Olympics. McEvoy, who lived in Europe, became the US representative for both Figoni et Falaschi and Talbot-Lago. A prominent Hollywood player, the fast-living McEvoy had access to celebrities like Errol Flynn, making him an ideal concessionaire for unusual and luxurious automobiles.

After World War II, the car's front end was reworked. Its original headlights, located behind the twin grilles, did not provide a great deal of light. They were replaced with externally mounted units that were faired into the car's body, a modification made to only a few Teardrop models.

After McEvoy's ownership, it was purchased by an unknown buyer in Nice, France. Later, an uncle of Jean-François du Montant, one of France's first vintage car dealers, bought it in Marseille in 1959 and then sold it in 1971 to R. Strinatti, a Swiss collector, who owned the car for the next 20 years. Eric Traber purchased the coupe in 1991 and raced it on the European vintage circuit. He brought it to the Historic Races in Monterey, California, in August 2000. J. Willard "Bill" Marriott admired the car and bought it directly from the racetrack.

Repainted gray with red fenders, it retains its original engine, driveline, and body and has been featured in many magazine articles, most prominently in the June 1987 issue of *Automobiles Classiques*. It has been displayed in several fine art museum exhibitions, including at the Museum of Fine Arts Houston and the Vero Beach Museum of Art.

Loaned from the Collection of J.W. Marriott, Jr.

LIQUID SCULPTURE AND THE SENSUOUS MACHINE

GENEVIEVE CORTINOVIS

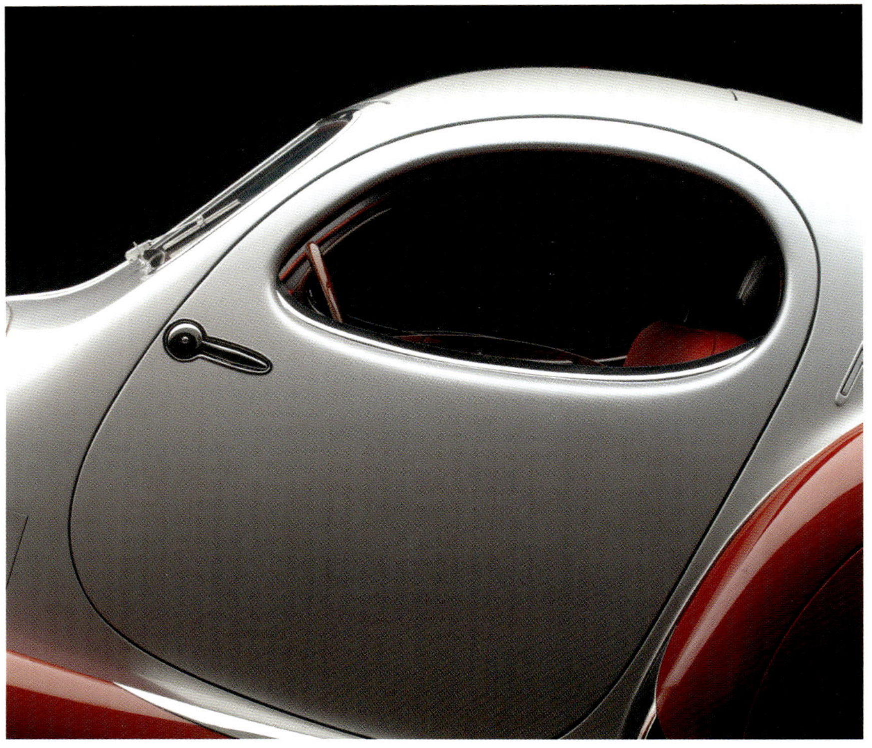

FIG. 156
Figoni et Falaschi, Boulogne-sur-Seine, France, active 1935–50s; Talbot-Lago, Suresnes, France, active 1936–59; *T150C SS Teardrop Coupe* (detail), 1938; steel chassis and aluminum alloy body; 50 × 174 × 64 in.; Collection of J.W. Marriott, Jr.

With the same uncanny presence of the android, the voluptuous aerodynamic automobiles of 1930s coachbuilders have the alluring and unsettling appeal of a machine made too sensuous. The softly slanted, oblong windows and swelling pontoon fenders of the Italian-born French coachbuilder Joseph Figoni's T150C SS Coupe seem animated by a life force beyond the power of mechanical production (FIG. 156).

A kind of liquid sculpture, Figoni's sloping bodies exemplified the "Goutte d'Eau" (drop of water) shapes captivating the French press since the Austrian engineer Edmund Rumpler's Tropfenwagen (drop of water car) first made the pages of the journal *Omnia* not long after its introduction at the 1921 Berlin auto show. Drawing on experience designing aircraft and wind-tunnel testing initially performed in Gustave Eiffel's research facilities, Rumpler posited the teardrop shape with its curved nose and tapered tail created less drag, allowing a car to achieve higher speeds without additional horsepower or fuel.[1] By the 1930s, it was widely accepted that, according to the principles of aerodynamics, "one of the best profiles is the deformation of a drop of water in the wind."[2]

In Figoni's hands, the engineer's complex calculations were subsumed by the visual expression of viscous material shaped by environmental forces. This skillful negotiation between knowledge and intuition distinguished the era's leading coachbuilders, who understood "the practical domain of aerodynamics" but who were first and

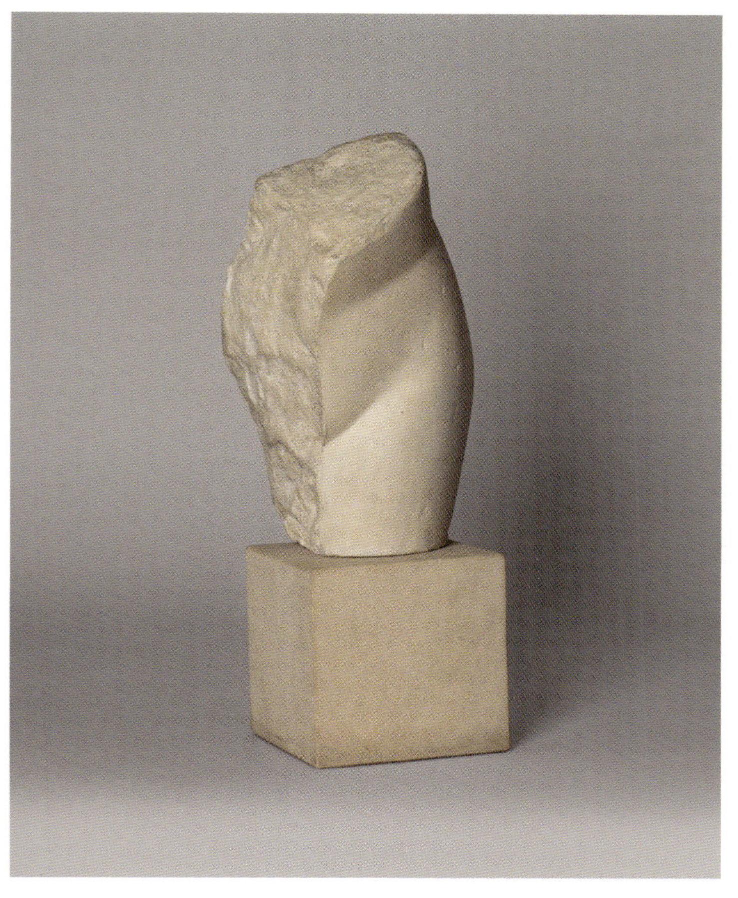

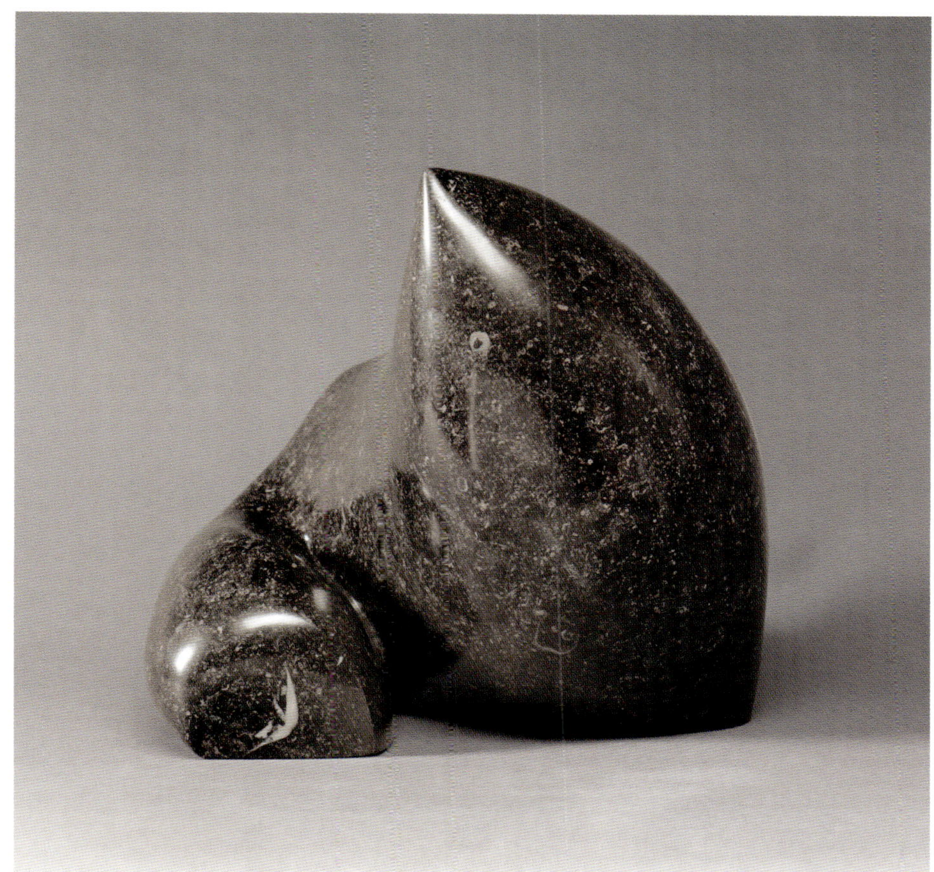

foremost artists capable of "revelations."[3] Fittingly, Figoni's coupe adopts the amoebic and softly distorted bodies of so-called biomorphic artworks, particularly sculpture, flourishing in 1930s France.

The English poet and critic Geoffrey Grigson was the first to employ the term "biomorphic" in the context of modern art in 1935.[4] In the opening issue of the journal *Axis*, he posited: "Abstractions are of two kinds, geometric, the abstractions which lead to the inevitable death; and biomorphic. The biomorphic abstractions are the beginning of the next central phase in the progress of art. They exist between Mondrian and Dalí, between idea and emotion, between matter and mind, matter and life."[5] One year later, Alfred Barr, Jr., director of the Museum of Modern Art in New York, described "biomorphism" in formal terms—where "the shape of the square confronts the silhouette of the amoeba"—applying it especially to works "associated with Surrealism."[6]

Biomorphic tendencies reflected longer-standing concerns by modern artists in defining the vitality of form and material in a modern technological world. The Romanian-born sculptor Constantin Brancusi literally chipped and sanded away detail in search of his subject's essence. Arriving in Paris in 1904, Brancusi established himself as a virtuosic carver, famously declining a position in Auguste Rodin's studio to develop his own practice. In 1908, he started a series of torsos that charted his increasing move toward simplification and abstraction. An early sculpture in the sequence describes the softly rounded contours of a young woman's hip, buttock, and thigh. Having mounted it on a smooth block, Brancusi instills the fragment—ostensibly excised or broken from a body—with the presence of the whole (FIG. 157). By 1922, the *Torso* had become a truncated and subtly distended teardrop—a vessel of organic energy—balanced on a rectangular base.

The artist and poet Jean (Hans) Arp was born a decade after Brancusi in Strasbourg and would come to exemplify the ambiguities and tensions inherent in modern biomorphism.[7] An energetic figure in the European avant-garde, Arp, while living in Zurich during World War I, founded with fellow expatriates Dada, an anarchic movement of artists and writers favoring collaboration and chance, approaches that informed his lifelong creative practice. In 1926, Arp settled in Meudon,

FIG. 157
Constantin Brancusi, Romanian (active France), 1876–1957; *Torso*, 1909; painted plaster; 10 × 6 ⅛ × 6 in.; Private collection

FIG. 158
Jean Arp, French (born Germany), 1886–1966; *Shell Crystal*, 1938; black granite; 13 × 14 × 11 in.; Saint Louis Art Museum, Gift of Alvin and Ruth Siteman 705:2018

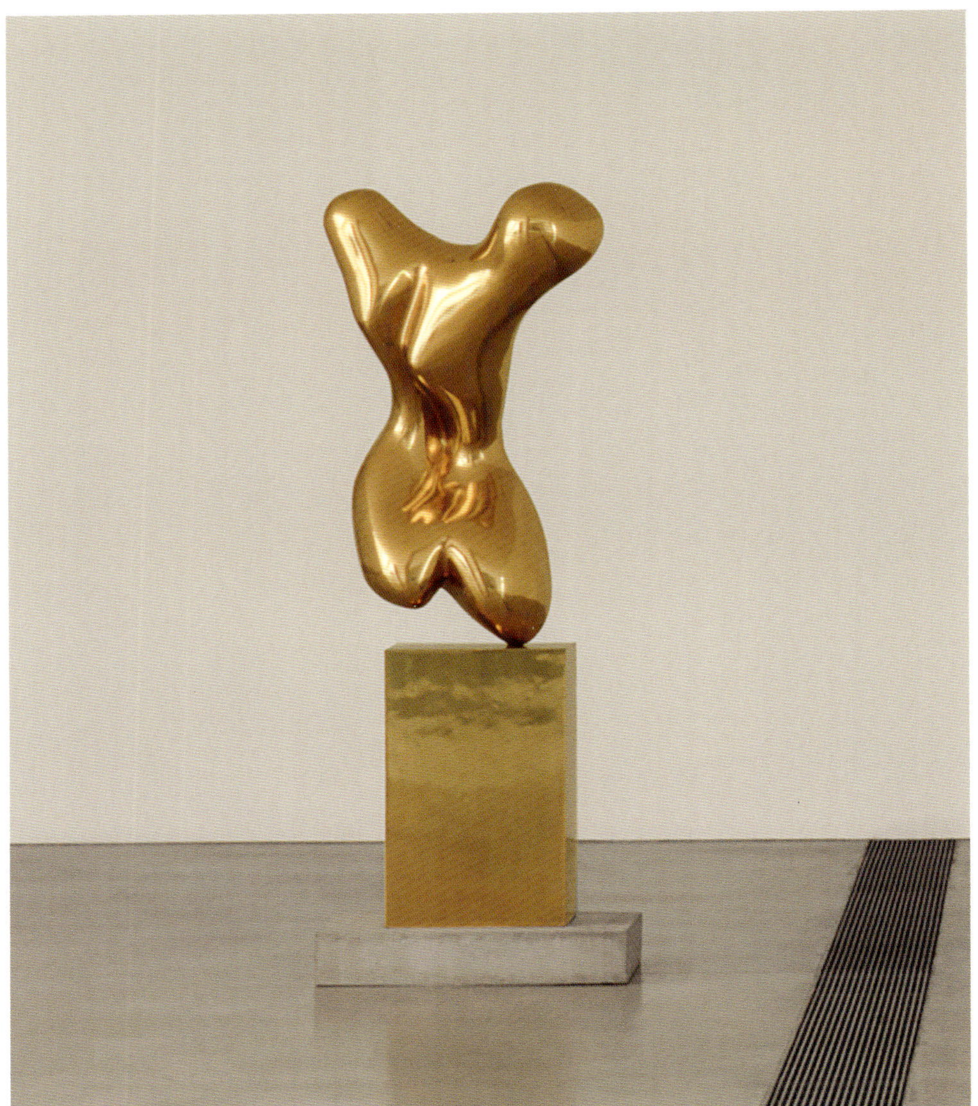

FIG. 159
Jean Arp, French (born Germany), 1886–1966; *Torso*, 1957; polished bronze; 36 × 23 × 15 in.; Private collection

France. After a career exploring sculptural relief, drawing, painting, and collage, he turned to sculptures in the round in about 1930.

Softly blending human, animal, and vegetal forms, Arp in his freestanding sculptures shifted between abstraction and representation, often suggesting embryonic development. From 1933, he called them "concretions," which he later defined as "the natural processes of condensation, hardening, coagulation, thickening, growing together."[8] The animated, upturned point of his 1938 *Shell Crystal* resists the weight of its sinuous, slumping base—a fusion of opposing phototropic and gravitational forces (FIG. 158). The black granite sculpture's beauty and strangeness encapsulate Arp's exaltation and subversion of natural forms and processes.

To achieve this dynamic organicism, Arp first modeled his sculptures in plaster using accretive and subtractive methods in a process akin to nature's own growth and decay. Not unlike Figoni, who modeled his body designs in clay before submitting them to draftsmen and craftsmen, Arp relied on technicians to realize his plaster sculptures in marble and metal.[9] The scholar Eric Robertson suggested that the collaborative opportunities in sculpture appealed to Arp, who consistently referenced the medieval guild as an aspirational arrangement for collective creative production.[10] Privileging conception, Arp happily distanced himself from the finished artwork. One of his earliest freestanding sculptures, *Torso*, was enlarged and cast in bronze in 1957, more than two decades after he first conceived in plaster its asymmetrical undulations—hips, thighs, and breasts wrung out like a wet towel (FIG. 159).[11]

Influenced by Freudian theories of sexuality and the unconscious, Surrealist imagery often distorted and fragmented women's bodies. Born Emmanuel Radnitzky in Philadelphia, Man Ray was a central figure in modernist circles of provocateurs in New York and later Paris. Shifting dexterously between media, he discovered in photography an

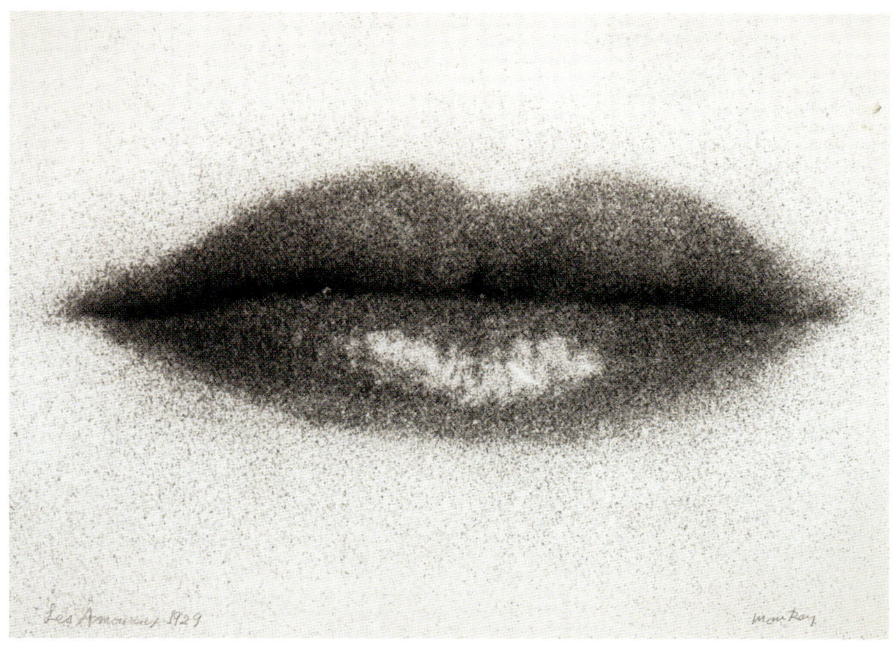

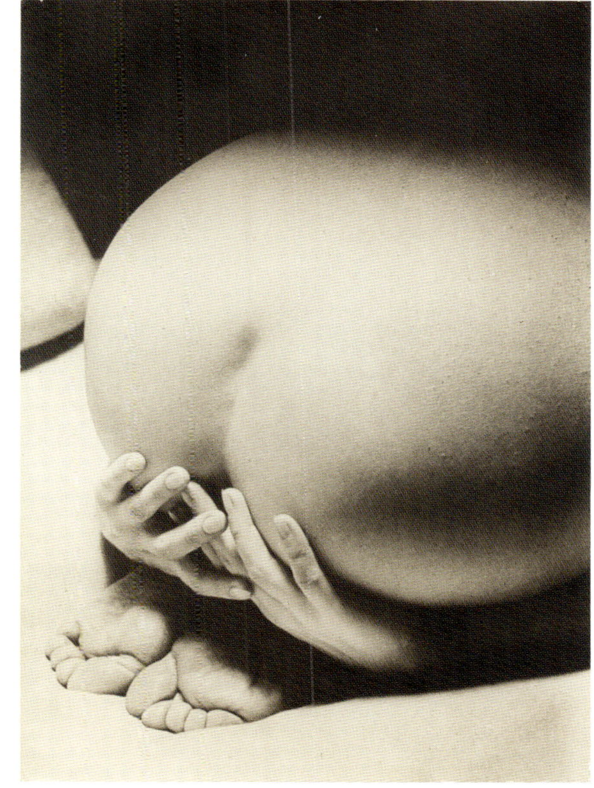

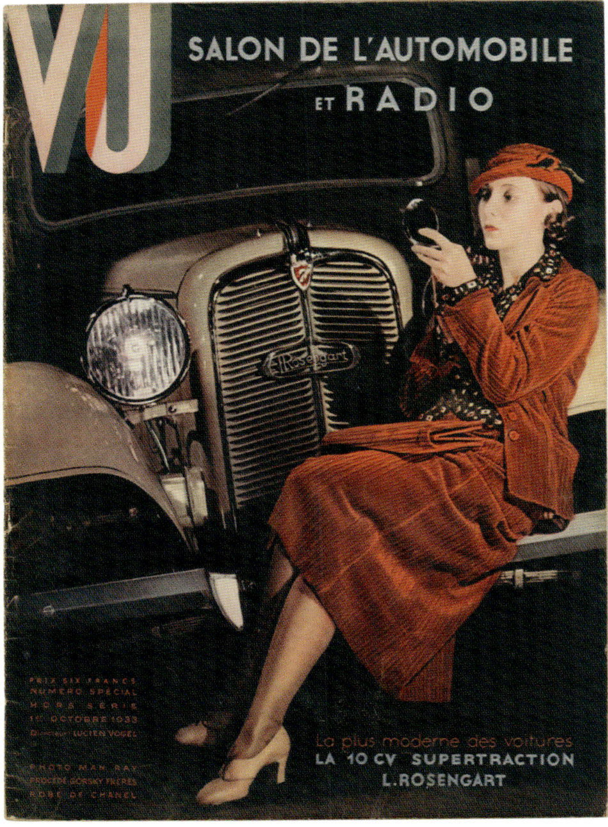

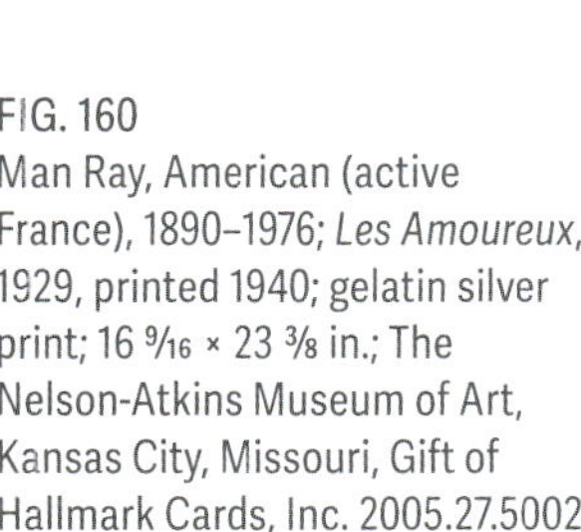

FIG. 160
Man Ray, American (active France), 1890–1976; *Les Amoureux*, 1929, printed 1940; gelatin silver print; 16 9/16 × 23 3/8 in.; The Nelson-Atkins Museum of Art, Kansas City, Missouri, Gift of Hallmark Cards, Inc. 2005.27.5002

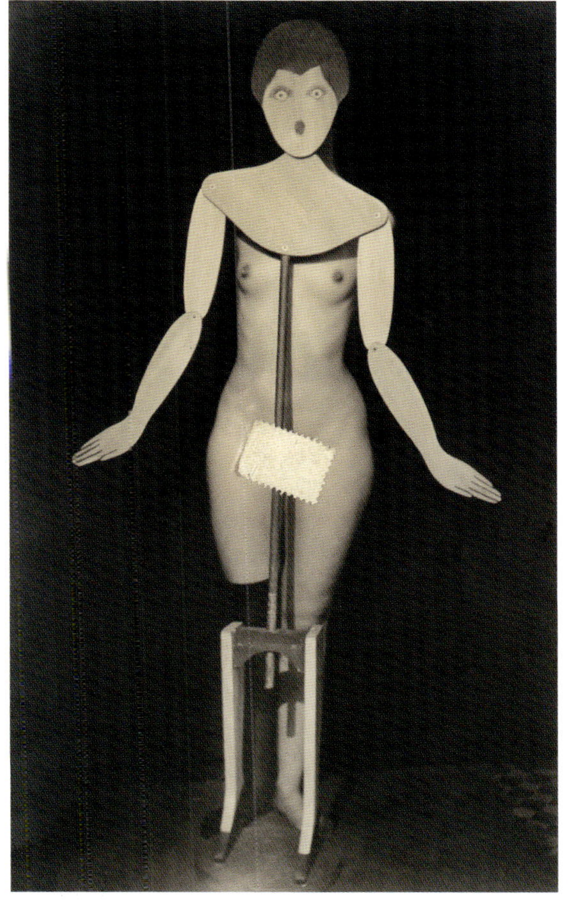

FIG. 161
Man Ray, American (active France), 1890–1976; *The Prayer*, 1930; gelatin silver print; 9 7/16 × 6 7/8 in.; Saint Louis Art Museum, Eliza McMillan Trust 20:1986

FIG. 162
Man Ray, American (active France), 1890–1976; cover for *Vu: Journal de la Semaine*, October 1, 1933

FIG. 163
Man Ray, American (active France), 1890–1976; *Dadaphoto*, 1920; gelatin silver collage; 9 × 5 5/8 in.; The Nelson-Atkins Museum of Art, Kansas City, Missouri, Gift of Hallmark Cards, Inc. 2005.27.4338

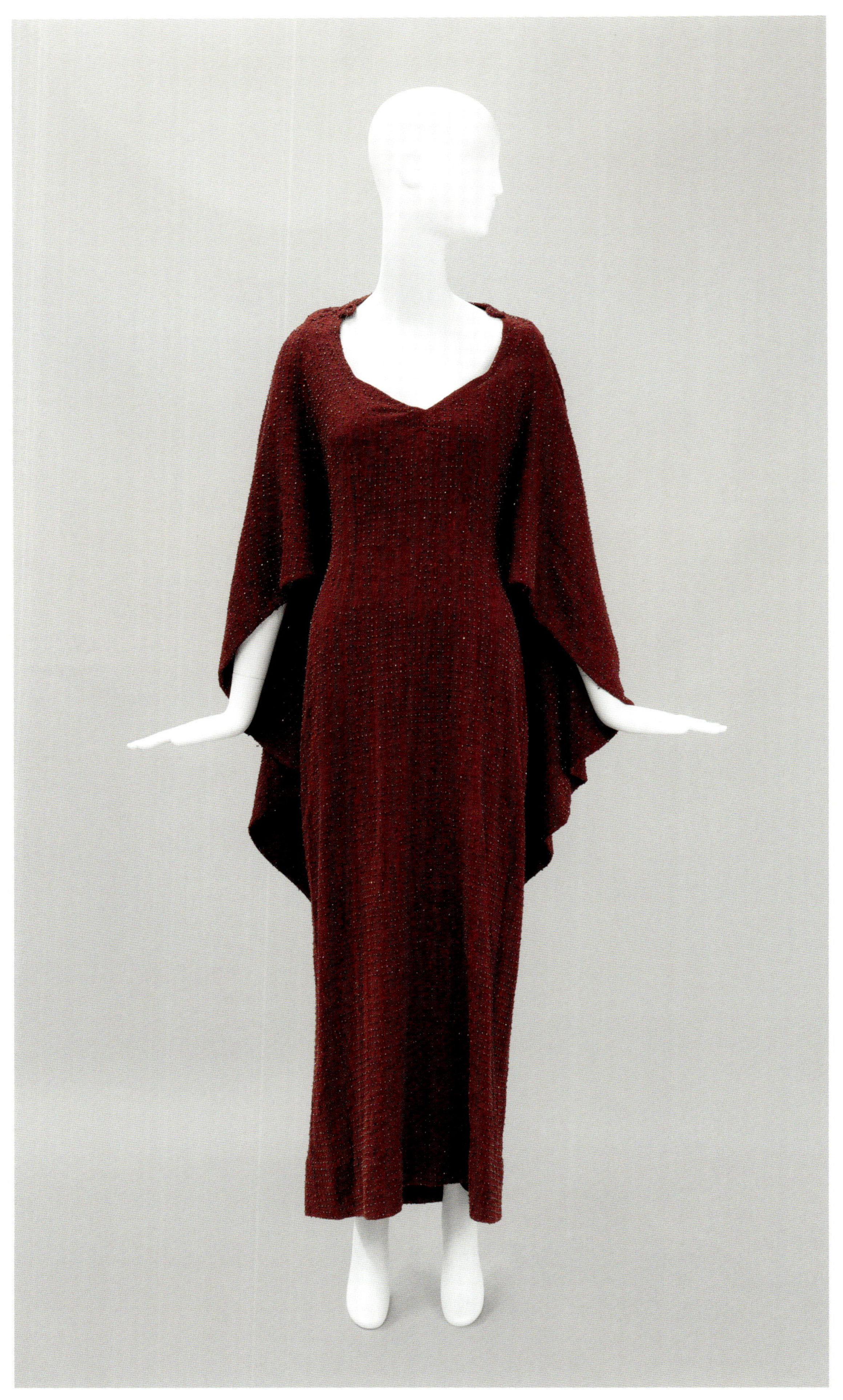

FIG. 164
Madame Grès (Germaine Émilie Krebs), French, 1903–1993; Maison Alix, Paris, active 1934–1942; *Evening Dress*, c.1936; wool crepe, cut steel beads, silk crepe, and satin; Courtesy of the Missouri Historical Society, St. Louis

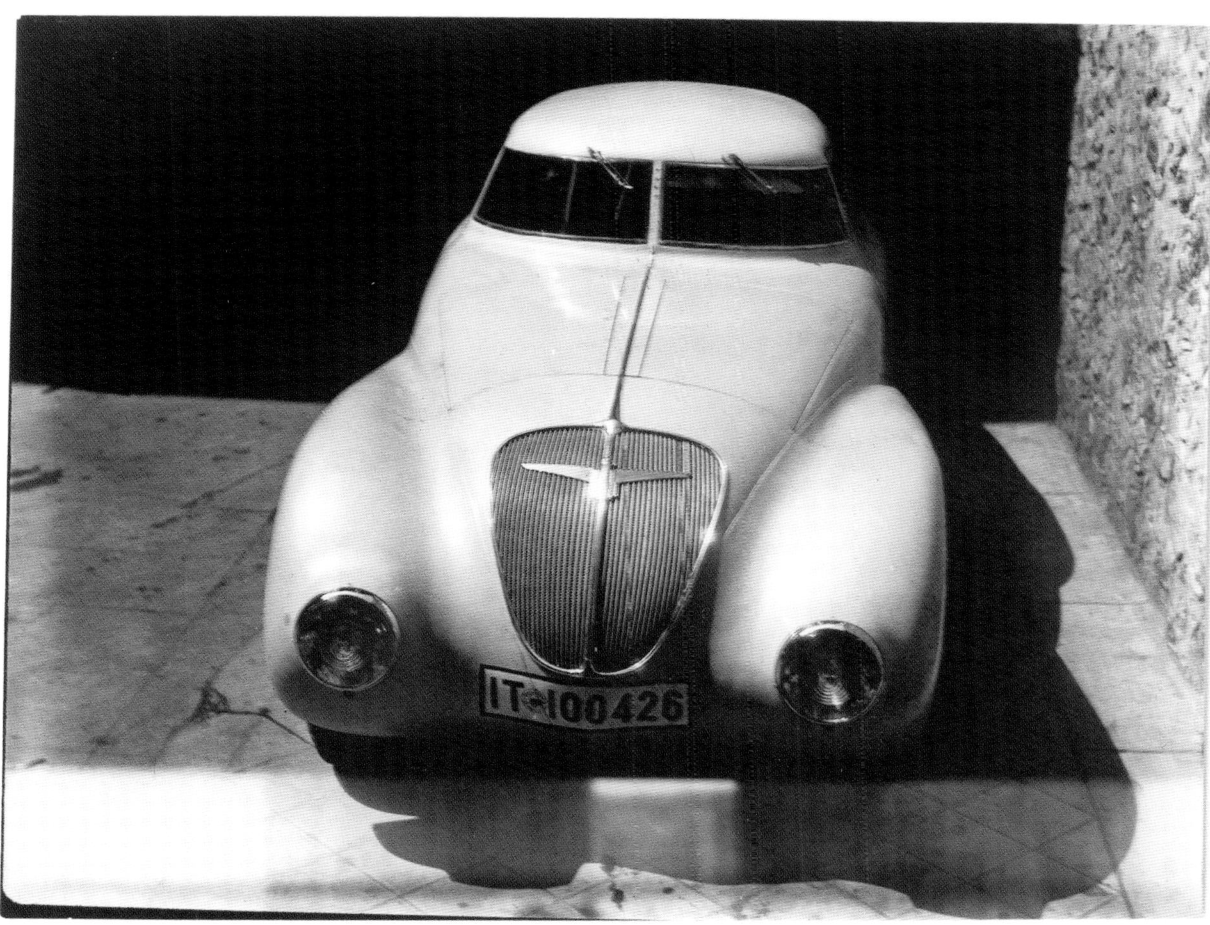

FIG. 165
Man Ray, American (active France), 1890–1976; *Voiture*, 1936; gelatin silver print; 3 1/3 × 4 3/7 in.; Centre Pompidou, Paris, Inventory no. AM 1994-394 (2456)

immediate and adaptable process unburdened by aesthetic convention. Edited with Marcel Duchamp, Man Ray's publication *New York Dada* included his image of a living coat rack—a woman's nude torso bisected by metal bars and cartoon cutouts—paired with a black box of text mordantly bidding readers to "Keep Smiling" (FIG. 163). Circulating in France before his own arrival in 1921, it anticipated Man Ray's indelible influence on the character of Surrealism.

By the 1930s, Man Ray's distortion of the female form had taken on an especially erotic dimension. In 1929 and 1930, he created two enigmatic photographs made of and with his lover, the American photographer Lee Miller. *Les Amoureux* enlarges Miller's lips until they fill the picture plane. Floating against a blown-out background, her pout becomes a grainy, glistening landscape of sexual longing frustrated by cool detachment (FIG. 160). In *The Prayer*, Man Ray photographed a prostrate woman, her fingers tangled as they simultaneously shield and caress her exposed backside (FIG. 161).[12] Sinking into the cushioned surface, the irregular contours of her toe pads appear as fleshy masses of ripe fruit. The close framing and intense light and shadows heighten the image's air of both carnality and disembodiment.

Man Ray oscillated between the artistic and commercial spheres. Deftly tempering his Surrealist lens, he became a genre-defining fashion photographer who stoked desire with a knowing wink. For the cover of a 1933 issue of *Vu* devoted to the Salon de l'Automobile, Man Ray perched a woman in a red Chanel suit on the precariously tilted bumper of an automobile (FIG. 162).[13] Gazing into a compact, her face and round mirror obscure its right headlamp, denying viewers the full toothy visage of its front grille. Dramatically lit, the woman's skin and the car's paint glow yellow as if made from the same incandescent flesh. Expertly employing studio lights but also negative printing and solarization, Man Ray transformed the classicizing drapery and romantic ruffles of 1930s couturiers—Elsa Schiaparelli, Jean Patou, and Alix, among others—into eerie, translucent silhouettes. Alluring and uneasy, Man Ray's images capture the slippage between body, object, and product.

Although cars were featured in Man Ray's earlier work, streamlined automobiles offered a new subject ripe with anthropomorphic allusions.

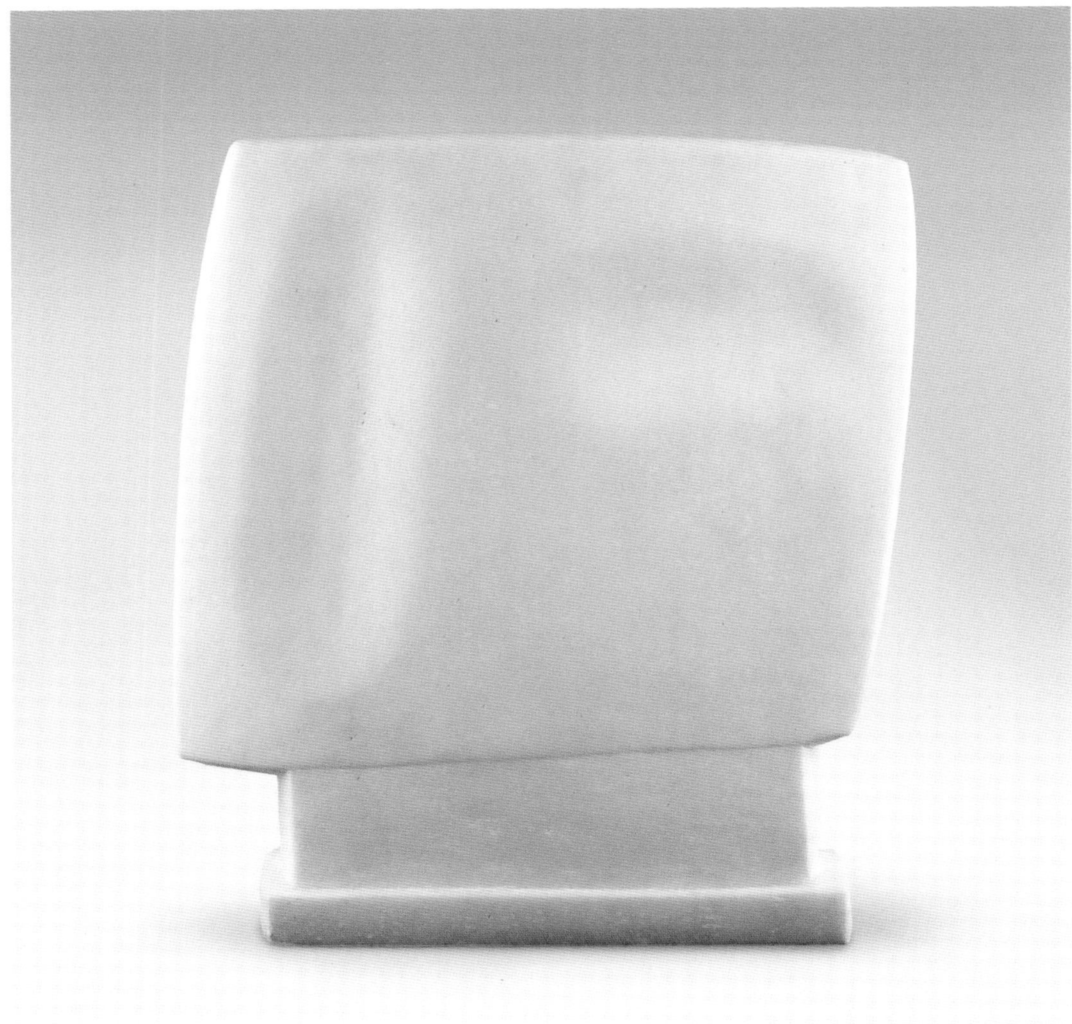

FIG. 166
Alberto Giacometti, Swiss, 1901–1966; *Tête qui regarde*, 1930; white marble; 16 ⅛ × 11 ⅝ × 3 ⅛ in.; Private collection

In a photograph from 1936, he captured an aerodynamic Adler Trumpf Rennlimousine in raking sunlight, its darkened headlamps protruding like nipples from conical breasts (FIG. 165). In 1937, he photographed his own round-nosed Peugeot overtaken by scrubby bush. Without a visible driver, both cars' bisected front windshields, dainty wipers falling over the glass like lashes, become vacant eyes masking unknown motivations. Man Ray imbued these machines, their sleek shapes informed by natural forces, with an autonomous power both beautiful and terrifying.

Twenty years later, sculptor Alberto Giacometti (FIG. 166), an influential voice in 1930s Parisian Surrealism, wrote an article about the 1957 Salon de l'Automobile for the French magazine *Arts* in response to the question of whether cars could be compared to sculpture. He concluded that they couldn't, citing their necessary utility and inherent redundancy, but mused on their perennially unsettling biomorphic and biomechanical qualities:

It does happen sometimes that I stop in the street to look at a car which reminds me of a toad, a bull, or a grasshopper; in the same way, perhaps, as I will gaze at a cloud, watching it ruffle into the shape of a head; or again, at a tree trunk, seeing there a tiger ready to spring. A car, like every other machine, is a recent discovery. It descends not only from the carriage but from the horse and carriage combined. The resulting product is certainly strange: a complete mechanical organism, having eyes, a mouth, a heart, and intestines; it will eat and drink and go on working until it breaks—what an odd parody of a living being.[14]

NOTES

1 Richard Adatto and Diana Meredith, "The European View," in *Curves of Steel: Streamlined Automobile Design at Phoenix Art Museum*, ed. Jonathan A. Stein and Michael Furman (Philadelphia: Coachbuilt Press, 2009), 74–76.

2 "M. André Dubonnet présente à nos lecteurs sa nouvelle voiture aérodynamique à moteur arrière," *Omnia, revue pratique de locomotion*, January 1, 1936, 290.

3 "Les Grandes Manifestations de la Saison d'été de l'Élégance en automobile," *Omnia, revue pratique de locomotion*, August 1, 1934, 99–104.

4 For a comprehensive analysis of the term "biomorphic/biomorphism," see Jennifer Mundy, "The Naming of Biomorphism," in *Biocentrism and Modernism*, ed. Oliver A. I. Botar and Isabel Wünsche (Farnham, UK: Ashgate, 2011), 61–73.

5 Geoffrey Grigson, "Comment on England," *Axis* (January 1935): 8.

6 Alfred H. Barr, *Cubism and Abstract Art: Painting, Sculpture, Constructions, Photography, Architecture, Industrial Art, Theatre, Films, Posters, Typography* (New York: Museum of Modern Art, 1936), 19.

7 See Brandon Taylor, *The Life of Forms in Art: Modernism, Organism, Vitality* (London: Bloomsbury Visual Arts, 2020), 92–126.

8 Jean Hans Arp, "Looking," in Carola Giedion-Welcker, Robert Melville, James Thrall Soby, Jean Arp, and Richard Huelsenbeck, *Arp* (New York: The Museum of Modern Art, 1958), 14–15.

9 "Mostly About People," *New York Herald Tribune*, February 10, 1950, 5: "The vehicular haute couture establishment was founded in 1921. Joseph Figoni handles the creative and Ovidio Falaschi runs the business operation. The firm employs 150 workmen and turns out two cars a week. M. Figoni showed us around. Workmen were hammering at sheets of metal, fabricating radiator grills by a blacksmith's forge, making steering wheels and door handles, and snipping leather. Everything by hand, M. Figoni noted proudly. None of this American mass production. M. Figoni creates all the designs himself. He makes a small clay model, from which his draftsmen make blueprints. Then a wooden skeleton as a guide."

10 Eric Robertson, *Arp: Painter, Poet, Sculptor* (New Haven: Yale University Press, 2006), 106.

11 This *Torso* is number two in an edition of three. Arp made the plaster model for this bronze cast in 1957, based on his 1931 plaster sculpture, *Torso, No. 8*. Charles Scott Chetham, *Modern Painting, Drawing, and Sculpture, Collected by Louise and Joseph Pulitzer, Jr.* (Cambridge, MA: Fogg Art Museum, 1971), 3:343–44.

12 Phillip Prodger writes that contrary to popular assumptions, Miller did not pose for *La Prière*, though he notes, "according to Miller, she . . . assisted Ray to photograph the model." See Phillip Prodger, "Lee Miller and Man Ray, The Ultimate Surrealist Object," in *Man Ray | Lee Miller: Partners in Surrealism*, ed. Prodger (New York: Merrell, 2011), 34.

13 *Vu*, October 1933, cover.

14 Alberto Giacometti, "Giacometti at the Salon d'Auto," trans. Elizabeth Faure, *Paris Review* 18 (Spring 1958): 118–20.

1939 BUGATTI TYPE 57C VANVOOREN CABRIOLET

KEN GROSS

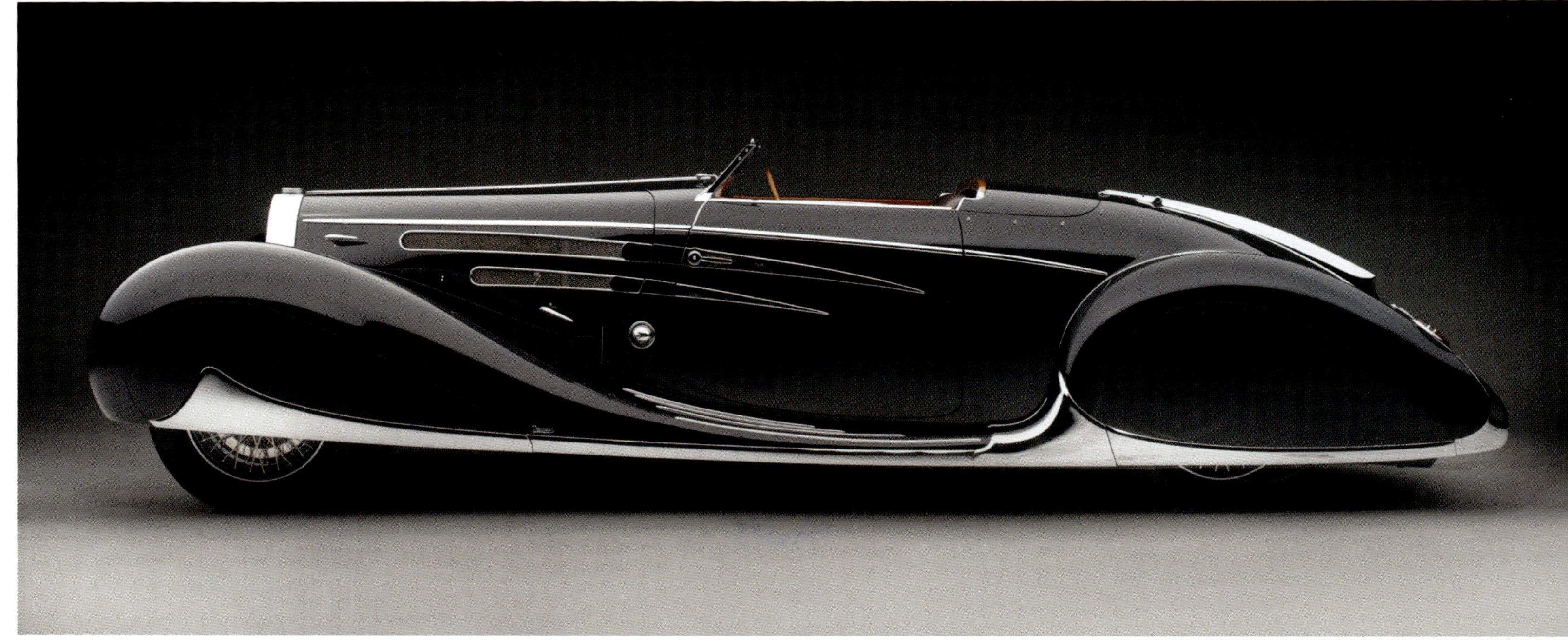

Carrosserie Vanvooren, Courbevoie, France, active 1888–1950; Automobiles Ettore Bugatti, Molsheim, France, active 1909–63; *Type 57C "Shah,"* 1939; 51 × 193 × 78 in.; Collection of Petersen Automotive Museum

From 1911 until the start of World War II, the automobiles of Ettore Bugatti (1881–1947), an authoritative and artistic Italian who lived in France for most of his life, competed successfully in international Grand Prix and sports-car racing. Bugatti's cars were stylish, temperamental, exclusive, and fast.

He experimented with aerodynamics and pioneered the use of lightweight metals like magnesium. Bugatti favored such engineering advances as self-adjusting de Ram shock absorbers, but he could also be conservative. He eschewed supercharging, at first, and clung to cable-operated brakes long after hydraulics proved superior.

The Great Depression of 1929 was slow to impact France, but by the early 1930s sales of luxury automobiles had dwindled. Ettore and his son Jean understood that a special new model was needed if their company was to survive. The styling of the resulting Type 57 was contemporary, and custom coachwork was available for those with means.

The Type 57 Atlantic, the inspiration for the later Atalante, debuted at the 1935 Paris and London motor shows. Initially called the Compétition Coupé Aérolithe (French for "meteor"), the car inspired four production versions called Atlantics. The Atlantic cockpit was sporty yet cramped and poorly ventilated. Forty luxurious and more civilized Atalante models were built on the standard Type 57 and the sports Type 57S chassis. An optional supercharger for the Type 57C and Type 57SC increased output to 170 hp and as much as 220, depending upon specifications.

For racing, a normally aspirated 3.3-liter, straight eight–powered Type 57, on the ultra-low "S" chassis, was fitted with streamlined open coachwork. The factory advertised its successes, which included averaging 135.45 mph for one hour, 123.8 mph for 2,000 miles, and 124.6 mph for 4,000 kilometers. An avid horseman, "Le Patron" was convinced automobile competition improved the breed, as it did with thoroughbred racing.

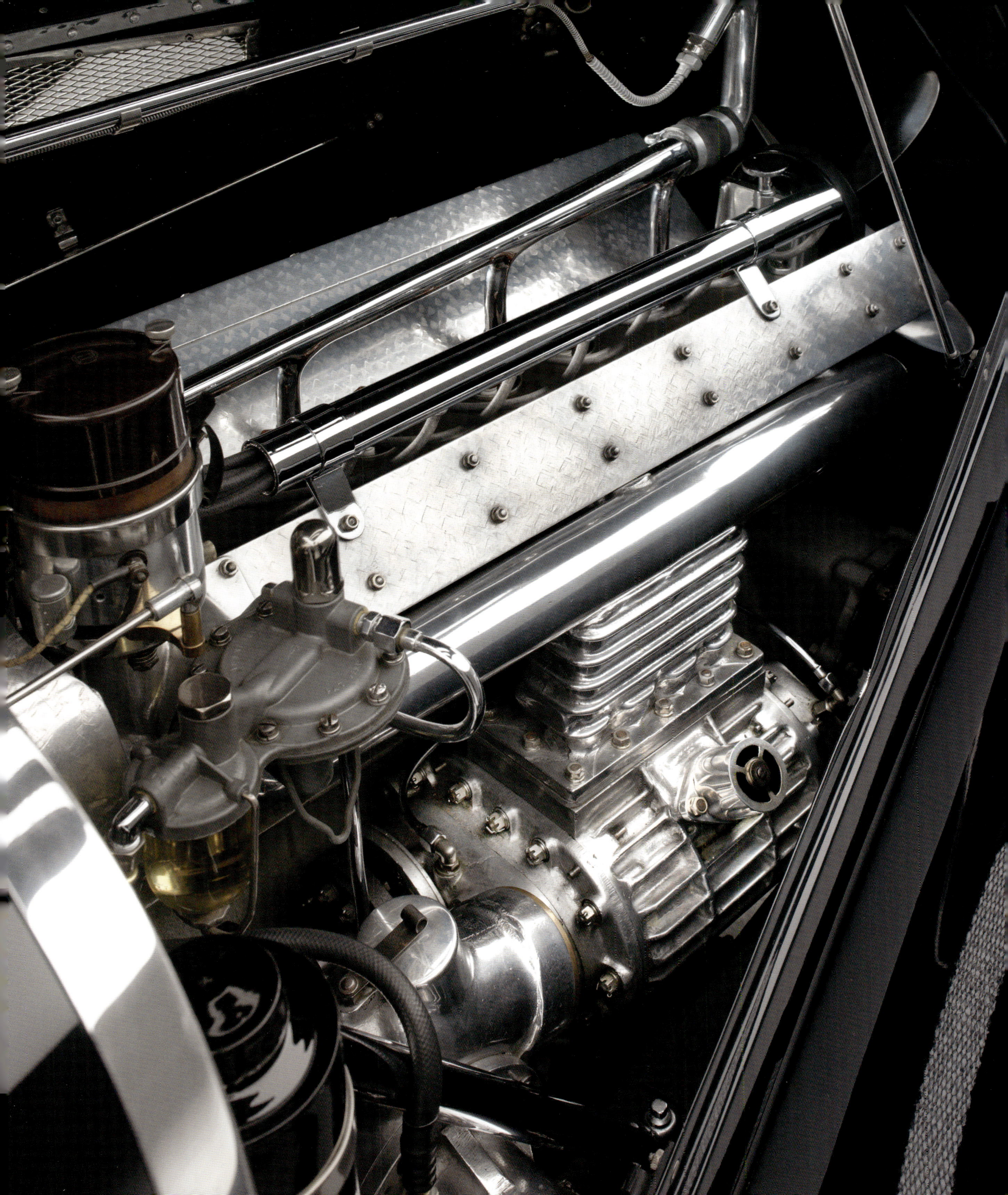

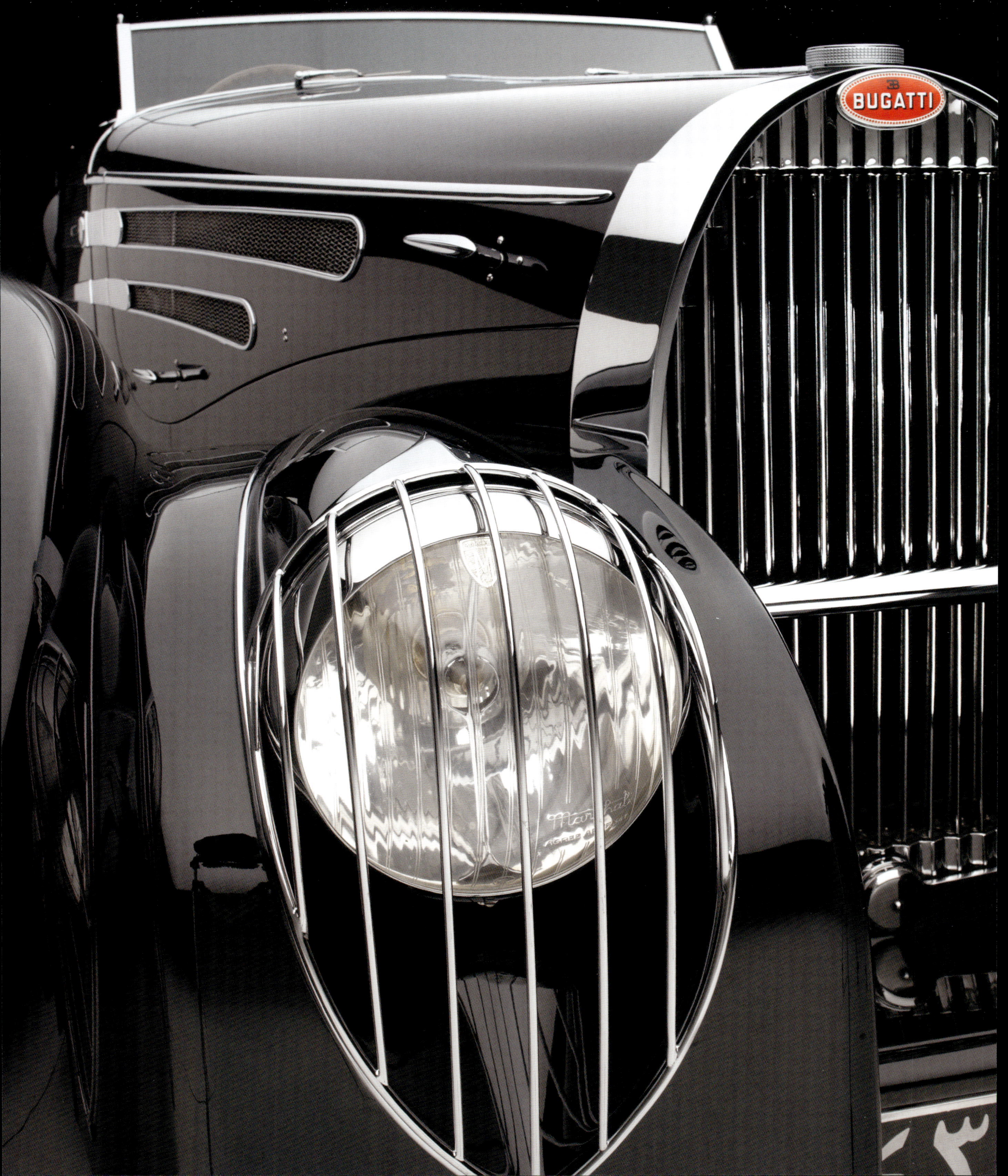
BUGATTI

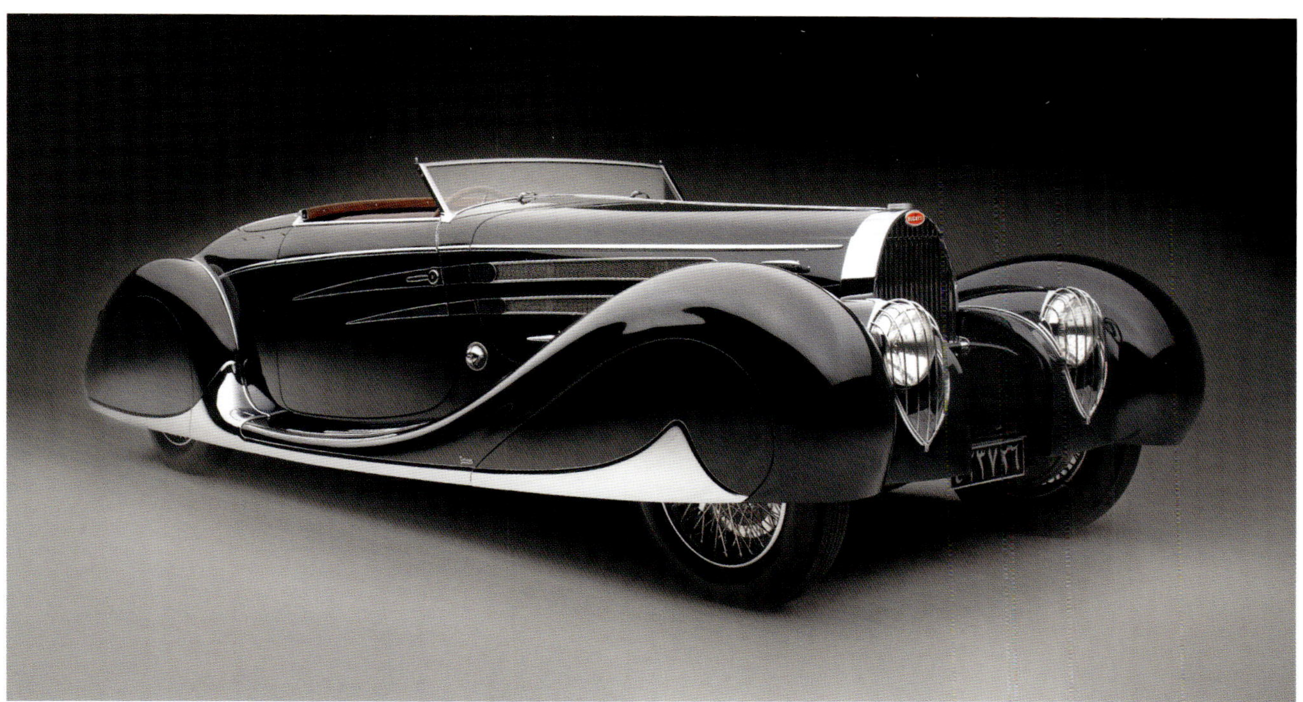

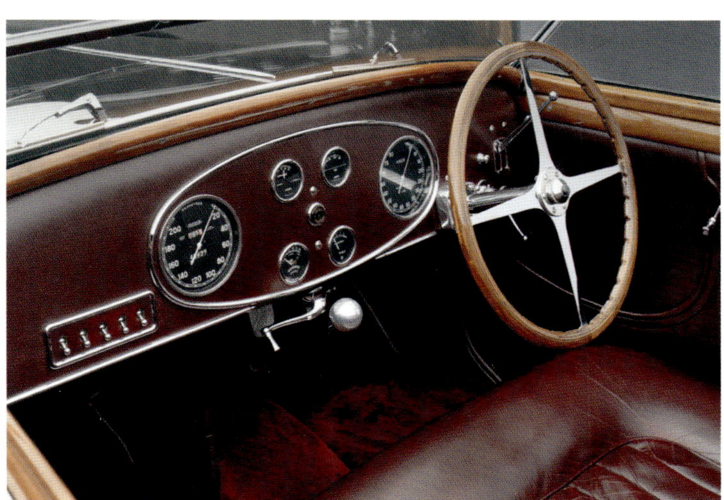

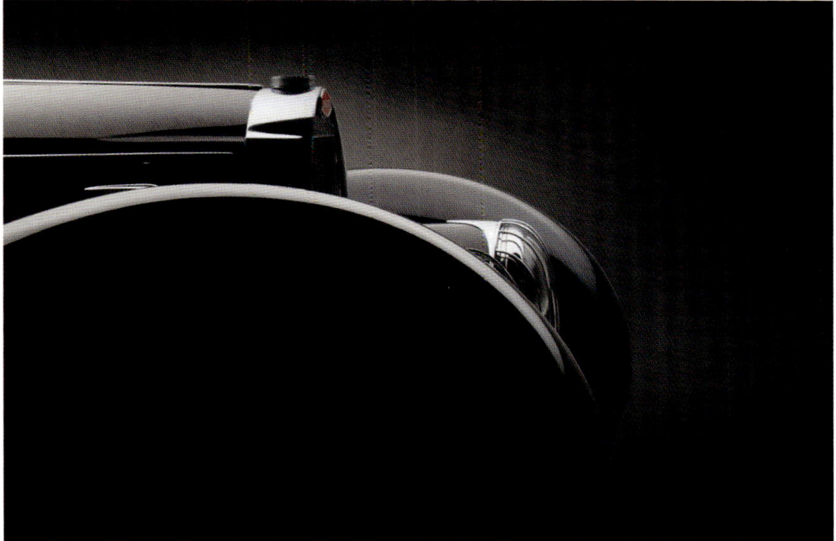

Near the end of 1938, all Type 57s were built to Series III specification, which included rubber (versus solid) engine mounts, chassis stiffening, and subtle engine updates. The most important change was Lockheed-designed hydraulic brakes with twin master cylinders. Riding comfort improved with Allinquant telescopic shock absorbers.[1]

This one-of-a-kind, supercharged Type 57C, chassis no. 57808, belonged to Mohammad Reza Pahlavi (1919–1980), the prince of Persia and future Shah of Iran. When Pahlavi married Princess Fawzia (1921–2013), a daughter of King Fuad I and sister of King Farouk I, their nuptials were celebrated in Cairo in 1939. To flatter the future leader of a key oil-producing country, many nations sent lavish wedding presents, such as a royal airplane and several luxurious cars, including this one.

This cabriolet's drophead coachwork, a study in sweeping lines and fluid Art Deco ornamentation, was constructed by Carrosserie Vanvooren of Paris. Figoni was offered the commission initially, but the firm could not meet the tight completion timeline, so Vanvooren offered to do the work "in the style of Figoni." The windscreen can be lowered into the cowl for a sportier appearance. In 1959, the Type 57C was sold from the Shah's Imperial Garage Collection, and after a succession of owners, it was purchased by Robert and Margie Petersen.

Loaned by the Petersen Automotive Museum, Los Angeles, California

1 Barrie Price, *57—The Last French Bugatti* (Poundbury, UK: Veloce Publishing, 1992), 116–17, 185.

MANNEQUINS, AUTOMOBILES, AND SALVADOR DALÍ'S *RAINY TAXI*

SARAH BERG

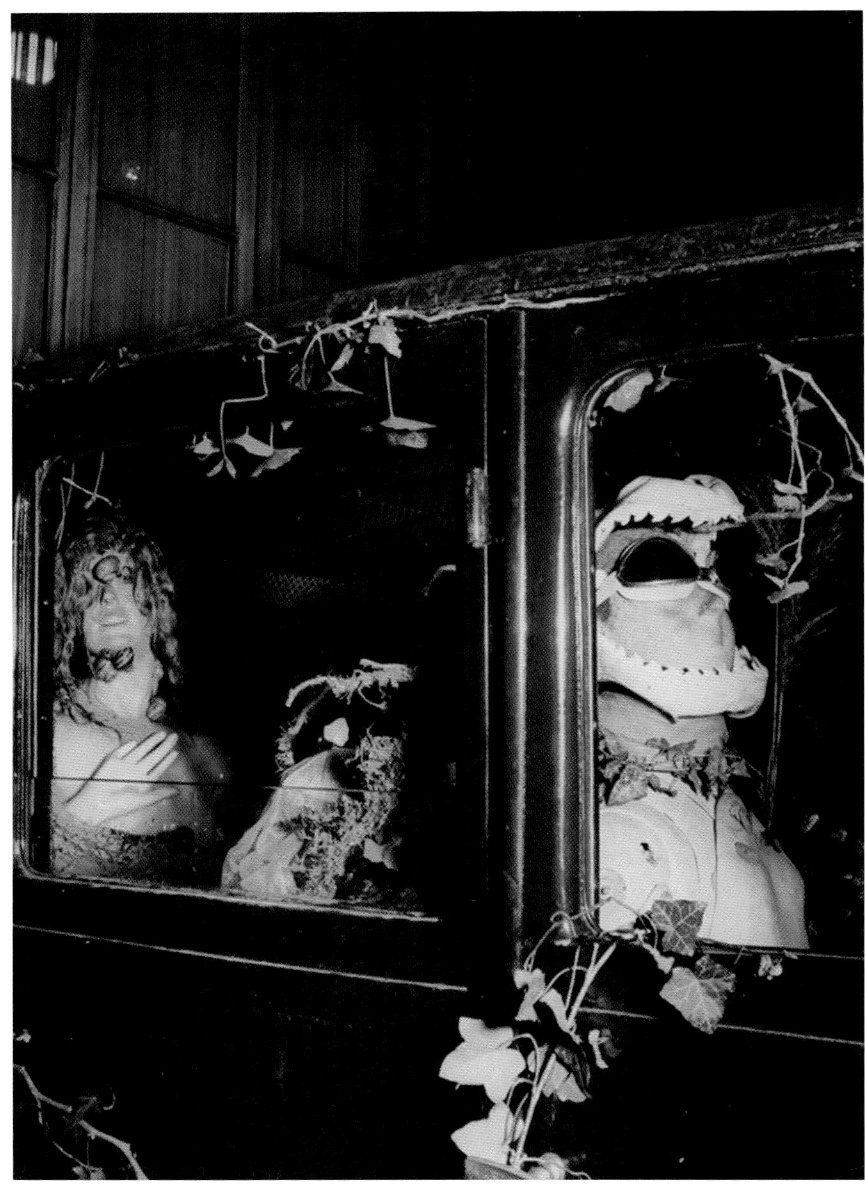

FIG. 167
Denise Bellon, French, 1902–1999; *"Rainy Taxi" of Salvador Dalí, International Surrealist Exhibition, Paris*, 1938, printed 1984; gelatin silver print; 24 × 30 in.; Fonds photographique Denise Bellon

A real black taxi strewn with ivy, with water leaking from an artificial rain system installed in the cab, Salvador Dalí's *Rainy Taxi* greeted guests to the 1938 Exposition Internationale du Surréalisme by soaking their evening slippers.[1] The life-size installation stood in the courtyard of the Galerie Beaux-Arts in Paris, its headlights on. Inside, the rain drenched its occupants: a dummy wearing a shark's head in the driver's seat, and a blonde shop-window mannequin covered in live snails in the back (FIG. 167). Beside the mannequin were a sewing machine, an omelet, and dripping foliage.

"Rainy Taxi" of Salvador Dalí, International Surrealist Exhibition, Paris (FIG. 168), captured by the photographer Denise Bellon, offers a voyeuristic view into the back seat. The mannequin's evening dress, decorated with reproductions of paintings by Jean-François Millet, falls from her shoulders. Burgundy snails—more than 200 in the cab—crawl over her exposed chest and neck. Her painted smile and outstretched hand, perhaps once elements of a charmingly posed window display, now affect a sense of distress beneath the unrelenting drizzle. Despite (or, perhaps, because of)

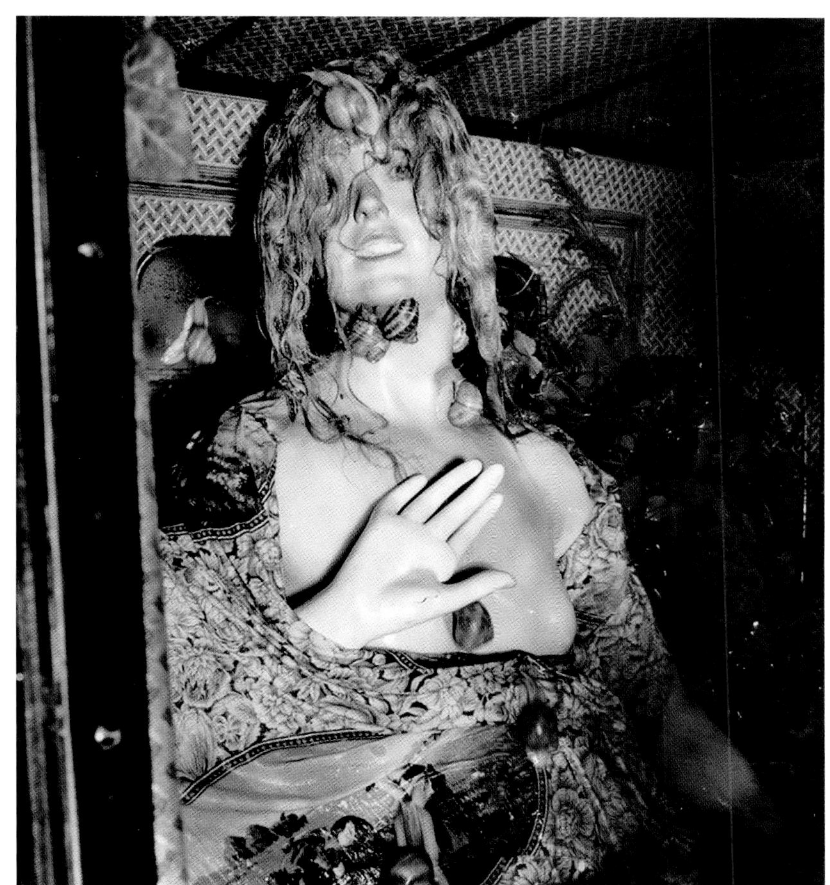

FIG. 168
Denise Bellon, French, 1902–1999; *"Rainy Taxi" of Salvador Dalí, International Surrealist Exhibition, Paris* (detail), 1938, printed 1984; gelatin silver print; 24 × 30 in.; Fonds photographique Denise Bellon

the feelings of discomfort it provoked in many visitors, the work was a resounding success and heralded the lasting influence of the Surrealist exhibition on modern art.

The use of mannequins, as in *Rainy Taxi*, was widespread not only in Surrealist art but also in the commercial landscape of 1930s Paris. The Surrealists, committed to the absurd and irrational, tended to appropriate and dissect aspects of their lived realities: shop-window mannequins, movie posters, glimmering metallic automobiles. Ilse Bing's 1932 photograph *Greta Garbo Poster, Paris* demonstrates the Surrealist eye as directed through a small, handheld camera (FIG. 169). A flaneuse's view of Parisian buildings and signage, the photograph foregrounds a tattered poster of Greta Garbo on a crumbling wall. With the actress's famously enigmatic gaze obscured, the picture is a Surrealist paradox of depth and flatness, displaying the tantalizing allure of celebrity and the city while rendering both completely unreachable.

Seeking ways to express the entanglement they perceived between art and commodity in their increasingly commercialized world, the Surrealists turned from literature and painting to a new obsession: the object. Often constructed using everyday materials, the Surrealist object complicated material reality, and the mannequin emerged as a critical component. For the Surrealists, the mannequin (usually female) represented a "subject of intense scrutiny: dismembered, fragmented, desecrated, eroticized, and eulogized in the pursuit of a range of psychological, sociological, and sexual concerns,"[2] in the words of the art historian and curator Ghislaine Wood.

This array of embodied themes was prominently on display at the 1938 exhibition, not least in Dalí's taxi. Just inside the Galerie Beaux-Arts, visitors encountered a corridor lined with sixteen female mannequins, each dressed by a different artist. Apart from the figure by Jean (Hans) Arp, which was almost completely obscured, the mannequins stood in various states of bizarre adornment and undress. Cast in roles of sexual allure through their decoration, they were frequently described as streetwalkers by visitors.[3] Artists and spectators alike also noted their "realness," a quality precedented by designer André Vigneau's pursuit to make mannequins for the 1925 International Exhibition of Modern Decorative and Industrial Arts that were even more

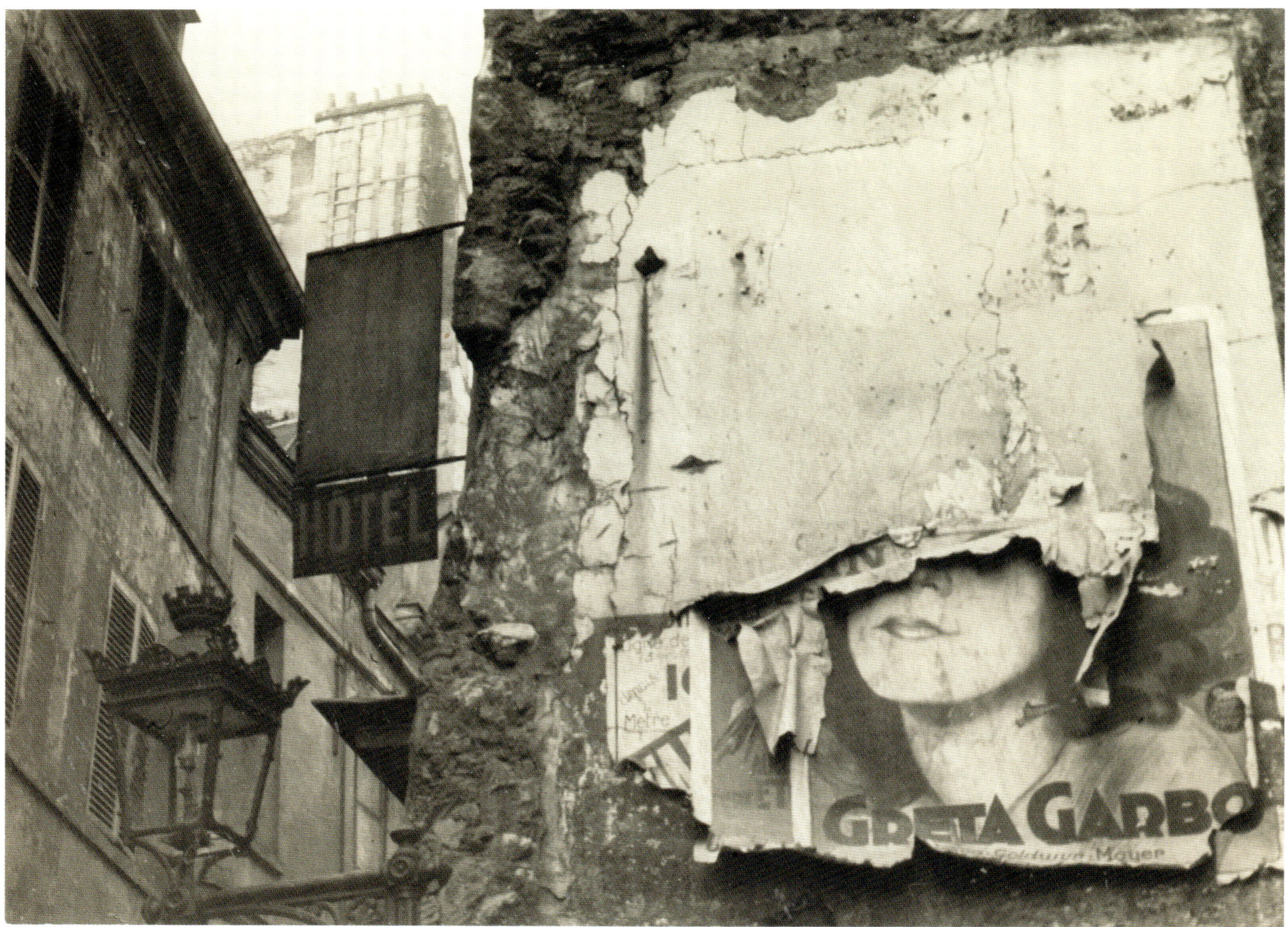

FIG. 169
Ilse Bing, American (born Germany), 1899–1998; *Greta Garbo Poster, Paris*, 1932; gelatin silver print; 5 ⅝ × 8 ¼ in.; Saint Louis Art Museum, Museum Purchase with funds donated by the St. Louis Friends of Photography, and Museum Funds 51:2006

lifelike than nature.[4] With finely painted features, the mannequins—including Dalí's taxi passenger—were perceived as realistic enough to be complicit, though helpless, participants in their encounters with the scintillated viewer.[5]

The slippery relationship between nature and artifice was a subject of fascination for many throughout this decade. Trompe l'œil spiderwebs and feathers sprung up on gowns by Jeanne Lanvin (FIGS. 170, 171); Elsa Schiaparelli collaborated with Dalí to make a dress decorated with a painted lobster, then another with padded ridges in the shape of the wearer's skeleton. False organic and biomorphic forms in art and fashion gestured toward a strange collision of the physical and fantastical. Dalí's depictions of a car being overtaken by foliage began with paintings such as *Solitude paranoïaque-critique* (1935), in which a landscape appears to materialize around the decaying shape of an old automobile. According to the art historian Ingrid Pfeiffer, Dalí used this imagery to depict nature overcoming civilization, and thus the rational becoming subservient to the unconscious.[6] The automobile already served to represent the forward drive of modernity in contemporary thought; juxtaposed with the wildness of nature, it became a useful foil to Dalí's pet notions of the organic, dreamlike, and absurd.

This is not to say that Dalí rejected the automobile entirely. Flippant toward strict artistic agendas,[7] he happily traveled by taxi or in one of his own cars on a regular basis, experiencing the new speeds that the automobile brought to modern life. The celerity of modernization subjected motorists to disillusionment and fragmentation—reality shattered into the world that existed inside the automobile and which sped past its windows. The split between these two realities was not unnoticed by Dalí. He told reviewers that the idea for the artwork came to him while waiting for a taxi under heavy rain in Milan,[8] where, upon entering the cab, he was struck by how suddenly the downpour stopped. He later wrote in 1942: "I cannot understand . . . why no one invents taxi-cabs

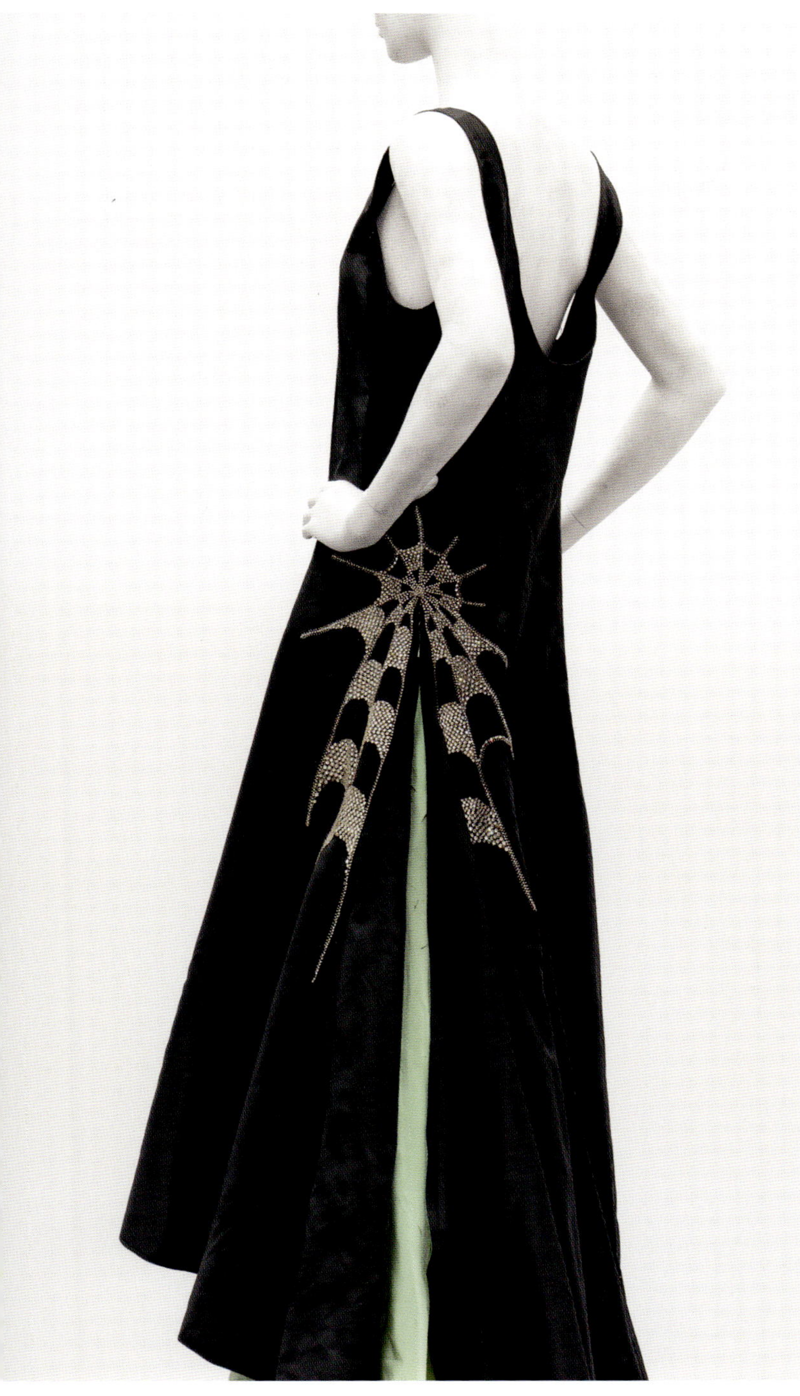

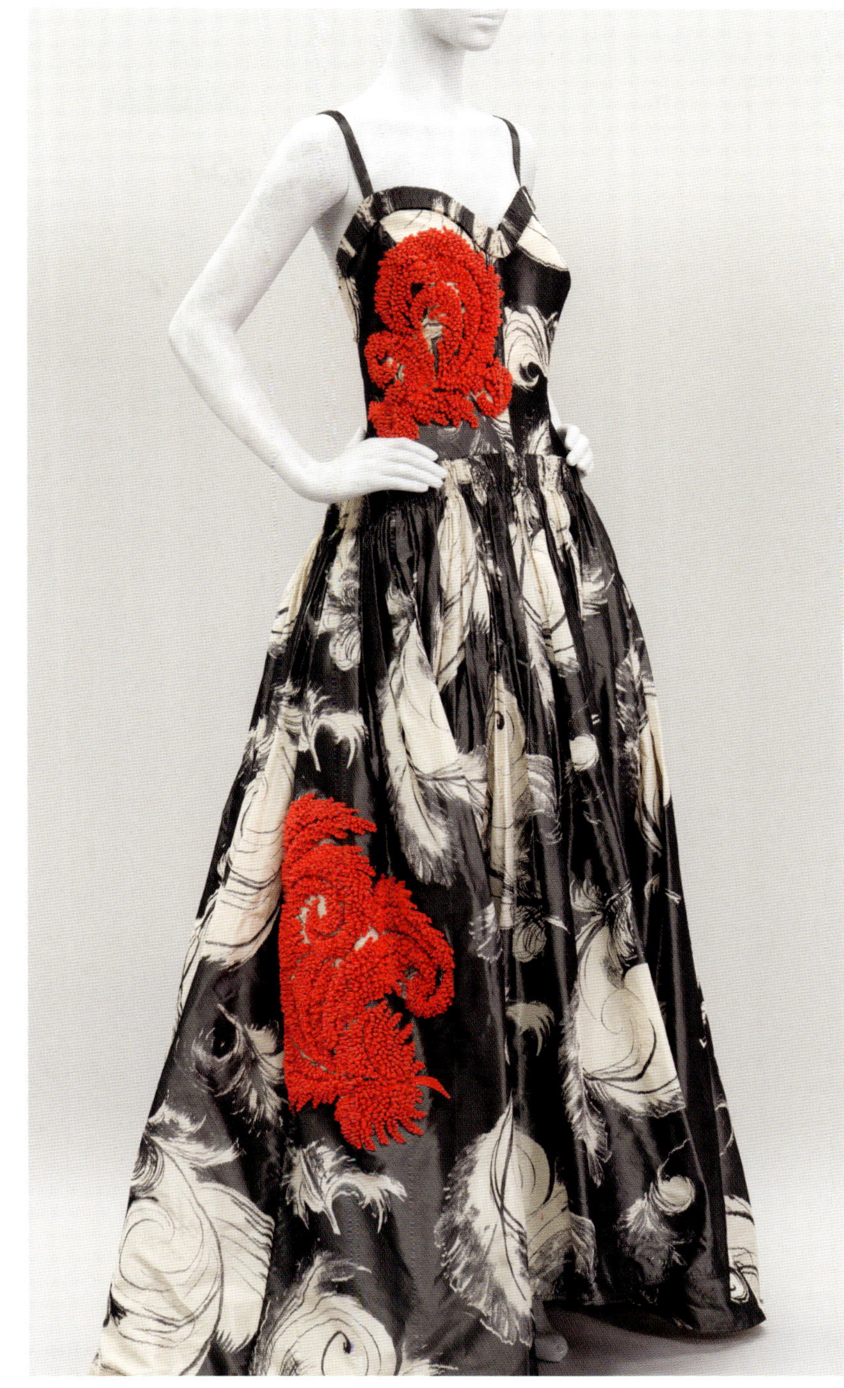

FIG. 170
Jeanne Lanvin, French, 1867–1946; Lanvin, Paris, founded 1889; *Evening Dress,* winter 1929/1930; silk faille, rhinestones, and glass beads; Courtesy of the Missouri Historical Society, St. Louis

FIG. 171
Jeanne Lanvin, French, 1867–1946; Lanvin, Paris, founded 1889; *Evening Dress, "Fusée,"* 1939; warp-printed silk taffeta and georgette ribbon trim; Courtesy of the Missouri Historical Society, St. Louis

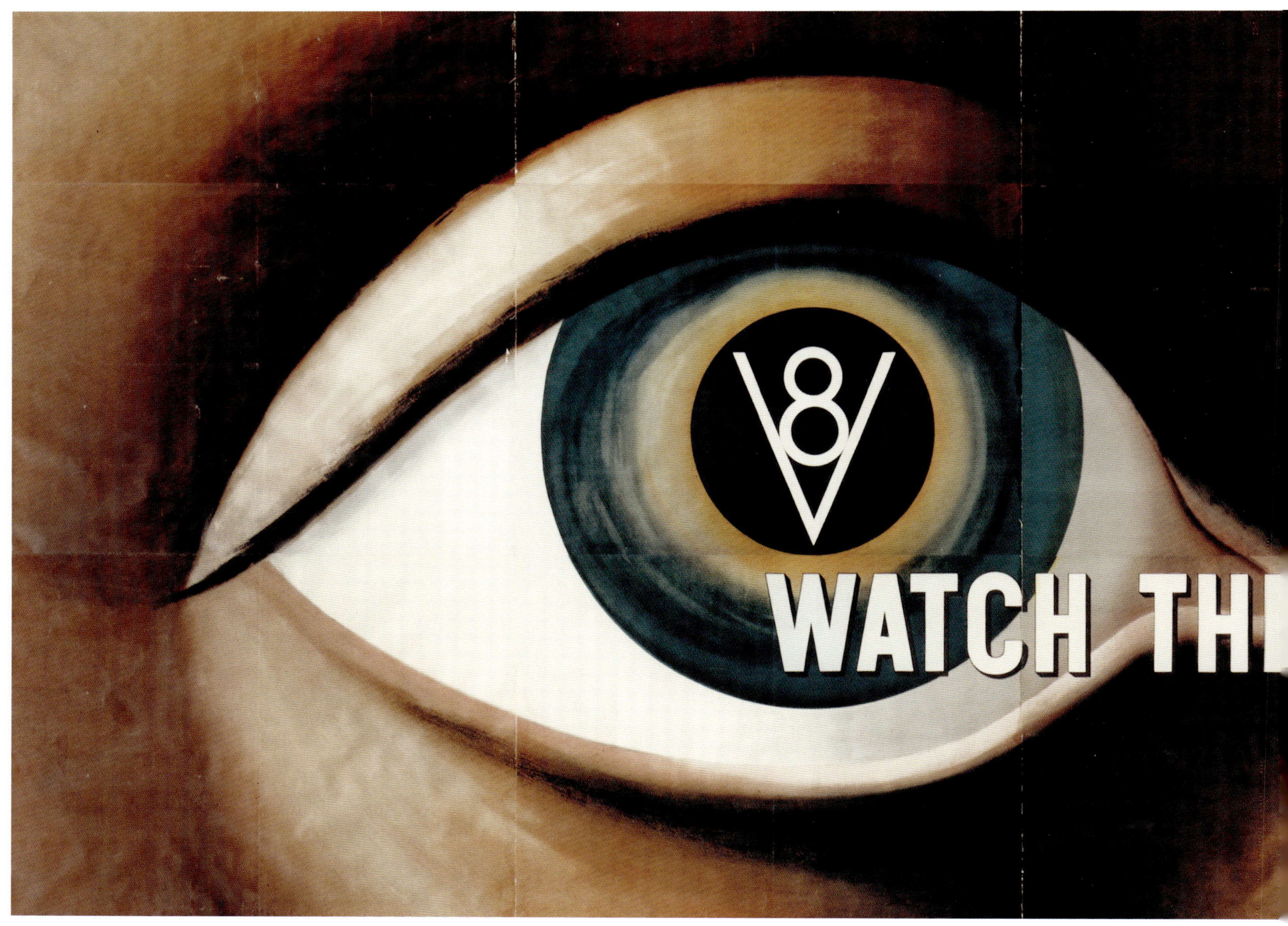

more expensive than the others fitted inside with a device for making artificial rain which would oblige the passenger to wear his rain coat when he got in while the weather was fine and sunny outside."[9] Through these experiences, the car became for Dalí a site of possible transformation—one that could be psychological, atmospheric, or even embodied.

It is worth acknowledging Dalí's mention of expense in his musings, lest we forget that the automobile was also a luxury. Even a defunct taxi connoted a relationship between passenger and driver.[10] In *Rainy Taxi*, Dalí's occupants sit in the tension of this as-of-yet unfulfilled transaction, an atmosphere made even more anxious by the various strange additions to the automobile, which indicate that expectations can no longer be trusted.

Demand for the automobile in interwar France was driven further by emerging fashionable designs. Upper-class enthusiasts delighted in *concours d'élégance* events, where luxurious vehicles were paraded by attractive women drivers and passengers. Much like the finely dressed mannequins that filled shop windows throughout Paris, the automobile was becoming a product manufactured for hungry eyes. A. M. Cassandre's poster *Watch the Fords Go By* (1937) illustrates this hunger using a giant, disembodied eye stamped with the V8 emblem—a design that literally imprints the desired commodity onto the act of seeing (FIG. 172). This gaze (assumed to belong to the male public) facilitated the entanglement of the body of the mannequin, the body of the woman, and the body of the automobile, seeing each as a commodity to be possessed. *Rainy Taxi* sits at the center of this entanglement. Revisiting it through Bellon's photographs today provides us with the evergreen opportunity to ponder whether we are looking out or looking in.

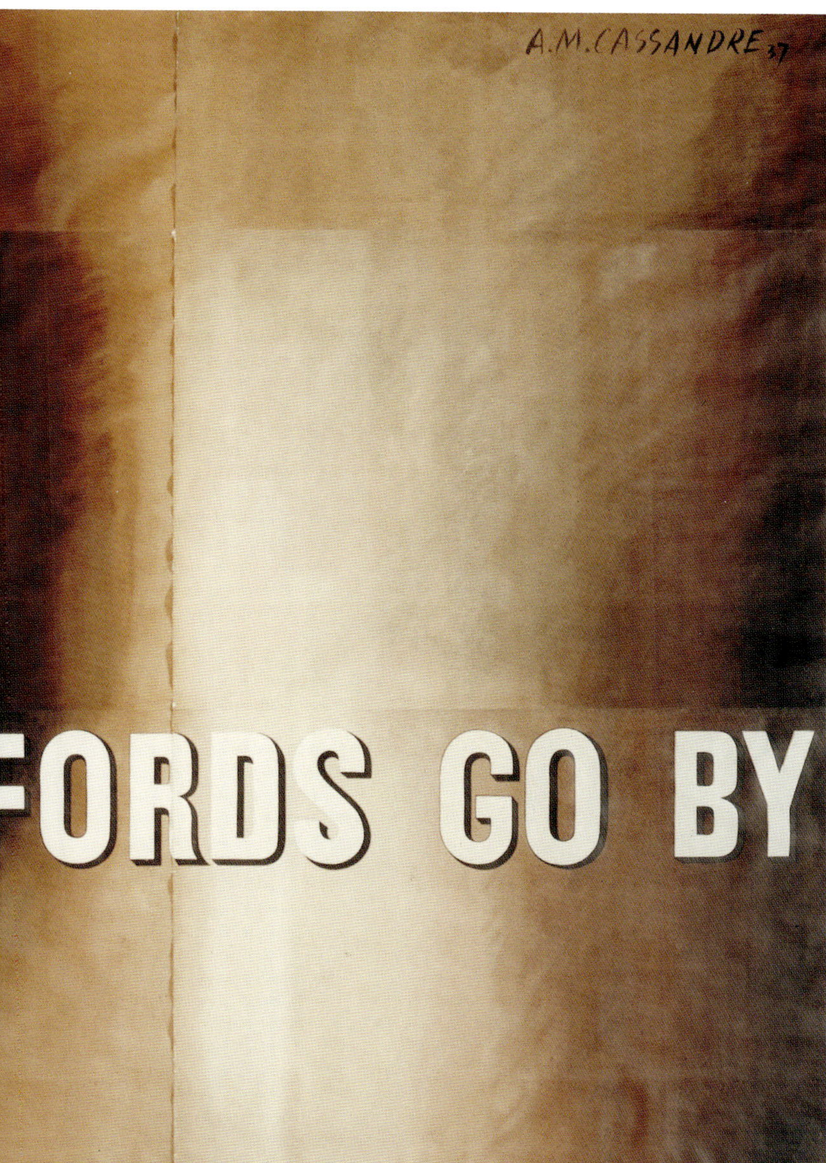

FIG. 172
A. M. Cassandre, French, 1901–1968; *Watch the Fords Go By*, 1937; offset lithograph; 8 ft. 11 in. × 19 ft. 6 ½ in.; Museum of Modern Art, New York, Gift of the designer

NOTES

1 Bettina Wilson, "Surrealism in Paris," *Vogue*, March 1, 1938, 144.

2 Ghislaine Wood, *Surreal Things: Surrealism and Design* (London: V&A Publications, 2007), 10.

3 Lewis Kachur, *Displaying the Marvelous: Marcel Duchamp, Salvador Dalí, and Surrealist Exhibition Installations* (Cambridge, MA: MIT Press, 2013), 39–40.

4 Nicole Parrot, *Mannequins* (New York: St. Martin's Press, 1982), 74.

5 Kachur, *Displaying the Marvelous*, 42.

6 Ingrid Pfeiffer, "Surreal Objects Yesterday and Today," in *Surreal Objects*, ed. Pfeiffer and Max Hollein (Ostfildern: Hatje Cantz, 2011), 20.

7 Despite his involvement with the Surrealists, Dalí would eventually be expelled from the group due to his refusal to agree with André Breton's political values.

8 Kachur, *Displaying the Marvelous*, 34.

9 Salvador Dalí, *The Secret Life of Salvador Dalí*, trans. Haakon M. Chevalier (New York: Dial Press, 1942), 271.

10 Sandra Zalman, "Salvador Dalí's *Rainy Taxi* at the Museum," in *Revisiting the Past in Museums and at Historic Sites*, ed. Anca I. Lasc, Andrew McClellan, and Änne Söll (New York: Routledge, 2022), 147.

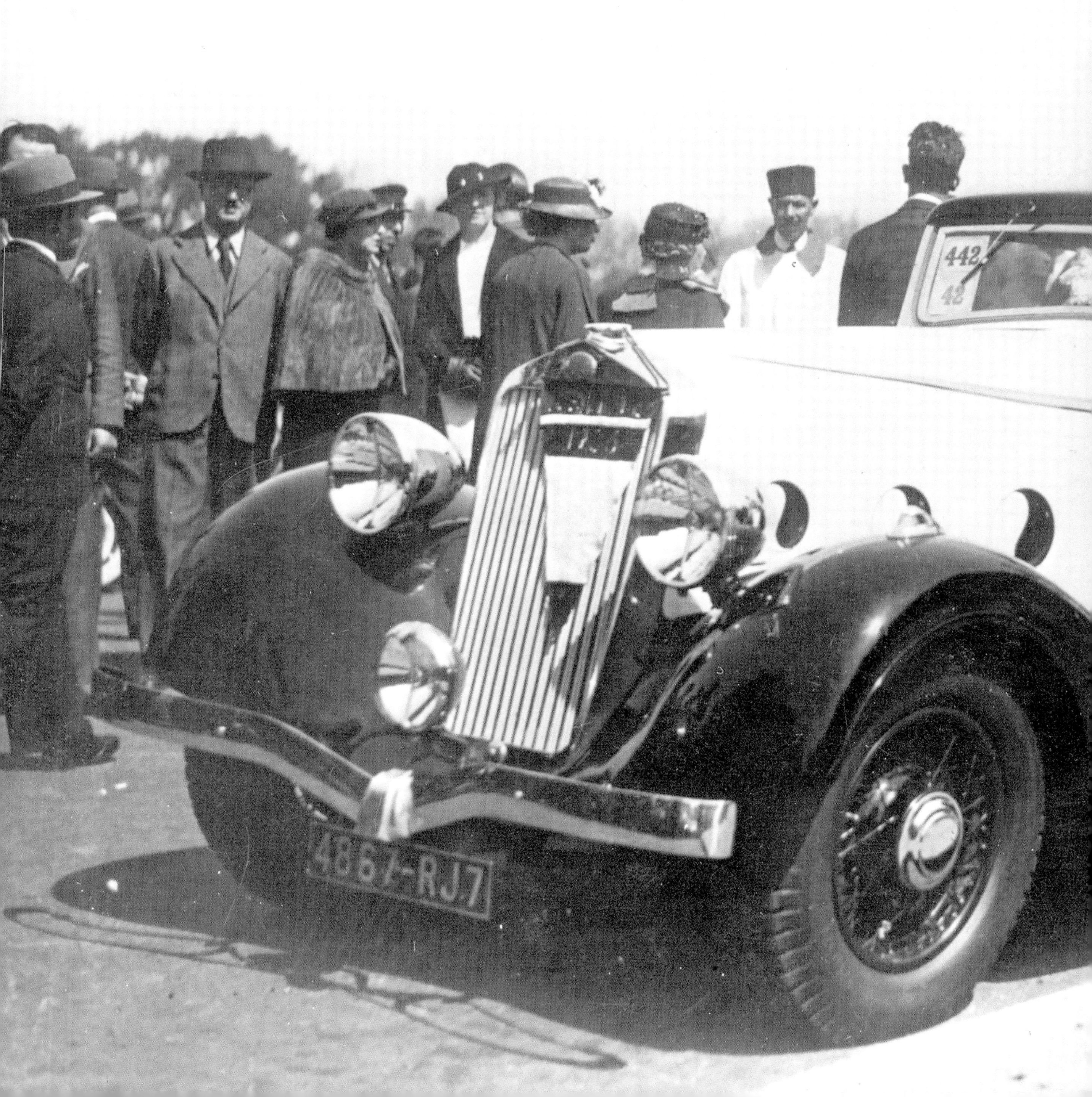
442
42
4867-RJ7

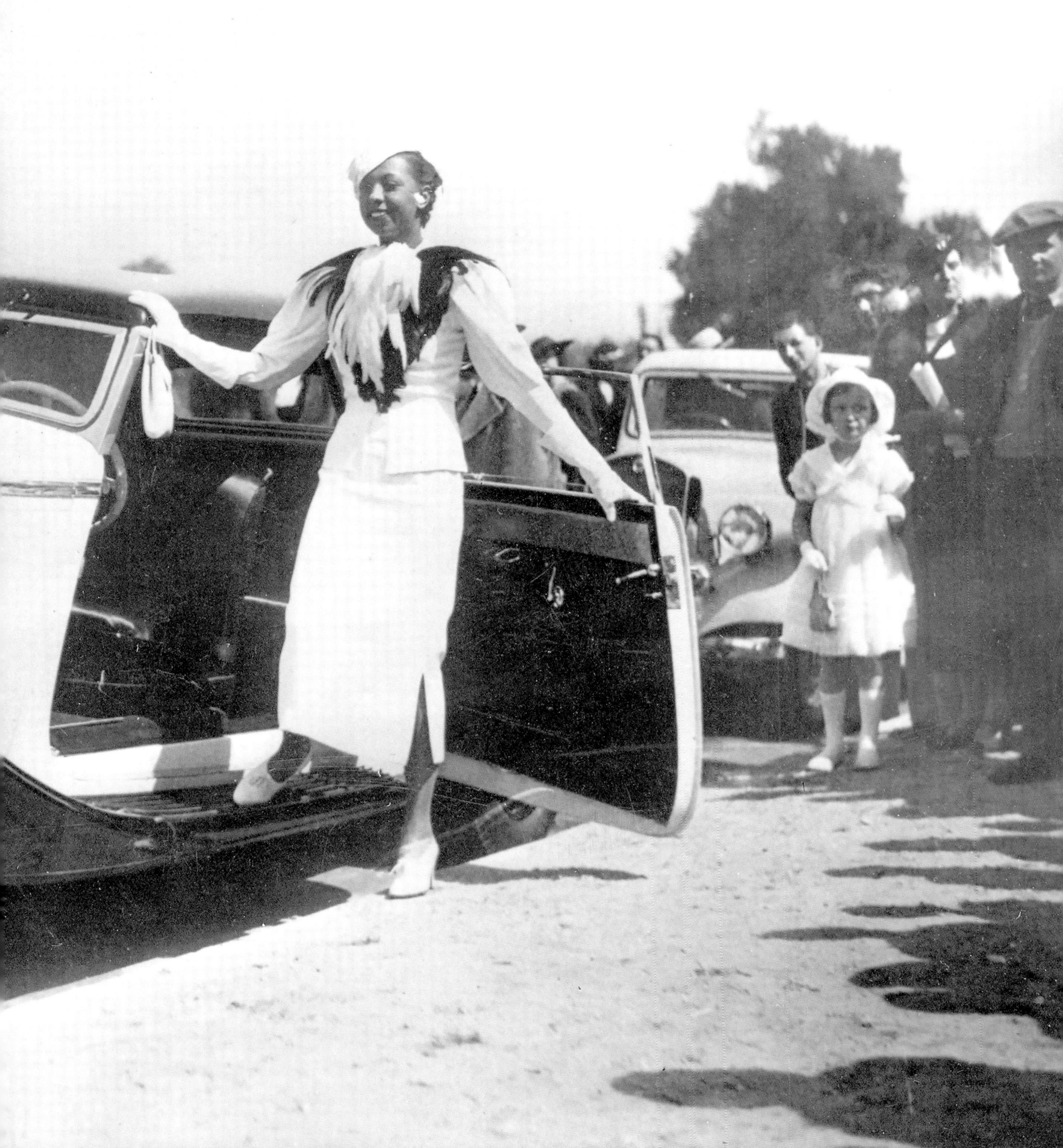

CHECKLIST OF THE EXHIBITION

The exhibition checklist is ordered by gallery and then alphabetically by the primary maker. All works followed by a page number are illustrated in the catalogue.

SCULPTURE HALL

Ettore Bugatti, French (born Italy), 1881–1947
Automobiles Ettore Bugatti, Molsheim, France, active 1909–63
Type 32, 1923; approx. 38 ½ × 164 × 47 in.; Courtesy of the Mathews Family (page 24)

TAYLOR HALL

Carrosserie Vanvooren, Courbevoie, France, active 1888–1950
Automobiles Ettore Bugatti, Molsheim, France, active 1909–63
Type 57C, 1939; 51 × 193 × 78 in.; Collection of Petersen Automotive Museum (page 176)

BRUTAL MACHINES MADE BEAUTIFUL

Citroën, Saint-Ouen-sur-Seine, France, founded 1919
Bernadette Ramaekers, Dutch, b. 1954
B14, 1928; 71 × 164 × 56 in.; Edward F. Niedzwiecki (page 56)

Robert Delaunay, French, 1885–1941
Eiffel Tower, 1924; oil on canvas; 63 ⅝ × 38 ⅛ in.; Saint Louis Art Museum, Gift of Mr. and Mrs. Morton D. May 536:1956 (pages 12, 85)

Sonia Delaunay, French (born Ukraine), 1885–1979
Maquette of Exhibition Catalogue, 1916; pochoir; 13 ½ × 17 ¾ in.; Private collection (page 20)

Published by Librairie des Arts Décoratifs, French; *Sonia Delaunay: Ses peintures, ses objets, ses tissus simultanés, ses modes*, c.1925; color illustrations; pochoir and relief process; 5⁄16 × 23 × 16 in.; Missouri State University Libraries, Springfield, Missouri (pages 90, 91)

Ferret Frères et Cie, Saint-Denis, France; *"Tissu simultané" n° 1*, 1924; printed silk; 14 ⅞ × 19 ½ in.; Musée des Tissus et des Arts décoratifs de Lyon (page 90)

Ferret Frères et Cie, Saint-Denis, France; *"Tissu simultané" n° 26*, June 1924; printed silk; 6 15⁄16 × 20 11⁄16 in.; Musée des Tissus et des Arts décoratifs de Lyon

Ferret Frères et Cie, Saint-Denis, France; *"Tissu simultané" n° 35*, 1923–24; printed silk; 18 5⁄16 × 18 ⅞ in.; Musée des Tissus et des Arts décoratifs de Lyon (page 90)

Ferret Frères et Cie, Saint-Denis, France; *"Tissu simultané" n° 33*, August 1924; printed silk; 9 1⁄16 × 6 ½ in.; Musée des Tissus et des Arts décoratifs de Lyon

Ferret Frères et Cie, Saint-Denis, France; *"Tissu simultané" n° 269p*, June 14, 1928; printed silk; 8 7/16 × 19 7/8 in.; Musée des Tissus et des Arts décoratifs de Lyon

Ferret Frères et Cie, Saint-Denis, France; *"Tissu simultané" n° 187*, 1926; printed silk; 7 7/8 × 19 5/8 in.; Musée des Tissus et des Arts décoratifs de Lyon

Ferret Frères et Cie, Saint-Denis, France; *"Tissu simultané" n° 186, color 4*, 1926; printed silk; 7 ½ × 19 5/16 in.; Musée des Tissus et des Arts décoratifs de Lyon (page 91)

Ferret Frères et Cie, Saint-Denis, France; *"Tissu simultané" n° 201 colors 4*, August 27, 1927; cotton and linen; 9 7/16 × 26 in.; Musée des Tissus et des Arts décoratifs de Lyon

René Lalique, French, 1860–1945
Cinq Chevaux (Five Horses), designed 1925; glass; 5 7/8 × 5 × 7 1/8 in.; The Baltimore Museum of Art (page 87)

Comète (Comet), designed 1925; glass, Carrara glass, and chrome; 4 1/8 × 4 × 7 7/8 in.; The Baltimore Museum of Art (page 87)

Victoire (Spirit of the Wind), designed 1928; glass, sterling silver, silver-plated copper, and granite; 11 ½ × 3 7/8 × 8 ½ in.; The Baltimore Museum of Art: Gift of Dr. and Mrs. Edward F. Lewison, Baltimore, in Memory of their Son, Richard Jay Lewison (1953–1996) (page 87)

Jacques-Henri Lartigue, French, 1894–1986
The Singer Racing Car "Bunny III," from "The Lartigue Portfolio," 1912, printed 1977; gelatin silver print; 6 3/8 × 8 3/8 in.; Saint Louis Art Museum, Gift of Frederick P. Currier 305:1995.8 (page 37)

Zissou Driving His "Bob on 4 Wheels" with Oléo and Louis as Passengers. Overloaded, The Bob Is Going To Crash…, from "The Lartigue Portfolio," 1910, printed 1978; gelatin silver print; 6 3/8 × 8 3/8 in.; Saint Louis Art Museum, Gift of Frederick P. Currier 305:1995.5 (page 10)

Fernand Léger, French, 1881–1955
Disque dans la Rue (Disk in the Street), 1919; oil on canvas; 19 ½ × 12 ½ in.; Private collection (page 21)

Sarah Lipska, French (born Poland), 1882–1973
Winter Sports Outfit, Vest with Leg Warmers, 1925; wool felt and twill with braided ribbons; Musées de Poitiers (page 81)

(attributed) *Textile*, 1927; silk; Brooklyn Museum Costume Collection at The Metropolitan Museum of Art, Gift of the Brooklyn Museum, 2009; Gift of Adelaide Goan, 1955 (page 34)

Made by Myrbor, Paris, active 1922–36; *Textile*, 1927; silk and metal; Brooklyn Museum Costume Collection at The Metropolitan Museum of Art, Gift of the Brooklyn Museum, 2009; Gift of Adelaide Goan, 1955 (page 18)

Pierre Louÿs, French, 1894–1976
Printed by Chaix, Paris, founded 1881; *Citroën Poster (Audace)*, 1923; lithograph; 62 × 45 ½ in.; Collection of Stephen F. Brauer (similar on page 88)

Henri Matisse, French, 1869–1954
The Windshield, On the Road to Villacoublay, 1917; oil on canvas; 15 1/16 × 21 ¾ in.; The Cleveland Museum of Art, Bequest of Lucia McCurdy McBride in memory of John Harris McBride II 1972.225 (page 41)

Unknown designer
Cocoon Coat, c.1929; silk brocade, silk charmeuse, and monkey fur; Courtesy of the Missouri Historical Society, St. Louis (page 79)

Cloche, c.1927; silk velvet, linen, and brass buttons; Courtesy of the Missouri Historical Society, St. Louis (page 79)

FROM THE AIR TO THE AVANT-GARDE

Avions Voisin, Issy-les-Moulineaux, France, 1905–46
C28 Aérosport, 1936; 65 × 194 × 58 in.; Private collection (page 130)

Georges Braque, French, 1882–1963
The Blue Mandolin, 1930; oil with sand on canvas; 46 × 35 in.; Saint Louis Art Museum, Museum Purchase 125:1944 (page 63)

Jean Cocteau, French, 1889–1963
Eduardo García Benito, Spanish, 1891–1981
Printed by Draeger Frères; Published by La "Société Spad"; *Dans le Ciel de la Patrie*, 1918; book; 9 ¾ × 11; Private collection

Gebrüder Thonet, Vienna, Austria, founded 1853
Armchair (Model No. 9), c.1904; beechwood and cane; 30 ½ × 23 ½ × 21 in.; Saint Louis Art Museum, Richard Brumbaugh Trust in memory of Richard Irving Brumbaugh and in honor of Grace Lischer Brumbaugh 250:1992 (page 94)

Jacques-Henri Lartigue, French, 1894–1986
Merlimont. First Flight of Gabriel Voisin in the Archdeacon Glider, from "The Lartigue Portfolio," 1904, printed 1978; gelatin silver print; 6 9⁄16 × 7 9⁄16 in.; Saint Louis Art Museum, Gift of Frederick P. Currier 305:1995.2 (page 124)

Jacques Le Chevallier, French, 1896–1987
René Koechlin, French, 1866–1951; *Lamp*, c.1927–30; aluminum; 10 × 9 in.; Saint Louis Art Museum, Marjorie Wyman Endowment Fund 104:2024a,b (similar on page 20)

Le Corbusier, Swiss (active France), 1887–1965
Le Plan Voisin, Paris, 1925, 1925; black pencil and India ink on tracing paper; 23 1⁄16 × 44 7⁄8 in.; Fondation Le Corbusier, Paris (page 95)

Le Plan Voisin, Paris, 1925, 1925; India ink on medium tracing paper; 29 1⁄8 × 40 3⁄16 in.; Fondation Le Corbusier, Paris (page 95)

Vers une architecture, 1924; book; closed: 9 ¾ × 6 ½ × ¾ in.; opened: 9 ¾ × 12 ¾ × ¾ in.; Steedman Architecture Collection, St. Louis Public Library

L'art décoratif d'aujourd'hui, 1925; book; closed: 9 ¾ × 6 ½ × ¾ in.; opened: 9 ¾ × 13 ½ × ¾ in.; Steedman Architecture Collection, St. Louis Public Library

Fernand Léger, French, 1881–1955
Still from the film *Ballet mécanique (Dudley Murphy)*, c.1923–24; gelatin silver print; 3 ½ × 4 5⁄8 in.; Saint Louis Art Museum, Funds given by donors to the 1995 Annual Appeal 5:1996 (page 62)

Published by Gustav Kiepenheuer, German, 1880–1949; *Composition à Deux Personnages*, 1920; lithograph; 14 7⁄16 × 11 7⁄16 in.; Saint Louis Art Museum, Gift of Julian and Hope Edison 336:2020 (page 61)

Marcel L'Herbier, French, 1888–1979
Directed by Marcel L'Herbier, French, 1888–1979; sets by Robert Mallet-Stevens, French, 1886–1945; still from the film *L'Inhumaine*, 1924 (page 62)

Jacques Lipchitz, French (born Lithuania), 1891–1973
The Standing Personage, 1916; bronze; height: 41 ¼ in.; Saint Louis Art Museum, Gift of Mr. and Mrs. Joseph Pulitzer Jr. 150:1973 (page 94)

Charles Loupot, French, 1892–1960
Printed by Devambez, Paris, founded 1826; *Voisin Automobiles*, 1923; lithograph; 64 × 47 ¾ in.; The Museum of Modern Art, Gift of The Lauder Foundation, Leonard and Evelyn Lauder Fund 159.1988 (page 129)

Jan Martel, French, 1896–1966
Joël Martel, French, 1896–1966
"Arrow" Mascot, c.1925–30, bronze, 3 9⁄16 × 7 1⁄16 × 6 7⁄8 in.; Collection of Tom van Oostende (page 22)

"Swallow" Mascot, c.1925–30, bronze, 5 ½ × 3 9⁄16 × 4 ½ in.; Collection of Tom van Oostende

"Pigeon" Mascot, c.1925–30, aluminum, 4 ¾ × 4 5⁄16 × 3 1⁄8 in.; Collection of Tom van Oostende (page 22)

Mascot for Sizaire Frères, c.1925–30, bronze, 3 15⁄16 × 2 15⁄16 × 7 1⁄16 in.; Collection of Tom van Oostende

Piet Mondrian, Dutch, 1872–1944
Composition of Red and White: Nom 1/Composition No. 4 with Red and Blue, 1938–42; oil on canvas; 39 ½ × 39 in.; Saint Louis Art Museum, Friends Endowment Fund 242:1972 (page 61)

François Roques, French, 1876–?
"Double Circle" Mascot, 1925–30, brassed and nickeled bronze, aluminum, height: 4 15⁄16 in.; Collection of Tom van Oostende (page 118)

"Bird of Prey" Mascot, 1925–30, aluminum, 8 ¼ × 2 ¾ in.; Collection of Tom van Oostende (page 118)

"Winged Wheel" Mascot, 1925–30, brassed and nickeled bronze, aluminum, 8 ¼ × 3 15⁄16 × 5 1⁄8 in.; Collection of Tom van Oostende (page 118)

Elsa Schiaparelli, Italian, 1890–1973
Schiaparelli, Paris, founded 1927; *Sweater*, c.1928; cashmere knit; Western Reserve Historical Society, Cleveland, Ohio (page 146)

Ugo Zagato, Italian, 1890–1968
Alfa Romeo Automobiles S.p.A., Milan, Italy, founded 1910
6C 1750 Spider, 1930; 43 × 144 × 64 in.; North Collection (page 64)

Atelier Martine, Paris, active 1911–29
Curtain Panel, c.1923; printed cotton with metal hardware; 105 × 46 in.; Saint Louis Art Museum, Richard Brumbaugh Trust in memory of Richard Irving Brumbaugh and Grace Lischer Brumbaugh 26:2016 (page 76)

Édouard Bénédictus, French, 1878–1930
Rug, c.1925; wool; plain weave with symmetrical knots; 121 × 79 in.; Lent by the Minneapolis Institute of Art, Gift of Ruth and Bruce Dayton and the Putnam Dana McMillan Fund (page 86)

Brunet-Meunié et Cie, Paris, founded 1815; *Fountains (Les Jets d'Eau) Textile*, 1925; cotton and rayon; 53 ¼ × 49 ¾ in.; Saint Louis Art Museum, Funds given by The Lea-Thi-Ta Study Group 464:2018 (page 86)

Robert Bonfils, French, 1886–1972
Printed by Vaugirard, Paris; *International Exposition of Modern Decorative Art, Paris, 1925, City Art Museum, July 20 to August 20, 1926*, 1926; lithograph; 9 × 13 ¾ in.; Museum Archives, Saint Louis Art Museum

Ettore Bugatti, French (born Italy), 1881–1947
Automobiles Ettore Bugatti, Molsheim, France, active 1909–63
Type 41 "Royale" Convertible, 1931; 62 ½ × 233 × 82 ½ in.; From the Collections of The Henry Ford, Dearborn, Michigan (page 102)

Callot Soeurs, Paris, active 1895–1937
Evening Dress, c.1920; moiré silk and metallic thread faille, silk charmeuse, and silk net; Courtesy of the Missouri Historical Society, St. Louis (page 78)

Pierre Chareau, French, 1883–1950
Desk and Stool, c.1927; wrought iron and palisander; desk: 37 × 63 × 40 in., stool: 14 ⅜ × 19 ¹¹⁄₁₆ × 15 ³⁄₁₆ in.; National Capital Bank, Courtesy of the Geoffrey Diner Gallery, Washington, DC (page 97)

Émile Decoeur, French, 1876–1953
Bowl, c.1920–25; glazed stoneware; 6 ¼ × 9 ⅝ in.; Saint Louis Art Museum, Museum Purchase 14:1927 (page 75)

Delaunay-Belleville, Saint-Denis, France, active early 20th century
Printed by Draeger, Paris, founded 1886; *Description des Chassis Delaunay Belleville 1924 suivie d'un essai sur les différentes manières de les carrosser par Benito, Lelong, Lepape, Martin, Ruhlmann*, 1924; ink on paper; 9 ½ × 10 ¼ in.; Private collection (pages 35, 72)

Charles Despiau, French, 1874–1946
Portrait of Line Aman-Jean, 1925; bronze; 21 × 15 ⅜ × 10 ¾ in.; Saint Louis Art Museum, Gift of Mr. and Mrs. Joseph Pulitzer Jr. 411:1952 (page 75)

Maurice Dufrêne, French, 1876–1955
Cornille Frères, Paris, active 1875–1926
Textile Length, c.1920; printed silk; 53 ⅛ × 51 ³⁄₁₆ in.; Musée des Arts décoratifs, Paris (pages i, ii)

Textile Sample, c.1920; printed silk; 31 ½ × 27 ⁹⁄₁₆ in.; Musée des Arts décoratifs, Paris

Jean Dunand, French (born Switzerland), 1877–1942
Jeune Archer, 1926; wood panel with colored lacquer and eggshell; 70 ⅞ × 48 ¹⁄₁₆ in.; Private collection (pages 68, 83)

Dresser Set, 1925–30; lacquer on copper, lacquer on wood, and crushed eggshell; tray: 10 ¾ × 10 ¾ in., covered box: 2 × 6 in., mirror: 13 ¾ × 6 ¼ in.; Minneapolis Institute of Art, Gift of Norwest Bank Minnesota (page 82)

Eileen Gray, Irish, 1878–1976
Design, early 1920s; pencil, chalk, India ink, and Chinese white; 9 ¹³⁄₁₆ × 11 ⅞ in.; Victoria and Albert Museum, London (page 83)

Tapis et Tissus de Cogolin, Cogolin, France, active 1879–1976; *Rug*, 1975, after 1926 design; cotton and wool; 42 ½ × 78 ⅜ in.; Saint Louis Art Museum, Funds given by the Decorative Arts Society 49:1980 (page 20)

Gustave Keller Frères, Paris, active 1856–1947
Handles, c.1910; ink, pencil, gouache, and gum arabic on paper; 19 × 12 ⅜ in.; Patrimoine Puiforcat, Paris, D-20536-1

Handles, c.1910; ink, pencil, and gouache on paper; 18 ¹¹⁄₁₆ × 12 ⁵⁄₁₆ in.; Patrimoine Puiforcat, Paris, D-20538-1

After Jean Henri-Labourdette, French, 1888–1972
Hispano-Suiza, Barcelona, Spain, founded 1904
H6B Skiff-Torpedo, 1925; 65 × 219 × 70 in.; North Collection (page 28)

Hermès, Paris, founded 1837
Automobile Travel Blanket, designed c.1925, made c.1950; lambskin and cashmere; Conservatoire des Créations Hermès, Paris (page 39)

Pocket Watch, c.1930; lacquer and silver; Conservatoire des Créations Hermès, Paris

Cigarette Case, 1930s; silver, lacquer, and vermeil; Conservatoire des Créations Hermès, Paris (page 39)

Georges Lepape, French, 1887–1971; Page from the Hermès Sellier catalogue *Maroquinerie, Voyage et Sport* (Leather goods, travel, and sport), 1926; Hermès Archives (page 157)

François Roques, French, 1876–?; Hermès; *Patterns for Leather Travel Cushions*, 1925; Hermès Archives

José Zinoview and Léon Benigni, French, 1892–1948; Draeger, Paris, founded 1886; Hermès catalogue cover, *L'Elégance et le Confort en Automobile* (Automobile elegance and comfort), 1925; lithograph; Hermès Archives (page 39)

House of Worth, Paris, active 1858–1956
Evening Dress, c.1925; silk charmeuse, silk plain weave, metallic thread lace, crystal, glass and plastic beads, and metallic thread; Courtesy of the Missouri Historical Society, St. Louis (page 78)

René Lalique, French, 1860–1945
René Lalique et Cie, Wingen-sur-Moder, France; *Hagueneau Water Glass*, designed 1924; glass; 7 ¾ × 3 ¾ in.; Saint Louis Art Museum, Museum Purchase 16:1927 (page 22)

Suzanne Lalique-Haviland, French, 1892–1989
René Lalique, French, 1860–1945
René Lalique et Cie, Wingen-sur-Moder, France; *Tourbillons Vase*, c.1925; press-molded glass and enamel; 7 ⅞ × 6 in.; Saint Louis Art Museum, Museum Purchase 63:1930 (page 84)

Jeanne Lanvin, French, 1867–1946
(attributed) *Robe de Style, "Fête galante,"* 1925; silk satin, silk velvet, silk net, metal and silk ribbon, rhinestones, glass and plastic beads, and metallic thread; Stephens College Costume Museum and Research Library, Columbia, Missouri (page 22)

Pierre Legrain, French, 1889–1929
Album de 96 dessins originaux et maquettes, ayant servi à l'exécution de reliures, 1916–27; manuscript with gilt and tooled leather binding; 17 ½ × 12 ¾ × 2 ½ in.; Spencer Collection, The New York Public Library, Astor, Lenox and Tilden Foundations

Émile Lenoble, French, 1875–1940
Jar, c.1930; glazed stoneware; 11 ¼ × 9 in.; Saint Louis Art Museum, Bequest of Ezra H. Linley by exchange 61:1937 (page 75)

René Nauny, French, active early 20th century
M. Desnet, French, died 1933
La Maison Desny, Paris, active 1927–33; *Tea and Coffee Service*, c.1927; silver-plated brass and ebony; overall: 5 ¼ × 15 × 8 ¾ in., coffeepot: 4 ⅝ × 8 × 2 ⅞ in., teapot: 4 × 6 ¾ × 2 ⅜ in., sugar: 3 ¼ × 5 ¾ × 2 in., creamer: 2 13⁄16 × 4 ½ × 1 ¾ in., tray: 1 × 15 × 8 ¾ in.; Saint Louis Art Museum, Museum Purchase 58:1997a–e (page 19)

Jean Patou, French, 1887–1936
House of Patou, Paris, founded 1914; *Cloak*, c.1926; silk crepe; Courtesy of the Missouri Historical Society, St. Louis (page 157)

Jean Puiforcat, French, 1897–1945
Vase for an Automobile, n° 7962, c.1925; silver and ivory; 5 13⁄16 × 3 ¼ × 1 1⁄16 in; Patrimoine Puiforcat, Paris, M-2024-003

Handle, 1939; pencil on tracing paper; 5 ⅜ × 8 ¼ in.; Patrimoine Puiforcat, Paris, D-32593-1

Handle, 1939; pencil on tracing paper; 4 7⁄16 × 5 ⅜ in.; Patrimoine Puiforcat, Paris, D-32594-1

Handle, 1939; pencil on tracing paper; 4 7⁄16 × 5 ⅜ in.; Patrimoine Puiforcat, Paris, D-32597-1

Paul Poiret, French, 1879–1944
Poiret, Paris, active 1903–29; *Evening Coat*, 1924; silk charmeuse, silk and metallic thread brocade, and brass buttons; Courtesy of the Missouri Historical Society, St. Louis (page 76)

Émile-Jacques Ruhlmann, French, 1879–1933
Table, c.1923; Kingwood veneer on mahogany and oak with ivory inlay; 22 ⅛ × 15 ⅜ × 30 ¾ in.; Brooklyn Museum, Purchased with funds given by Joseph F. McCrindle, Mrs. Richard M. Palmer, Charles C. Paterson, Raymond Worgelt, and an anonymous donor (page 73)

Side Chair, 1926; Macassar ebony, silvered bronze, replacement silk, and cotton velvet; 37 ¼ × 17 ¾ × 20 in.; Saint Louis Art Museum, Gift of Mr. and Mrs. Stanley Hanks 110:1972 (page 75)

Jenny Sacerdote, French, 1868–1962
Jenny, Paris, active 1909–1940; *Jacket*, c.1926; silk crepe, karakul [Persian lamb fur], silk braid, metallic thread, and silk plain weave; Courtesy of the Missouri Historical Society, St. Louis (page 152)

PHOTO CREDITS

©2025 Artists Rights Society (ARS), New York: FIGS. 13, 31, 36–37, 40, 63, 93–94, 148, 157–62, 164–65, 171; p. 105. ©2025 Artists Rights Society, Image: Banque d'Images, ADAGP / Art Resource, NY: cover. ©Les Arts Décoratifs, Paris: FIG. 149. ©Les Arts Décoratifs / Jean Tholance: end sheets. Carlos Azevedo: FIG. 121. ©Rene Buthaud: FIG. 57. Chelles Helio Faucheux: p. 6, FIG. 35B. Marie Clérin Photographe: FIG. 98. David Cooper: FIG. 106. ©René André Coulon: FIG. 69. ©Estate of Denise Bellon: FIGS. 166–67. ©Estate of Ilse Bing, Courtesy Edwynn Houk Gallery: FIG. 168. ©Estate of Émile Deschler: FIG. 125. ©Estate of Louis Gaudin: FIG. 128. ©Estate Germaine Krull, Museum Folkwang, Essen / Art Institute of Chicago / Art Resource, NY: FIGS. 33–34. ©The Estate of Jason Rhoades, Courtesy the Estate of Jason Rhoades and Hauser & Wirth, Photo: Thomas Barratt: FIGS. 16A, B. ©Fondation Henri Cartier-Bresson / Magnum Photos: FIGS. 9, 131. Michael Furman: pp. 50–55. gallica.bnf.fr / Bibliothèque nationale de France: FIG. 3. ©Gooding & Company / Josh Hway: pp. 56–59. Peter Harholdt: FIG. 155; pp. 1, 28–31, 64–67, 120–23, 136–39, 164–67, 176–79. From the Collections of The Henry Ford: pp. 102–3. ©Hermès 2025: FIGS. 18–22, 137, 150. Mitro Hood, FIGS. 75–77. ©Lanvin Heritage: FIG. 153. ©Boris Lipnitzki / Roger-Viollet: FIG. 151. ©Lyon, Musée des Tissus et des Arts décoratifs / Sylvain Pretto: FIGS. 45, 82, 83, 86. ©Roberto Martinez Baldrich: pp. 2–3. The Menil Collection, Photo by Paul Hester: FIG. 27. ©The Metropolitan Museum of Art / Art Resource, NY: FIGS. 4, 135. Minneapolis Institute of Art: FIG. 6. ©The Museum of Modern Art / Licensed by SCALA / Art Resource, NY: FIG. 122. ©Musées de Poitiers / Christian Vignaud: FIGS. 62A, B. ©National Museum of Ireland: FIG. 65. ©Pracusa: FIG. 80. REP: FIG. 56. Sinh Truong: pp. 24–27. ©2025 Succession H. Matisse / Artists Rights Society (ARS), New York: FIGS. 24–25. Michel Zumbrunn: pp. 130–31.

Details

Front cover: FIG. 31; Back cover: FIG. 1; Endpapers: Maurice Dufrêne, *Textile Length*, c.1920 (see checklist); p. 1: detail of *Skiff-Torpedo* on page 28; pp. 2–3: Roberto Martinez Baldrich illustration in *Art, goût, beauté* 51, November 1924, Courtesy of National Gallery of Victoria, Melbourne, Campbell-Pretty Fashion Research Collection ©Roberto Martinez Baldrich; p. 4: Josephine Baker with her Delage, 1935; p. 6: FIG. 35B (detail); p. 7: FIG. 10 (detail); pp. 10–11: Jacques-Henri Lartigue, *Zissou Driving His "Bob on 4 Wheels,"* 1910 (see checklist); pp. 32–33: Fashion spread from *Art, goût, beauté*, July 1924, Courtesy of National Gallery of Victoria, Melbourne, Campbell-Pretty Fashion Research Collection ©Roberto Martinez Baldrich; p. 34: Sarah Lipska, *Textile*, 1927 (see checklist); pp. 68–69: FIG. 66 (detail); p. 70: FIG. 73 (detail); pp. 106–7: Jacques-Henri Lartigue, *Grand Prix of the A.C.F.—A Delage*, 1912 (see checklist); p. 108: *Talbot-Lago Coupe*, page 164 (detail); pp. 140–41: Jacques-Henri Lartigue, *Deauville: Daisy Spéranza*, 1916 (see checklist); p. 142: FIG. 145 (detail); pp. 186–87: FIG. 124 (detail); p. 200: Georges Lepape illustration for *Vogue*, January 1, 1924.

CONTRIBUTORS

Sarah Berg is the research assistant for Decorative Arts and Design at the Saint Louis Art Museum.

Genevieve Cortinovis is the Andrew W. Mellon Foundation Associate Curator of Decorative Arts and Design at the Saint Louis Art Museum.

Pierre-Jean Desemerie is a fashion historian and doctoral candidate in the Decorative Arts, Design History, and Material Culture program at Bard Graduate Center.

Ken Gross is a writer, automotive historian, and former director of the Petersen Automotive Museum in Los Angeles, California.

Justice Henderson is the 2023–2025 Romare Bearden Graduate Museum Fellow at the Saint Louis Art Museum.

Daniel Marcus is the curator of collections and exhibitions at the Columbus Museum of Art in Columbus, Ohio.

LENDERS

The Saint Louis Art Museum thanks all lenders to the exhibition. This list recognizes the lenders who had committed loans to the exhibition at the time this catalogue was published.

Art Institute of Chicago
The Baltimore Museum of Art
Collection of Hamish Bowles
Collection of Stephen F. Brauer
Brooklyn Museum
The Cleveland Museum of Art
William E. Connor Collection
The Costume Institute, The Metropolitan Museum of Art, New York
The Design Museum, London
Fondation Henri Cartier-Bresson, Paris
Fondation Le Corbusier, Paris
Fonds photographique Denise Bellon
Linda and Paul Gould
The Henry Ford, Dearborn, Michigan
International Center of Photography, New York
Keller Collection
Laffanour Galerie Downtown, Paris
Collection of J.W. Marriott, Jr.
The Mathews Family
Miles Collier Collections at Revs Institute, Naples, Florida
Minneapolis Institute of Art
Missouri Historical Society
Missouri State University Libraries
Musée des Arts décoratifs, Paris
Musée des Tissus et des Arts décoratifs de Lyon
Musées de Poitiers
Museum of Modern Art, New York
National Capital Bank, courtesy of the Geoffrey Diner Gallery, Washington, DC
The Nelson-Atkins Museum of Art
Edward F. Niedzwiecki
North Collection
Patrimoine Hermès, Paris
Patrimoine Puiforcat, Paris
Petersen Automotive Museum
Spencer Collection, The New York Public Library
Steedman Architecture Collection, St. Louis Public Library
Stephens College Costume Museum and Research Library
Collection of Mary Strauss
Universitätsbibliothek Augsburg
Collection of Tom van Oostende
Victoria and Albert Museum, London
Western Reserve Historical Society, Cleveland

Private collections

INDEX

This book is published in conjunction with the exhibition *Roaring: Art, Fashion, and the Automobile in France, 1918–1938*, presented at the Saint Louis Art Museum from April 12, 2025, to July 27, 2025.

This exhibition is presented with generous support from the Enterprise Mobility Foundation and Barbara and Andy Taylor. Additional support provided by the Betsy & Thomas Patterson Foundation, the E. Desmond Lee Family Endowment for Exhibitions, and the Edward L. Bakewell Jr. Endowment for Special Exhibitions.

Saint Louis Art Museum
One Fine Arts Drive, Forest Park
St. Louis, Missouri 63110
USA
www.slam.org

Hirmer Verlag GmbH
Bayerstrasse 57–59
80335 Munich
Germany
www.hirmerpublishers.com

Head of Publications, Saint Louis Art Museum
Valerie Lazalier Edmison
Image Rights Manager, Saint Louis Art Museum
Jason Gray
Senior Editor, Hirmer Publishers
Elisabeth Rochau-Shalem
Project Manager, Hirmer Publishers
Rainer Arnold
Designer, Hirmer Publishers
Hannes Halder
Copyediting
Susan Higman Larsen
Proofreading
Mike Pilewski
Indexing
Anne Holmes
Prepress
Reproline Genceller 2.0, Germering
Fonts
Adelle Sans, Dashiell Text, DK Hokitika
Paper
170 g/sqm GardaMatt Art
Printing/binding
Printer Trento

Printed in Italy

ISBN: 978-3-7774-4458-1
LCCN: 2024053950

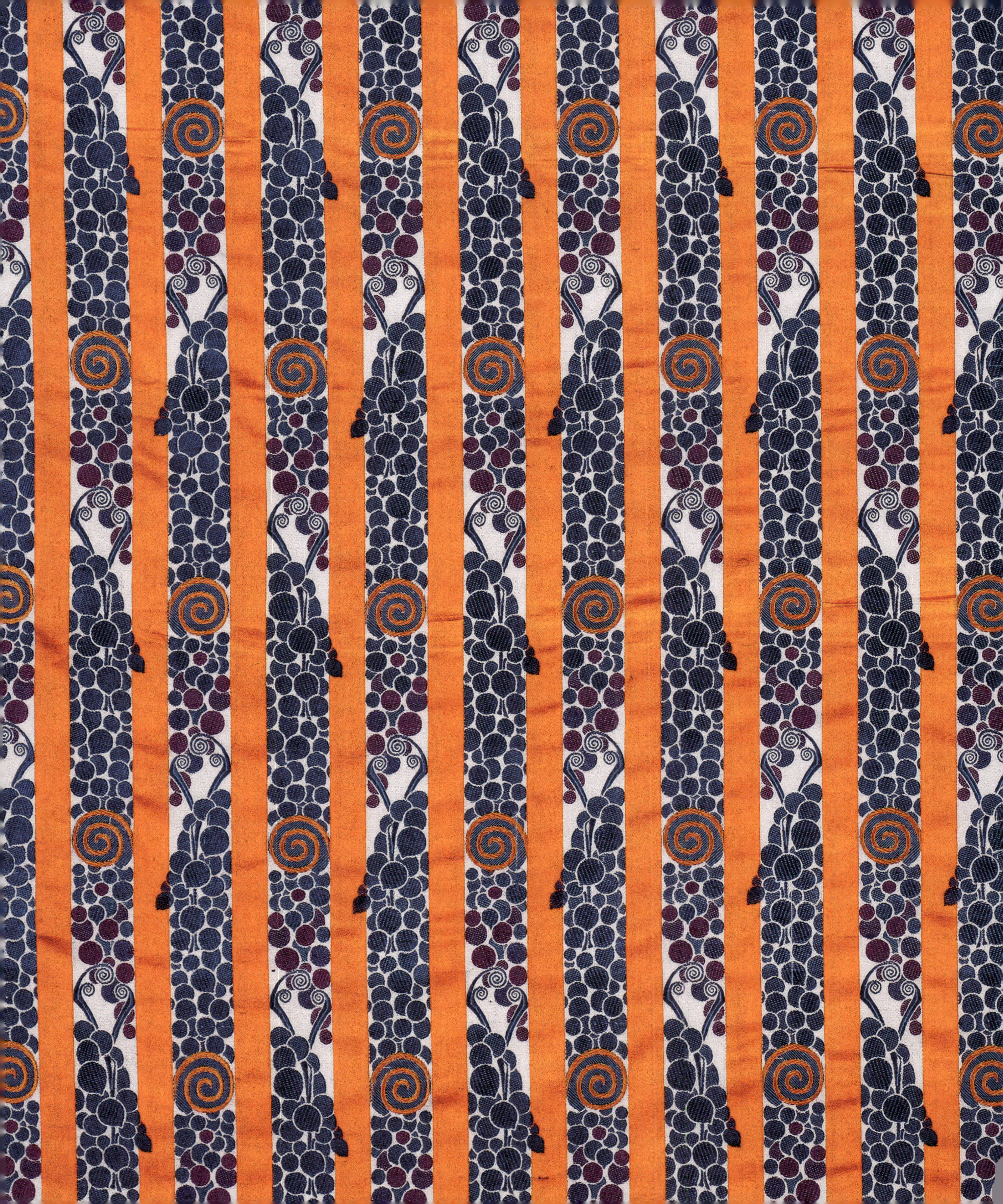

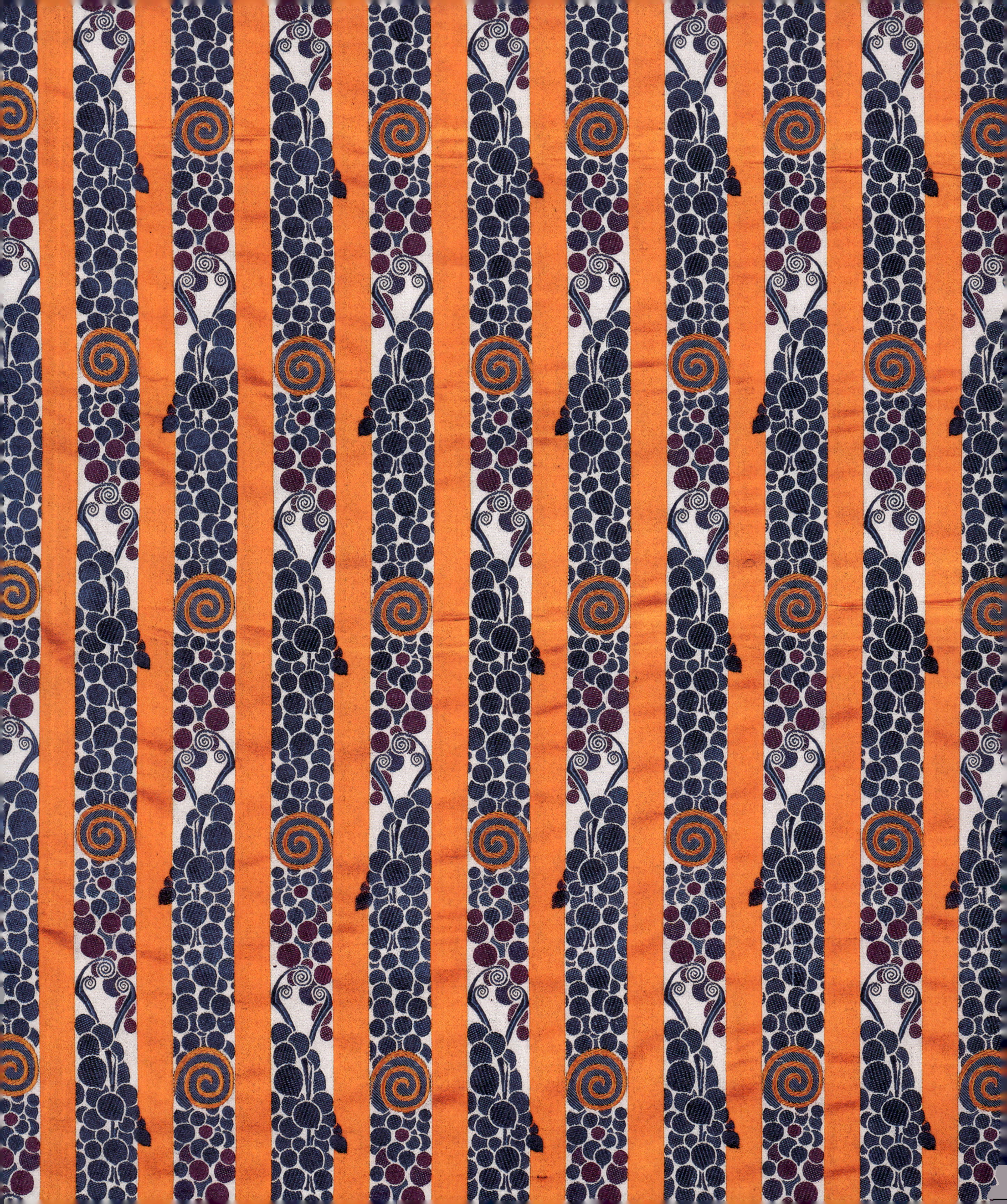